The Learning Region

The Learning Region

Foundations, State of the Art, Future

Edited by

Roel Rutten

Assistant Professor of Organization Studies, Department of Organization Studies, Tilburg University, The Netherlands

Frans Boekema

Professor of Economic Geography and Extraordinary Professor of Euregional Management, Radboud University Nijmegen and Associate Professor of Regional Economics, Tilburg University, The Netherlands

Edward Elgar

Cheltenham, UK • Northampton, MA, USA

Published by
Edward Elgar Publishing Limited
Glensanda House
Montpellier Parade
Cheltenham
Glos GL50 1UA
UK

Edward Elgar Publishing, Inc.
William Pratt House
9 Dewey Court
Northampton
Massachusetts 01060
USA

A catalogue record for this book
is available from the British Library

Library of Congress Cataloguing in Publication Data

The learning region: foundations, state of the art, future/edited by
  Roel Rutten, Frans Boekema.
      p.   cm.
    Includes bibliographical references and index.
    1. Regional economics. 2. Learning—Economic aspects.
  3. Social capital (Sociology). 4. Space in economics.
  5. Technological innovations—Economic aspects. I. Rutten,
  Roel, 1971–   . II. Boekema, Frans.
  HT388.L4   2007
  330—dc22
                                                    2006102953

ISBN 978 1 84376 938 5

Printed and bound in Great Britain by MPG Books Ltd, Bodmin, Cornwall

Contents

Figures and tables

FIGURES

TABLES

About the editors

Roel Rutten and Frans Boekema have been working as a team on the learning region for the better part of a decade. In 1998 they organized their first international seminar on the learning region, the results of which were published in an edited volume in 2000. Another conference followed in 2000, and again the outcomes were published in an edited volume in 2003. These two projects laid the groundwork for the present book. Two further seminars followed in 2002 and 2004. Although these seminars did not focus exclusively on the learning region, they dealt with the same questions and concepts that underlie the subject. The outcomes of these seminars were published in two special issues of *European Planning Studies* in 2004 and 2005 respectively. The seminars that Rutten and Boekema organized also served to build a network of international scholars working in the field of regions and innovation. Attending conferences in order to present their work was another element of the same strategy. Most notably, Rutten and Boekema participated in the conferences of the Regional Studies Association (in Europe) and the Western Regional Science Association (in the USA). The work that Rutten and Boekema presented and discussed at these conferences was often published in the form of book chapters.

The networking, the discussions at conferences, and the publications culminated, as if by an inescapable logic, in the present volume. Over the years, Rutten and Boekema have made connections with several of the most renowned scholars in the field of regions and innovation, and have developed their own approach to the learning region. Based on this combination of people and ideas, the present volume aims to make an important contribution to the literature on the learning region.

To date, Rutten and Boekema continue to work on follow-up projects on the learning region.

Roel Rutten (b. 1971) is Assistant Professor of Organization Studies in the Department of Organization Studies at Tilburg University, the Netherlands. He began his career as a consultant for ERAC (European Regional Affairs Consultants) in 1994. Among other things, ERAC specialized in European regional innovation policy, and it is in this field that Rutten was working during his ERAC years, from 1994 through 2001. During that same period he wrote a PhD thesis on regional innovation networks. The thesis was based on an in-depth case study of the innovation network of Océ (a manufacturer of copiers and printers in the Netherlands) and its suppliers. Rutten began his present occupation in 2001. Among other things, he was involved in an evaluation study of approximately 100 temporary product development networks of small and medium-sized enterprises in the Eindhoven region in the Netherlands.

Frans Boekema (b. 1949) is Professor of Economic Geography and Extraordinary Professor of Euregional Management at Radboud University Nijmegen, the Netherlands and Associate Professor of Regional Economics at Tilburg University, the Netherlands. He studied regional economics and economic geography at Tilburg University and began his career as Assistant Professor in the department of Regional Economics in 1976. In 1986 he completed his dissertation on local initiatives and regional development. In 1990 he was appointed Associate Professor of Regional Economics and Economic Geography at Tilburg University and became part-time Professor in Economic Geography at the Faculty of Management Sciences of Radboud University in Nijmegen, the Netherlands in 1995. During this time he was also working as manager of the Regional Economic Department of the Economic Institute Tilburg, a research and consultancy institute. In 2006 he was appointed Extraordinary Professor of Euregional Management at Radboud University in Nijmegen. His main fields of research activities are: local and regional development, technological development and regional innovation systems, borders, border regions and border-crossing activities, clusters, networks and learning regions. He has published many articles and books on these subjects in the past decades.

Contributors

Bjørn T. Asheim is Professor in Economic Geography at the Institute for Cultural and Economic Geography at Lind University in Sweden. He is also deputy director of the Centre for Innovation, Research and Competence in the Learning Economy (CIRCLE) at the same university.

Nicola Bellini is Professor of Business Economics at the Sant' Anna School of Advanced Studies in Pisa, Italy. He is director of a research centre on innovation and territorial systems at the same institute.

Frans Boekema is Professor of Economic Geography and Extraordinary Professor of Euregional Management, Radboud University Nijmegen and Associate Professor of Regional Economics, Tilburg University, the Netherlands.

Philip Cooke is Professor of Regional Development and Director of the Centre for Advanced Studies at Cardiff University in Wales, UK.

Richard Florida is the Hirst Professor at George Mason University's School of Public Policy in Fairfax, VA, USA, and a non-resident senior fellow at the Brookings Institution in Washington, DC, USA.

Robert Hassink is Professor of Human Geography in the Department of Sociology and Human Geography at Oslo University, Norway.

Gert-Jan Hospers is Assistant Professor of Economics at the School of Public Administration and Technology at the University of Twente, the Netherlands.

Patrick Kenis is Professor of Policy and Organization Studies in the Department of Organization Studies at Tilburg University, the Netherlands.

Mikel Landabaso is a senior researcher for the European Commission in Brussels at the Department of Regional Innovation Strategies and Technology Transfer, Directorate General Regional Policy.

Mark Lorenzen is Associate Professor in the Department of Industrial Economics and Strategy at the Copenhagen Business School. He is also affiliated with Imagine Creative Industries Research and Danish Research Unit on Industrial Dynamics (DRUID).

Ed Malecki is Professor of Geography in the Department of Geography at the Ohio State University, Columbus, OH, USA.

Marius Meeus is Professor of Innovation and Organization in the Department of Organization Studies at Tilbury University, the Netherlands.

Kevin Morgan is Professor of European Regional Development at the School of City and Regional Planning, Cardiff University in Wales, UK. He is also director of the Regeneration Institute at the same university.

Leon Oerlemans is Professor of Organizational Dynamics in the Department of Organization Studies at Tilburg University, the Netherlands and Professor of Economics and Innovation at the Faculty of Engineering, Built Environment and Information Technology, University of Pretoria, South Africa.

Roel Rutten is Assistant Professor of Organization Studies, Department of Organization Studies, Tilburg University, the Netherlands.

Michael Storper is Professor of Economic Sociology at the Centre de Sociologie des Organisations in Paris, France. He is Professor of Economic Geography at the London School of Economics (LSE) in London, UK, and Professor of Regional and International Development at the University of California at Los Angeles (UCLA) in Los Angeles, CA, USA.

Acknowledgements

The publishers wish to thank the following who have kindly given permission for the use of copyright material.

Elsevier Science Ltd for article: Florida, Richard (1995), 'Toward the learning region', *Futures*, **27** (5), 527–36.

Taylor & Francis Ltd for articles: Storper, Michael (1993), 'Regional "worlds" of production', *Regional Studies*, **27**, 433–55, Morgan, Kevin (1997), 'The learning region: institutions, innovation and regional renewal', *Regional Studies*, **31**, 491–503, Asheim, Bjørn T. (1996), 'Industrial districts as learning regions', *European Planning Studies*, **4**, 379–400.

Every effort has been made to trace all the copyright holders, but if any have been inavertently overlooked the publishers will be pleased to make the necessary arrangements at the first opportunity.

1. The learning region: foundations, state of the art, future

Roel Rutten and Frans Boekema

This history of the learning region perhaps began at the 1991 annual meeting of the Association of American Geographers, when Michael Storper, in a session on 'The geography of rationality and collective action', presented a paper about learning regions. Although it is lost to history whether the term 'learning region' was actually coined at that particular session, there is no mistaking that the 'learning-based regional production systems' that Storper discussed in his talk were renamed as learning regions shortly thereafter. From the early 1990s onward, the term learning region begins to surface in the literature on economic geography. In the decade and a half since, a wealth of publications on the learning region has appeared in both journals and books. The thinking about learning regions was triggered by several studies, the above study by Michael Storper and the classic study on the competitive advantage of nations by Michael Porter (1990) among them, that showed trade specialization among advanced economies to be increasing. This specialization followed from the discovery of absolute advantage based on superior localized technological learning. In other words, learning-specialized sectors and industries were found to have a distinct geography of agglomeration in a limited number of sub-national core regions. These regions often developed specific conventions of learning, which led Storper (1993) to call them 'regional worlds of production'. In Storper's words: 'Much of the way a given production complex functions relies on the untraded interdependencies of the actors in that complex . . . The different regional worlds of production that are found in each of these cases also correspond to different product-based worlds . . . They correspond to different regional–sectoral combinations of elements from those worlds . . . Each of these systems is therefore a regional economy of relational assets' (Storper, 1997: 162–3). Contrary to the belief to which many subscribed at the time, globalization of the economy reinforced regional differences; it did not eradicate them. That is the fruit of the early work on the learning region. From then on, the quest was on to explain how and why regions differed in the global economy.

A TRAIL THROUGH THE LITERATURE

By the early 1990s, the regional level had become a hot topic in scientific discourse. Kenichi Ohmae, in his 1995 book, *The End of the Nation State: The Rise of Regional Economies*, stressed the role of regions as new engines of prosperity, while reshaping global markets. Once efficient engines of wealth creation, nation states, their fates increasingly determined by economic choices made elsewhere, had become inefficient in creating and distributing wealth. The new engines of prosperity, Ohmae argued, were region states. They had emerged in places such as the area between San Diego and Tijuana, in Singapore and in parts of Malaysia and Indonesia, in Silicon Valley, in the Bay Area and in the adjacent portion of the Chinese mainland. Ohmae concluded that the emergence of the nation state changed deeply and forever the global logic of what defines how corporations operate and how governments of nation states understand their proper roles in (regional) economic affairs. Managers and policy makers must remember that people (with their knowledge, know-how, expertise and capacity for learning) came first and borders second.[1]

Many authors have contributed to the growing field of the learning region. Some of them already had a well-established reputation in economic geography; others earned one because of their work on the learning region, such as Phil Cooke, Annalee Saxenian and many others. After Richard Florida made explicit use of the term 'learning region' in his 1995 article in *Futures*, the term became en vogue. By now, the idea had taken root that

> Regions are becoming focal points for knowledge creation and learning in the new age of global, knowledge-intensive capitalism, as they in effect become learning regions. These Learning Regions function as collectors and repositories of knowledge and ideas, and provide the underlying environment or infrastructure which facilitates the flow of knowledge, ideas and learning. In fact, despite continued predictions of the end of geography, regions are becoming more important modes of economic and technological organization on a global scale. (Florida, 1995: 527)

A related growing body of literature that is older than the learning region is the systems of innovation approach. Earlier work on systems of innovation was conducted at the national level. The discourse about national systems of innovation, e.g. Lundvall (1988, 1992), was in part a response to the question whether or not globalization was undermining the ability of individual nations to influence their own technological sovereignty. Studies into national (and regional) innovation systems have found that regional communities of firms and supporting networks of institutions that share a common knowledge base and benefit from their shared access to a unique set of skills and resources are instrumental in furthering innovation. What the innovation systems literature contributed, then, is the insight that innovation is fundamentally a geographical process. In other words, innovation is facilitated, though not necessarily contained by, spatial clustering of the actors involved within the same region. (See also Boekema et al., 2000; Rutten and Boekema, 2004, 2005.)

Another body of literature from which the learning region draws is the industrial districts literature. Bjørn Asheim (1996), for example, argued that collective learning of small and medium-sized enterprises in industrial districts is the key to understanding conditions for prosperity. Asheim's focus was on factors enabling and constraining the formation of sufficient learning capacity. Asheim's publication is also interesting from another point of view, that is, the difference between the American and the European approaches. Florida's (1995) conception of the learning region focuses on the extent and quality of the institutional infrastructure that constitutes a key element of the regional innovation system. So, in the North American context, learning regions are associated with the presence or absence of a dense network of research institutions as well as a broader set of environmental and social amenities that attract highly skilled workers to a locale and keep them there. In the European context, however, the analysis of learning regions focuses much more on the contributions that social capital and trust make to supporting dense networks of inter-firm relationships and the process of interactive learning.

Another groundbreaking article about learning regions is Kevin Morgan's 1997 contribution in *Regional Studies*. It has been quoted many times over the past ten years. A potentially significant theoretical convergence between the two hitherto distinct fields of innovation studies and economic geography seemed to be under way at that time. Through the prism of the learning region, the article examined some of the theoretical and policy implications of this convergence. Drawing on the work of evolutionary political economy, it highlighted the significance for regional development of the interactive model of innovation. At the same time, the policy implications were examined. This was done in two ways: through a new generation of European Union regional policy measures and through a case study of regional innovation in Wales. The main aim of Morgan's paper was to try to connect some of the concepts of the network paradigm (such as interactive innovation and social capital) to the problems of regional development in Europe. Finally, the paper offered a critical assessment of the distributional consequences of such a strategy. This was done by posing the central question: 'Is regional policy enough to address the socio-economic problems of old industrial regions?'

The aforementioned articles of Storper, Florida, Asheim and Morgan on learning regions play an important role in the remainder of this volume. Full reprints of these articles can be found in Part I. Their role will be explained further in the next section. But one other development remains to be discussed before we can move on. Also in the 1990s, key political bodies such as the World Bank, the OECD and the European Union, as well as many national governments, became convinced that the global economy was a knowledge-based economy. As a consequence, they believed competitive success to be dependent on the ability to produce and utilize knowledge effectively. Thus a pressing need arose for firms, communities, regions and nations to invest a greater share of resources in education and training than they had in the past (European Commission, 1995; OECD, 1992; Hague, 1996). Because of the high dependency of innovation on learning within and between regional-based agents and (re)sources, some authors prefer to speak of a learning economy rather than a knowledge-based economy. By stressing the process of learning, they also stress the fact that learning is a social process that works best in a situation of spatial proximity, as this allows frequent interaction between human agents and thus results in richer and thicker flows of knowledge being exchanged among them more efficiently. In other words, innovative capabilities are sustained through regional communities that share a common knowledge base (see Morgan, 2004). In this respect, it may be concluded that the regional level is of critical importance because of the fact that both space (i.e. an actual geographic area) and proximity contribute to producing, distributing and utilizing the very tacit knowledge and the capacity for learning that support innovation (see Rutten, 2003).

From the above it follows that, concerning this topic, several literatures contribute to a better understanding of the phenomenon of the learning region. Put simply, too simply perhaps, the learning region draws from three main literatures: regional learning; clusters and networks; and institutions of innovation. Regional learning highlights the process of learning and the spatial dimensions of this process. Clusters and networks draw attention to how the process of learning can be organized. Institutions of innovation point to tangible and intangible 'infrastructures' that support learning and innovation. These concepts overlap. That is, some clusters and networks have a regional dimension, whereas others have a wider scope. Institutions of innovation may pertain to a region, but also to a nation. Where these three concepts overlap, we argue, is where, conceptually, we will find learning regions. When regional learning takes places in regional networks and is supported by regional institutions of innovation, we can speak of a learning region (see Figure 1.1). This book aims to develop this rough outline into a conceptualization of the learning region.

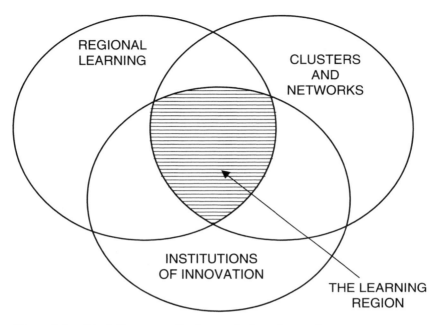

Figure 1.1   Disciplines contributing to the learning region

AIM AND STRUCTURE OF THE BOOK

The main target of this book, expressed in a single sentence, is to conceptualize the learning region. From the previous sections it becomes clear that, although a wealth of literature has been published about learning regions, we are nowhere nearer to saying what a learning region is than we were 15 years ago. Based on the existing literature, however, we feel that such a conceptualization can be made and we intend to do so in this volume. It is not our intention to produce a checklist as a tool for identifying a 'real' learning region. Instead, we argue that the learning region should be an analytical concept that can help us understand how learning takes place in regions and why regions are important for learning. Nowadays, the importance of learning is hardly contested in the literature. On the contrary, the consensus is that we live in a globalized, knowledge-based economy, which, at the same time, is also a regional learning economy. The spatial dimension of learning, in our view, has two different but equally important aspects. First, it concerns distance, or proximity. That is, it pays to learn in proximate relations because tacit knowledge is most easily exchanged in those kinds of relations. Second, some regions have a milieu of innovation that facilitates learning and innovation better than in other regions. In this volume, from a diversity of disciplines, we undertake to explain how companies learn in networks, how their spatial environment (or regional milieu) is important to learning and why and when proximity is important to inter-firm learning. The multidisciplinary approach of this volume is obvious from the different backgrounds of the authors involved: organization studies, economics, human and economic geography, spatial economics, sociology and regional economic policy making.

As can be derived from the subtitle, this volume has three parts: foundations, state of the art, and future. In the foundations part we present four articles from renowned scientists that have contributed to the birth of the learning region. Chapter 2 is a reprint of Michael Storper's 1993 article in *Regional Studies*, 'Regional "worlds" of production: learning and innovation in the technology districts of France, Italy and the USA'. A revised version of this paper was later published as a book chapter in *The Regional World* (Storper, 1997). As argued earlier, this was one of the very first articles to discuss the learning region. Richard Florida's 'Toward the learning region', in Chapter 3, is the second contribution in this part. It is a reprint of this article as it appeared in *Futures* in 1995. Many publications about the learning region refer to this article. Chapter 4 is a reprint of 'Industrial districts as "learning regions": a condition for prosperity', by Bjørn Asheim, which first appeared in *European Planning Studies* in 1996. In this contribution Asheim discussed constraints to learning in regions. The final contribution in Part I, Chapter 5, is a reprint of Kevin Morgan's 1997 article in *Regional Studies*: 'The learning region: institutions, innovation and regional renewal'. These four articles were key contributions to the debate on the learning region over the past 15 years. Of course, in view of the wealth of contributions on the learning region, this selection can only be arbitrary. On the other hand, it does provide a good overview of the theoretical diversity concealed behind the deceptively straightforward term, learning region. The complexity demonstrated by these articles is the very reason that the concept of the learning region merits thorough investigation. This is the purpose of Part II, which presents the state of the art of the learning region. In Chapter 6 we dissect the learning region on the basis of the above four articles. The key theoretical concepts that emerge from this exercise are the starting point for the discussion in the next chapters of Part II.

In this part, a selection of authors elaborates these key concepts. The authors were specifically selected because of their expertise regarding the concepts on which they have written about. Without exception, these authors have published ground-breaking contributions in their fields of expertise. This collection of chapters forms the state of the art of conceptual thinking about regions, learning and innovation in the first decade of the twenty-first century.

Chapter 7 is a completely adapted version of an earlier article by Ed Malecki, which was published in *Erdkunde* in 2000. The version here has been largely rewritten by Gert-Jan Hospers and has as its title 'Knowledge and the competitiveness of places'. Ed Malecki is one of the leading scholars from the USA in the field of regions and learning. Gert-Jan Hospers, although relatively new to this field, is an exponent of a much broader group of Dutch economic geographers working on regions and innovation. This chapter discusses the role of space in relation to knowledge and learning. Nowadays, knowledge has emerged as one of the most important aspects influencing regional economic growth and development. Space has often been argued to be of importance with regard to learning; in fact, it is one of the foundations of the learning region. If we take into account empirical studies, however, the results are mixed (Breschi and Lissoni, 2001). In this chapter several notions regarding space and learning are discussed. In particular the chapter looks at why proximity may be important with respect to learning. Second, the relation between learning and space can be studied by using the region as a starting point in explaining why some regions support learning better than others.

In Chapter 8, Leon Oerlemans, Marius Meeus and Patrick Kenis discuss regional innovation networks. Oerlemans and Meeus have published intensively on innovation networks since the early 1990s. Kenis is one of the leading network sociologists in Europe. The main questions that these authors address are: why are regional networks important with respect to learning and how do they work? Learning, they argue, should be seen as a process that takes place within an organizational context, for example, a network. For a number of reasons, these networks may have a spatial dimension. However, the relation between space, i.e. proximity, and learning in the case of innovation networks is not a straightforward one. The challenge is to explain when it is efficient for companies to organize their learning in regional networks. In order to find the answer to this question, the authors interrogate several theoretical perspectives, such as innovative milieu, industrial districts and new industrial spaces.

The next chapter, by Phil Cooke, elaborates on the literature on regional innovation systems. The author is particularly competent for this task given his many publications in this field. His main aim in this chapter is to explain why, conceptually, the promise of learning and, particularly in this context, the learning region, waxed and then waned so swiftly. Though institutional learning has a respectable pedigree, going back to Argyris (1962) and Arrow (1962) and their question as to whether organizational hierarchy or hetrarchy best nurtured it, the neoclassical economics community has

largely ignored it. On the other hand, many learning discourses have not
fulfilled their promises. Ultimately, what will matter is how well developing
organizations promote learning and the wise use of knowledge. But this
cannot be achieved without paying proper attention to an organization's
place in the broader innovation system.

Social capital is the subject of Chapter 10, where Mark Lorenzen links
this potentially elusive concept to regions. Lorenzen is from a Danish
network of scholars (DRUID[2]) that has become something of a brand name
in the field of learning and regions. Although consensus has emerged that
social capital is of great importance in economic relations, exactly how
social capital 'works' in these relations is the subject of fierce debate.
Lorenzen takes a stand in this debate by arguing that the 'social' in social
capital is the key to understanding this concept. He argues that, because it
is a social phenomenon, social capital may be seen as a characteristic of
regions. Seen in this way, social capital may help explain regional differences
in the performance of innovation networks.

In Chapter 11, Nicola Bellini and Mikel Landabaso shift attention
towards the policy dimension of regional innovation. Bellini, from Italy,
has written many publications on regional innovation policy from a theoretical perspective. His co-author, Landabaso, from Spain, is one of the
founding fathers of the modern European Union's regional innovation
policy. The authors present their reflections on the state of the art of innovation policy in Europe's regions. Whereas in former times practitioners
who argued in favour of a regional dimension of innovation policy were
like an avant-garde compared to mainstream 'grand' industrial policy,
which was often national or European in nature, today the need for regional
innovation policy is commonplace. However, the 'right' approach to
regional innovation policy has not yet been found and evaluation studies
on the effects of various regional policies have shown mixed results
(European Commission, 2004). Inspired by the so-called 'Lisbon Agenda'
of the European Union, several policy experiments on the regional level
have seen the light of day. Herein lies the key to innovative regional policy
for the future.

In the final chapter of Part II, Robert Hassink takes a critical look at
the learning region. Hassink has repeatedly criticized the learning region
for being a fuzzy concept. He bases his critique on years of experience in
the field of regions and learning, which he acquired in Korea and Europe.
In his chapter, Hassink points to a number of conceptual weaknesses of
the learning region in need of answer. He argues that the learning region
may 'work' as a concept for policy but that it remains to be seen whether
it will be useful beyond that. What is really new about this concept and
what are the characteristics of learning regions? As it is, Hassink argues,

the learning region overlaps with many other theories in the field of regions and innovation. In his view, the learning region should develop into a new approach in which 'learning clusters' play a crucial role. The new direction that Hassink sees forms a natural bridge to the last part of this volume.

The final part of this volume concerns the future of the learning region. The single chapter in this part is perhaps the most challenging one, as it seeks to distinguish the learning region from other theories in the field, some of which have been around for much longer than the learning region. The various chapters in Part II have identified a large number of variables that play a role in the concept of the learning region. Of course, these variables could be neatly organized into a conceptual model in Part III, but that would be to miss the point. After all, many of these variables can also be found in the other theories referred to above. If the learning region is to secure its own place in the literature on regions and learning, it must offer something new. The novelty, we argue, should be in a particular approach rather than in the variables or the phenomena that are the object of study. For the learning region, we propose that a relational approach to studying regions and learning is the most promising way to set the learning region apart from other theories in the field. The relational approach advocates that actors should be studied within the context of their real social relations with other actors. In the case of learning between actors, this approach seems particularly relevant, as learning is a decidedly social process, something consistently put forward by the authors in Part II. The relational approach, rather than a purely economic approach, borrows from sociology in understanding social relations. Probably the best-known representative of the relational perspective to date is Mark Granovetter, with his account of 'embeddedness' (Granovetter, 1985). However, the relational approach really goes back to the work of the French sociologist Émile Durkheim in the late nineteenth century. Chapter 13 spends some time on developing the relational perspective from the work of Granovetter and Durkheim (Durkheim, 1893/1997).

In our view, the future of the learning region lies in the way in which regional learning is best explained. This means that the actual social context of actors must be accounted for. The social context not only includes relations with other actors but also refers to the fact that a region as such is a social context that affects how actors behave, albeit in varying degrees from region to region. At the very least, the more sociological approach that we suggest, although in need of further development, offers something new to the literature on regions and innovation that is in danger of becoming monopolized by transactionist, economic approaches.

NOTES

1. 'Whereas at one time the decisive factor of production was land, and later capital . . . today the decisive factor is increasingly man himself, that is, his knowledge.' Pope John Paul II in his 1991 encyclical *Centesimus annus.*
2. DRUID: Danish Research Unit for Industrial Dynamics.

REFERENCES

Argyris, C. (1962), *Interpersonal Competence and Organizational Effectiveness*, Homewood, IL: Dorsey.

Arrow, K. (1962), 'The economic implications of learning-by-doing', *Review of Economic Studies*, **29**, 155–73.

Asheim, B. (1996), 'Industrial districts as "learning regions": a condition for prosperity', *European Planning Studies*, **4** (4), 379–400.

Boekema, F., Morgan, K., Bakkers, S. and Rutten, R. (eds) (2000), *Knowledge, Innovation and Economic Growth. The Theory and Practice of Learning Regions*, Cheltenham, UK and Northampton, MA, USA: Edward Elgar.

Breschi, S. and Lissoni, F. (2001), 'Localised knowledge spillovers vs. innovative milieux: knowledge "tacitness" reconsidered', *Papers in Regional Science*, **80** (3), 255–74.

Durkheim, É. (1893/1997), *The Division of Labour in Society*, New York: The Free Press.

European Commission (1995), *The Green Paper on Innovation*, Brussels: European Commission.

European Commission (2004), *Regions Matter: EU Regional Policy and Structural Funds*, Brussels: European Commission.

Florida, R. (1995), 'Toward the learning region', *Futures*, **27** (5), 527–36.

Granovetter, M. (1985), 'Economic action and social structure: the problem of embeddedness', *American Journal of Sociology*, **91** (3), 481–510.

Hague, I. (ed.) (1996), *Trade, Technology and International Competitiveness*, Washington, DC: The World Bank.

Lundvall, B. (1988), 'Innovation as an interactive process: from user–producer interaction to the National System of Innovation', in G. Dosi, C. Freeman, R. Nelson, R. Silverberg and L. Soete (eds), *Technical Change and Economic Theory*, London: Pinter.

Lundvall, B. (ed.) (1992), *National Systems of Innovation: Towards a Theory of Innovation and Interactive Learning*, London: Pinter.

Malecki, E. (2000), 'Knowledge and regional competitiveness', *Erdkunde*, **54**, 334–51.

Morgan, K. (1997), 'The learning region: institutions, innovation and regional renewal', *Regional Studies*, **31** (5), 491–503.

Morgan, K. (2004), 'The exaggerated death of geography: learning, proximity and territorial innovation systems', *Journal of Economic Geography*, **4** (1), 3–21.

OECD (1992), *Technology and the Economy: The Key Relations*, Paris: OECD.

Ohmae, K. (1995), *The End of the Nation State: The Rise of Regional Economies*, London: HarperCollins.

Porter, M. (1990), *The Competitive Advantage of Nations*, London: Macmillan.

Rutten, R. (2003), *Knowledge and Innovation in Regional Industry. An Entrepreneurial Coalition*, London: Routledge.

Rutten, R. and Boekema, F. (eds) (2004), 'The quest for spatial embeddedness: knowledge, proximity and capabilities', Special Issue, *European Planning Studies*, **12** (5).

Rutten, R. and Boekema, F. (eds) (2005), 'Innovation, policy and economic growth: theory and cases', Special Issue, *European Planning Studies*, **13** (8).

Storper, M. (1993), 'Regional "worlds" of production: learning and innovation in the technology districts of France, Italy and the USA', *Regional Studies*, **27** (5), 433–55.

Storper, M. (1997), *The Regional World: Territorial Development in a Global Economy*, New York: The Guilford Press.

PART I

Foundations

2. Regional 'worlds' of production: learning and innovation in the technology districts of France, Italy and the USA

Michael Storper

A NEW ERA OF COMPETITION

There is now widespread agreement that the forms of production organization which characterized the most dynamic industries of the post-war
period in the advanced economies, i.e. mass production in the consumer
durables sectors and their associated capital goods, are no longer as central
to economic growth, change and capital accumulation as they once were.
The social science literatures are replete with tales of the restructuring of
the Chandlerian–Galbraithian firm, the spread of programmable technologies, the shortening of product cycles, the deepening of contracting
and subcontracting relations, the revival of the role of small and medium-
sized units of production, and the emphasis on quality as much as on price
in competition (Piore and Sabel, 1984; Becattini, 1987; Sabel, 1989; Best,
1990; Sengenberger and Loveman, 1990; Hirst and Zeitlin, 1992). There is
an emerging consensus that the most advanced competitive standard in the
evolving system of open global markets is that of *continuous technological
change* (Amendola and Gaffard, 1990; Amsden, 1990; Best, 1990). There is
also evidence of increasing specialization in world trade patterns as a result
of uneven distribution of specialized technical skills and learning (Dosi
et al., 1990; Gerstenberger, 1990; Porter, 1990; Guerrieri, 1992).

Many of these technologically dynamic, export-oriented sectors are
found in localized concentrations within their respective national territories: examples include the high technology zones of the USA, the strong
concentration of mechanical engineering in southern Germany, the famous
pockets of design-oriented production in northeast-central Italy, or the
concentration of high technology and high fashion in the Paris region
(Storper, 1992). In this paper, I investigate and compare the social relations
and institutions at the regional level that underpin technologically

dynamic, export-oriented production networks in France, Italy and the USA. I argue that localized rules, institutions and practices are key both to their geographical concentration and their technological performance.

Agglomeration and Technological Dynamism

In recent years, it has been demonstrated that vertical disintegration is positively associated with geographical agglomeration: as the level of external transactions in a production system increases in the face of growth or uncertainty, and to the extent that those transactions have geographically sensitive cost structures, there is a tendency for the producers caught up in that division of labour to cluster in territorial space in order to minimize the time and costs of transacting (Scott, 1988a).

In technologically dynamic industries (whether in sectors where product technology is highly uncertain, such as the high technology industries, or in dynamic versions of a sector characterized by relatively mature technologies), vertical integration of the production system tends to be inhibited by the need of firms to avoid 'lock-in' to a given technology and instead to retain the flexibility needed to travel down a pathway of technological change whose contours cannot be fully defined at the outset (Nelson and Winter, 1982; Dosi et al., 1988). As a result, technologically dynamic industries typically are organized in the form of production *networks*, based on an elaborate *and shifting* interfirm and inter-unit divisions of labour (Amendola and Gaffard, 1990; Foray, 1990).

The technologically dynamic production complex is a special case, because the uncertainty which underlies its division of labour is, *a priori*, both greater than the cases of uncertainty and qualitatively different. First, a given transactional relationship in the presence of learning tends to be qualitatively more dense than in the case of simple market fluctuations, for it involves knowledge that is not only not yet standardized, but which is often not yet developed (Lorenz, 1988; Håkansson, 1989; Lundvall, 1990). User–producer interactions thus involve the difficult and not easily objectifiable process of interpretation. Second, the whole transactional structure may be subject to redefinition as new types of products and new firms enter the structure and as whole new sub-nodes, channels and codes of transaction are defined (Russo, 1986; von Hippel, 1987). Where rapid learning is taking place, the transactional structure is likely to involve constant negotiation, renegotiation and dependence on achieved understandings as the basis of achieving common reinterpretations of new evidence and opportunities (Bellandi, 1989).

Yet even this explanation of the relationship between agglomeration and technological dynamism, based on input–output transactions, is at best partial. Some such agglomerations appear to have relatively low levels of direct interfirm transactions and are instead characterized by untraded or non-market interdependencies between innovative firms. The analytical task is, then, to comprehend the basis for both the complex interfirm transactional relations noted above, and these untraded interdependencies. In this paper, I emphasize the behavioural basis for such interrelations which lead to learning, arguing that rules, institutions and practices of key collective agents enable local technological learning. Particular sets of such behaviours select the local economy into particular sectors, on the basis of the compatibility between local forms of learning and the underlying technological possibilities of sectors (or, more accurately, subsectors).

Agglomeration thus seems to be tied to all three of the principal dimensions of technological change: technological (lock-in vs flexibility); economic (cost minimization, knowledge spillovers and externalities); and behavioural (qualities of transactions and learning) – Dosi et al., 1990.[1] As a result, we may call the agglomerations in which technologically dynamic industries are located 'technology districts' (Storper, 1992).

Technological Learning and Regional Context: Conventional 'Worlds' of Production

If we assume that, in a given industry, there is an outer technological frontier of existing or currently anticipatable fundamental or applied knowledge, the question is why some producers act upon it more than others, and why they act upon it as they do. One obvious reason is that information is imperfect, and some sets of producers have better institutions that reduce the uncertainty associated with this information in a way that they learn more from it. But this is again just the weak version of uncertainty. We can say, more positively, that the use and development of information in such a way that technological learning takes places has to do with the qualitative behaviours of agents in a network.

There is significant evidence that all agents are not alike when it comes to transactional activity (Granovetter, 1985).[2] If the behaviours of producers and users – their expectations, preference structures, and so on – differ considerably from place to place, it stands to reason that some types of behavioural routines, and the rules and institutions that underlie them, are more effective at promoting interactions which sustain technological learning than others. This suggests, in other words, that the potential positive externalities of production networks, in the form of technological learning, are only realized – or, are differentially realized – according to the concrete qualities of the transacting that is carried out.

While some of these differences in outcome could, in principle, reflect different behavioural preferences of the people who constitute the production network, the question would still arise as to why some preferences are shared or why, in any case, the preferences of some people become the norms of the network (see Elster, 1984). Stated another way, only some preferences take the form of mutual engagements and thus become enforceable social habits of the transactional activity which underlies technological learning. It is, therefore, necessary to identify the key principles of mutual engagement of the critical agents in the production system, or what may be called the *conventions* of that production network and its agglomeration. Conventions are practices, routines, agreements and their associated informal or institutional forms. They bind economic actors together so that mutual behavioural expectations co-ordinate their actions. In essence, a set of conventions defines a local 'world of production'. Such a 'world' consists of practices, institutions and material objects/tools, but it is also a coherent universe of action – what political philosophers call a *cité* – which incorporates specific forms of cognition, theories, doctrines, institutions and rules (see, *inter alia*, Centre d'Etudes de l'Emploi, 1987; Choffel et al., 1988; Eymard-Duvernay, 1989; Salais, 1989; Thevenot, 1989).

This, then, is the field of inquiry into the behavioural sources of technologically dynamic or learning-rich production systems, and the differences between these systems and others. It involves a structured conceptualization of a broad set of features of a regional political–economic culture, its institutions and the behavioural routines of its individual and collective agents.[3]

In this paper, I present brief case studies of conventions underlying technology districts in France, Italy and the USA.[4] The case study sketches presented focus on two principal conventions which define the behavioural dimensions of technological learning in these production systems: the *identities* of the key innovating agents; and the ways in which their *participation* in the production system is organized *vis-à-vis* other groups.

NORTHEAST-CENTRAL ITALY: HIGH ENTRY, CLOSE CO-ORDINATION AND REGIONAL CLOSURE

Introduction

The story of industrial growth in northeast-central (NEC) Italy has now been told many times (Bagnasco, 1977; Becattini, 1978, 1987; Balestri, 1982; Brusco, 1982; Piore and Sabel, 1984; Russo, 1986). In regions such as

Emilia-Romagna, Tuscany, the Veneto, and parts of Lombardy, Trentino-Alto Adige and Friuli-Venezia-Guilia, especially over the 1960s and 1970s, there was a remarkable growth of employment and output in the design-intensive or craft-based industries, producing mostly fashion goods – clothing, leather, fabrics, furniture, personal accessories – but also frequently extending to the machinery sectors associated with these final outputs, and occasionally including other metalworking or mechanical industries (such as food processing or packaging machinery). In a number of sectors, these regions produce very high proportions of Italian exported outputs and, in a few, they are absolutely dominant in world markets (Balestri, 1982; Becattini, 1987; Nuti, 1990; Sforzi, 1990). These areas are distinguished by their dense clusters of very small firms (hundreds or even thousands of firms, whose size averages ten employees or fewer, depending on industry or locality). It is important to note that other local industrial areas in Italy share these characteristics of small size, large numbers and dense local concentration in narrow sectoral specializations, but that only in NEC Italy has rapid growth in per capita income relative to these other areas occurred in tandem with the growth process in general (Del Monte, 1986). Numerous quantitative and qualitative analyses have shown that NEC Italy is different from the other areas in that the firms partake of a local, vertical division of labour, whereas in other areas they tend to be clusters of firms which do the same thing; and that in NEC Italy, the local production system is richly endowed with commercial agents who organize the production activities and market the local products as final outputs, with a local independent brand name, whereas, in other areas, firms are frequently either subcontractors to larger external firms (especially to Piemontese or Milanese firms), or they sell intermediate inputs on open markets (Nuti, 1990).

The experience of NEC Italy has attracted a great deal of attention because it is rare for a wealthy developed country to specialize heavily in fashion-oriented and semi-customized industrial outputs, and to do so via production systems which are rooted overwhelmingly in small, often very small, firms. Even when other developed economies do show similar trade specializations (e.g. German textiles and textile machinery), the production systems tend to be more normal, in the sense that they involve bigger firms, more bureaucratic forms of work organization and lower levels of geographical concentration than are found in NEC Italy. As a consequence, much of the vast literature on NEC Italy has devoted its attention to the structural properties of the region's production systems: firm size; productivity; wages; prices; scale; and scope. In some cases, the characteristics of these systems are said to define an ideal type of flexible specialization, and in other cases an ideal type of industrial backwardness and petty entrepreneurship.

Southern European Latin–Catholic Capitalism

There exists a long line of thought on the specificities of capitalist development in the Latin countries of Southern Europe. These places have developed along fundamentally different lines from the Protestant, Anglo-Saxon capitalism of the Rhenish–Lotharingian system (with Lombardy, however, included in the latter). Barrington Moore's well-known thesis of a 'conservative modernization' which preserves political stability at the price of more rapid growth and technological change is the key point of reference (Moore, 1966). Southern Europe is distinguished by: the importance of its *petite bourgeoisie* (20–30 per cent of total workforce, against 8–12 per cent in Northern Europe); by political institutions rooted in clientelism (frequently church-, class- and family-based, sometimes Mafia-based), whose exchanges of favours secure political stability but slow down economic adjustments by impeding factor mobility; and by a conflictual and group-based form of democracy where rights are secured through hard, active social conflicts, as opposed to the individualistic forms of citizenship and the administered quality of Northern European democracies (Berger, 1981; Carboni, 1991).

All this is, of course, a background to NEC Italian development. But it cannot help us understand why the NEC Italian economic experience has been so different from most areas in Italy, Spain and France: on the one hand, why the systems of NEC Italy have not stagnated as in Southern Italy; on the other, why the decentralized model of production has so much more force here than in France. In NEC Italy, for example, the traditional *petite bourgeoisie* has transformed itself into a rich and privileged entrepreneurial middle class; extremely rapid economic growth has now been joined to high levels of political stability; and clientelism seems to have assumed highly modern forms that do not, at least to the degree envisioned by Moore's theory, impede economic adjustments, but instead channel them in qualitatively specific ways.

The point of departure of virtually all the detailed studies of the NEC Italian production systems – by both admirers and detractors – is that they should not be regarded as collections of small firms, but rather something akin to multi-product organizations, and that the internal institutional arrangements of the systems are deeply inscribed in broader social arrangements (or what economists might call the 'institutional environment'). The original contribution of the present analysis is to systematize the understanding of how these arrangements constitute conventions that underlie the economic performance of these production systems.[5]

Entry, Membership, Reciprocity, Voice and Loyalty

Figure 2.1 schematizes the conventions of participation in Emilian and Tuscan export-specialized production systems. On the left-hand side of the figure may be found (somewhat modified) equivalents to the economic components of the system which are analysed above (markets, firms and the division of labour, labour, innovation, economic efficiency), which are the *economic outcomes of participation*; on the right-hand side may be found the *sources of identities of key actors*, while the middle column refers to the *ways those actors interact or participate*, the mechanism that connects forms of participation to economic outcomes.

Selection and entry: resource mobilization and class structure
There are five basic communities which have been mobilized to construct the production systems of NEC Italy: (1) the buyers, designers and innovators; (2) middle-class entrepreneurs; (3) new entrepreneur/artisans; (4) homeworkers; and (5) skilled workers. The sources of these groups are quite diverse, and the borders between some of them are quite fluid.

In the case of fashion industries, there are almost always special agents who take care of buying products from producing firms, intermediating between the production system and the market; alternatively, there are designers who possess brand names or skills which are recognized directly on national and international markets. The ranks of these key agents are difficult to join in that there are skill and reputation barriers to entry; what is surprising is that the ranks of these agents show considerable turnover. Historically, designers are the modern heirs of aristocratic tastes (in Tuscany), where ranks were never fully closed as in the case of French guilds (*corporations*). In Emilia, designers are less important than product innovators, who frequently are former skilled workers who have gone to technical schools, or who have teamed up with scientists and technicians via those schools.

Participation in the production systems in question is thus characterized by the possibility of entry into the key technology-mastering groups. Entrepreneurial activity is mobilized by a series of push and pull factors in Emilia and Tuscany. Middle-class entrepreneurs are usually just one-generation inheritors of enterprises started by their parents; the stratified class barriers typical of the industrial north do not exist in the industrial economies of these regions. More recent firms are frequently of the smaller artisanal (less than ten workers) type. Here, entrepreneurs in the twentieth century have had three principal avenues of access to industrial activity. Many were released from agriculture, and specifically from *mezzadria* (metayage; share-cropping activity), which was the dominant form

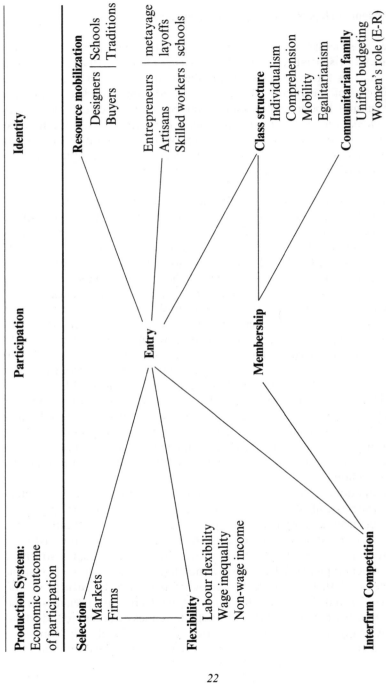

Production System:
Economic outcome
of participation

Participation

Identity

Selection
Markets
Firms

Flexibility
Labour flexibility
Wage inequality
Non-wage income

Entry

Membership

Interfirm Competition

Resource mobilization
Designers | Schools
Buyers | Traditions

Entrepreneurs | metayage
Artisans | layoffs
Skilled workers | schools

Class structure
Individualism
Comprehension
Mobility
Egalitarianism

Communitarian family
Unified budgeting
Women's role (E-R)

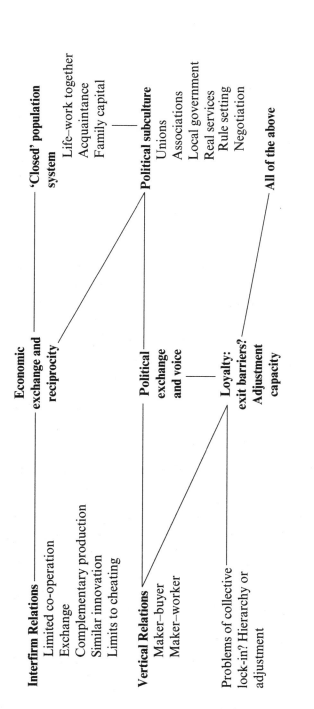

Figure 2.1   Conventions of identity and participation in NEC Italy

of agricultural organization in both these regions. Share-cropping is dominant only in NEC Italy; historically it is fully dominant in no other European region (Todd, 1990). As a result, there is an unusually strong experience in organizing independent, small-scale and family-based economic activity, and an extremely strong ideology of economic independence, i.e. the wish not to work directly as a wage labourer. As late as 1950, 40 per cent of the population of these regions was in agriculture, and that proportion dropped to less than 10 per cent by the end of the 1970s (Tinacci Mosello, 1983). A second source of entrepreneurs, principally in the metalworking sector of Emilia, is technical schools, which have a long history in that region. Those schools combine theoretical and practical training, thus making possible independent, innovative but applied activity and, because they were founded and operated in a region noted for its socialist orientation, access to them has frequently involved people from all classes (Cappecchi, 1990a). Third, in the post-war period, both regions suffered massive layoffs of workers from large industrial plants, and those workers typically did not migrate from the region but instead turned to entrepreneurial activity. Many of these were highly skilled workers who were provided with machines by their former employers to start up their own firms. Finally, even those families that remained in agriculture, and some that turned to urban work, often had at least one member who was available for industrial homework; many homeworkers were women who had skills in pre-existing specialities of these regions (weaving straw hats in Emilia, for example, a predecessor of the knitwear industry). In Emilia, women homeworkers have been politically organized for many decades, formalizing their work and institutionalizing their position in the regional economy.

In both these regions, but especially in Emilia-Romagna, the class structure is compressed: the structural differentiation typical of centres of large-scale industry has not been heavily in evidence in the twentieth century, as manifested in qualities of the region's class system – such as a spirit of egalitarianism, and high levels of upward mobility from working to entrepreneurial class – and in quantitative dimensions such as the low level of regional income inequality when compared to the North and the South (Cappecchi, 1990b).

These forms of participation have had a clear functional effect: the rate of entry into entrepreneurial activity has been extraordinarily high. In turn, the economic outcomes of entry are to select regional production activity into markets for products whose qualities are most amenable to a structure with low barriers to entry and resulting high levels of productive decentralization.

Flexibility: resources, membership and the family

NEC Italy is characterized by a family structure most unusual in Europe: the 'communitarian family'. This family type consists of extended family households, where parental (usually father) authority is secure, hierarchical and multi-generational, coupled with the tradition of fully equal inheritance among siblings (Todd, 1990). The economic logic in this kind of situation is unified family budgeting, i.e. the sharing of family income and the goal of maximizing the income of the whole, rather than the individual parts. It is enforced by the authority wielded by the *capofamiglia*. The logic of individual labour is not predominant (Paci, 1985), nor the logic of individual survival, which makes economic fluctuations relatively untraumatic for individuals (Becattini, 1987). Work, entrepreneurship and participation in NEC Italy cannot be understood by looking at the individual in the labour market, but must be analysed in terms of the individual within the family unit, in relation to labour and product markets.

The effects of this membership on the structure of the production system are many. Smaller firms are generally characterized by lower productivity and wages per hour than larger firms. Lower wage incomes are in general compensated by income redistribution within the communitarian family. For both entrepreneurs and workers, boom times offer profit as a source of income. The quasi-rents that are earned on the kinds of products made in the region come directly to entrepreneurs, and are, in some cases, shared out in higher wages for loyal skilled employees. It is precisely this mechanism, in combination with family income pooling, that has allowed so much capital accumulation and firm formation to occur in the region. The principal way of raising incomes over the 1960s and 1970s was not, in any case, through productivity-led price reductions, but by moving up the price–performance curve to 'better' goods, and by enlarging markets in the geographical sense, i.e. further internationalization (see Rey, 1989).

For entrepreneurs, the advantages are clear. But why are workers willing to tolerate wage inequalities *vis-à-vis* larger firms? There are, apparently, two reasons. On the one hand, many have few formal skills and cannot secure positions in larger firms; this is certainly true of a significant number of workers in the smaller firms, and homeworkers, who are frequently overworked and underpaid. On the other hand, interviews with workers in the small firms suggest another reason: many hope to become entrepreneurs themselves, and prefer smaller firms because they are connected by relations of family and friendship and they use their experience in these firms to learn about entrepreneurship (Solinas, 1982). In the case of extended family relations, these workers will often be partially financed by their 'employers' later on (Dei Ottati, 1991). That this is a trajectory for workers is suggested by the fact that, in one recent survey, 56 per cent had had voluntary interfirm mobility up to three times, and 10 per cent more than three times (Trigilia, 1990). As a representative of the Confederazione Generale Italiana del Lavoro put it recently:

> The features of work in industrial districts are at the root of the difference between district workers and workers in traditional businesses. In districts, for example, work may be paid for by a combination of earnings and a share in company ownership. Those workers who possess the greatest professional skills are in a position to use this as a level on the labour market and hence to move from one firm to the next until they are offered a real stake in the ownership of the firm for which they work. (Brutti, 1990, p. 3)

In short, membership has a redistributive, income-smoothing effect which provides enormous labour flexibility to firms, while providing non-wage income for a large number of entrepreneurs and training for a certain number of workers. The group which is largely left out is the homeworkers.

This circumstance calls our attention to a critical dimension of the role of labour in the production system – the motivations of workers, the ways they interpret their own circumstances, have to do with the wider net of social relations to which they belong. Their overall income and life-chance structures are as important in mobilizing them as a collective resource as their immediate hourly pay conditions and their status as wage labour.

Interfirm competition: entry and membership
The ease and continuity of entry virtually guarantee that there are high levels of interfirm competition. It is precisely the ideologies of economic independence, combined with a compressed class structure, which make entrepreneurs equals among equals, with little of the paternalism and local hierarchy, which limit the possibility of interfirm competition, found in many other local production systems for these types of goods elsewhere in Europe. Interfirm competition is assured, moreover, by the system of com-mercialization, for buyers, designers or final output manufacturers are keenly aware of the prices and qualities that can be offered by the best pro-ducers in an area, and enforce these standards on all firms to whom they give orders (Bursi, 1988). Fierce, though bounded, local competition is the order of the day.

Interfirm relations: reciprocity and social closure
The regions of NEC Italy are characterized by high levels of closure of their local population systems; that is, high percentages of those living and working in the area were born there (Bellandi, 1992). In strictly economic terms, this relative closure is mirrored in the very low levels of internation-alization of ownership and control of firms, and in the very high levels of

ownership and control by natives of the regions (Mutinelli et al., 1991). This does not imply that capital and resources from outside the regions, or outside of Italy, are not present. Indeed, the levels of strategic alliances and external capital participation have tended to rise in recent years. But even with a rising number of acquisitions, the overall extraregional and international participation remain strikingly low.

Economic reciprocity rests essentially on the dense interpersonal ties between individuals and families who know each other for life, which is structurally underpinned by this population closure. First, there are limited co-operative exchanges between firms, the typical form of which is work sharing. When a firm has too much work, it may share it out with other firms, on the expectation of a return when the shoe is on the other foot. At times, firms will even permit their equipment to be used by workers from another firm, on their premises (Becattini, 1989).

Second, there are limits to cheating. Cheating may take two principal forms in the contexts under discussion. On the one hand, in a fiercely competitive environment when workloads are low, producers may bid below their average costs, rather than have no work at all, in an effort to build their connections to the buyers. On the other hand, buyers may bid down prices to untenable levels when their power is great. Both of these types of behaviour do occur, but they have been surprisingly rare, even in the very difficult decade of the 1980s. One can only assume that the circulation of information is such that the negative reputation effects outweigh, in most cases, the temptation to cheat.

Third, in both the fashion and the mechanical engineering sectors, complementary technological developments are promoted by dense connections between people. In the latter, there are numerous documented instances of firms aiding skilled workers to set up their own firms, but in complementary or cognate rather than competitive product lines (Cappecchi, 1990b). In the former, the information flows between producers and equipment makers are known to be extremely thick; in Prato, for example, this supports a robust textile machine and equipment sector, as it does in the Sassuolo tile equipment industry. User–producer relations for complementary technological improvements and market-widening are forms of reciprocity (Bursi, 1982; Russo, 1986).

Vertical relations: voice and political subcultures
The regions of NEC Italy are characterized by distinctive political subcultures: whether communist areas as in Emilia and Tuscany, or 'white' (Christian Democratic) areas of the Veneto or Friuli-Venezia-Giulia, they have distinctive, non-contested local political majorities. In essence, these unified political subcultures aggregate fragmented demands and free the

local political system from pressures of divided loyalties (Trigilia, 1986). In lieu of having to contest power, their absolute local dominance provides them with the opportunity to construct mechanisms for voice between the principal parties in the local economy, through which solutions to problems are negotiated. Note that neither the red nor the white regimes are heavily associated with the ideologically motivated programmes those labels normally suggest. Both are fundamentally neo-localist regimes, where agents bundle the principals' demands, and give them voice, although the organizations through which voice is exercised do have different ideological colours: in the red areas, they are unions and co-operatives, as well as artisanal associations and local government agencies, while in the white areas they are linked to the local church (rural savings banks, charities, agricultural organizations).

In Emilia, unions have been considerably more favourable to the system of decentralized production than in Tuscany, where they have kept up an ideological opposition to small firms as backward and opposed to the interests of the working class (Pezzini and Brusio, 1990; Regini, 1988). In both, only about one-third of the workers in the very smallest artisanal firms are organized, as opposed to much higher percentages (exceeding 70 per cent) in firms with more than 100 workers in Emilia. In both, however, unions have been critical in securing district-wide agreements that protect wages even in the smallest artisanal firms, even when, as in Tuscany, they refuse to participate actively and ideologically in political projects to build the decentralized production structure (Trigilia, 1986). Other critical organizational bases of voice include the local branches of the Confederazione Nazionale d'Artigianato (CNA), who negotiate for the smallest firms, as well as the kinds of industry associations found elsewhere. Thus, the local system is highly negotiated and inclusive, but in the form of a four-party local corporatism – artisans, political party locals, unions and local–regional governments. The leadership of each of these groups is strongly interlocking in Emilia-Romagna and Tuscany. In combination with the relatively low level of entry–exit into the regional population system, and the communitarian family system, there is very high motivation for problem-solving at the regional level and for avoidance of deep distributional conflicts.

The outcome is what Trigilia (1990), borrowing from Dore's (1987) characterization of the negotiated character of Japanese production systems, calls 'flexible rigidities'. Unions secure district-wide wage and working conditions agreements. In the Prato woollen textiles district, the unions have negotiated an agreement on the production calendar covering hundreds of mills which partake of the same production cycles, agreeing to reduce the workweek but allowing overtime (without hourly wage premiums) to take place when demand is high, with the overtime hours banked against slack periods of the year. The agreement's preamble states that 'both unions and industry recognize the need to find solutions to plant restructuring, above all regarding personnel redundancy' (*The Bridge*, 1988). This type of agreement is important for the mutual obligations it creates. Unions support the modernization of firms, and do not take advantage of boom times to press for conditions which are untenable across the entire production cycle, including the busts which are inherent to the fashion industries. Employers bind themselves to paying wages in the slack parts of the production cycle, and to avoid redundancy when there are cyclical downturns. How important are these mechanisms? Perulli (1987) surveyed a large number of firms in Modena (Emilia-Romagna) and found that fully 60 per cent had agreements for working time flexibility over the year.

There are certain differences between the ways these flexible rigidities are maintained in the red and the white areas; the former tend to have more labour conflicts than the latter, but they are less severe. But in both cases there are almost never severe, prolonged attempts on the parts of employers to deunionize or to severely reduce the terms of worker protections in the district-wide agreements (Trigilia, 1986, p. 1990).

There are two weak points in employer–worker relations, it should be noted. First, homeworkers are rarely unionized, although they have secured legal protections via the action of the regional governments in recent years (indeed, homework is highly regulated in Emilia and Tuscany). This means that homeworkers enjoy certain legal minima, but do not have much collective bargaining power (Lazerson, 1989). Second, a critical group of employers, the buyers, are largely outside the system of flexible rigidities. They retain an extremely high level of flexibility with respect even to the established middle-sized firms in the fashion industries, with everybody else absorbing the effects of such flexibility. Buyers transmit, directly, the force of the market to the production system, and generate significant stress on firms and workers who are party to the kinds of flexibly rigid agreements described here.

Local political solidarity also takes the more traditional form of sectionalism, i.e. lobbying in the local interest with respect to the national government. Even this sectionalism can involve strong vertical solidarities. Artisanal firms, for example, have been steadily institutionalized in the form of a series of national laws (the Sabatini Laws on financial assistance for machinery purposes; R&D support (374/76; 675/77; 46/82); the Marcora Law supporting co-operatives; and the basic artisanal statute which deregulates labour markets for firms with fewer than ten employees). The CNA, which has powerful branches throughout Italy, has

been instrumental in securing such protections for small firms. Local governments in the red areas have helped passage of these laws by contributing to the national majorities required, in spite of the fact that the national
government has been dominated by the Christian Democrats throughout
the post-war period, in another example of solidity of the local structure
for exercising voice on behalf of particular strata in the local production
systems. While sectionalism on behalf of local *firms* is not foreign to
observers in other countries, consider the lengths to which vertical solidarity can go in the presence of local voice systems such as those described
here: national protections for homeworkers (largely unenforced elsewhere)
were supported by the entirety of the political spectrum in Emilia, including employers of all types.

Collective lock-in or adjustment and innovation? Loyalty and exit barriers
After the spectacular successes of the post-war period, some Italian industrial districts suffered in the late 1980s. The woollen district of Prato, for
example, suffered a 19 per cent drop in units of production from 1984 to
1990, and an employment loss of 11 per cent, with cutbacks especially
severe in the firms with more than 100 employees (Balestri, 1991). In the
Carpi district in Emilia-Romagna, there was a 10.5 per cent drop in employment and units of production from 1981 to 1988 (Bursi, 1989). Elsewhere,
as in the mechanical engineering industries of Emilia-Romagna, and some
of the DIC districts in Lombardy and Friuli-Venezia-Giulia, production
has been stable or with marginal cutbacks. Thus, the picture is one of
difficulty in some places, especially the fashion industries of Tuscany and
Emilia, and stability without growth elsewhere.

Some observers have claimed that these difficulties must mean that
decentralized production was merely a parenthesis between two periods of
normal, large-firm dominated, scale-oriented production in these industries (Harrison, 1990). As part of this general reprise of normal industrial
history, they claim that the degree of localism of these industries is now
eroded by internationalization of control and markets.

The evidence is much more ambiguous. The share of employment held
by large firms in Italy continued to drop throughout the 1980s while that of
small firms held steady (Bianchi, 1989). The penetration of international
capital into key Italian production systems is a minor phenomenon,
amounting to only 13 per cent in mechanical engineering, 2 per cent in
textiles and less than 1 per cent in clothing. On a regional basis, the vast
majority of inward investment is in Milan and Turin and has barely
touched Emilia, Tuscany and the Veneto (Mutinelli et al., 1991; Bellandi,
1992); the control of employment by extra-regional firms is also quite low.
Overall firm size distributions do not exhibit any coherent tendency

towards vertical integration in the industries and regions at hand. The recent period has not spelt the end of decentralized production.

Clearly, the question is how well the localized production systems will be able to compete under conditions of declining demand (e.g. in woollen textiles: a world-wide demand decline) or stiffened competition (e.g. in knitwear) or quality-based competition (e.g. from Japanese producers in the case of Emilian mechanical engineering). A number of the forms of local economic participation described above – compressed class structure, communitarian family, closed population structure and strong local political subcultures – not only create propitious conditions for voice and political exchange, but also discourage exit from the region in general and from the production system in particular. There is a high degree of loyalty to the local economic and social systems which, in effect, creates strong exit barriers (Giovannini, 1987). The effects of such loyalty–exit barriers are not fully understood, nor easily formalized or quantified, but virtually all of the close analysts of the NEC Italian production systems agree that they create pressures towards innovation, adjustment and, perhaps, stagnation of the local systems that are manifestly different from those found in, say, American production regions with their high levels of labour entry and exit (Hickmann, 1989).

While existing entrepreneur–artisans are heavily supported not only by the CNA and local governments, but also by their moral 'first-comer' rights inside the production system, they do not oppose the entry of new entrepreneurs because they often know, or identify with, the newcomers. In this case, given the existence of exit barriers, there is a strong pressure for periodic adjustments of the precise field of production and learning, as local supply outstrips demand or as extra-regional competitors enter (Nuti, 1990). In Bologna, Modena and Prato, this has been reflected in pressure to move up the price–performance curve into increasingly high quality products, because high levels of exit and mobility are not politically viable options (Bellandi and Trigilia, 1990). Here, we rejoin our point of departure about the particular relationships of economic growth and political stability in Southern European capitalism.

Attempts to move up the price–quality curve for regional production take many different forms: Carpi's knitwear producers moved into 'fantasy' fabrics; Prato's woollen producers went from industrial-quality carded wools to high-quality combed wools, and are now attempting to move into other markets; Bologna's machinery industries have continually branched out into new closely related outputs, and to improve the quality of existing models. The conventions of learning have been quite resilient in the late 1980s; whether they are adequate to the current challenge remains to be seen (Bellandi and Trigilia, 1990; Forlai and Bertini, 1990).

SPLENDOUR, CADRE AND CORPORATION IN THE ÎLE-DE-FRANCE

France has not been a favoured subject of analysis of either the literatures on technological innovation (where the subjects are almost always Japan and the USA) or on production flexibility (where the subjects are almost always Italy and Germany). In large part, this is because France is a weak specializer at this moment in history; she has few dramatic strong points – in the sense of whole clusters of related industries like the broad American position in high technology or the Italian position in craft-based industries – in international trade, although she has many moderately good positions (Lafay and Herzog, 1989).

France has also been ignored because there is no single, most visible model of technological dynamism underlying its international successes. There are *many Frances*, an observation which may carry some irony in that European nation with the longest-lasting, highly centralizing, state economic policy apparatus (Le Bras and Todd, 1981). The *Francilien* model is that of high technology and, to a lesser extent, design-intensive craft industries in the Paris region: the Île-de-France. The *Rhodanien* model concerns design-intensive and craft-based industries, and metalworking–mechanical sectors in the Rhône–Alpes region. The *système sud* refers to the growth of high technology manufacturing and services in selected areas of southern France. A fourth model, that of the *nouvelle ouest* (Vendée, parts of Brittany), refers to a form of low wage, highly flexible, rural industrialization which is not technologically dynamic. Length limitations permit me to analyse only the Francilien system here.[6]

The Pieces of the Puzzle: Foundations of the Conventions of Production

There are common features to the way that conventions of economic activity are structured in France, whatever the region. All of the systems have three basic building groups, each of which is highly internally (horizontally) organized: (1) employers or the *patronat*; (2) the state (including both the central state and local political brokers or *notables*); (3) workers, and their communities and cultures of *métier* (craft). The different regions are distinguished by the qualities of these groups and their modes of insertion into their respective regional political economies. All of the systems are also *vertically conflictual*, in a way that the Third Italy is not. In each of the cases of a successful regional specialization, one of the groups has the ability and incentive to define the advanced products. A set of detailed practices for mobilizing innovative knowledge, creating markets and regulating labour market transactions, either resolves, in a very specific way, the underlying vertical conflict which is typical of French economic life or allows the group with innovative capacity to impose its will on the others.

Different as they are, both the high fashion and the high technology industries of the Île-de-France, both producing export specializations of France, derive their dynamism from the existence of steep organizational hierarchies and the power of parallel elites in creating, defining and organizing their markets. In the Francilien model, we observe a stop-and-go system of innovation in the high technologies which is dependent on decisions of the state technocracy; in the *haute couture* industries of the same region, the equivalent of the state are the couturiers, who make and impose decisions about fashion innovation.

Fashion clothing in the Île-de-France

The high fashion industries of the Paris region include two basic segments: true *haute couture*, where the product is made in batches of fewer than ten, and the production process is truly artisanal (St Laurent has fewer than 50 in-house couturiers), and the much larger brand-name ready-to-wear market (i.e. moderately expensive clothes produced in small to medium-sized batches on a strictly seasonal basis). Notwithstanding the decentralization of significant amounts of production in the latter segment to other regions of France or even abroad, the production complex has not only held its own in the central Paris neighbourhood known as the *sentier*, but has grown somewhat in recent years (Brunet, 1986).

What are now known as the *maisons de haute couture*, of course, date back to the early part of the twentieth century when Paris – as the cultural capital of the western world – took the lead in developing clothes for the woman liberated from bourgeois dress of the nineteenth century (Lipovetsky, 1987). But the Chanels of the world are really just the latest phase in Paris's role as capital of fashion and luxury goods production. Under Louis XIV, Colbert established the various royal manufactories, such as the one at Sèvres for porcelain and crystal, and at the Gobelins for tapestries and rugs (Boissonade, 1931). These systems of production did not rely on industrial methods; the centralization of royal commands mobilized resources and made possible shifts in commands according to the whims of royal fashion. It was a means to quality control: the establishment of *conventions of product quality*.

Paris was already a centre of clothing fashion in the seventeenth century because it was the political capital of Europe, locus of Europe's most centralized court: men and women from England to the west and Poland and Russia to the east looked to Paris to know how to dress (but not the Italians, who had their own skills in this domain!). Clothes were made to order by individual artisans, of which the Paris region counted a considerable number. What consolidated the whole system was the centralized fashion authority of the court. Because of its commitment to luxury and refinement, many refer to this type of production as based on the French commitment to *splendeur* (splendour). Throughout the eighteenth century, this system grew ever more splendid (see, *inter alia*, De Goncourt, 1982). In the bourgeois society that succeeded the Revolution, the fetish of fashion lived on and clothing design was considered to be one of the *beaux arts*. Bourgeois men engaged in dandyism in the nineteenth century (Prévost, 1957); for women, the situation is summed up in the slogan of the *Magasin des Modes*: '*l'ennui naquit un jour de l'uniformité*' (Lipovetsky, 1987).[7]

The modern *haute couture* system is, in many ways, a natural reincarnation of the old royal system, where the designers occupy a key position in dictating the norms of fashion. Like their royal counterparts, they are the authority behind the convention of quality for the fashion good: they give it material form and organizational continuity. As long as their ranks are stable, there are no shake-ups in the structure of the production system because they control the brand name (Simon, 1931). Splendour, as a convention of product quality, has been carried forth to the present day.

With the rise of new social groups, especially the urban professional classes, new forms of social distinction in fashion have also come about: strict high fashion has been replaced by more widely marketed but none the less not mass-produced garments (Bourdieu and Delsaut, 1975). These garments cannot be produced in-house if costs are to be controlled. The *prêt-à-porter* (ready-to-wear) system is a kind of half-way house between high fashion and the competitive sweatshop system found in the USA. The principal resource is the design of the garment, i.e. the trade-mark which carries the signification of quality, and this is still well guarded by the fashion houses (Latour, 1961). A classic system of subcontract cutting and sewing is used, where ethnic solidarity characterizes each level of the system: the design houses and better boutiques (French); the cutters (middle eastern or Jewish); and the sewers (Turkish, north African) and knock-off (*degriffe*) outlets (middle eastern or Jewish). The labour market for this industry, while relying on ethnic selection, is essentially a *liberal* one, lacking unions and any determining role for families. Only the more highly skilled workers, such as cutters, are what the French call *gens de métier* (craftpersons, with a strong craft identity): their work rules are their own, and their labour processes are not to be rationalized or codified by any outside force, including their employers. Jewish-owned sewing houses, I was told in an interview, have an informal cartel which has maintained constant real prices over the last 20 years and this explains why manufacturers (design houses) have not eliminated them through the price squeeze tactics used in many other garment districts of the world. The key way that vertical conflict is dampened is that the whole industry turns on considerable quasi-rents owing to the brand names of the garments and the relatively closed ranks of the Paris boutique trade. As a result, there is still a great deal of cost pass-through in the fashionable ready-to-wear market (Montagne-Villette, 1987).

A third level of the fashion system is 'young look', or knock-off apparel, which are copies of better *prêt-à-porter* at much lower quality, and aimed at younger buyers at lower prices. Fashions have a short lifespan so proximity to the design community is essential. This is the sweatshop segment of the industry, yet it does not threaten *prêt-à-porter* because of the strong vertical control noted above, and its dependence on those same designers. Spatial proximity and organizational separation are the rules.

To summarize: the dynamism of the system is the design apparatus which controls conventions of product quality and the distribution network. This dynamism is also the source of what might be dubbed the 'technological conservatism' of the system, since it prevents major new groups from entering the ranks of designers; the system remains 'royal', in the sense of hierarchical and closed. The conservatism of the system, due to the oligopoly that controls it, prevents the liberal labour market from becoming a sweatshop market, by enabling the designers to pass through quasi-rents for these relatively expensive garments; it also avoids (at least in part) the temptation to move much of the subcontracting outside Paris altogether. Yet, this is not, in the end, an inclusive system as in NEC Italy and in overseas markets the knock-off industries of other countries, including Italy and Germany, have grown more rapidly than the French, for both cost and design reasons (Montagne-Villette, 1987).

High technology in the Île-de-France
The high technology industries of the Île-de-France are also organized by an elite and they are conservatively innovative. In aerospace and electronics, there are only a few important systems integrators and components producers in France, such as Thomson, Matra, Dassault, Aerospatiale and SNECMA. The products in which French high technology has been internationally successful are overwhelmingly those in which the state's purchases are important, and include: nuclear reactors; digital processors; off-line data processing equipment; radar equipment; telecommunications switching gear; and large aircraft. It must also be remembered that since the 1950s, French industrial planning has been based on a technological concept – that of the *filière* (commodity chain) – and not on final markets: the idea is that industrial competence includes the entire commodity chain (Bauchet, 1986). The convention of quality is a *technological* one and the tradition of splendour continues here, where French industrial planners are noted for undertaking ambitious high technology projects. Thus, when a

command for an existing or developing high technology product is received by a prime contractor in France, it may also be accompanied by an analysis of the *filière*, and an offer on the part of the state (in the form of a plan or a set of co-ordinated incentives) to support further development of that *filière*. The most recent example of this is the *plan calcul* (computer development plan). This differs from the American defence contracting system, where the development of the *filière* (through subcontracting or in-house divisions) is largely left up to the prime contractors themselves.

The definition of the convention of quality comes out of a restricted *milieu* of agents. As is well known, France has an extremely able and highly prestigious state technocracy, coming out of the *grandes écoles* (Suleiman, 1979). These engineers and administrators not only occupy the upper ranks of various ministries and state-owned consumers of high technology systems (such as France Télécom), but also most of the private or semi-private high technology firms (Bourdieu, 1989). The first tier of the production system, the large contractors and the state bureaucracies, are run by a closed elite. There is, as a result, very little user–producer feedback in the way this is normally understood: markets are concentrated and the key producers are also members of the key user (state) group.

Resources are mobilized in a very different way in the second tier, i.e. the network of input suppliers. In spite of the centralizing traditions of both state and employers in France, the Paris region is an extremely large and diversified economy; the opportunity grid is enormous and the rate of new firm start-ups in high technology industries has been very high over the past decade (Carroue, 1984; Lakota and Milleli, 1987). But there are few examples, in France, of a start-up company becoming a major high technology enterprise, as in the story of Apple in the USA in the 1970s, or Hewlett-Packard in the 1950s. This is because the system of commands, of access to markets, is highly organized by the state and the large companies.

The counterpart, however, is that networks are more faithful: a subcontractor firm which curries the right relationships can enjoy a high degree of loyalty, although access is still determined in large measure by the type of connections the principal of the firm possesses: an engineer from a *grande école* has a much greater probability of receiving state or large-firm commands than someone who lacks this title. In sum: the rate of spin-off is lower than in the USA, but the interfirm relations between these two levels of the production network are likely to be more faithful, due to smaller numbers and social solidarity at both levels.

Labour relations play an important role in technological dynamism and its limits. The *Bassin Parisien* is often taken to be *the* model of French labour relations, but in fact its labour markets are constructed on a cultural base and political history which is relatively specific to the region (Le Bras and Todd, 1981). The old guild-like organizations (*corporations*) of arti-sans (*compagnons*), were destroyed in the Revolution but their spirit, para-doxically, lives on in another form, in French working habits, where the spirit of craft is the guide for conduct (Sewell, 1980; Guedez, 1981; d'Iribarne, 1990). As a result, one can find a kind of disrespect for organi-zational–bureaucratic rules, and weak organizational capacity among the French working class of the Paris region – its famous 'anarcho-syndicalist' mix (Terrail and Tripier, 1986). The French employer class has historically reacted with great resistance to the demands of workers, whether this be the strictly private *patronat* or their *confrères* in state-owned companies. French large companies have a well-documented mix of Taylorist work processes and a tendency towards patriarchal and personalistic treatment of workers, including frequent violations by employers of their own Tayloristic rules (d'Iribarne, 1990). The result is that French industry has, for much of the twentieth century, been characterized by strong vertical conflict, in the form of occasional violent labour–capital struggles.

It is the state that has intermediated between these two groups, usually through the system of branch agreements which set the standards of work and pay for each branch of industrial activity. These agreements have a mixed record; while they serve to standardize conditions for each branch, thus encouraging horizontal solidarity for both workers and employers, they also tend to rigidify work and pay conditions, and they do nothing to offset the fundamental vertical conflict between employers and workers. The system of values related to *métier* counteracts, to some extent, the *accords de branche* by precluding strong organizational loyalty for the worker, while the employer's essential hostility to workers and general unwillingness to engage in on-the-job training also remains in place (Segrestin, 1985). This is as much the case in high technology industries as anywhere else, and it has led to a rather persistent inability of French high technology industries to reach the manufacturing quality and price stan-dards of its major competitors. Labour markets are orderly, but at the price of inability to meet best-practice standards.

The state and its closely associated (or owned) companies, then, remains the key to the specializations of the Île-de-France's high technol-ogy industries, where state technocrats and their equivalents in private industry pursue a market that mobilizes their technological talents and reproduces the commercial weaknesses of French high technology (Stoffäes, 1983). With enough resolve, isolation from civilian markets and financial support from the state, the blockages of the labour process, too, can be overcome. The result is that when the decisions of the technocratic *cadres* are good ones, the Francilien (essentially 'royal') system succeeds, often splendidly.

INNOVATION, MATURITY AND SUCCESSION IN CONTEMPORARY CALIFORNIAN HIGH TECHNOLOGY DISTRICTS

High technology and advanced services are just the latest in a series of innovative American products in the twentieth century. The logic of American industrial development over this period has been to invent or – where the USA is not the first mover in purely scientific or inventive terms – to commercialize production and create mass markets for new types of goods, based on the utilization of new *basic* technologies.

Much of the debate on technological dynamism and American economic growth has centred on the relative influence of demand conditions and factor supplies. The notion that the USA has presented a special, perhaps unique, set of demand conditions for new technologies has been central to the analyses of Fishlow (1965), Rosenberg (1972) and others. In the nineteenth century, the occupation of a largely empty continent generated a demand for goods that were light, fast and cheap, rather than durable, steady, precise or heavily ornamented. In virtually all the intermediate or producer goods sectors (guns, locomotives, industrial machinery, bicycles, agricultural equipment), American industry came up with versions that shared these three characteristics and were available to much larger markets than their European counterparts. The advent of consumer society came early on in the USA, and it was based on a technological configuration of daily life which included capital-intensiveness (household consumer durables), large personal spaces (the need for a lot of personal goods) and a high degree of spatial separation (cars, aeroplanes, telephones). For much of this century the American economy has been the global leader in one after another of the industries producing different elements of this package.

This demand-side explanation, while important, is insufficient to account for the sources of American specializations. I shall argue that the mobilization of factor supplies, in the form of the identities and participation of key actors, is central to the developmental trajectory of these complexes. This trajectory may be schematized as follows:

1. The USA is the pioneer of the basic product group.
2. Localized industrial complexes develop rapidly through proliferation of independent firms – spin-off by new groups of entrepreneurs – involving identity creation and participation at the local level.
3. Entrepreneurs typically sell out at a certain point to larger companies, who then concentrate the market; these companies are, at least in terms of their key facilities, mostly located in product-pioneering industrial agglomerations.

4. Taylorization and high average productivity are attained through product standardization.
5. The USA loses its position as producer of state-of-the-art products in that sector, but its role in the US economy is succeeded by another product-pioneering industry.

This sequence of events, and the particular way that the system operates at each of its stages, has deep and coherent causes in the conventions of identity and participation that we shall now investigate with respect to Californian technoloy districts in electronics and aerospace. We shall observe high levels of horizontal inflow into new activities and new markets, but we shall see that the principal solution to long-term problems of adjustment is *exit* of capital and labour resources rather than the search for new markets within those sectors.

The Mobilization of Resources: Innovations and Start-ups

Key resource mobilizing and innovating groups in the American economy have, of course, varied according to the period and the industry at hand; if, in the early nineteenth century, it was the frontier settler, and from the mid-nineteenth to the mid-twentieth it was the industrial capitalist, it is certainly now the entrepreneur/professional or scientist, especially the engineer-turned-entrepreneur. Each of these groups, while sharing the basic American faith in individual achievement, has been constituted by a distinctive convention of identity, and each has ultimately come to be identified with a particular region of the USA.

In the 1930s, 1940s and 1950s, the initial resource-mobilizers in what were to become the American high technology industries were entrepreneurs whose identities were defined by their membership in a scientific–professional culture (Ramo, 1988). As in France, formal knowledge and training are the key elements which underlie admission to this group, but unlike the engineers and scientists who graduate from France's prestigious *École des Mines* or *École Polytechnique*, the American scientist–engineer receives his/her greatest social approval when formal knowledge is applied to entrepreneurial activity, not to the direction of large, technologically important public or semi-public bureaucracies.[8] Whereas in the one case, professionalism means insertion into a prestigious hierarchy, in another it is a means to break away. The professional–scientific culture of the USA is not like *métier* in France or artisanship in Italy either, for in both these cases the mastery of the skill involves solidarity and creativity within the rules, not innovation in the American sense of technological experimentation whose purpose is to break away from the existing, normal path of technological adaptation (Nelson, 1988). The American system is, in this sense, extraordinarily effective at motivating and mobilizing talent to do new things (see Kenney and Florida, 1990).

It should be remembered that the founding entrepreneurs in the high technology sectors did have prior industrial or institutional experience. In the microelectronics industry, the scientists and engineers who were eventually to become the scions of Silicon Valley were originally associated either with university research programmes or with defence-oriented research laboratories. In the case of the aircraft industry, the founders of the important firms were initially associated with one or another kind of machine-building industry in the eastern USA. In aerospace as well, many of today's important companies were started by individuals who had prior experience in a related sector. In some cases, these formative experiences occurred in the locality which would ultimately come to dominate the new industry (Silicon Valley); just as often, they did not (Los Angeles, aerospace).

The other conditions which facilitate entrepreneurial activity in the USA, despite the overwhelming importance of the large-firm sector, are well known and include the well-developed and highly fluid capital market, and relatively low social wage and overhead costs (Bucaille and Beauregard, 1987). But there are other routes as well, which depart from this purely entrepreneurial model. A number of the most important high technology specializations of the USA have, for considerable periods of their history, been supported by military procurement or by regulated oligopolistic markets (as in the civilian aircraft industry in the 1950s and 1960s, where the big airlines supported much of Boeing's research and development and product planning). My purpose here is not to resolve the debate over the sources of all innovation in American high technology, but rather that all the high technology industries, even those whose development ultimately may have depended heavily on various forms of market regulation and protection, none the less had their origins in the technological experimentation alluded to above, even if they later developed under highly subsidized or regulated conditions. This experimentation is currently unfolding in the biotechnology and medical instruments industries (de Vet, 1990).

The convention of quality which underlies the innovative small firm in contemporary Californian high technology is clearly the (difficult to attain) combination of adherence to a scientific rule, while coming up with a novelty. This may involve the new application of existing scientific knowledge, or it may involve research and development prospecting to serve a market which is yet to come into existence (Salais and Storper, 1993). One can find this same phenomenon in the early history of the aircraft industry (the Loughhead [Lockheed] Brothers and Donald Douglas, in the 1920s and 1930s), the microelectronics industry in Silicon Valley (Fred Terman,

Stephen Jobs and others) and in the defence-related equipment sector (Simon Ramo and Howard Hughes).

Interfirm Relations: Spin-off and Agglomeration

In the Californian industrial districts of the twentieth century, once a new domain of products becomes identified in technological terms, i.e. once we know that the industry is the semiconductor industry or the aircraft industry, the process of new firm formation takes on a much more regular pattern – that of spin-off (Scott, 1988a, 1988b). Spin-off essentially consists of a process where *key personnel* separate themselves from existing companies in the now-established industry and set up their own firms. Two dimensions of spin-off may be noted here. On the one hand, the fact that key personnel have such a strong impulse to separate themselves from existing companies and to start up their own is evidence of the deep, underlying rationality of entrepreneurialism in the USA; it is a career path unimaginable for similarly competent engineers in France, for example, where loyalty to prestigious large companies is the rule. On the other hand, these key personnel are no longer precisely the same genre of entrepreneurs who start up the industry: they are formed within an industry which is already institutionalized. Not only is the basic technological scope of the industry now defined, but its professional culture is now considerably more specific.

Spin-off begins to create a more dense transactional tissue in the industry: the proliferation of new product-pioneering companies, as well as of specialized input suppliers, deepens the vertical and horizontal divisions of labour and is manifest in the growth of the local industrial complex and a tendency for average firm size to decline in early years. This has been the history of the semiconductor and aerospace industries in Silicon Valley and Los Angeles, respectively; and the process is currently unfolding in the medical instruments industry of Orange County, just south of Los Angeles (Saxenian, 1988; Scott, 1988a; de Vet, 1990).

The existence of industry-specific human capital, i.e. a professional culture which is now rather precisely delimited, is an important basis of the regulation of interfirm relations and their geographical configuration. New firm founders are linked by their strong professional culture, which defines the rules of the game, and this is reinforced by relatively small numbers and personal reputation effects. Interviews with the founders of the military equipment industry and the semiconductor industry confirm that these two mechanisms give a powerful order and co-ordination to transactional relations, while allowing them remarkable fluidity (Ramo, 1988; see also note 8). At the same time, the fact that such relations are so fluid encourages producers to group themselves together in geographical space

so as to minimize the costs of contracting and re-contracting, and to maximize the probability of successful market search, where formal contracts
do not govern the transactional relationship. This helps to explain the
paradox of agglomeration in the USA, where the extraordinary geographical mobility of resources and the highly developed system of transport and
absence of customs barriers might otherwise be thought to encourage a dispersed set of spatial production relations.

As the industry develops, different specialized production complexes
may come into existence (as in the cases of Dallas, Boston, Minneapolis in
the microelectronics and computer industries, in addition to Silicon
Valley). Although a high proportion of interfirm transactions may remain
local, as in the case of Silicon Valley, certain highly specialized inputs may
only be available from other production areas. These specialized production complexes are marked by professional cultures which are now
industry-, product- (intra-industry) and agglomeration-specific; thus the
identities of mainframe engineers in Minneapolis are different from those
of semiconductor engineers in Silicon Valley or personal computer makers
in Route 128 (Saxenian, 1988; de Vet, 1990).

Industrial Maturity

Industrial maturity in innovative American industries is neither strictly an
outcome of product standardization nor evidence of the failure of the
American system of innovation, as is nowadays frequently claimed. It
is a logical outcome of a system of conventions that privileges product-
pioneering innovations but discourages certain forms of incremental
innovation.

From spin-off to sell-out
In the highly regulated military-oriented industries, the problem of
interfirm co-ordination is resolved by the establishment of a hierarchical
system directed by the prime contractors. But this is a special case. In other
sectors, many observers have noted the relative absence of strong associational ties at the industry level, and a resistance to government regulation
(Saxenian, 1990). Market relations and 'arm's-length' contracting appear
to dominate (Stowsky, 1987).

Once a product-pioneering industry grows to the point where reputation
effects weaken, i.e. where entrepreneurs are linked only by a formal
technical–professional culture, a qualitative change in interfirm relations
appears to take place. Most of the surveys of start-up firms reveal that small
entrepreneurs feel that they have no time to co-ordinate among each other.
They feel enormous pressures from their lenders (whether private lenders or

capital markets, especially in the case of impatient venture capital), the existence of legal barriers to collaboration and the sense that there is a race to the market because others are doing what they are doing. Under these conditions, the temptations to engage in opportunistic behaviour grow and with them the possibilities of business failure. Opportunism includes both the large final output firm that cannot secure sufficient loyalty on the part of its input suppliers and the behaviour of large firms who use their superior legal and market power to unload risk on their smaller suppliers.

The high rate of sell-out of even successful small and medium-sized firms is a rational response to this system of interfirm relations; that is, a high percentage of those firms which do not fairly rapidly go beyond a certain threshold of size and product diversity, and which do not die in their first few years, are sold to larger companies by their founders. The motivations cited by these entrepreneurs are very clear: they are successful at innovation and, faced with the hazardous transactional environment of American industry and the vastly superior financial resources of the large firms, they decide to capitalize a portion of their possible stream of innovative quasi-rents by selling out to the large firm (Bass, 1991). They avoid a risk which is largely created by the transactional environment itself. That environment, however, is a product of the ideology of creating and taking risks which is deeply ingrained in the key actors' culture; those who sell out often claim that they prefer to move on to something else rather than struggle to survive in a morally hazardous transactional environment (Ramo, 1988). The result is not simply a process of development characterized by high rates of spin-off but, via sell-out, a generally high rate of *turbulence* (Hickmann, 1989).

Much of this is well predicted by transactions cost theory, for what we observe is, indeed, a series of market failures followed by a tendency towards vertical integration. My point here is that this market failure is in fact central to the logic of the market itself in American high technology agglomerations. The markets are ordered by conventions in such a way that they fail. The sell-out process is deeply rooted in the rationalities that lead entrepreneurs to create markets in the first place.

Selecting innovation

The idea of *craft* – in the sense of long-term commitment to incremental improvement – is largely absent from the notion of *innovation* in the context described above. It has been closely documented that American industries lead either in very new breakthrough technologies, or in applying breakthroughs that come from elsewhere directly to very standardized production processes (Kelley and Brooks, 1989). Japanese, German and Italian industries, by contrast, appear to be much better at implementing continuous innovations through either factory-level learning-by-doing or production-level learning-by-doing, *where the key to both is close transactional co-ordination* (for an excellent case study of Californian failure in this regard, see Stowsky, 1987).

From breakthrough to maturity
Innovation, followed by transactional failure, ultimately encourages vertical integration. Moreover, managerial practices in large American firms are consistently more oriented towards imposing very rigid and hierarchical role distinctions and limited information feedbacks as compared to Japanese or German firms (Hyman and Streeck, 1988; Aoki, 1990; Coriat, 1990; Sabel et al., 1990). Under these circumstances, it is perfectly logical that American large firms will do better in the manufacture of standardized products than those which require either incremental improvement or co-ordination of many components, or than competitors who are better at co-ordinating transactional systems, whether external or internal. It helps to explain why American product-pioneering industries enjoy a period of very high productivity, hence maturity, after they cease to be product-pioneering.

The American System in Perspective: The Importance of Exit

Product-pioneeering industries in the USA are not only typically agglomerated, but these agglomerations are located outside of zones of traditional industrialization. In the case of high technology, most of the important agglomerations are both outside of the northeastern and midwestern industrial regions (Silicon Valley, Orange County and Dallas), and located in suburban areas rather than cores of large metropolitan regions. In the new industrial spaces of the USA, there is initially no well-defined local elite that organizes the new system of social relations and mediates between interests; new industrial elites (consisting of successful entrepreneur/professionals) are formed and they are integrated into the structure of landowning elites already in place, who profit from the rapid rise in land prices that results from the local industrialization process (Molotch, 1975; Di Lellio, 1987; Bloch, 1992).

In such places, professional culture consists not just of identity based on mastery of scientific or technical knowledge, but also on individual achievement via the use of that knowledge. The deeply rooted themes of American culture are strongly present: equal chances via professionality or training; unequal fates via differences in level of intelligence, hard work or luck (Hartz, 1955; Bellah et al., 1985). The Californian technology district is seen as a place for this individual effort to unfold in propitious conditions, not as a milieu which should encourage equality and solidarity. Indeed, the latter set of conditions are held to be inimical to the product-pioneering which brings the industrial complex into being in the first place (see note 8).

Thus, to use Hirschman's (1970) terminology, we find in contemporary Californian technology districts the paradox of a social order based on agreement about the rationality and disciplining force of exit, and this includes the phenomenon of spin-off, which is a key form that exit takes. In contrast, in the industrial communities of NEC Italy, entry is followed by loyalty and voice; in the Francilien system, the barriers to entry are extremely high, and hierarchy combined with loyalty governs the transactional system.

Another supposed anomaly of the American innovation and manufacturing system is that it excels at basic technological innovations (breakthroughs), but does less well at follow-through, i.e. at commercializing innovations and maintaining market shares (Cohen and Zysman, 1986). Some have even recently claimed that the American system of breakthroughs is breaking down (Kenney and Florida, 1990).

On the basis of the account given here, it may be seen that follow-through is not absent in the American system; in the form of product standardization, Taylorization and the introduction of mass production methods, American industry does follow through on its basic innovations. With the dramatic evidence of loss of American share in many high technology markets (such as merchant semiconductors, consumer electronics and capital goods in the electronics sector), the correct question to pose is – why does this specific form of follow-through not succeed in maintaining market shares? The provisional answer that follows from our account is that this follow-up privileges standardization and the efficiencies of mass production to the detriment of incremental innovation, as seems to be so strongly in evidence in the Japanese and German manufacturing systems (Cusumano, 1985; Aoki, 1990; Best, 1990; Coriat, 1990). While much of the now extensive literature on American production methods has centred on the commitment to mass production methods as the source of this problem (e.g. Jaikumar, 1986); it may very well be that the conventions of the system which so effectively encourage invention and initial innovation also encourage exit on the part of innovators and do little to encourage resulting large firms to turn their talents to incremental improvements. Two sectors of the economy – the highly innovative and the highly productive – have relatively little long-term interaction as compared to other countries. Moreover, at a larger scale, the American economy has had a developmental path in which sectoral succession compensates for maturity and decline; the latter is tolerated because of a faith in replacement of old sectors by new sectors (Bluestone and Harrison, 1982). The failures of the American system, which are so often discussed today, must be seen not as aberrations, but as deeply inscribed in the conventions of identity and participation of the American economy.

REGIONAL SYSTEMS COMPARED: IDENTITY, PARTICIPATION AND INNOVATION

In this section, I turn to an explicit comparison of the technology districts studied above. The technological dynamism of these systems arise when key resources are mobilized through a convention of *identity* and when the group holding that identity is co-ordinated with other key groups in the production system through a convention of *participation* such that the key resource can be used for innovation which corresponds to the basic technological possibilities of a particular sector or sub-sector; the conventions that encourage learning are thus economic selection devices for their production systems (on selection, see Dosi et al., 1990).

The definition of distribution of key production skills and competences, by which is meant the stock of knowledge and practice which is key to the particular technological dynamism, i.e. the field in which learning takes place, are based on socially constituted identities. The identities of key skill groups is normally associated with recognized important institutions: in NEC Italy, the artisans have the Confederazione Nazionale d'Artigianato (CNA), which is organized into regional groups. In Bologna, a visit to the CNA is very impressive. One goes to the outskirts of town and finds oneself in front of a 23-storey office tower. The regional CNA occupies the entire building. Its programmes for small entrepreneurs range from research, training and finance to strong local political interventions (through political parties as well as through relations directly to elected administrations) to ensure that the entrepreneurial environment is highly regulated and supported by regional government. In France, organization at each horizontal level of the system is very strong: Francilien technocrats have both narrow class origins and they share the rigorous socializing experience of the *grandes écoles*, to the point where they have recently been named 'the aristocracy of the State' (Bourdieu, 1989). It is also brought together for workers at the branch level through the *accords de branche* which are imposed on all workers in each industry by the state. In the USA, as we noted, scientific–professional culture is strongly imparted by the university training system and its counterpart, formal credentialing.

These key resource mobilizers do not exist in isolation, of course, and so their relations to other groups in the production system and regional society are crucial to whether their competences get used to promote learning and

Table 2.1   Identity, participation and innovation compared

Identity \\ Participation	Entry difficult system 'closed'	Entry easy system 'opened'
Local identity: small numbers; acquaintance; reputation	Southern Germany[1]	NEC Italy[2]
National identity: large numbers; anonymity; formalized, codified	Francilien[3] High technology High fashion	California[4] High tech

Notes:
1. Innovation is gradual, i.e. concentrated within a field of traditional excellence, based on local identities. Because the system is relatively closed, there is little expansionist tendency and all resources are concentrated on improvement within the traditional field. Local system of difficult entry drives system into industries with entry barriers.
2. Identities are similar to the first case, but the system is much more open to entry. Hence there is a tendency for stiff local competition, overproduction, and necessity for periodic overhaul of the system, usually by expanding or altering product lines, but in the same technological field. Selection for industries with relatively low barriers to entry.
3. A system based on large numbers, but with relatively fixed hierarchy whose role is to introduce innovation by establishing standards. In high technology, this is large-scale technology programmes; in high fashion, it is the fashion season.
4. A scientific–entrepreneurial system with high rates of entry and failure in early technology stages and consolidation around major companies as base technologies stabilize. Selection for low barriers early on, and high barriers later on.

technological dynamism. Table 2.1 shows, in a highly schematic way, the conventions of identity and participation of key groups. The horizontal axis describes participation: is it a fixed population or one subject to what we have called horizontal mobility through entry? The vertical axis captures identities: whether the group is constituted on the basis of a local membership, i.e. with relatively small numbers and personal knowledge or reputation effects, or a national membership, implying larger numbers, greater anonymity and formal codified relations. This generates four types of cases, of which our case studies represent three.

The NEC Italian design-intensive and craft-based goods production complexes are characterized by medium-run possibilities of entry to the key technology-mastering group, the artisan–entrepreneurs, but this fluid participation is coupled to very strong integrative, identity-creation mechanisms at regional level. Entry is sustained in part because existing entrepreneur–artisans are heavily supported not only by the CNA and local governments, but also by their moral 'first-mover' rights inside the production system. We might say that participation involves 'voice and *community loyalty*'. Learning takes place within a well-defined domain of activity, but because the system is locally expansionist there is pressure for periodic adjustments of the precise field of production and learning, as markets become saturated; in NEC Italy, this has been reflected in a rapid move up the price–performance curve into increasingly high quality, sophisticated products.

The Francilien system, too, rests on the command over key technological or knowledge resources by groups whose memberships are not only highly restricted but also rather highly formalized. In the case of high technology, this is the technocracy of the *grandes écoles* and, in the case of high fashion, it is the restricted community of designers who hold the brand names. Let us concentrate, for the sake of brevity, on the example of high technology. The leading groups have little competition from (via entry) on the day-to-day level (although there is severe competition to get in, in the first place to the *grandes écoles*). Moreover, the other groups in the production system are frequently protected from immediate competition (state-dependent subcontractors, for example, and labour unions among their workers). In the face of fixed, conflictual participation, learning is discontinuous: it works when the dominant group can reorganize the system around specific large-scale projects, essentially buying its way out of conflict by stabilizing its commands to partners over the medium run. The result is that the system is technologically conservative (not product-pioneering), but also technologically excellent. This decision-making process has its strength in *dynamic imitation*, and thus its technological conservatism.

Finally, the convention of participation in contemporary Californian technology districts is characterized by ease of entry for those who are credentialed and the fact that this group is formed on the basis of a large, impersonal, national resource pool. The kind of direct control of interfirm relations which is characteristic of the French companies and their allies in the ministries is absent; nor do the universities and professional associations of the USA provide the same kind of interpersonal group cohesion as do the *grandes écoles* in France. Pentagon control is indirect and relies on contracting, whereas in the French case it rests on planning for the entire *filière*. The scientific–entrepreneurial system, with high rates of entry and failure (exit) in early technology stages, promotes consolidation around major companies as technologies stabilize. The bias of learning in a system where participation is structured in such a manner should be breakthrough and Taylorization, rather than incremental improvement.

CONCLUSION

Many growth models, especially those based on the importance of technological change, now centre on endogenous supply-side sources of productivity increases (Dosi et al., 1990; Romer, 1990). I have analysed in detail
one specific component of that supply side, the behavioural–institutional
sources of technological learning, which I have dubbed the 'conventions' of
identity and participation.[9]

In all of the cases examined in preceding sections, there are strong points
of resemblance: technologically dynamic production systems consist of
clusters of firms in which the presence of an intricate social divison of
labour – both horizontal and vertical in nature – is in evidence at the
regional level. All display high levels of external economies of scale (a large
number of firms in the regional complex) and external economies of scope
(a large variety of phases in the division of labour accounted for by
different firms in the regional complex).

Yet the mere existence of this form of production organization –
although perhaps necessary to the attainment of a high level of technological dynamism and product quality in the face of dynamism – does not constitute an explanation of the origins or developmental tendencies of such
systems. There is no global condition in different product markets which
positively defines, *a priori*, the nature of 'best practice', and the keys to
increasing market shares. The basic general condition – the increasing
volume of trade in many markets – may be the result of such technological
dynamism. These production systems, which are leaders in international
trade, continually re-define the best practices (in the sense of product and
process-based technology gaps) for their respective markets (Dosi et al.,
1990). The analytical paradox, then, is that even though all such systems
do seem to share certain basic organizational characteristics, their routes to
developing such dynamism are very different. The analysis of the conventions of different production systems can help us understand how they
select themselves into specific product markets and define their technological trajectories.

ACKNOWLEDGEMENTS

This paper was originally presented to the Annual Meeting of the
Association of American Geographers, Miami, 16 April 1991, in a session
entitled 'The Geography of Rationality and Collective Action'. It is based
on research carried out while the author was a research fellow of the
German Marshall Fund, and later while he was supported by funding from

the Fulbright Programme and the French Ministry of Research and Technology. Their support is gratefully acknowledged. Additional support came from the International Studies and Overseas Programmes of UCLA, the Academic Senate of the University of California, Los Angeles Division, the Center for German and European Studies at the University of California–Berkeley, and the Groupement de Recherche, 'Institutions, Emploi, et Politique Economique' (Paris). I wish to thank a number of people for comments on earlier drafts, notably Jonathan Zeitlin, Robert Salais and Edward Lorenz.

NOTES

1. Obviously all three, i.e. economic, technological and behavioural, components are important in determining the rate and direction of innovation and learning. A central question is whether there are principles of coherence among the three dimensions that can be identified (see Dosi et al., 1990).
2. For a case study of trust relations in French subcontracting networks, see Lorenz (1988).
3. One major recent theory purporting to capture the interactions between economic forces and such institutional–behavioural forces is the French regulationist approach. The regulation school acknowledges the sociological foundations of viable economic systems, and in this sense my approach has much sympathy with theirs. The regulation school acknowledges these non-economic foundations in the restricted sense of the need for coherence between institutional supports for a macroeconomic structure (described as a regime of accumulation in the regulationist approach). The regulationist approach, however, does nothing in particular to develop the analysis of the generation and properties of these foundations. They tell us little about how the production system and its mode of regulation actually might come into being and function coherently; the theory resorts to claims about the 'openness' of history and these appropriate institutional–economic matches as 'discoveries'.
   The approach upon which the present analysis is based is distinctive from the regulationist approach in four ways. First, it concentrates on the meso-economic level of organization, of groups of actors in production systems, not on the macroeconomic and macro-social levels (i.e. regimes of accumulation at national level and 'historical blocs' at national or international level). Second, it holds open the possibility that causality runs in two directions, i.e. endogenous product-technology dynamics may generate best-practice techniques, and so the object of coherence (the production system) is defined by the subjects, and not the other way around, as in the regulationist approach. The sense of history is different because an evolutionary theory of economic growth is used, in which micro and macro interact and in which micro-dynamics are much more open than in the regulationist approach (see following points). Third, the present approach considers that normative bases of mobilization and distribution differ from place to place and so the rules of coherence are not universal (i.e. the constraints on performance are not defined exclusively within the economic domain; they are mutually determined by institutions and economy, especially in the domain of wage–effort bargains and reservation wages). Fourth, the economics of conventions holds that different normative bases of action could set up a wide variety of rational micro-calculations in the economy. For a more extensive discussion of the regulationist approach, see Salais and Storper (1993), chapter 6.
4. All of these districts produce products which are export specializations for their home countries. In a large number of cases, export specialization is due to superior technology, as is shown in Dosi et al. (1990).

5. In a country such as Italy, not only is it difficult to speak of a national set of conventions of participation, but even at the level of NEC Italy, there are important interregional and intercommunal variations in history, structure and functioning of economic participation; there are a number of important 'Italian success stories of local development' (Camagni and Cappello, 1987). What follows is not an attempt to efface such differences, but rather an analysis of a broad story line which, in varying degrees, applies to the specific cases; participation in the different parts of NEC Italy is broadly similar and manifests important common differences with the rest of Italy, Western Europe and North America.
6. See Salais and Storper (1993), chapter 5, for an analysis of these other French cases.
7. 'Boredom was born one day out of uniformity.'
8. Many of these observations are gleaned from interviews conducted with several successful high technology entrepreneurs in the Los Angeles region in the autumn of 1990 and winter of 1991.
9. By definition, the export-oriented industrial clusters examined here are highly dependent on movements in demand. In at least two cases examined, French and American aerospace, they are directly dependent on government investment decisions. In the case of Italian and French design-based and precision metalworking industries, the participation of external decision-makers is quite low, but the localized clusters are none the less caught up in an ongoing process whereby parts of the value chain are relocated as they become subject to comparative advantage dynamics. Why, then, the emphasis on local and supply-side factors in this analysis? In the former cases, remember that many externally motivated investment programmes have failed; the question remains why, in the cases of French and American aerospace, the production systems stimulated by government spending were successful and why they generated important commercially successful products as well. In the DIC industry cases, those parts of the production systems that remain in high cost, high wage production centres must reinvest new, less cost–price sensitive roles for themselves through technological learning in order to maintain high market shares in the face of global competition. They have done so successfully over several decades; global shifting of parts of the value chain is, simply speaking, nothing new to these places.

REFERENCES

Amendola, M. and Gaffard, J.L. (1990), *La Dynamique Economique de l'Innovation*, Paris: Economica.

Amsden, A. (1990), *Asia's Next Giant*, New York: Oxford University Press.

Aoki, M. (1990), *Information, Incentives and Bargaining in the Japanese Economy*, New York: Cambridge University Press.

Bagnasco, A. (1977), *Tre Italie*, Bologna: Il Mulino.

Balestri, A. (1992), 'Industrial organization in the manufacture of fashion goods: the textile district of Prato, 1950–1980', unpublished MA thesis, Department of Economics, University of Lancaster.

Balestri, A. (ed.) (1991), *La Produzione di Impianti e Macchinari Tessile nell'Area Pratese*, Prato: Unione Industriale Pratese.

Bauchet, P. (1986), *Le Plan dans l'Economie Française*, Paris: Presses de la Fondation National des Sciences Politiques.

Bass, S. (1991), 'Prospects for local industrial policy in the age of the Keiretsu: Japanese direct investment in Southern California's biotechnology industry', unpublished MA thesis, Department of Urban Planning, UCLA, Los Angeles.

Becattini, G. (1978), 'The development of light industry in Tuscany: an interpretation', *Economic Notes*, 7 (2–3), 107–23, Monte dei Paschi di Siena.

Becattini, G. (ed.) (1987), *Mercato e Forze Locale: Il Distretto Industriale*, Bologna: Il Mulino.

Becattini, G. (1989), 'Riflessione sul distretto industriale marshaliano come concetto socio-economico', *Stato e Mercato*, **25**.

Bellah, R., Madsen, R., Sullivan, W., Swidler, A. and Tipton, S. (1985), *Habits of the Heart: Individualism and Commitment in American Life*, Berkeley: University of California Press.

Bellandi, M. (1989), 'Capacitá innovativa diffusa e distretti industriali', Working Paper, Department of Economics, University of Florence.

Bellandi, M. (1992), Personal communication (letter) to Michael Storper, January.

Bellandi, M. and Trigilia, C. (1990), 'Come cambia un distretto industriale: l'industria tessile di Prato', Working Paper, Department of Economics, University of Florence.

Berardi, D. and Romagnoli, M. (1984), *L'area Pratese: Tra Crisi e Mutamento*, Prato: Consorzio Centro Studi.

Berger, S. (1981), 'The petite bourgeoisie', in S. Berger and M. Piore (eds), *Dualism and Discontinuity in Industrial Societies*, New York: Cambridge University Press.

Best, M. (1990), *The New Competition: Institutions of Industrial Restructuring*, Cambridge: Polity Press.

Bianchi, P. (1989), 'Riorganizzazione proddutiva e crescita esterna delle imprese Italiane', in M. Regini and C. Sabel (eds), *Strattegie di Riaggiustamento Industriale*, Milan: Franco Angeli.

Bloch, R. (1993), 'The making of an outer city: industry, culture and land in Oakland County, Michigan', unpublished PhD dissertation, Department of Planning, UCLA, Los Angeles.

Bluestone, B. and Harrison, B. (1982), *The Deindustrialization of America*, New York: Basic Books.

Boissonade, P. (1931), *Le Socialisme de l'Etat*, Paris: Champion.

Bourdieu, P. (1989), *La Noblesse d'Etat*, Paris: Les Editions de Minuit.

Bourdieu, P. and Delsaut, Y. (1975), 'Le couturier et sa griffe', *Actes de la Recherche en Sciences Sociales*, **1**, 3–22.

Brunet, R. (1986), *Le Rédéploiement Industriel*, Montpellier: GIP/RECLUS.

Brunet, R. and Sallois, J. (eds) (1986), *France: les Dynamismes du Térritoire*, Montpellier: GIP/RECLUS.

Brusco, S. (1982), 'The Emilian model: productive decentralization and social integration', *Cambridge Journal of Economics*, **6**, 167–84.

Brutti, P. (1990), 'Industrial districts: the point of view of the unions', ILO Conference on Industrial Districts and Local Economic Regeneration, Geneva, October.

The Bridge (1988), 'Italian textile workers: innovation and new industrial relations', The Bridge Association, Rome.

Bucaille, A. and Costa de Beauregard, B. (1987), *PMI: Enjeux Régionaux et Internationaux*, Paris: Economica.

Bursi, T. (1982), *Il Settore Meccano-Ceramico nel Comprensorio della Ceramica: Struttura e Processi di Crescita*, Milan: Franco Angeli.

Bursi, T. (1989), *Piccole e Media Imprese e Politiche di Adattamento: Il Distretto della Maglieria di Carpi*, Milan: Franco Angeli.

Camagni, R. and Cappello, R. (1987), 'Italian success stories of local development: theoretical conditions and practical experience', paper, Department of Economics and Business Administration, Bocconi University, Milan.

Cappecchi, V. (1990a), 'L'industrializzazione a Bologna nel Novecento: dagli inizi del secolo alla fine della seconda guerra mondiale', *Storia Illustrata di Bologna*, **18** (4), 341–60.

Cappecchi, V. (1990b), 'L'industrializzazione a Bologna nel Novecento: dal secondo dopoguerra ad oggi', *Storia Illustrata di Bologna*, **9** (5), 161–80.

Carboni, C. (1990), *Lavoro Informale ed Economia Diffusa: Costanti e Trasformazione Recenti*, Rome: Edizione Lavoro.

Carroue, L. (1984), 'L'électronique professionel en région parisienne: recherche à propos d'un tissu industriel régional', *Analyse de l'Espace*, **3/4**, 22–44.

Centre d'Etudes de l'Emploi (1987), 'Les entreprises et leurs produits', *Cahiers du Centre d'Etudes de l'Emploi*, **30**, Paris.

Choffel, P., Cuneo, P. and Kramarz, F. (1988), 'Des trajéctoires marquées par la structure de l'entreprise', *Economie et Statistique*, **213** (September).

Cohen, S. and Zysman, J. (1986), *Manufacturing Matters*, New York: Basic Books.

Colombo, M., Mariotto, S. and Mutinelli, M. (1991), *The Internationalization of Italian Industry*, Milan: Bocconi University for OECD.

Coriat, B. (1990), *Penser à l'Envers*, Paris: C. Bourgois.

Cusumano, M. (1985), *The Japanese Automobile Industry*, Cambridge, MA: Harvard University Press.

Dei Ottati, G. (1987), 'Distretto industriale, problemi della transazione e mercato communitario: prime considerazioni', *Economia e Politica Industriele*, **51**, 93–122.

Dei Ottati, G. (1991), 'Il finanziamento dello sviluppo locale', paper presented to a conference on Possibilities and Limits of Local Development', Prato, September.

Del Monte, A. (1986), 'Job generation in small and medium-sized enterprises: Italy', paper, Department of Economics, University of Naples.

de Vet, J.M. (1990), 'Innovation and new firm formation in Southern California's medical device industry', unpublished MA thesis, Department of Geography, UCLA, Los Angeles.

di Lellio, A. (1987), 'Changing citizenship in "high tech" communities: the case of Dallas and Grenoble', paper presented at the International Sociological Association Conference on Technology, Restructuring, and Urban–Regional Development, Dubrovnik, June.

d'Iribarne, P. (1990), *La Logique d'Honneur: Gestion des Entreprises et Traditions Nationales*, Paris: Editions du Seuil.

Dore, R. (1987), *Flexible Rigidities*, Stanford, CA: Stanford University Press.

Dosi, G., Pavitt, K. and Soete, L. (1990), *The Economics of Technical Change and International Trade*, New York: New York University Press.

Dosi, G., Freeman, C., Nelson, R., Silverberg, G. and Soete, L. (eds) (1988), *Technical Change and Economic Theory*, London/New York: Frances Pinter.

Elster, J. (1984), *Ulysses and the Sirens*, New York: Cambridge University Press.

Eymard-Duvernay, E. (1989), 'Conventions de Qualité et Formes de Coordination', *Révue Economique*, **40** (2), 329–58.

Fishlow, A. (1965), *American Railroads and the Transformation of the Antebellum Economy*, Cambridge, MA: Harvard University Press.

Foray, D. (1990), 'The secrets of industry are in the air: éléments pour un Cadre d'Analyse du Phénomène de Reseau d'Innovateurs', paper presented at the Workshop on Networks of Innovators, Montreal, May.

Forlai, L. and Bertini, S. (1990), 'Evoluzione e prospettive del distretto Pratese: alcune considerazione teoriche', NOMISMA paper, Industrial Policy Laboratory of the Emilia-Romagna Region/University of Bologna.

Gerstenberger, W. (1990), 'Reshaping industrial structures', paper presented to the International Conference on Technology and Competitiveness, OECD, Paris, June.

Giovannini, P. (1987), 'La "Societá" Toscana e le sue Trasformazioni', in Istituto Gramsci Toscano (ed.), *Verso una Riflessione sul Modello Toscano di Sviluppo*, Atti del Seminario tenutoso a Firenze nell'aprile, pp. 31–52.

Goncourt, E. de (1982), *La Femme an XVIIIième Siècle* (originally published 1862), Paris: Flammarion.

Granovetter, M. (1985), 'Economic action and social structures: the problem of "embeddedness"', *American Journal of Sociology*, **91**, 481–510.

Guedez, A. (1981), 'Travail ouvrier et travail humain: l'exemple du Compagnonnage', *Cahiers Internationaux de Sociologie*, **81**, 239–54.

Guerrieri, P. (1992), 'Technology and trade performance of the most advanced countries', paper, Department of Economics, University of Rome.

Håkansson, H. (1989), *Corporate Technological Behavior: Co-operation and Networks*, New York: Routledge.

Harrison, B. (1990), 'The big firms are coming out of the corner', Working Paper, School of Urban and Public Affairs, Carnegie–Mellon University, Pittsburgh.

Hartz, L. (1955), *The Liberal Tradition in America*, New York: Harcourt, Brace, Jovanovich.

Hickmann, R. (1988), 'The job creation process: implications for regional economic development', Report to the French Ministry of Employment and Social Affairs, Paris.

Hirschman, A. (1970), *Exit, Voice, and Loyalty: Responses to Decline in Firms, Organizations, and States*, Cambridge, MA: Harvard University Press.

Hirst, P. and Zeitlin, J. (1992), 'Flexible specialization versus post-Fordism: theory, evidence, and policy implications', in M. Storper and A.J. Scott (eds), *Pathways to Industrialization and Regional Development*, London: Routledge, pp. 70–115.

Hyman, R. and Streeck, W. (eds) (1988), *New Technologies and Industrial Relations*, Oxford: Basil Blackwell.

Jaikumar, R. (1986), 'Post-industrial manufacturing', *Harvard Business Review*, **113** (6), 69–76.

Kelley, M. and Brooks, H. (1989), 'From breakthrough to follow-through', *Issues in Science and Technology*, **5** (3), 42–7.

Kenney, M. and Florida, R. (1990), *The Breakthrough Illusion*, New York: Basic Books.

Lafay, G. and Herzog, C. (1989), *Commerce International: La Fin des Avantages Acquis*, Economica, Paris.

Lakota, A. and Milleli, C. (1987), *Emploi, Entreprises et Équipements en Ile-de-France: une Géographie de la Turbulence*, Modes d'Emploi No. 10, Collection Reclus, Montpellier: GIP/RECLUS.

Latour, A. (1961), *Magiciens de la Mode*, Paris: Juilliard.

Lazerson, M. (1989), 'A new phoenix; the return of the putting-out mode of production', ILO Workshop on Industrial Districts, Florence, April.

Le Bras, H. and Todd, E. (1981), *L'invention de la France*, Paris: Livre de Poche.

Lipovetsky, G. (1987), *L'empire de l'Ephémère: la Mode et son Destin dans les Sociétés Modernes*, Paris: Gallimard.

Lorenz, E. (1988), 'Neither friends nor strangers: informal networks of subcontracting in French industry', in D. Gambetta (ed.), *Trust: Making and Breaking Co-operative Relations*, Oxford: Basil Blackwell.

Lundvall, B.-Å. (1990), 'User–producer interactions and technological change', paper presented to the Conference on Technological Change organized by the TEP (Technology, Employment, Productivity) programme of the OECD, Paris/La Villette, June.

Molotch, H. (1975), 'The city as growth machine', *American Sociological Review*, **82**, 226–38.

Montagne-Villette, S. (1987), 'L'industrie de prêt-à-porter en France', Thèse de doctorat es Lettres en Sciences Humaines, Université de Paris IV.

Moore, B. (1966), *Social Origins of Dictatorship and Democracy*, Boston, MA: Beacon Press.

Nelson, R. (1988), 'Institutions supporting technical change in the United States', in G. Dosi et al., *Technical Change and Economic Theory*, London: Frances Pinter, pp. 312–29.

Nelson, S. and Winter, S. (1982), *An Evolutionary Theory of Economic Change*, Cambrige, MA: Harvard University Press.

Nuti, F. (1990), 'I distretti dell'industria manifatturiera (L'indagine del sottoprogetto CNR "Sistema delle Imprese")', Department of Economics, University of Bologna (mimeo).

Paci, M. (1985), *La Struttura Sociale Italiana: Costanti Storiche e Trasformazione Recenti*, Bologna: Il Mulino.

Perulli, P. (1987), 'Flexibility strategies: employers, trade unions and local government', paper presented to MIT Conference on New Technologies and Industrial Relations, Cambridge, MA.

Pezzini, M. and Brusco, S. (1990), 'Small scale enterprises and the ideology of the Italian left', in F. Pyke, G. Becattini and W. Sengenberger (eds), *Industrial Districts and Inter-Firm Co-operation in Italy*, Geneva: ILO, pp. 142–60.

Piore, M. and Sabel, C. (1984), *The Second Industrial Divide*, New York: Basic Books.

Porter, M. (1990), *The Competitive Advantage of Nations*, London: Macmillan.

Prévost, J.C. (1957), *Le Dandyisme en France, 1817–1839*, Paris: Flammarion.

Ramo, S. (1988), *The Business of Science*, New York: Hill and Wang.

Regini, M. (ed.) (1988), *La Sfida della Flessibilitá: Impresa, Lavoro, e Sindacati nella Fase Post-Fordista*, Milan: Franco Angeli.

Rey, G. (1989), 'Profile and Analysis, 1981–1985', in D. Goodman and J. Bamford (eds), *Small Firms and Industrial Districts in Italy*, London: Routledge, pp. 69–93.

Romer, P. (1990), 'Endogenous technological change', *Journal of Political Economy*, **98** 5(2), S71–S102.

Rosenberg, N. (1972), *Technology and American Economic Growth*, New York: Harper and Row.

Russo, M. (1986), 'Technical change and the industrial district: the role of interfirm relations in the growth and transformation of ceramic tile production in Italy', *Resources Policy*, **14**, 329–43.

Sabel, C. (1989), 'Flexible specialization and the resurgence of regional economies', in P. Hirst and J. Zeitlin (eds), *Reversing Manufacturing Decline?*, Oxford: Berg, pp. 17–70.

Sabel, C., Kern, H. and Herrigel, G. (1990), 'Collaborative manufacturing: new supplier relations in the automobile industry and the redefinition of the industrial corporation', Department of Political Science, MIT, Cambridge, MA.

Salais, R. (1989), 'L'analyse économique des conventions du travail', *Révue Economique*, **40** (2), 43–73.

Salais, R. and Storper, M. (1992a), 'The four worlds of contemporary production', *Cambridge Journal of Economics*, **16**, 169–93.

Salais, R. and Storper, M. (1993), *Les Mondes de Production*, Paris: Editions de l'Ecole des Hautes Etudes en Sciences Sociales.

Saxenian, A. (1988), 'Regional networks and the resurgence of Silicon Valley', Working Paper No. 508, Institute of Urban and Regional Development, Berkeley, CA.

Saxenian, A. (1990), 'The origins and dynamics of production networks in Silicon Valley', Working Paper No. 516, Institute of Urban and Regional Development, Berkeley, CA.

Scott, A.J. (1988a), *Metropolis: From the Division of Labor to Urban Form*, Berkeley and Los Angeles: University of California Press.

Scott, A.J. (1988b), *New Industrial Spaces: Flexible Production and Regional Economic Development in the USA and Western Europe*, London: Pion.

Sengenberger, W. and Loveman, G. (1987), *Smaller Units of Employment: A Synthesis Report on Industrial Reorganization in Industrialized Countries*, Geneva: International Institute for Labour Studies.

Segrestin, D. (1985), *Le Phénomène Corporatiste: Essai sur l'Avenir des Systèmes Professionnels Fermés en France*, Paris: Fayard.

Sewell, W. (1980), *Work and Revolution in France: the Language of Labour from the Old Regime to 1848*, Cambridge: Cambridge University Press.

Sforzi, F. (1990), 'The quantitative importance of Marshallian industrial districts in the Italian economy', in F. Pyke, G. Becattini and W. Sengenberger (eds), *Industrial Districts and Interfirm Co-operation in Italy*, Geneva: International Institute for Labour Studies.

Simon, P. (1931), *Monographie d'une Industrie de Luxe: la Haute Couture*, Paris: Seuil.

Solinas, G. (1982), 'Labor market segmentation and workers' careers: the case of the Italian knitwear industry', *Cambridge Journal of Economics*, **6**, 331–52.

Stoffäes, C. (1983), *Politique Industrielle*, Paris: Droit.

Storper, M. (1992), 'The limits to globalization: technology districts and international trade', *Economic Geography*, **68**, 60–93.

Stowsky, J. (1987), 'The weakest link: semiconductor production equipment, linkages, and the limits to international trade', BRIE Working Paper No. 27, Berkeley, CA.

Suleiman, E. (1979), *Les Élites en France: Grands Corps et Grandes Écoles*, Paris: Editions du Seuil.

Terrail, J. and Tripier, M. (1986), *Destins Ouvriers, Cultures d'Entreprise, Pratiques Syndicales*, Paris: CRESF.

Thevenot, L. (1989), 'Economie et Politique de l'Entreprise. Economie de l'Efficacité et Confiance', in L. Boltanski and L. Thevenot (eds), *Justesse and Justice dans le Travail*, Cahiers du CEE no. 33, série PROTEE, Paris: Presses Universitaires de France, pp. 135–207.

Tinacci Mosello, M. (1983), 'Modernitá e Tradizione di un Sistema Industriale Locale: Il Modello Pratese della "Fabbrica Diffusa" e la sua Evoluzione Storica', *Acts of the 23rd Italian Geographical Congress*, **2** (2), 294–305.

Tinacci Mosello, M. (1989), 'Innovative capacities of industrial districts. Hypothesis and Verification: the case study of Prato in Tuscany', Discussion Paper No. 59, Department of Economics, University of Florence.

Todd, E. (1990), *L'invention de l'Europe*, Paris: Seuil.

Trigilia, C. (1986), *Grandi Partiti e Piccole Imprese*, Bologna: Il Mulino.

Trigilia, C. (1990), 'Italian industrial districts: neither myth nor interlude', paper delivered to the Conference on Industrial Districts and Local Economic Regeneration, Geneva, October.

von Hippel, E. (1987), *The Sources of Innovation*, New York: Oxford University Press.

3.   Toward the learning region
Richard Florida

A new age of capitalism is sweeping the globe. In Silicon Valley, a global
centre for new technology has emerged, where entrepreneurs and technolo-
gists from around the world backed by global venture capital invent the new
technologies of software, personalized information and biotechnology that
will shape our future. In the financial centres of Tokyo, New York and
London, computerized financial markets provide instantaneous capital
and credit to companies and entrepreneurs across the vast reaches of the
world. In the film studios of Los Angeles, computer technicians work
alongside actors and film directors to produce the *software* that will run on
new generations of home electronics products produced by television and
semiconductor companies in Japan and throughout Asia. Computer scientists and software engineers in Silicon Valley and Seattle work with computer game makers in Kyoto, Osaka and Tokyo to turn out dazzling new
generations of high-technology computer games. In Italy, highly computerized factories produce designer fashion goods tailored to the needs of consumers in Milan, Paris, New York and Tokyo almost instantaneously.
Teams of automotive designers in Los Angeles, Tokyo and Milan create
designs for new generations of cars, while workers in Kyushu work to the
rhythm of classical music in the world's most advanced automotive assembly factories to produce these cars for consumers across the globe.
Throughout Japan, a new generation of knowledge workers operate the
controls of mammoth automated factory complexes to produce the most
basic of industrial products – steel. A new industrial revolution sweeps
through Taiwan, Singapore, Korea, Malaysia, Thailand, Indonesia, and
extends its reach to formerly undeveloped nations such as Mexico and
China. And, once-written-off regions, like the former Rustbelt of the USA,
are being revived through international investment and the creative
destruction of traditional industries.

Despite continued predictions of the 'end of geography', regions are
becoming more important modes of economic and technological organization in this new age of global, knowledge-intensive capitalism. Although
there have been numerous excellent studies of the dynamics of individual
regions,[1] the role of regions in the new age of knowledge-based, global

capitalism remains rather poorly understood. And, while several outstanding studies have chronicled the rise of knowledge-based capitalism, outlined the contours of learning organization, and described the knowledge-creating company,[2] virtually no one has developed a comparable theory of what such changes portend for regions and regional organization.

This article suggests that regions are a key element of the new age of global, knowledge-based capitalism. Its central argument is that regions are themselves becoming focal points for knowledge creation and learning in the new age of capitalism, as they take on the characteristics of *learning regions*. Learning regions, as their name implies, function as collectors and repositories of knowledge and ideas, and provide an underlying environment or infrastructure which facilitates the flow of knowledge, ideas and learning. Learning regions are increasingly important sources of innovation and economic growth, and are vehicles for globalization. In elaborating this thesis, the following sections provide brief descriptions of the new era of knowledge-based capitalism and its global scope, before turning to our discussion of the dynamics of learning regions.

THE KNOWLEDGE REVOLUTION

Capitalism, as writers as diverse as Peter Drucker and Ikujiro Nonaka point out, is entering into a new age of knowledge creation and continuous learning.[3] This new system of knowledge-intensive capitalism is based on a synthesis of intellectual and physical labour – a melding of innovation and production – or what I have elsewhere termed *innovation-mediated production*.[4] In fact, the main source of value and economic growth in knowledge-intensive capitalism is the human mind. Knowledge-intensive capitalism represents a major advance over previous systems of Taylorist scientific management or the assembly-line system of Henry Ford, where the principal source of value and productivity growth was physical labour.[5] The shift to knowledge-based capitalism represents an epochal transition in the nature of advanced economies and societies. Ever since the transition from feudalism to capitalism, the basic source of productivity, value and economic growth has been physical labour and manual skill.[6] In the knowledge-intensive organization, intelligence and intellectual labour replace physical labour as the fundamental source of value and profit.

The new age of capitalism makes use of the entirety of human intellectual and creative capabilities. Both R&D scientists and workers on the factory floor are the sources of ideas and continuous innovation. Workers on the factory floor use their deep and intimate knowledge of machines and production processes to devise new, more efficient production processes. This new system of economic organization harnesses the knowledge and intelligence of the team – the group social mind – a sharp break with the conception of individual knowledge embodied in the lone inventor or great scientist. Teams of R&D scientists, engineers and factory workers become collective agents of innovation. The lines between the factory and the laboratory blur.

The factory is itself becoming more like a laboratory – a place where new ideas and concepts are generated, tested and implemented. Like a laboratory, the knowledge-intensive factory is an increasingly clean, technologically advanced and information-rich environment. In an increasing number of factories, workers perform their tasks in clean-room environments, alongside robots and machines which conduct the physical aspects of the work. In some knowledge-intensive factories, laboratory-like spaces are available for workers, which may include sophisticated laboratory-like equipment – computerized measuring equipment, advanced monitoring devices and test equipment. Workers use these laboratory-like spaces together with R&D scientists and engineers to analyse, fine-tune and improve products and production processes.

THE GLOBAL SHIFT

This new age of capitalism is taking the form of an increasingly integrated economic system, with globe-straddling networks of transnational corporations and high levels of foreign direct investment between and among nations. Such investment is a vehicle for diffusing advanced technologies and state-of-the-art management practices and is a powerful contributor to the global flow of knowledge. Indeed, international investment has surpassed global trade as the defining feature of the new global economy. A United Nations report shows that today transnational corporations operate some 170 000 factories and branches throughout the globe. In 1992, this worldwide network of foreign affiliates generated $5.5 trillion in sales, exceeding world exports of $4 trillion, one-third of which took the form of intra-firm trade.[7]

Globalization is increasingly taking place through *transplant* companies and in some instances through integrated complexes of transplant factories and surrounding supplier and product development activities. The best examples of such complexes include Toyota and Honda's massive production complexes in the USA. In fact, Japanese automotive production in North America takes the form of an integrated transplant complex comprising seven major automotive assembly complexes and more than

400 suppliers located in and around the traditional industrial heartland region of the USA.[8]

Transplant investment is the source of important productivity improvement and economic growth. According to a recent study by the McKinsey Global Institute, transplants increase productivity by accelerating the adoption and diffusion of best-practice organization and management, and placing pressure on domestic industries to adopt those best practices.[9] The McKinsey study notes that:

> Transplants from leading-edge producers: (1) directly contribute to higher levels of domestic productivity, (2) prove that leading-edge productivity can be achieved with local inputs, (3) put competitive pressure on other domestic producers, and (4) transfer knowledge of best-practices to other domestic producers through natural movement of personnel. Moreover, foreign direct investment has provoked less political opposition than trade because it creates jobs instead of destroying them. Thus, it is likely to grow faster in years to come.

A recent OECD study provides additional empirical evidence of the link between foreign direct investment, productivity improvement and economic growth.[10] Comparing investment and productivity patterns in 15 advanced industrial nations, the OECD study found that foreign-owned companies are typically more efficient than domestic firms in both absolute levels and in rates of productivity growth. The study found that these productivity gains resulted from more advanced technology than domestic industries, or from adding capacity. By contrast, productivity increases at locally owned companies more often resulted from downsizing and lay-offs. The study also found that international investment has been a key source of employment growth across the advanced industrial nations. In 10 of 15 countries studied, foreign-owned companies created new employment more rapidly than did their domestically owned counterparts, sometimes expanding their operations while domestic firms were contracting. In three others, they eliminated jobs, but they did so more slowly than domestically owned enterprises. The study found that the largest employment declines occurred in Japan and Germany, where soaring costs during the 1980s caused international investors to cut a significant number of jobs. Furthermore, the OECD study points to a link between investment and trade, as foreign subsidiaries tended to export and import more than domestic firms, with most of the imports taking the form of intra-firm trade.

Foreign direct investment has played a key role in the economic revival of the USA.[11] For example, productivity grew more rapidly in foreign-owned transplant manufacturing companies in the USA than for the manufacturing sector as a whole during the 1980s. The real output of transplant manufacturers rose nearly four times as fast as all manufacturing establishments between 1980 and 1987. Transplant companies generated productivity increases and value-added which outdistance US-owned companies. From 1987 to 1990, for example, the rate of increase in plant and equipment expenditures for transplant industrial enterprises (e.g. non-bank, non-agricultural business) was five times greater than that for US-owned business. As of 1989, value-added per employee was substantially higher in transplants than for US-owned manufacturers. And, transplant companies have played an important role in the economic resurgence of the US industrial midwest – a region which produced more than $350 billion in manufacturing output, making it the third largest manufacturing economy in the world.[12]

Technology and innovative activity are also undergoing considerable globalization. For most of the Cold War, the USA was the world's overwhelming generator of research and technology. However, by the early 1990s, the combined R&D expenditures of the EC and Japan exceeded those of the USA, and their R&D efforts were much more focused on commercial technology. Furthermore, the share of patents to non-US inventors has increased dramatically, with non-US inventors accounting for nearly half of all US patents in 1992.[13]

As the pace of innovation has accelerated and the global sources of technology have grown, corporations have expanded their global innovative activities and cross-border alliances. A global survey of companies in the USA, Europe and Japan found that corporations are substantially increasing their reliance on external sources of research and technology for both basic research and product and development.[14] Furthermore, a growing number of corporations are establishing R&D facilities abroad. US companies conducted roughly 12 per cent of their total R&D activities abroad in 1991, the most recent year for which reliable data are available. Japanese companies have established a global network of more than 200 research, development and design facilities.

The past decade has seen the progressive globalization of the US technology base, as the USA has become the hub in the global science and technology system.[15] Since 1980, foreign companies have invested tens of billions of dollars in roughly 400 research, development and design centres in the USA. The annual R&D outlays of these facilities has risen from $4.5 billion in 1982 to $10.7 billion in 1992, and the share of total industrial R&D they comprise has grown from 9 per cent to nearly 17 per cent over the same period, roughly one out of every six dollars of industrial R&D spending in the USA. R&D spending by foreign companies is highly concentrated in sectors where foreign industries are highly competitive – European companies in chemicals and pharmaceuticals and Japanese and German companies in automotive-related technologies and electronics. The globalization of innovation is required to tap into the sources of knowledge and ideas, and scientific and technical talent which are embedded in cutting-edge regional innovation complexes such as Silicon Valley in the USA, Tokyo or Osaka in Japan, Stuttgart in Germany, and many others.

TOWARD THE LEARNING REGION

The shift to knowledge-intensive capitalism goes beyond the particular business and management strategies of individual firms. It involves the development of new inputs and a broader infrastructure at the regional level on which individual firms and production complexes of firms can draw. The nature of this economic transformation makes regions key economic units in the global economy.[16] In essence, globalism and regionalism are part of the same process of economic transformation. In an important and provocative essay in *Foreign Affairs*, Kenichi Ohmae suggests that regions, or what he calls *region states*, are coming to replace the nation state as the centrepiece of economic activity.[17]

> The nation state has become an unnatural, even dysfunctional unit for organizing human activity and managing economic endeavor in a borderless world. It represents no genuine, shared community of economic interests; it defines no meaningful flows of economic activity. On the global economic map the lines that now matter are those defining what may be called region states. Region states are natural economic zones. They may or may not fall within the geographic limits of a particular nation – whether they do is an accident of history. Sometimes these distinct economic units are formed by parts of states. At other times, they may be formed by economic patterns that overlap existing national boundaries, such as those between San Diego and Tijuana. In today's borderless world, these are natural economic zones and what matters is that each possesses, in one or another combination, the key ingredients for successful participation in the global economy. (pp. 78–9)

Region states, Ohmae points out, are fundamentally tied to the global economy through mechanisms such as trade, export, and both inward and outward foreign investment – the most competitive region states are home not only to domestic or indigenous companies, but are attractive to the best companies from around the world. Region states can be distinguished by the level and extent of their insertion in the international economy and by their willingness to participate in global trade.

> The primary linkages of region states tend to be with the global economy, and not with host nations. Region states make such effective points of entry into the global economy because the very characteristics that define them are shaped by the demands of that economy. Region states tend to have between five million and 20 million people. A region state must be small enough for its citizens to

share certain economic and consumer interests but of adequate size to justify the infrastructure – communications and transportation links and quality professional services – necessary to participate economically on a global scale. It must for example, have at least one international airport and, more than likely, one good harbor with international-class freight-handling facilities. A region state must also be large enough to provide an attractive market for the broad development of leading consumer products. In other words, region states are not defined by their economies of scale in production (which, after all, can be leveraged from a base of any size through exports to the rest of the world) but rather by having reached efficient economies of scale in their consumption, infrastructure and professional services. (p. 80)

For most of the twentieth century, successful regional as well as national economies grew by extracting natural resources such as coal and iron ore, making materials such as steel and chemicals, and manufacturing durable goods such as automobiles, appliances and industrial machinery. The wealth of regions and of nations in turn stemmed from their abilities to leverage so-called natural comparative advantages that allowed them to be mass producers of commodities competing largely on the basis of relatively low production costs. However, the new age of capitalism has shifted the nexus of competition to ideas. In this new economic environment, regions build economic advantage through their ability to mobilize and to harness knowledge and ideas. In fact, regionally based complexes of innovation and production are increasingly the preferred vehicle used to harness knowledge and intelligence across the globe.

The new age of capitalism requires a new kind of region. In effect, regions are increasingly defined by the same criteria and elements which comprise a knowledge-intensive firm – continuous improvement, new ideas, knowledge creation and organizational learning. Regions must adopt the principles of knowledge creation and continuous learning; they must in effect become *learning regions*. Learning regions provide a series of related infrastructures which can facilitate the flow of knowledge, ideas and learning.

Regions possess a basic set of ingredients that constitute a production system (see Table 3.1). They all have a *manufacturing infrastructure* – a network of firms that produce goods and services. Mass production organization was defined by a high degree of vertical integration and internalization of capabilities. External supplies tended to involve ancillary or non-essential elements, were generally purchased largely on price, and stored in huge inventories in the plant. Knowledge-intensive economic organization is characterized by a much higher degree of reliance on outside suppliers and the development of co-dependent complexes of end-users and suppliers. In heavy industries, such as automobile manufacturing, large assembly facilities play the role of hub, surrounding themselves with a spoke network of customers and suppliers in order to harness

Table 3.1   From mass production to learning regions

	Mass production region	Learning region
Basis of competitiveness	Comparative advantage based on: • natural resources • physical labour	Sustainable advantage based on: • knowledge creation • continuous improvement
Production system	Mass production • physical labour as source of value • separation of innovation and production	Knowledge-based production • continous creation • knowledge as source of value • synthesis of innovation and production
Manufacturing infrastructure	Arm's-length supplier relations	Firm networks and supplier systems as sources of innovation
Human infrastructure	• Low-skill low-cost labour • Taylorist work force • Taylorist education and training	• Knowledge workers • Continuous improvement of human resources • Continuous education and training
Physical and communication infrastructure	Domestically oriented physical infrastructure	• Globally oriented physical and communication infrastructure • Electronic data exchange
Industrial governance system	• Adversarial relationships • Command-and-control regulatory framework	• Mutually dependent relationships • Network organization • Flexible regulatory framework

innovative capabilities of the complex, enhance quality and continuously reduce costs.

Regions have a *human infrastructure* – a labour market from which firms draw knowledge workers. Mass production industrial organization was characterized by a schism between physical and intellectual labour – a large mass of relatively unskilled workers who could perform physical tasks but had little formal involvement in managerial, technical or intellectual activities, and a relatively small group of managers and executives responsible for planning and technological development. The human infrastructure system of mass production – the system of public schools, vocational training, and college and university professional programmes in business and engineering – evolved over time to meet the needs of this mass production system turning out a large mass of 'cogs-in-the-machine' and a smaller technocratic elite of engineers and managers. The human infrastructure required for a learning region is quite different. As its name implies, a learning region requires a human infrastructure of knowledge workers who can apply their intelligence in production. The education and training system must be a learning system that can facilitate life-long learning and provide the high levels of group orientation and teaming required for knowledge-intensive economic organization.

Regions possess a *physical and communications infrastructure* upon which organizations deliver their goods and services and communicate with one another. The physical infrastructure of mass production facilitated the flow of raw materials to factory complexes and the movement of goods and services to largely domestic markets. Knowledge-intensive firms are global players. Thus, the physical infrastructure of the new economy must develop links to and facilitate the movement of people, information, goods and services on a global basis. Furthermore, knowledge-intensive organization draws a great portion of its power from the rapid and constant sharing of information and increasingly electronic exchange of key data between customers, end-users and their suppliers. For example, seat suppliers for Toyota receive a computer broadcast of what seats to build as Toyota cars start down the assembly line. A learning region requires a physical and communication infrastructure which facilitates the movement of goods, people and information on a just-in-time basis.

To ensure growth of existing firms and the birth of new ones, regions have a capital allocation system and financial market which channel credit and capital to firms. Existing financial systems create impediments to the adoption of new management practices. For example, interviews with executives and surveys of knowledge-intensive firms in the USA indicate that banks and financial institutions often require inventory to be held as collateral, creating a sizeable barrier to the just-in-time inventory and supply practices which define knowledge-intensive economic organization. The capital allocation system of a learning region must create incentives for knowledge-based economic organization, for example, by collateralizing knowledge assets rather than physical assets.

Regions also establish mechanisms for *industrial governance* – formal rules, regulations and standards, and informal patterns of behaviour between and among firms, and between firms and government organizations. Mass production regions were characterized by top–down relationships, vertical hierarchy, high degrees of functional or task specialization, and command-and-control modes of regulation. Learning regions must develop governance structures which reflect and mimic those of know-ledge-intensive firms, that is co-dependent relations, network organization, decentralized decision making, flexibility, and a focus on customer needs and requirements.

Learning regions provide the crucial inputs required for knowledge-intensive economic organization to flourish: a manufacturing infrastructure of interconnected vendors and suppliers; a human infrastructure that can produce knowledge workers, facilitates the development of a team orientation, and which is organized around life-long learning; a physical and communication infrastructure which facilitates and supports constant sharing of information, electronic exchange of data and information, just-in-time delivery of goods and services, and integration into the global economy; and capital allocation and industrial governance systems attuned to the needs of knowledge-intensive organizations.

BUILDING THE FUTURE

For most of the past two decades, experts predicted a shift from manufacturing to a post-industrial service economy, or from basic industries to high technology.[18] In the wake of the predictions, efforts were undertaken to invest in new critical technologies and industries.[19] But, the change under way is not one of old sectors giving way to new, but a more fundamental change in the way goods are produced and the economy itself is organized – from mass production to a knowledge-based economy. The implications of the epochal economic transformation are indeed sweeping.

For firms and organizations, the challenge will be to shift towards the principles of knowledge-based organization, and to adopt new organizational and management systems which harness knowledge and intelligence at all points of the organization from the R&D laboratory to the factory floor. Maintaining a balance between cutting-edge innovation and high-quality and efficient production will be a critical issue. To do so, organizations will increasingly adopt best-practice techniques throughout the world, creating new and more powerful forms of knowledge-intensive organizations. Such organizational mechanisms are likely to blend the ability of 'Silicon Valley' style high-technology companies to spur individual genius and creativity, with strategies and techniques for continuous improvement and the collective mobilization of knowledge. Knowledge-intensive firms and organizations will be called on to build integrated and dense global webs of innovation and production. And these firms will increasingly be forced to build and maintain new regional infrastructures which can support knowledge-based production systems.

The new age of capitalism holds even greater challenges for regions. The very fabric of regional organization will change, as regions gradually adopt the principles of knowledge creation and learning. Learning regions will be called on to supply the human, manufacturing and technological infrastructures required to support knowledge-intensive forms of innovation and production. Rather than ushering in the 'end of geography', globalization is likely to occur increasingly through complex systems of regional interdependence and integration. And, as the nation state is squeezed between the poles of accelerating globalization and rising regional economic organization, regions will become focal points for economic, technological, political and social organization.

At a broader level, there is likely to be a shift from strategies and policies which emphasize national competitiveness to ones which revolve around the concept of *sustainable advantage* at the regional as well as national scale. Sustainable advantage means that organizations, regions and nations shift their focus from short-run economic performance to re-creating, maintaining and sustaining the conditions required to be world-class performers through continuous improvement of technology, continuous development of human resources, the use of clean production technology, elimination of waste, and a commitment to continuous environmental improvement. Indeed, the concept of sustainable advantage has the potential to become the central organizing principle for economic and political governance at the international, national and regional scales. In this sense, there is some possibility that over time it may come to replace the increasingly dysfunctional *Fordist* model of nationally based political–economic regulation.

The industrial and innovation systems of the twenty-first century will be remarkably different from those which have operated for most of the twentieth. Knowledge and human intelligence will replace physical labour as the main source of value. Technological change will accelerate at a pace heretofore unknown: innovation will be perpetual and continuous. Knowledge-intensive organizations based on networks and teams will replace vertical bureaucracy, the cornerstone of the twentieth century. The intersection of relentless globalization and the emergence of learning regions are likely to erode the power and authority of the nation state – the paragon of nineteenth and twentieth century political economy. Whole new institutions for international trade, investment, environment and security will doubtless be created. While the new century holds out great hope, it will require tremendous energy and effort to set in motion the necessary changes, and an unparalleled collective effort to bring them about.

ACKNOWLEDGEMENTS

Research support provided by the Sloan Foundation, National Science Foundation, Ford Foundation, Joyce Foundation and US Economic Development Administration is gratefully acknowledged. Discussions with Joyce-Nathalie Davis Florida, Martin Kenney, Timothy McNulty and Richard Walker have stimulated the line of thinking developed in this article.

NOTES AND REFERENCES

1. By far the best attempt to understand the role of regions in the new age of capitalism is: Kenichi Ohmae, 'The rise of the region state', *Foreign Affairs* 1993, pp. 78–87. See also David Wolfe, 'The wealth of regions', paper presented at the Workshop on Institutions of the New Economy, Canadian Institute for Advanced Research, Toronto, 21–23 May 1994, and Philip Cooke, 'The new wave of regional innovation networks', unpublished Working Paper, Centre for Advanced Studies, University of Wales College of Cardiff, March 1994. See also Annalee Saxenian, *Regional Advantage: Culture and Competition in Silicon Valley and Route 128* (Cambridge, MA, Harvard University Press, 1994); and Michael Piore and Charles Sabel, *The Second Industrial Divide* (New York, Basic Books, 1984), which describe the role of firm networks in regional organization.
2. See Peter Drucker, *Postcapitalist Society* (New York, Harper Business, 1993); and Ikujiro Nonaka, 'The knowledge creating company', *Harvard Business Review*, November–December 1991, pp. 69–104.
3. Ibid.
4. See Richard Florida and Martin Kenney, 'The new age of capitalism: innovation-mediated production', *Futures*, **25** (6), July–August 1993, pp. 637–52; and Richard Florida, 'The new industrial revolution', *Futures*, **23** (6), July–August 1991, pp. 559–76.
5. See Shoshana Zuboff, *In the Age of the Smart Machine* (New York, Basic Books, 1989); David Hounshell, *From American System to Mass Production, 1800–1932* (Baltimore, MD, Johns Hopkins University Press, 1994).
6. See William Lazonick, *Competitive Advantage on the Shopfloor* (Cambridge, MA, Harvard University Press, 1990).
7. United Nations, *World Investment Report, 1993: Transnational Corporations and Integrated International Production* (New York, United Nations, 1993). Also see Peter Dicken, *Global Shift* (London, Guilford Press, 1992).
8. See Martin Kenney and Richard Florida, *Beyond Mass Production: The Japanese System and Its Transfer to the United States* (New York, Oxford University Press, 1993).
9. McKinsey Global Institute, *Manufacturing Productivity* (Washington, DC, McKinsey Global Institute, October 1993).
10. Organization for Economic Cooperation and Development, *The Performance of Foreign Affiliates in the OECD Countries* (Paris, OECD, 1994).
11. See Richard Florida, 'International investment: neglected engine of the global economy', in Cynthia Beltz (ed.), *The Foreign Investment Debate: Opening Markets Abroad, Closing Markets at Home* (Washington, DC, American Enterprise Institute, 1995); United States, Department of Commerce, *Foreign Direct Investment in the United States* (Washington, DC, US Government Printing Office, June 1993); Edward Graham and Paul Krugman, *Foreign Direct Investment in the United States* (Washington, DC, Institute for International Economics, 1991).
12. See Richard Florida, 'Regions and creative destruction: changing production organization and the industrial revival of the US industrial Midwest', *Economic Geography* (forthcoming).

13. See Richard Florida, 'Technology policy for a global economy', *Issues in Science and Technology*, Spring 1995, pp. 49–56.
14. Edward Roberts, *Strategic Management of Technology: Global Benchmarking* (Cambridge, MA, MIT Sloan School of Management, December 1993).
15. Richard Florida and Martin Kenney, 'The globalization of Japanese R&D: the economic geography of Japanese R&D in the US', *Economic Geography*, October 1994, pp. 344–69.
16. See Federal Reserve Bank of Chicago, *Regional Economics in Global Markets* (Chicago, IL, Federal Reserve Bank of Chicago, 1993).
17. Ohmae, 'The rise of the region state'.
18. See, for example, the classic work of Daniel Bell, *The Coming of Post-Industrial Society* (New York, Basic Books, 1973). Also see Fred Block, *Postindustrial Possibilities: A Critique of Economic Discourse* (Berkeley, CA, University of California Press, 1990).
19. For a critique of these strategies, see Richard Florida and Martin Kenney, *The Breakthrough Illusion* (New York, Basic Books, 1990).

4. Industrial districts as 'learning regions': a condition for prosperity

Bjørn T. Asheim

1. INTRODUCTION

The future of industrial districts has been critically discussed during the past years. Some observers have raised questions about the long-term stability of industrial districts, arguing that they will be fragmented either through the take-over of the most successful small and medium sized enterprises (SMEs) by transnational corporations (TNCs) or the formation of hierarchies of firms inside the districts led by the most dynamic SMEs (Harrison, 1994a, 1994b). Others suggest that some industrial districts will develop a 'post-Marshallian' organization of production, i.e. to become Marshallian nodes within global networks (Amin and Thrift, 1992). As this will imply a reduced level of vertical disintegration locally, one could ask how 'Marshallian' such nodes would eventually become (Harrison, 1994b).

While this position basically treats the changing role and function of industrial districts as problematic, caused by the globalization process, another position looks at industrial districts as a specific stage of development in a process of industrialization (Dimou, 1994). Garofoli has presented a typology of Italian industrial districts representing a redynamization of the concept (Dimou, 1994). This implies that industrial districts can pass through a possible development process from 'areas of productive specialization' via 'local productive systems' to 'system areas' as the most advanced form (Garofoli, 1992). In this view, industrial districts do not represent a stable organizational model of industrial production. On the contrary, development and change should be looked upon as a 'natural' part of the history of industrial districts.

Such a process of change could either result in a strengthening and reproduction of the typical 'Marshallian' characteristics of the districts, as is the case with 'system areas', in a 'post-district' (in the meaning 'post-Marshallian') organizational model, which were able to secure the continual growth of the regions involved, or in a circular and cumulative process of fragmentation leading to stagnation and decline in the previously prosperous districts. Most observers seem to agree, however, that technological capabilities are an important differentiating factor concerning the development and future prospects of industrial districts (Asheim, 1994a; Bellandi, 1994; Brusco, 1990; Crevoisier, 1994; Garofoli, 1991a).

Thus, the endogenous innovative capacity of the districts is of strategic importance for their future development. Bellandi sees 'the assessment of the endogenous innovation capacities of the industrial districts . . . [as] . . . a key issue' (Bellandi, 1994, p. 73). More specifically, this means the capability of SMEs in industrial districts to break path-dependency and change technological trajectory through radical innovations. Crevoisier emphasizes the importance of understanding how industrial districts 'react to or generate radical innovations. Without making this point clear, it is not possible to make any prediction about the reproduction and the duration of such systems' (Crevoisier, 1994, p. 259).

In my view, the core of the question is related to the collective learning capacity of SMEs in industrial districts, which will be crucial to their innovativeness and flexibility (Johnson and Lundvall, 1991). In this article, factors enabling and constraining the formation of a sufficient learning capacity to bring about the necessary structural changes will be discussed. Special focus will be directed towards analysing the role and function of the specific 'Marshallian' characteristics of industrial districts (i.e. the domination of small firms, the balance between competition and cooperation, and in the industrial atmosphere of agglomeration economies) in securing a successful transformation of the districts into 'learning regions', which could exploit 'the benefits of learning-based competitiveness' (Amin and Thrift, 1995, p. 11).

2.   THE 'MARSHALLIAN' INDUSTRIAL DISTRICT AND ENDOGENOUS TECHNOLOGICAL DEVELOPMENT

2.1   Industrial Districts and Incremental Innovations

Piore and Sabel (1984) highlighted permanent innovation as a vital characteristic of industrial districts, and a precondition for their continuous growth. According to Piore and Sabel 'the fusion of productive activity, in the narrow sense, with the larger life of the community' represents 'the common solution' to the problems of 'the reconciliation of competition and cooperation' as well as of 'the regeneration of resources required by the collectivity but not produced by the individual units of which it is composed' (Piore and Sabel, 1984, p. 275). The development of industrial districts confirms that such 'fusion' can solve the first problem, and also – conditioned by a supporting local organizational and institutional infrastructure – can increase the collective resources of a district. However, it is much more doubtful whether it – without further public intervention – has the potential to secure the permanent innovation and adoption of new technologies.

What Piore and Sabel here emphasize is an understanding of industrial districts as a 'social and economic whole', where the success of the districts is as dependent on broader social and institutional aspects as on economic factors in a narrow sense (Pyke and Sengenberger, 1990). Bellandi emphasizes that the economies of the districts originate from the thick local texture of interdependencies between the small firms and the local community (Bellandi, 1989). Becattini maintains that 'the firms become rooted in the territory, and this result cannot be conceptualised independently of its historical development' (Becattini, 1990, p. 40). This 'Marshallian' view on the basic structures of industrial districts expresses the idea of 'embeddedness' as a key analytical concept in understanding the functioning of industrial districts (Granovetter, 1985). It is precisely the embeddedness in broader socio-cultural factors, originating in a pre-capitalist civil society, that is the material basis for Marshall's view of agglomeration economies as the specific territorial aspects of geographical agglomeration of economic activity (Asheim, 1992, 1994a).

Thus, in contrast to traditional regional economics, Marshall attaches a more independent role to agglomeration economies. In traditional regional economics, agglomeration economies is understood as agglomerated external economies, normally specified as localization and urbanization economies, i.e. it is used as a functional concept describing an intensification of the external economies of a production system by territorial agglomeration. According to Marshall, external economies are obtained through the geographical concentration of groups of small firms belonging to the same industry (i.e. localization economies), while in traditional regional economies the achievement of external economies of scale is not conditioned by a territorial agglomeration of industrial complexes. According to Perroux, it is possible to talk about growth poles in an 'abstract economic space' (Perroux, 1970). Thus, by defining agglomeration economies as social and territorial embedded properties of an area, Marshall abandons 'the pure logic of economic mechanisms and introduces a sociological approach in his analysis' (Dimou, 1994, p. 27).

Marshall maintains that the two most important aspects of his understanding of agglomeration economies, 'mutual knowledge and trust' and the 'industrial atmosphere', will together have a positive effect on the promotion of innovations and innovation diffusion among small firms within industrial districts. However, Marshall was also aware of the fact that agglomeration economies as such do not guarantee that product and process innovations will take place.

Indeed, studies have shown that the 'industrial atmosphere' of industrial districts can support the adoption, adaptation and diffusion of innovations among SMEs (Asheim, 1994a). In the same way, the presence of trust can stimulate the introduction of new technology into industrial districts, since mutual trust – in addition to reducing transaction costs – seems to be crucial for the establishment of non-contractual inter-firm linkages.

However, the importance of territorial embedded agglomeration economies in promoting innovations concerns largely incremental innovations: 'Industrial districts can generate innovations by incremental steps, through a gradual improvement of the final product, of the process and of the overall production organization' (Bianchi and Giordani, 1993, p. 31). Garofoli also maintains that industrial districts have a larger capacity to deal with gradual innovations than with 'ruptures' (Garofoli, 1991b).

Thus, agglomeration economies can represent important basic conditions and stimulus to incremental innovations through informal 'learning-by-doing' and 'learning-by-using', primarily based on tacit knowledge (Asheim, 1994a). Becattini conceives of this as a social process of collective self-awareness in which the decision to introduce a new technology, partly owing to the common system of values and attitudes prevailing in the districts, is perceived as 'an opportunity to defend an already acquired position' (Becattini, 1990, p. 47). It is in this sense that Becattini's statement that 'a MID (i.e. a Marshallian industrial district) is either creative or it is not a (true) MID' (Becattini, 1991, p. 104) should be understood.

As Bellandi suggests, such learning, based on practical knowledge (experience) of which specialized practice is a prerequisite, may have significant creative content (Bellandi, 1994). Thus, as a result of what Bellandi calls 'decentralized industrial creativity' (DIC), the collective potential innovative capacity of small firms in industrial districts is not always inferior to that of large, research-based companies (Bellandi, 1994). The fact remains, however, that, in general, the individual results of DIC are incremental, even if 'their accumulation has possible major effects on economic performance' (ibid., p. 76).

2.2   Incremental Innovations and Competitive Advantage

In an increasingly globalized world economy, however, it is rather doubtful whether incremental innovations will be sufficient to secure the competitive advantage of SMEs in industrial districts. Crevoisier argues that the reliance on incremental innovations 'would mean that these areas will very quickly exhaust the technical paradigm on which they are founded'

(Crevoisier, 1994, p. 259). In addition, Bellandi underlines that 'consistency (between DIC and MID) does not mean necessity. A number of difficulties may arise which can constrain and even bring to a halt DIC within an industrial district' (Bellandi, 1994, pp. 80–81).

Bellandi (1994) emphasizes the private and public institution-making as a condition for the reproduction of dynamic industrial districts with growth potentials. When difficulties concerning institution-making or the supporting local industrial policy arise in an industrial district, 'the basic conditions which sustain DIC are easily impaired, and the life-expectancy of such a district is relatively short' (ibid., p. 81). Such institution-making is part of what Amin and Thrift (1994) call 'institutional thickness', which they claim is of critical importance for 'the performance of local economies in a globalizing world' (Amin and Thrift 1994, p. v).

In his advocacy for a transition from the original 'industrial district Mark I' (i.e. districts without local government intervention) to 'industrial district Mark II' (i.e. districts with considerable government intervention) Brusco points out that 'industrial districts eventually face the problem of how to acquire the new technological capabilities which are necessary to revive the process of creative growth. It is here that the need for intervention appears' (Brusco, 1990, p. 17). In another context, Brusco has claimed that 'industrial districts are slow to adopt new technologies, lack expertise in financial management, have little of the know-how required for basic research, and are unable to produce epoch-making innovations' (Brusco, 1992, p. 196).

However, perhaps a more fundamental problem of Marshallian industrial districts is that their basic characteristics do not represent the most adequate means to meet the challenge of remaining competitive in a globalized world economy. The original rationale for industrial districts rests on the creation of 'external economies of scale' (i.e. economies that are external to the firm but internal to the area) for groups of small firms as a competitive alternative to the 'internal economies of scale' of big companies (Asheim, 1994a). Thus, external economies concern the productivity of the single firm and the efficiency of the production system, obtained through an external, technical division of labour between firms, 'which can often be secured by the concentration of many small businesses of a similar character in particular localities: or, as is commonly said, by the localization of industry' (Marshall, 1891, p. 325). Marshall underlines the possibilities of dividing 'the process of production into several stages, each of which can be performed with the maximum of economy in a small establishment' (Marshall in Whitaker, 1975, pp. 196–7; here quoted from Becattini, 1989, p. 131).

Thus, Marshall's perspective was to secure the productivity and competitiveness of small firms through economies of localization achieved by an extensive division of labour and strong product specialization between firms in territorial agglomerations (industrial districts). The standard of comparison was the internal economies of scale of large firms. Even if the specific Marshallian interpretation of agglomeration economies can be said to stimulate the innovation process at the district level, their major impact was to secure the (informal) skills and 'social and ideological qualifications' of the workforce. When using the term 'industrial atmosphere' Marshall refers to factors of a 'public good' character (Becattini, 1990) emergent within industrial districts 'in which manufacturers have long been domiciled, a habit of responsibility, of carefulness and promptitude in handling expensive machinery and materials becomes the common property of all' (Marshall, 1986, p. 171). In this way 'the agglomeration of industry in a district generates, in time, an aptitude for industrial work, and this aptitude communicates itself to most of the people who live in the district' (Bellandi, 1989, p. 143).

These characteristics of a traditional MID represent at least two fundamental problems with respect to generating endogenous technological development in contemporary industrial districts. The first problem is the one-dimensional focus on efficiency and productivity as understood within a Fordist frame of reference, i.e. productivity growth as a result of standardized production. Even if this has significantly changed in contemporary industrial districts as economies of scope within SMEs – as a result of new computerized production technique and a large increase in the demand for customized products – are as important as economies of scale in achieving high productivity, this does not guarantee a large enough innovation capacity to retain competitiveness in the globalized world economy. In a post-Fordist economy, competition through innovativeness has gained increasingly greater importance. Camagni also argues that the industrial district approach represents a static perspective as it 'considers the local relationships mainly in terms of locational efficiency' (Camagni, 1991, p. 2).

The second problem concerns the 'functionality' of Marshallian agglomeration economies with respect to endogenous innovation capacity. As already pointed out, the territorial embedded agglomeration economies can promote incremental innovations. However, this is conditioned by the productive balance between the functional and territorial modes of integration (Asheim, 1994a). It is precisely the combination of functionally integrated external economies and territorially integrated (Marshallian) agglomeration economies that have made the industrial districts so successful, but at the same time so vulnerable to changes in the international capitalist economy (Asheim, 1992). If a 'lock-in' situation occurs, for example as a result of the inability of SMEs in industrial districts to change technological trajectory, the existence of a strong 'industrial atmosphere' could be used to squeeze wages to remain competitive, which consequently would result in a functional incapacity of the system of SMEs to promote technological development. However, in more dynamic industrial districts with a less strong path-dependency the presence of 'industrial atmosphere' can provide additional competitive strength through the willingness of committed workers to engage in the formation and workings of 'learning organizations'.

Lastly, it should be remembered that Marshall in his writings on the progressive role of industrial districts in generating industrial and economic growth is strongly influenced by the ideas of Spencer that evolutionary progress meant differentiation and integration (Hodgson, 1993; Sunley, 1992). However, while Sunley argues that Marshall's biological analogies result in a 'consequent exaggeration of the efficiency and potential of industrial localizations' (Sunley, 1992, p. 306), Hodgson (1993), from a perspective of the history of ideas of economics, sees the introduction of biological analogies as representing an improvement towards making economic theory more dynamic ('bringing life back into economics') compared with the dominating mechanical, static analogies. According to Hodgson, 'Marshall saw the limitations of mechanical reasoning, and turned to biology in his search for inspiration and metaphor' (ibid., p. 99).[1]

3. INDUSTRIAL DISTRICTS IN A POST-FORDIST 'LEARNING ECONOMY'

3.1 Innovation and Territorial Agglomeration

The major impact of Porter's book *The Competitive Advantage of Nations* (1990) reflects a change in the understanding of the strategic factors which promote innovation and economic growth. Porter's main argument for the importance of clusters is that they represent the material basis for an innovation-based economy. This argument is clearly fundamental to Schumpeter's idea that 'competition in capitalist economies is not simply about prices, it is also a technological matter: firms compete not by producing the same products cheaper, but by producing new products with new performance characteristics and new technical capabilities' (Smith, 1994, p. 10). This is what Storper and Walker (1989) call 'strong competition' between 'quality-competitive' firms, i.e. firms which base their competitiveness on innovative activity resulting in product and process innovations, in contrast to 'weak competition' between 'price-competitive' firms, i.e. firms which meet tougher competition with cost (normally wage) and price reductions.

Porter's cluster is basically an economic concept indicating that 'a nation's successful industries are usually linked through vertical (buyer/ supplier) or horizontal (common customers, technology, channels, etc.) relationships' (Porter, 1990, p. 149). However, he emphasizes that 'the process of clustering, and the interchange among industries in the cluster, also works best when the industries involved are geographically concentrated' (ibid., p. 157).

These ideas are more or less the same as the ones Perroux, another Schumpterian-inspired economist, presented in the early 1950s. Perroux argued that it was possible to talk about 'growth poles' (or 'development poles') in an 'abstract economic space', i.e. firms which are linked together with an innovative 'key industry' to form an industrial complex. According to Perroux the growth potential and competitiveness of a growth pole could be intensified by territorial agglomeration (Haraldsen, 1994; Perroux, 1970).

Thus, the main argument for territorial agglomerations of economic activity in a contemporary capitalist economy is that they provide the best context for an innovation-based economy. This is supported by modern innovation theory, originating from new institutional economics, which argues that 'regional production systems, industrial districts and technological districts are becoming increasingly important' (Lundvall, 1992, p. 3). According to Amin and Thrift,

> agglomerated learning capability becomes a condition for both dominating the relevant global economic networks *and* securing the cumulative industrial development of the 'home base' by attracting and supporting the best quality domestic and overseas firms. (Amin and Thrift, 1995, p. 12)

Modern innovation theory is developed as a result of criticism of the traditional dominating linear model of innovation as the main strategy for national R&D policies. The 'linear model of innovation' was part of the Fordist era of industrial organization and production, based on formal knowledge generated by R&D activity (codified scientific and engineering knowledge), large firms and national systems of innovation. Smith (1994) identifies the problem of this model along two dimensions. The first problem was 'an overemphasis on research (especially basic scientific research) as the source of new technologies' (ibid., p. 2). Within this perspective a low innovative capacity could be explained by a low R&D activity. Consequently, technology policy in most Western countries was directed towards increasing the level of basic research. The second problem was a 'technocratic view of innovation as a purely technical act: the production of a new technical device' (ibid.). The linear innovation model is, thus, 'research-based, sequential and technocratic' (ibid.).

However,

> it is now recognized that technological innovation and its contribution to eco-
> nomic growth is punctuated by discontinuities, nonappropriabilities, and
> process of learning by doing, using and failing. Evolutionary theories of eco-
> nomic and technological change have now replaced the determinism of the
> linear model. (Felsenstein, 1994, p. 73)

This criticism implies another and broader view on the process of innovation as a technical as well as a social process; as a non-linear process,
'involving not just research but many related activities' (Smith, 1994, p. 6);
and as a process of interaction between firms and their environment
(Smith, 1994). This implies a more sociological view on the process of
innovation, in which interactive learning is looked upon as 'a fundamental
aspect of the process of innovation' (Lundvall, 1993, p. 61). Lundvall
emphasizes that 'learning is predominately an interactive and, therefore, a
socially embedded process which cannot be understood without taking into
consideration its institutional and cultural context' (Lundvall, 1992, p. 1).
Also Camagni emphasizes that

> technological innovation . . . is increasingly a product of social innovation, a
> process happening both at the intra-regional level in the form of collective learn-
> ing processes, and through inter-regional linkages facilitating the firm's access to
> different, though localised, innovation capabilities. (Camagni, 1991, p. 8)

Moreover, this emphasis on regional specific 'context conditions' points to
the importance of the 'lifeworld', which is constituted by the embedded
socio-cultural structures of the civil society, especially to the innovative performance of territorial agglomerated SMEs (Asheim, 1990; Nootenboom,
1988). Habermas defines the lifeworld as the spheres of society where the
interaction between people is based on communicative action (Habermas,
1987). In the perspective of innovation theory the main point is that 'system'
and 'lifeworld' are characterized by different forms of rationality. While the
'system' of the 'economy' and 'politics' spheres of society is dominated by
strategic, instrumental rationality, the 'lifeworld' is dominated by a non-
instrumental, communicative rationality. The dominating position of the
instrumental, techno-economic rationality of modern industrial societies
results in a colonization of the lifeworld by the system, i.e. the reorganization and instrumentalization of the lifeworld to become part of the system
(Habermas, 1987).

This tendency of the 'system' of colonizing the 'lifeworld' has consequences for innovative activity in a modern economy, as the non-
instrumental, creative work of researchers and inventors will always

represent an aspect of the instrumental innovation processes of firms and organizations. This implies that the contradiction between 'system' and 'lifeworld' can manifest itself even within central institutions of the 'system' like firms, and can, thus, play a significant role with respect to 'the innovative performance of the economy' (Lundvall, 1993, p. 63).[2] Lundvall maintains that 'the economy would become stagnant and plagued by tremendous transaction costs if economic agents were limited to actions based on instrumental and strategic behaviour' (Lundvall, 1993, p. 58).

According to Lundvall,

> the importance of interactive learning explains why instrumental and strategic behaviour, including opportunism, is mixed with communicative action and discursive rationality. The specific mix prevailing at a certain time and place affects the institutional set-up as well as the rate and direction of the process of innovation. (Ibid., p. 61)

Thus, in this perspective interactive learning includes technical learning, communicative learning as well as social learning (Lundvall, 1993). Lundvall adds that 'cooperation in processes of technical learning tend to stimulate "social learning" and reinforce communicative rationality' (ibid., p. 60).[3]

Lundvall and Johnson maintain that the concept of 'learning economies' refers 'first of all to the ICT (information, computer and telecommunication)-related techno-economic paradigm of the post-Fordist period. It is through the combination of widespread ICT-technologies, flexible specialization and innovation as a crucial means of competition in the new techno-economic paradigm, that the learning economy gets firmly established' (Lundvall and Johnson, 1994, p. 26). These perspectives of the 'learning economy' are based on the view that 'knowledge' is the most fundamental resource in a modern capitalist economy, and 'learning' the most important process (Lundvall, 1992), thus making the learning capacity of an economy of strategic importance to its innovativeness and competitiveness.

One of the consequences of considerably more knowledge-intensive modern economies is that 'the production and use of knowledge is at the core of value-added activities, and innovation is at the core of firms' and nations' strategies for growth' (Archibugi and Michie, 1995, p. 1). Thus, in a 'learning economy' 'technical and organizational change have become increasingly endogenous. Learning processes have been institutionalized and feed-back loops for knowledge accumulation have been built in so that the economy as a whole . . . is "learning by doing" and "learning by using" (Lundvall and Johnson, 1994, p. 26).

3.2 Cooperation and Innovation

The emphasis on interactive learning as a fundamental aspect of the process of innovation points to cooperation as an important strategy in order to promote innovations. The rapid economic development in the 'Third Italy', based on territorially agglomerated SMEs, has drawn an increased attention towards the importance of cooperation between firms and between firms and local authorities in achieving international competitiveness.

> It is the success of the industrial districts in securing inter-firm co-operation and channelling the competitive forces towards such constructive ends of quality upgrading and technical change that brought them to the attention of the international research community. (You and Wilkinson, 1994, p. 276)

According to Dei Ottati,

> this willingness to cooperate is indispensable to the realization of innovation in the ID which, due to the division of labour among firms, takes on the characteristics of a collective process. Thus, for the economic dynamism of the district and for the competitiveness of its firms, they must be innovative but, at the same time, these firms cannot be innovative in any other way than by cooperating among themselves. (Dei Ottati, 1994, p. 474)

Many observers have pointed to the importance of collaboration between territorially agglomerated firms in promoting international competitiveness. Pyke (1994) underlines the close inter-firm cooperation and the existence of a supporting institutional infrastructure at the regional level (e.g. centres of real services) as the main factors explaining the success of Emilia-Romagna. Camagni points out 'the collective learning processes that enhance the local creativity, the capability of product innovation and of "technological creation"' (Camagni, 1991, p. 3). And You and Wilkinson are also of the opinion that 'a high degree of cooperation may be an important ingredient of industrial success' (You and Wilkinson, 1994, p. 275).

Thus, if these observations are correct, this represents new 'forces' in the promotion of technological development in capitalist economies, implying a modification of the overall importance of competition between individual capitals. Of course, the fundamental forces in a capitalist mode of production constituting the technological dynamism are still caused by the contradictions of the capital–capital relationship (Asheim, 1985). However, the combined effects of the globalized and deregulated world economy and the reduced power of nation states due to transfer of authority to supranational organizations (e.g. the EU and the World Trade Organization) have resulted in an increased need for firms to establish organizational microregulation to improve the ability to control the growing complexity and insecurity in the increasingly competitive world economy through inter-firm cooperation. Lazonick argues, referring to Porter's empirical evidence (Porter, 1990), that

> domestic cooperation rather than domestic competition is the key determinant of global competitive advantage. For a domestic industry to attain and sustain global competitive advantage requires continuous innovation, which in turn requires domestic cooperation. Domestic rivalry is an important determinant of enterprise strategies. But the substance of these competitive strategies – specifically whether they entail continuous innovation or cut-throat price-cutting – depends on how and to what extent the enterprises in an industry cooperate with one another. (Lazonick, 1993, p. 4)

The organizational form of the new microregulation securing inter-firm cooperation is achieved either through global or local networks of close inter-firm relations as an independent, third form of governance as an alternative to markets (of a globalized world economy) and hierarchies (of large corporations).[4] Through networking, the ambition is to create 'strategic advantages over competitors outside the network' (Lipparini and Lorenzoni, 1994, p. 18). However, to achieve this it is important that the networks are organized in accordance with the principle of the 'strength of weak ties' (Granovetter, 1973). Grabher argues that

> loose coupling within networks affords favourable conditions for interactive learning and innovation. Networks open access to various sources of information and thus offer a considerably broader learning interface than is the case with hierarchical firms. (Grabher, 1993, p. 10)

Using this perspective on networks when discussing the relation between competition and cooperation within industrial districts, competitive advantage is achieved internally through inter-firm cooperation and exploited externally through competition with firms of the 'outside' world. Lazonick argues that

> to fight foreign rivals requires a suspension of rivalry in order to build value-creating industrial and technological communities. Unless social organizations are put in place that can engage in innovation, heightened domestic rivalry will lead to decline. (Lazonick, 1993, p. 8)

3.3 The Role of Cooperation and Competition and the Innovative Capacity of Industrial Districts

In the literature on industrial districts from Piore and Sabel's book (1984) and until today the emphasis has been that 'the central feature of the "industrial district" is the balance between competition and co-operation among firms' (You and Wilkinson, 1994, p. 259). Dei Ottati asserts that

> the cooperate elements contribute in a decisive way to the integration of the system, while forces of competition keep it flexible and innovative. This is because competition in the particular socio-economic district environment encourages better utilization of available resources and above all, development of latent capabilities and diffuse creativity. (Dei Ottati, 1994, p. 476)[5]

Porter (1990) also has similar problems of acknowledging the large and increasing influence of cooperation on the promotion of innovations and competitiveness. According to Porter,

> two elements – domestic rivalry and geographic industry concentration – have especially great power to transform the 'diamond' into a system, domestic rivalry because it promotes upgrading of the entire national 'diamond', and geographic concentration because it elevates and magnifies the interactions within the 'diamond'. (Porter, 1990, p. 131)

And he concludes

> that the most striking findings from our reasearch . . . is the prevalence of several domestic rivals in the industries in which the nation had international advantage. Rivalry has a direct role in stimulating improvement and innovation. (Ibid., p. 143)

Furthermore, Porter maintains that

> the broader effects of domestic rivalry are closely related to an old but often neglected notion in economics known as external economies. (Ibid., p. 144)

This ambivalence regarding the relationship between, and the relative importance of, competition and cooperation is basically caused by a traditional, Marshallian perception of industrial districts and of the achievement of external economies through vertical cooperation.[6] In my view, one of the constraining factors in moving beyond the domination of incremental innovations in industrial districts is the fierce competition between subcontractors specializing in the same products or phases of production, and vertically linked to the commissioning firms. This limits the potential for horizontal technological cooperation (Asheim, 1994a). In addition, a characteristic of industrial districts is that they are made up of independent small firms with no single big firm acting as a centre of strategic decision-making. The problem, in this respect, is that owing to a shortage of both human and financial resources, formal R&D activity has normally been out of reach for the majority of SMEs. As a consequence, they lack the capacity to build up and support a necessary level of research and development capacity in accordance with the linear model of innovation and, thus, should exploit more systematically the broader social basis of innovative activity.[7]

This means that the possibilities and potentials of the 'learning economy' are not fully recognized. In this connection an important aspect of a 'learning economy' is that

> the organisational modes of firms are increasingly chosen in order to enhance learning capabilities: networking with other firms, horizontal communication patterns and frequent movements of people between parts and departments, are becoming more and more important. (Lundvall and Johnson, 1994, p. 26)

This can be illustrated by an example from the 'Third Italy', where a firm started to cooperate with its suppliers in developing new products (i.e. product innovations) in order to institutionalize a continual organizational learning process. This cooperation played a central role in shortening the product cycle, improving the product quality and increasing the competitiveness of the firm (Bonaccorsi and Lipparini, 1994). The firm redefined the relations to its major suppliers based on the recognition that

> a network based on long-term, trust-based alliances could not only provide flexibility, but also a framework for joint learning and technological and managerial innovation. To be an integral partner in the development of the total product, the supplier must operate in a state of constant learning, and this process is greatly accelerated if carried out in an organizational environment that promotes it. (Ibid., p. 144)

Generally, Semlinger notes that

> modern purchasing policies are heading towards an intensification of interfirm cooperation referred to as 'integration of suppliers' or 'dissolving the boundaries of the enterprise'. (Semlinger, 1993, p. 169)

This implies an understanding of flexibility as primarily a function of the innovative capability of firms and districts, i.e. a more dynamic perspective than the traditional focus on internal and external flexibility caused by new computerized production equipment and vertical disintegration.

3.4   Forms of Inter-firm Cooperation

The importance of horizontal inter-firm cooperation with respect to promoting innovations highlights the qualitative aspects of networking, i.e. specifically the governance structure of the networks. Networking within local and global production systems results in new, planned forms of industrial organization in contrast to the anarchic results of a market-based externalization process.[8] However, these new ways of organizing industrial production can take various forms. The specific new form of industrial organization resulting from close inter-firm networking is represented by 'quasi-integration' (Leborgne and Lipietz, 1988). Quasi-integration refers to relatively stable relationships between firms, where the principal firms (i.e. the buyers) aim at combining the benefits of vertical integration as well as vertical disintegration in their collaboration with suppliers and subcontractors (Haraldsen, 1995). According to Leborgne and Lipietz,

> quasi-integration minimizes both the costs of coordination (because of the autonomy of the specialized firms or plant), and the costs of information/transaction (because of the routinized just-in-time transactions between firms). Moreover the financial risks of R&D and investments are shared within the quasi-integrated network. (Leborgne and Lipietz, 1992, p. 341)

Leborgne and Lipietz distinguish between three different forms of quasi-integration. The most extreme case is called 'vertical quasi-integration', where 'the buyer has at its disposal the know-how of the subcontractor' (ibid.). By contrast, there is the case of 'horizontal quasi-integration', when 'partnership and strategic alliance link a supplier with specific technology to a regular customer of another sector of the division of labor' (ibid.). The general case is, however, the intermediate situation of 'oblique quasi-integration', where the customer orders 'specific goods which are part of the process of production' (ibid., p. 342), but where the supplier 'is fully responsible for the process of production' (ibid.).

Haraldsen (1995) maintains that the relations between 'differentiated suppliers' and the buyers are characterized by 'horizontal quasi-integration'; the relation between 'specialized suppliers' and the buyers by 'oblique quasi-integration'; while 'vertical quasi-integration' corresponds to the relations between capacity subcontractors and their principal firms.

'Vertical quasi-integration' represents an externalization of the technical division of labour from a unit of production (i.e. a factory) to a production system. Such networks are characterized by an intensive 'weak' competition between potential subcontractors, and, consequently, they are not very innovative.

In contrast, 'oblique quasi-integration' can typically be constituted by 'user–producer' relations which imply potentially good opportunities for 'learning by interacting', based on an externalization of the technical division of labour within a production system. As interactive learning is at the core of the process of innovation in a 'learning economy', this form of inter-firm cooperation represents important possibilities for carrying out radical product and process innovations.

'Horizontal quasi-integration' represents a form of inter-firm coopera-tion, where the supplier delivers goods which are not an integrated part of the production process of the principal firm, as opposed to the two previ-ous categories. In this case it is more a question of complementary prod-ucts or services, which imply that such horizontal relations are based on a social division of labour (Haraldsen, 1995).

Leborgne and Lipietz (1992) maintain that the more horizontal the ties between the partners in the network are (i.e. networks dominated by oblique or horizontal quasi-integration), the more efficient the network as a whole is. This is also emphasized by Håkansson, who points out that

> collaboration with customers leads in the first instance to the step-by-step kind of changes (i.e. incremental innovations), while collaboration with partners in the horizontal dimension is more likely to lead to leap-wise changes (i.e. radical innovations). (Håkansson, 1992, p. 41)

Generally Leborgne and Lipietz argue that 'the upgrading of the partner increases the efficiency of the whole network' (Leborgne and Lipietz, 1992, p. 399).

This reorganization of networking between firms can be described as a change from a domination of vertical relations between principal firms and their subcontractors based on a technical division of labour to horizontal relations between principal firms and suppliers based on a social division of labour. Patchell refers to this as a transformation from production systems to learning systems, which implies a transition from 'a conven-tional understanding of production systems as fixed flows of goods and services to dynamic systems based on learning' (Patchell, 1993, p. 797). Patchell argues that Japan has developed 'a social technology that resolves the transaction cost trade-offs . . . between internal and external gover-nance structures' (ibid.). This social technology can be conceptualized by using Asanuma's reformulation of Williamson's static concept 'asset-specific relation' to the more dynamic concept 'relation-specific skill' (Asanuma, 1989). According to Patchell, 'relation-specific skill' is 'the crux for comprehending the shift from production systems to learning systems' (Patchell, 1993, p. 797). Such a transformation requires 'organizational integration', which is a result of the organizational capability of firms (Lazonick and Smith, 1995). Organizational integration is manifest when 'the relationships among participants in a specialized division of labour permit their activities to be planned and co-ordinated to achieve specified goals' (ibid., p. 9).

'Relation-specific skill' is defined as

the skill required on the part of the supplier to respond efficiently to the specific needs of a core firm. Formation of this skill requires that learning through repeated interactions with a particular core firm be added to the basic techno-logical capability which the supplier has accumulated. (Asanuma, 1989, p. 28)

On this background the distinction is made between 'design-supplied' (DS) and 'design-approved' (DA) suppliers, which is constituted by the difference between 'the technological dependency of DS firms on the core firm to design the product that they produce' (Patchell, 1993, p. 811), and DA firms, which 'will exchange technological information on an equal level of sophis-tication with core firms, and these DA suppliers serve regional, national, and international markets' (ibid., p. 812). The qualitative difference between these two forms of inter-firm cooperation is represented by the difference between vertical relations of core firms and subcontractors (i.e. a DS firm) on the one hand, and horizontal relations of core firms and suppliers (i.e. DA firms) on the other hand, where 'core firm and supplier share informa-tion and participate in an evolving learning and creative process' (ibid., p. 814).[9] Thus, the promotion of horizontal inter-firm cooperation must have a central role in the future industrial policy.

3.5 'Learning Economies' and Organizational and Institutional Innovations

A contrast to traditional Marshallian industrial districts is the increased importance of 'the collectivist and institutional basis for successful co-ordination' (You and Wilkinson, 1994, p. 265). According to You and Wilkinson, Marshall meant that

the role of employers' and workers' organizations and the state was limited. By contrast, in recent discussions of industrial districts, collectivity in the form of direct inter-firm relationships, formal and informal institutions and public policy play a central role in establishing and guaranteeing business and labour standards, fostering innovations and technology diffusion and organizing edu-cation and training. (Ibid., p. 266)

This is in accordance with a 'learning economy' in which 'a wide array of institutional mechanisms can play a role' (Morgan, 1995, p. 6). Thus, gen-erally speaking 'the institutional characteristics of the learning economy becomes a crucial question' (Lundvall and Johnson, 1994, p. 30).

Furthermore, Lundvall and Johnson underline that 'the firms of the learning economy are to a large extent "learning organizations"' (ibid.,

p. 26). A dynamic flexible 'learning organization' can be defined as one that promotes the learning of all its members and has the capacity of continuously transforming itself by rapidly adapting to changing environments by adopting and developing innovations (Pedler et al., 1991; Weinstein, 1992). Thus, important organizational and institutional innovations in a 'learning economy' are the formation of 'learning organizations' not only at an intrafirm, but also at an inter-firm level as well as at a district or regional level.

Intra-firm cooperation
Lundvall and Johnson argue that 'the firm's capability to learn reflects the way it is organized. The movement away from tall hierarchies with vertical flows of information towards more flat organizations with horizontal flows of information is one aspect of the learning economy' (Lundvall and Johnson, 1994, p. 39). This is in line with Scandinavian experiences, which have shown that flat and egalitarian organizations have the best characteristics of being flexible and learning organizations, and that industrial relations characterized by strong involvement of functional flexible, central workers is important in order to have a working 'learning organization'. Such organizations will also result in well-functioning industrial relations, where all the employees (i.e. the (skilled) workers as well as the managers) will have a certain degree of loyalty towards the firm. All experience shows that 'the process of continuous improvement through interactive learning and problem-solving, a process that was pioneered by Japanese firms, presupposes a workforce that feels actively committed to the firm' (Morgan, 1995, p. 11).[10]

Brusco – with special reference to the industrial districts of Emilia-Romagna – points to the dominating model of production in the districts 'that was able to be efficient and thus competitive on world markets, in which efficiency and the ability to innovate were achieved through high levels of worker participation and were accompanied by working conditions that were acceptable' (Brusco, 1995, p. 5). In general, Porter points out that

> differences in managerial approaches and organizational skills create advantages and disadvantages in competing in different types of industries. Labor–management relationships are particularly significant in many industries because they are so central to the ability of firms to improve and innovate. (Porter, 1990, p. 109)

According to modern organizational theory and practice the challenges of the 'learning economy' are increasingly being institutionalized as firm internal 'development organizations'. They represent the framework for carrying out the process of continuous improvement in productivity and competitiveness. The strategy behind such an organizational innovation is to make 'labour productivity "endogenous" and raise it above market levels, hence not transferable to other firms' (Perulli, 1993, p. 110).

A strong and broad involvement within an organization will also make it easier to use and diffuse informal or 'tacit', non-R&D-based, knowledge, which in a 'learning economy' has a more central role to play in securing continuous innovation. 'Transactions' with 'tacit' knowledge within and between networking organizations require trust, which is easier to establish and reproduce in flat organizations than in hierarchical ones. In a study of successful intra-firm reorganization of SMEs in Baden-Württemberg Herrigel reports that one company

> set out to constitute 'trusting' relations among all actors within the firm, regard- less of role or position in the organization, which were informed by mutual respect. It discouraged thinking in terms of hierarchy and status and made all information about the company available to everyone within it. (Herrigel, 1996, p. 46)

According to Lipparini and Lorenzoni 'a high dose of trust serves as sub- stitute for more formalized control systems' (Lipparini and Lorenzoni, 1994, p. 18; see also Lorenz, 1992 and Sabel, 1992). In organizations char- acterized by an authoritarian management style the attitude of the employ- ees will often be to keep 'the relevant information to themselves' (You and Wilkinson, 1994, p. 270).

Inter-firm cooperation
Generally, inter-firm networking is of strategic importance to SMEs due to their lack of financial and human resources and/or marketing capabilities, which restrict their innovative capacity. According to Brusco, it is 'the fact of being a "system" rather than being a "single firm" that defines the degree of sophistication of these industrial structures' (Brusco, 1986, p. 194). In this way, the internal skill and competence of firms are strengthened through inter-firm collaboration, and can, furthermore, be supported by local structures outside the firm. This strategy could be characterized as 'learning-by-interacting', of which the interactions between producers and users of intermediate products and between suppliers and users of machine tools and business services represent the main forms of cooperation. Herrigel refers to cases of successful adjustment and restructuring of SMEs in Baden-Württemberg, where 'relations with suppliers . . . were intensified so that important providers were drawn directly into the devel- opment process' (Herrigel, 1996, p. 47). Such cooperation can result in a largely improved innovative capacity of SMEs within industrial districts. Russo concludes her analysis of technological development in Sassoulo, Emilia-Romagna, by underlining the importance of 'the interrelationships

between firms and their proximity to each other. Together these provide the basis for the process of generation and adoption of new techniques' (Russo, 1989, p. 215).

The spatial proximity of interacting firms is an important enabling factor in stimulating inter-firm 'learning networks' involving long-term commitment. Håkansson claims that 'the importance of proximity is particularly noticeable in horizontal relationships, but it is not altogether absent in the case of vertical relations' (Håkansson, 1992, p. 125). In this way, the ability to generate 'new knowledge by combining internal and external learning could then be a critical variable in understanding SMEs innovative capabilities' (Lipparini and Sobrero, 1994, p. 136).[11]

However, this may require a change in the industrial organization towards a more hierarchical group-formation of firms, which can be observed in several industrial districts in the 'Third Italy' (Zeitlin, 1992). According to Cooke, 'recent evidence from . . . the Third Italy, suggests group-formation has enabled firms in industrial districts to outperform their sector generally' (Cooke, 1994a, p. 24). Most commonly these groups are formed by SMEs under competitive pressure aiming to stay competitive (Zeitlin, 1992). In addition to providing SMEs with financial and human resources to increase the innovative capacity so as to improve their international competitiveness, the formation of groups can be a strategy for establishing more systematic horizontal inter-firm networking promoting technological cooperation.

Furthermore, in this perspective the organization of innovation network between industrial districts and the external world (Camagni, 1991), giving priority to horizontal inter-firm technological cooperation to ensure the adoption and diffusion of radical innovations, is very important.[12]

Regional cooperation

An important innovation in the institutional set-up of 'learning regions' would be the establishment of territorial embedded regional systems of innovation (Asheim, 1995) – which could improve what has been called 'systemic innovation' with reference to Baden-Württemberg (Cooke and Morgan, 1994) – as a strategic part of a regional innovation policy. The aim of such a policy is through public intervention to support organizational innovations such as 'centres of real services' in the industrial districts of Emilia-Romagna (Brusco, 1992), which have turned out to be successful in modernizing the economic structure of the districts and, thus, have strengthened their competitive advantage. In general, Amin and Thrift emphasize 'the need for enterprise support systems, such as technology centres or service centres, which can help keep networks of firms innovative' (Amin and Thrift, 1995, p. 12). And, according to Cooke, 'the region is a most appropriate economic and administrative entity around which to plan networking approaches' (Cooke, 1994b, p. 33).

The need for such public intervention could be illustrated with reference to what the GREMI group calls 'innovative milieu', i.e.

> the set, or the complex network of mainly informal social relationships on a limited geographical area, often determining a specific external 'image' and a specific internal 'representation' and sense of belonging, which enhance the local innovative capability through synergetic and collective learning processes. (Camagni, 1991, p. 3)

In this perspective, creativity and continuous innovation are considered to be a result of

> a collective learning process, fed by such social phenomena as intergenerational transfer of know-how, imitation of successful managerial practices and technological innovations, interpersonal face-to-face contacts, formal or informal cooperation between firms, tacit circulation of commercial, financial or technological information. (Ibid., p. 1)

However, the basic problem with the 'innovative milieu' approach is that, beyond referring to 'industrial atmosphere' and different forms of incremental innovations, it does not specify the mechanisms and processes which promote innovative activity more successfully in some regions than in others, i.e. 'why localization and territorial specificity should make technological and organizational dynamics better' (Storper, 1995a, p. 203). Their focus is too much on what they call the 'territorial logic' of development processes, which on the one hand misses the central point of the 'productive' balance of the functional and territorial modes of integration, which has been the key to the industrial and economic success of the industrial districts (Asheim, 1992, 1994a), without fully understanding the challenges of the 'learning economy' on the other hand.[13]

Furthermore, the strong focus on the advantages of the territorial mode of integration increases the possibilities of ignoring the danger of supporting economic and social structures which create 'lock-in' situations through the 'weakness of strong ties' (Granovetter, 1973), which often characterizes old industrial agglomerations of SMEs (Glasmeier, 1994).[14] Porter argues that 'geographic concentration does carry with it some long-term risks, however, especially if most buyers, suppliers, and rivals do not operate internationally' (Porter, 1990, p. 157). And Grabher points out what he calls an 'embeddedness dilemma' with respect to major social, economic and technological changes (Grabher, 1993). However, Camagni warns about such development tendencies when he maintains that innovation networks and cooperation agreements become the strategic instruments that local environments may utilize in order to avoid an 'entropic death' which always threatens too closed systems, and to keep on exploiting at the same time the advantages provided by their internal synergies, their industrial 'memory' and atmosphere. (Camagni, 1991, p. 5)

The challenge of 'learning regions' is to increase the innovative capability of SME-based industrial agglomerations through identifying 'the economic logic by which milieu fosters innovation' (Storper, 1995a, p. 203). According to Porter, 'competitive advantage is created and sustained through a highly localized process' (Porter, 1990, p. 19). At the regional level, this points to the importance of disembodied technical progress, i.e. progress 'which can occur independently of changes in physical capital stock' (de Castro and Jensen-Butler, 1993, p. 1), and 'untraded interdependencies', i.e. 'a structured set of technological externalities which can be a collective asset of groups of firms/industries within countries/regions' (Dosi, 1988, p. 226), with respect to establishing regional systems of innovation. Together with territorial embedded Marshallian agglomeration economies, disembodied technical knowledge and 'untraded interdependencies' constitute the material basis for the formation of territorially embedded regional systems of innovation as an alternative to regionalized national systems of innovation represented by science parks and other top–down technology policies based on the linear model of innovation (Asheim, 1995; Henry et al., 1995). According to de Castro and Jensen-Butler, 'rapid disembodied technical progress requires . . . a high level of individual technical capacity, collective technical culture and a well-developed institutional framework . . . [which] . . . are highly immobile in geographical terms' (de Castro and Jensen-Butler, 1993, p. 8). Dosi argues that 'untraded interdependencies' represent 'context conditions' which generally are country- or region-specific, and of fundamental importance to the innovative process (Dosi, 1988, p. 226; see also Storper, 1995a, 1995b). Amin and Thrift precisely underline 'the role of localized "untraded interdependencies" in securing learning and innovation advantage in interregional competition' (Amin and Thrift, 1994, p. 12).

4. CONCLUSION: INDUSTRIAL DISTRICTS AS 'LEARNING REGIONS'

In this article I have aimed to discuss the future of industrial districts in the perspective of the 'learning economy'. I agree that 'there exists a viable, dynamic, competitive and socially desirable paradigm of small and medium-sized enterprise development, following the principle of the Italian industrial districts prototype' (Lyberaki and Pesmazoglou, 1994, p. 509), conditioned by a transformation of the districts into 'learning regions'.

The viability, dynamism and competitiveness of SMEs in industrial districts has basically been the result of the way

> flexible specialization works by violating one of the assumptions of classical political economy: that the economy is separate from society. Markets and hierarchies . . . both presuppose the firm to be an independent entity. . . . By contrast, in flexible specialization it is hard to tell where society ends, and where economic organization begins. (Piore and Sabel, 1984, p. 275)

However, as emphasized by Bellandi (1994) and Brusco (1990), it is a question of a potential collective innovative capacity of territorial agglomerated SMEs, which has to be systematically developed and supported both at the intra-firm, the inter-firm and the district or regional level. This perspective emphasizes the importance of organizational innovations to promote cooperation, primarily through the formation of dynamic flexible learning organizations within firms, between firms in network and between firms and society regionally. Such learning organizations must be based on strong involvement at the intra-firm level, on horizontal cooperation at the inter-firm level, and on the embeddedness of regional systems of innovation at the regional level. This could, together with other necessary organizational and social innovations in the regional institutional set-up, contribute to turning industrial districts into 'learning regions'.

Such 'learning regions' would be in a much better position than 'traditional' industrial districts to avoid a 'lock-in' of development caused by localized path-dependency. In a 'learning economy' the competitive advantage of firms and regions is based on innovations, and innovation processes are seen as socially and territorially embedded, interactive learning processes. Thus, based on modern innovation theory, it could be argued that SMEs in industrial districts can develop a large innovative capacity.

This new understanding of the institutional and cultural context of a 'learning economy' stresses the importance of the 'fusion' of the economy with society, where socio-cultural structures and other broader historical factors are not only looked upon as reminiscences from pre-capitalist civil societies, but as necessary prerequisites for regions in order to be innovative and competitive in a post-Fordist global economy. This forces a re-evaluation of 'the significance of territoriality in economic globalization' (Amin and Thrift, 1995, p. 8).

In this way 'learning regions' could have the possibilities of transcending the contradictions between functional and territorial integration through a new, regionalized integration of the traditional, 'contextual' knowledge of industrial districts and the 'codified' knowledge of the global economy within the framework of territorially embedded regional systems of innovation.[15]

ACKNOWLEDGEMENTS

Earlier versions of this paper were presented at the conference of the IGU Commission on the Organization of Industrial Space on 'Interdependent and uneven development: Global-local perspectives', Seoul, South Korea, August 1995; and at the ESST conference, San Sebastian, Spain, September 1995. I would like to thank discussants at these conferences together with Marco Bellandi and two anonymous reviewers for valuable comments. The usual disclaimers apply.

NOTES

1. It is in this perspective that the often quoted statement of Marshall (also quoted by Sunley, 1992) that 'the Mecca of the economist lies in economic biology rather than in economic dynamics' should be understood. Hodgson (1993) points out that the rest of the paragraph is very seldom referred to. Here Marshall writes: 'But biological conceptions are more complex than those of mechanics; a volume on Foundations must therefore give a relatively large place to mechanical analogies; and frequent use is made of the term "equilibrium", which suggests something of a statical analogy' (Marshall, *The Principles of Economics*, 9th edn, Macmillan, London 1949, p. xii; here quoted from Hodgson, 1993, p. 99).
2. Lundvall points out that 'R&D departments are more oriented to communicative action while the legal and accounting departments are oriented most to strategic rationality' (Lundvall, 1993, p. 59).
3. This view on the relations between 'system' and 'lifeworld' with respect to innovative activity resembles to a certain degree the opinion of the young Schumpeter when emphasizing the central role of the entrepreneur in the innovation process, and his scepticism about the innovative capacity of large companies. Even if he later strongly modified this opinion, it is still an empirical fact that SMEs often are more innovative than large companies, especially with respect to product innovations in certain high-tech industries. Some large corporations even try to solve problems in connection with a weak innovativeness through systematic take-overs of innovative SMEs.
4. In this connection it is important to distinguish between global and local networks. Global networks are constituted by functionally integrated global production systems dominated by large firms (TNCs), while the typical local network is a territorial integrated local production system consisting of SMEs (e.g. the industrial district as the ideal type).
5. This assertion obviously weakens her earlier referred statement (p. 474).
6. Porter has an explicit reference to Marshall (in a footnote) when he discusses the relation between domestic rivalry and external economies.
7. In addition, the emphasis on the importance of domestic rivalry and competition in influencing factor creation (Porter, 1990), could reflect the survival of the view of 'the orthodox economics in which co-operation is regarded exclusively as an attempt to distort prices and is therefore inefficient' (You and Wilkinson, 1994, p. 275).
8. The externalization of specific tasks to a network of specialized subcontractors, which increase the level of vertical disintegration, must in my view be seen as an attempt to

deepen what Marx called the despotism of the (originally internal) technical division of labour (i.e. the capitalist division of labour within a unit of production based on functional specialization) rather than as an extension of the anarchy of the (external) social division of labour (i.e. the traditional division of labour within a society producing specific goods (use-values) for a market) (Asheim, 1994b).

9. In a comparison of the typology of Patchell with the one of Leborgne and Lipietz, 'design-supplied' subcontractors correspond to 'vertical quasi-integration', while 'design-approved' suppliers can be represented by 'oblique quasi-integration' as well as 'horizontal quasi-integration'.

10. Becattini underlines similar aspects when he discusses the socio-material basis for creativity within industrial districts: 'Consequently, if creativity is regarded by some societies as a valuable asset, these societies should curb or even forbid those forms of organization of the process of production which involve physical stress and tedium, and at the same time promote research and investment into the production of means of mitigating human fatigue, and methods of production capable of eliminating excessive repetitiveness in human activities' (Becattini, 1991, p. 106).

11. Camagni points out that such 'interfirm networks may enrich the respective territorial environments or "milieux" through the opportunities they provide for information interchange, explicit or tacit know-how transmission, and skilled factors mobility through the networks' (Camagni, 1991, p. 5).

12. According to Camagni the formation of innovation networks with external and specialized milieux may provide local firms with 'the complementary assets they need to proceed in the economic and technological race' (Camagni, 1991, p. 4).

13. Dimou argues along the same lines that 'the industrial district appears as an organizational fact, stemming from the interactions between an industrial dynamic defined at a global level and a social dynamic defined at a territorial level. As long as these two components of the district evolve in the same way – that is, as long as the territory regulates efficiently the industrial process – the district structure subsists through time' (Dimou, 1994, p. 28).

14. However, the balance between functional and territorial integration is also exposed to threats towards stronger functional integration from an extension of the time–space distanciation of the production system through increased external ownership and control of local industry (Asheim, 1992; Tolomelli, 1990).

15. These new views of the workings of a modern economy are also shared by 'social economics' (or 'socio-economics') (Amin and Thrift, 1995) and the 'embeddedness approach' (Grabher, 1993).

REFERENCES

Amin, A. and Thrift, N. (1992), 'Neo-Marshallian nodes in global networks', *International Journal of Urban and Regional Research*, **16**, 571–87.

Amin, A. and Thrift, N. (eds) (1994), *Globalization, Institutions, and Regional Development in Europe*, Oxford: Oxford University Press.

Amin, A. and Thrift, N. (1995), 'Territoriality in the global political economy', *Nordisk Samhällsgeografisk Tidskrift*, **20**, 3–16.

Archibugi, D. and Michie, J. (1995), 'Technology and innovation: an introduction', *Cambridge Journal of Economics*, **19**, 1–4.

Asanuma, B. (1989), 'Manufacturer–supplier relationships in Japan and the concept of the relation-specific skill', *Journal of the Japanese and International Economies*, **3**, 1–30.

Asheim, B.T. (1985), 'Capital accumulation, technological development and the spatial division of labour: a framework for analysis', *Norwegian Journal of Geography*, **45**, 87–97.

Asheim, B.T. (1990), 'Innovation diffusion and small firms: between the agency of lifeworld and the structure of systems', in N. Alderman, E. Ciciotti and A. Thwaites (eds), *Technological Change in a Spatial Context: Theory, Empirical Evidence and Policy*, Berlin: Springer-Verlag, pp. 37–55.

Asheim, B.T. (1992), 'Flexible specialization, industrial districts and small firms: a critical appraisal', in H. Ernste and V. Meier (eds), *Regional Development and Contemporary Industrial Response. Extending Flexible Specialization*, London: Bellhaven Press, pp. 45–63.

Asheim, B.T. (1994a), 'Industrial districts, inter-firm co-operation and endogenous technological development: the experience of developed countries', in *Technological Dynamism in Industrial Districts: An Alternative Approach to Industrialization in Developing Countries?*, New York and Geneva: UNCTAD, United Nations, pp. 91–142.

Asheim, B.T. (1994b), 'The Small Firm Squeeze: Globalization, Flexibilization and the Power of TNCs', paper presented at the workshop on 'The boundaries of the firm', European Management and Organization in Transition (EMOT), European Science Foundation, Como, October.

Asheim, B.T. (1995), 'Regionale innovasjonssystem – en sosialt og territorielt forankret teknologipolitikk?', *Nordisk Samhällsgeografisk Tidskrift*, **20**, 17–34.

Becattini, G. (1989), 'Sectors and/or districts: some remarks on the conceptual foundations of industrial economics', in E. Goodman and J. Bamford (eds), *Small Firms and Industrial Districts in Italy*, London: Routledge, pp. 123–35.

Becattini, G. (1990), 'The Marshallian industrial district as a socio-economic notion', in F. Pyke, G. Becattini and W. Sengenberger (eds), *Industrial Districts and Inter-firm Cooperation in Italy*, Geneva: International Institute for Labour Studies, pp. 37–51.

Becattini, G. (1991), 'The industrial district as a creative milieu', in G. Benko and M. Dunford (eds), *Industrial Change and Regional Development*, London: Belhaven Press, pp. 102–14.

Bellandi, M. (1989), 'The industrial district in Marshall', in E. Goodman and J. Bamford (eds), *Small Firms and Industrial Districts in Italy*, London: Routledge, pp. 136–52.

Bellandi, M. (1994), 'Decentralized industrial creativity in dynamic industrial districts', in *Technological Dynamism in Industrial Districts: An Alternative Approach to Industrialization in Developing Countries?* New York and Geneva: UNCTAD, United Nations, pp. 73–87.

Bianchi, P. and Giordani, M.G. (1993), 'Innovation policy at the local and national levels: the case of Emilia-Romagna', *European Planning Studies*, **1**, 25–41.

Bonaccorsi, A. and Lipparini, A. (1994), 'Strategic partnerships in new product development: an Italian case study', *Journal of Product Innovation Management*, **11**, 135–46.

Brusco, S. (1986), 'Small firms and industrial districts: the experience of Italy', in D. Keeble and E. Wever (eds), *New Firms and Regional Development in Europe*, London: Croom Helm, pp. 184–202.

Brusco, S. (1990), 'The idea of the industrial district: its genesis', in F. Pyke, G. Becattini and W. Sengenberger (eds), *Industrial Districts and Inter-firm Co-operation in Italy*, Geneva: International Institute for Labour Studies, pp. 10–19.

Brusco, S. (1992), 'Small firms and the provision of real services', in F. Pyke and W. Sengenberger (eds), *Industrial Districts and Local Economic Regeneration*, Geneva: International Institute for Labour Studies, pp. 177–96.

Brusco, S. (1995), 'Global Systems and Local Systems', paper presented at an OECD seminar on 'Local systems of small firms and job creation', Paris, June.

Camagni, R. (1991), 'Introduction: from the local "milieu" to innovation through cooperation networks', in R. Camagni (ed.), *Innovation Networks: Spatial Perspectives*, London: Belhaven Press, pp. 1–9.

Castro, E. de and Jensen-Butler, C. (1993), *Flexibility, Routine Behaviour and the Neo-classical Model in the Analysis of Regional Growth*, Institute of Political Science, University of Aarhus.

Cooke, P. (1994a), 'The Baden-Württemberg Machine Tool Industry: Regional Responses to Global Threats', paper presented at the workshop of the Centre of Technology Assessment in Baden-Württemberg on 'Explaining regional competitiveness and the capability to innovate – the case of Baden-Württemberg', Stuttgart, June.

Cooke, P. (1994b), 'The co-operative advantage of regions', paper prepared for Centenaire Harald Innis Centenary Celebration Conference on 'Regions, Institutions, and Technology: Reorganizing Economic Geography in Canada and the Anglo-American World', University of Toronto, September.

Cooke, P. and Morgan, K. (1994), 'Growth regions under duress: Renewal strategies in Baden-Württemberg and Emilia-Romagna', in A. Amin and N. Thrift (eds), *Globalization, Institutions, and Regional Development in Europe*, Oxford: Oxford University Press, pp. 91–117.

Crevoisier, O. (1994), Book review (of G. Benko and A. Lipietz (eds), *Les régions qui gagnent*, Paris, 1992), *European Planning Studies*, **2**, 258–60.

Dei Ottati, G. (1994), 'Cooperation and competition in the industrial district as an organization model', *European Planning Studies*, **2**, 463–83.

Dimou, P. (1994), 'The industrial district: a stage of a diffuse industrialization process – the case of Roanne', *European Planning Studies*, **1**, 23–38.

Dosi, G. (1988), 'The nature of the innovative process', in G. Dosi et al. (eds), *Technical Change and Economic Theory*, London: Pinter Publishers, pp. 221–38.

Felsenstein, D. (1994), Book review essay (on D. Massey et al., *High tech fantasies*, London, 1992), *Economic Geography*, **70**, 72–5.

Garofoli, G. (1991a), 'Local networks, innovation and policy in Italian industrial districts', in E.M. Bergman et al. (eds), *Regions Reconsidered*, London: Mansell, pp. 119–40.

Garofoli, G. (1991b), 'The Italian model of spatial development in the 1970s and 1980s', in G. Benko and M. Dunford (eds), *Industrial Change and Regional Development*, London: Belhaven Press, pp. 85–101.

Garofoli, G. (1992), 'Diffuse industrialization and small firms: the Italian pattern in the 1970s', in G. Garofoli (ed.), *Endogenous Development and Southern Europe*, Aldershot: Avebury, pp. 83–102.

Glasmeier, A. (1994), 'Flexible districts, flexible regions? The institutional and cultural limits to districts in an era of globalization and technological paradigm shifts', in A. Amin and N. Thrift (eds), *Globalization, Institutions, and Regional Development in Europe*, Oxford: Oxford University Press, pp. 118–46.

Grabher, G. (1993), 'Rediscovering the social in the economics of interfirm relations', in G. Grabher (ed.), *The Embedded Firm. On the socioeconomics of industrial networks*, London: Routledge, pp. 1–31.

Granovetter, M. (1973), 'The strength of weak ties', *American Journal of Sociology*, **78**, 1360–80.

Granovetter, M. (1985), 'Economic action and social structure: the problem of embeddedness', *American Journal of Sociology*, **91**, 481–510.
Habermas, J. (1987), *The Theory of Communicative Action* (Vol. 2). *Lifeworld and System: A Critique of Functionalist Reason*, Cambridge: Polity Press.
Håkansson, H. (1992), *Corporate Technological Behaviour. Co-operation and Networks*, London: Routledge.
Haraldsen, T. (1994), *Teknologi, økonomi og rom – en teoretisk analyse av relasjoner mellom industrielle og territorielle endringsprosesser*. Doctoral dissertation, Department of Social and Economic Geography, Lund University, Lund University Press, Lund.
Haraldsen, T. (1995), 'Spatial Conquest – the Territorial Extension of Production Systems', paper presented at the Regional Studies Association conference on 'Regional futures: Past and present, east and west', Gothenburg, May.
Harrison, B. (1994a), 'The Italian industrial districts and the crisis of the cooperative form: Part I', *European Planning Studies*, **2**, 3–22.
Harrison, B. (1994b), 'The Italian industrial districts and the crisis of the cooperative form: Part II', *European Planning Studies*, **2**, 159–74.
Henry, N. et al. (1995), Along the road: R&D, society and space, *Research Policy*, **24**, 707–26.
Herrigel, G. (1996), 'Crisis in German decentralized production: unexpected rigidity and the challenge of an alternative form of flexible organization in Baden-Württemberg', *European Urban and Regional Studies*, **3**, 33–52.
Hodgson, G. (1993), *Economics and Evolution. Bringing Life Back into Economics*, Cambridge: Polity Press.
Johnson, B. and Lundvall, B.-Å. (1991), 'Flexibility and institutional learning', in B. Jessop et al. (eds), *The Politics of Flexibility. Restructuring State and Industry in Britain, Germany and Scandinavia*, Aldershot: Edward Elgar, pp. 33–49.
Lazonick, W. (1993), 'Industry cluster versus global webs: organizational capabilities in the American economy', *Industrial and Corporate Change*, **2**, 1–24.
Lazonick, W. and Smith, K. (1995), *Organization Innovation and Competitive Advantage: Long-term Investment and Public Policy*, Project Proposal, Oslo: STEP Group.
Leborgne, D. and Lipietz, A. (1988), 'New technologies, new modes of regulation: some spatial implications', *Environment and Planning D: Society and Space*, **6**, 263–80.
Leborgne, D. and Lipietz, A. (1992), 'Conceptual fallacies and open questions on post-Fordism', in M. Storper and A.J. Scott (eds), *Pathways to Industrialization and Regional Development*, London: Routledge, pp. 332–48.
Lipparini, A. and Lorenzoni, G. (1994), 'Strategic Sourcing and Organizational Boundaries Adjustment: A Process-based Perspective', paper presented at the workshop on 'The changing boundaries of the firm', European Management and Organizations in Transition (EMOT), European Science Foundation, Como, October.
Lipparini, A. and Sobrero, M. (1994), 'The glue and the pieces: Entrepreneurship and innovation in small-firm networks', *Journal of Business Venturing*, **9**, 125–40.
Lorenz, E. (1992), 'Trust, community, and cooperation: towards a theory of industrial districts', in M. Storper and A.J. Scott (eds), *Pathway to Industrialization and Regional Development*, London: Routledge, pp. 195–204.
Lundvall, B.-Å. (1992), 'Introduction', in B.-Å. Lundvall (ed.), *National Systems of Innovation*, London: Pinter Publishers, pp. 1–19.

Lundvall, B.-Å. (1993), 'Explaining interfirm cooperation and innovation: limits of the transaction-cost approach', in G. Grabher (ed.), *The Embedded Firm. On the Socioeconomics of Industrial Networks*, London: Routledge, pp. 52–64.

Lundvall, B.-Å. and Johnson, B. (1994), 'The learning economy', *Journal of Industry Studies*, **1**, 23–42.

Lyberaki, A. and Pesmazoglou, V. (1994), 'Mirages and miracles of European small and medium enterprise development', *European Planning Studies*, **2**, 499–521.

Marshall, A. (1891, 2nd edn), *Principles of Economics*. London: Macmillan.

Marshall, A. (1986, 8th edn), *Principles of Economics*. London: Macmillan.

Morgan, K. (1995), 'Institutions, Innovation and Regional Renewal. The Development Agency as Animateur', paper presented at the Regional Studies Association conference on 'Regional futures: past and present, east and west', Gothenburg, May.

Nooteboom, B. (1988), 'The facts about small business and the real values of its "life world"', *The American Journal of Economics and Sociology*, **47**, 299–314.

Patchell, J. (1993), 'From production systems to learning systems: lessons from Japan', *Environment and Planning A*, **25**, 797–815.

Pedler, M. et al. (1991), *The Learning Company*, London: McGraw-Hill.

Perroux, F. (1970), 'Note on the concept of "growth poles"', in D. McKee, R. Dean, N. Leahy (eds), *Regional Economics: Theory and Practice*, New York: The Free Press, pp. 93–103.

Perulli, P. (1993), 'Towards a regionalization of industrial relations', *International Journal of Urban and Regional Research*, **17**, 98–113.

Piore, M. and Sabel, C. (1984), *The Second Industrial Divide: Possibilities for Prosperity*, New York: Basic Books.

Porter, M. (1990), *The Competitive Advantage of Nations*, London: Macmillan.

Pyke, F. (1994), *Small Firms, Technical Services and Inter-firm Cooperation*, Geneva: International Institute for Labour Studies.

Pyke, F. and Sengenberger, W. (1990), 'Introduction', in F. Pyke, G. Becattini and W. Sengenberger (eds), *Industrial Districts and Inter-firm Cooperation in Italy*, Geneva: International Institute for Labour Studies, pp. 1–9.

Russo, M. (1989), 'Technical change and the industrial district: the role of inter-firm relations in the growth and transformation of ceramic tile production in Italy', in E. Goodman and J. Bamford (eds), *Small Firms and Industrial Districts in Italy*, London: Routledge, pp. 198–222.

Sabel, C. (1992), 'Studied trust: building new forms of cooperation in a volatile economy', in F. Pyke and W. Sengenberger (eds), *Industrial Districts and Local Economic Regeneration*, Geneva: International Institute for Labour Studies. pp. 215–50.

Semlinger, K. (1993), 'Small firms and outsourcing as flexibility reservoirs of large firms', in G. Grabher (ed.), *The Embedded Firm. On the Socioeconomics of Industrial Networks*, London: Routledge, pp. 161–78.

Smith, K. (1994), 'New directions in research and technology policy: identifying the key issues', *STEP-report*, I, Oslo: The STEP Group.

Storper, M. (1995a), 'The resurgence of regional economies, ten years later: the region as a nexus of untraded interdependencies', *European Urban and Regional Studies*, **2**, 191–221.

Storper, M. (1995b), 'Territorial development in the global learning economy: the challenge to developing countries', *Review of International Political Economy*, **2**, 394–424.

Storper, M. and Walker, R. (1989), *The Capitalist Imperative. Territory, Technology, and Industrial Growth*, New York: Basil Blackwell.

Sunley, P. (1992), 'Marshallian industrial districts: the case of the Lancashire cotton industry in the inter-war years', *Transactions of the Institute of British Geographers*, **17**, 306–20.

Tolomelli, C. (1990), 'Policies to support innovation in Emilia-Romagna: experiences, prospects and theoretical aspects', in N. Alderman, E. Ciciotti and A. Thwaites (eds), *Technological Change in a Spatial Context: Theory, Empirical Evidence and Policy*, Berlin: Springer-Verlag, pp. 356–78.

Weinstein, O. (1992), 'High technology and flexibility', in P. Cooke et al. (eds), *Towards Global Localization*, London: UCL Press.

Whitaker, J.K. (ed.) (1975), *The Early Economic Writings of Alfred Marshall, 1867–1890*, Vol. 2, London: Macmillan.

You, J.-I. and Wilkinson, F. (1994), 'Competition and co-operation: toward understanding industrial districts', *Review of Political Economy*, **6**, 259–78.

Zeitlin, J. (1992), 'Industrial districts and local economic regeneration: overview and comment', in F. Pyke and W. Sengenberger (eds), *Industrial Districts and Local Economic Regeneration*, Geneva: International Institute for Labour Studies, pp. 279–94.

5. The learning region: institutions, innovation and regional renewal

Kevin Morgan

INTRODUCTION

As we prepare to enter a new millennium the classical paradigms of social and economic development seem to have exhausted themselves. The paradigms of the Left, ranging from neo-Keynesian to Marxist, are impaired by an exaggerated and naive faith in the capacity of the state. Less credible still is the neo-liberal paradigm of the Right, whose adherents are unable or unwilling to recognize the shortcomings of the market as a mechanism for promoting economic development and social welfare. For all their differences the classical paradigms are afflicted by dualisms – state versus market, public versus private, etc. – which need to be transcended rather than affirmed in a one-sided fashion. In contrast, some of the more eclectic 'third wave' conceptions of development consciously try to eschew such binary thinking so as to open up to inquiry regional processes and intermediate institutions that were marginalized by the inordinate attention devoted to 'state' and 'market'.

Over the past few years in particular we have witnessed the spread of a new paradigm, variously referred to as the *network* or *associational* paradigm. Whatever the shortcomings of this new paradigm, it is clearly fuelled by the pervasive belief that 'markets' and 'hierarchies' do not exhaust the menu of organizational forms for mobilizing resources for innovation and economic development (Illeris and Jakobsen, 1990; Powell, 1990; Camagni, 1991; OECD, 1992; Lundvall, 1992; Cooke and Morgan, 1993; Grabher, 1993; Sabel, 1994; Storper, 1995; Amin and Thrift, 1995). A new, more sceptical conceptual landscape is beginning to emerge, and this may be no bad thing if we are to make sense of, and engage with, the complex and sometimes bewildering changes that are under way in economy, society and polity in the world today. A new century may be upon us, but some of the challenges ahead are already clear. Indeed some of them have a depressingly familiar ring to them, like mass unemployment, environmental degradation, uneven economic development, social polarization and shallow democracy.

For the European Union one of the key institutional challenges will be to manage the twin processes of widening and deepening, a tension which could eventually wreck the Union unless the principle of subsidiarity is given more practical expression. In developmental terms another challenge will be to overcome the knowledge transfer problem. Relative to Japan and the USA, for example, the EU has a poor record of converting scientific and technological knowledge into commercially successful products and services; that is, an inability to transfer knowledge from laboratory to industry and from firm to firm (Commission of the European Communities (CEC), 1993). At bottom the EU lacks a robust networking culture, that is, the disposition to collaborate to achieve mutually beneficial ends. Although there are regional exceptions to this rule, the fact remains that in aggregate terms much more needs to be done to promote interorganizational flows of information and knowledge. One of the underlying arguments here is that this problem might be addressed most effectively at the regional level, providing regional policy is conceived as a dimension of innovation policy rather than just a social welfare measure.

The main aim of this paper is to try to connect some of the concepts of the network paradigm – like interactive innovation and social capital – to the problems of regional development in Europe. In an attempt to 'earth' these concepts the paper presents two concrete case studies of new departures in policy and practice. The first is the European Commission's new programme of Regional Technology Plans (RTPs), which tries to give practical expression to the network paradigm.[1] The second examines the role of the Welsh Development Agency as an *animateur* of innovation in Wales.

INSTITUTIONS, INNOVATION AND THE LEARNING ECONOMY

Over the past two decades, innovation – understood in the broad sense to include product, process and organizational innovation in the firm as well as social and institutional innovation at the level of an industry, region and nation – has assumed an ever more central role in theories of economic development. Whatever the limitations of their work, Marx and Schumpeter were pioneers for their time in recognizing that innovation was the premier source of competitive advantage in capitalist economies, a force that could exert devastating effects, socially and economically, on traditional centres of production. Who can ever forget the poignant passage in *Capital* devoted to the battle between hand-weaving and new power-weaving technology, a battle in which the bones of cotton-weavers ended up 'bleaching the plains of India' (Marx, 1976)?

Schumpeter, too, was alive to the revolutionary potential of innovation, or what he called 'quality competition' as opposed to 'ordinary competition' (i.e. price competition). In this conception, innovation was the driving force of economic development and it assumed a number of forms, like 'the new commodity, the new technology, the new source of supply, the new type of organisation' etc. This kind of 'quality competition', he argued, 'strikes not at the margins of the profits and the outputs of the existing firms but at their foundations and their very lives' (Schumpeter, 1943). The key agents of the innovation process changed over time in Schumpeter's conception: initially he had admired the individual as 'heroic' entrepreneur; later, he resigned himself to the fact that the process of innovation had become *routinized* in the form of the R&D department, one of the key organizational innovations of the twentieth century (Freeman et al., 1982).

While Schumpeter did not have what we might call a 'theory of innovation', a new school of economic theory has developed over the past few years which has tried to build on some of his key insights: that capitalism is an *evolutionary* process driven by technical and organizational innovation; a process in which firms face a greater degree of *uncertainty* and *instability* than is ever admitted in neoclassical theory; a process in which social *institutions* other than the market play a major role. Sometimes referred to as 'neo-Schumpeterian', this school of evolutionary economic theory has done much to advance our understanding of innovation and technological change (Dosi et al., 1988; Freeman, 1994). Equally significant, it has also opened up some rich seams of inquiry for the cognate fields of industrial organization, economic sociology, regional studies and science and technology policy.

In this section I want to highlight two propositions which are normally associated with (but not exclusive to) this evolutionary school and then try to connect these to some new theoretical departures in the field of regional development.

Let us begin with the first proposition, namely that *innovation is an interactive process*. While this may seem a rather banal proposition, it is only over the past decade that it has begun to be treated seriously in economic theory and corporate practice. It arose from a critique of the *linear* model of innovation, in which innovation was thought to proceed sequentially from research to marketing as a result either of technology-push or market-pull pressures. There are a number of fatal weaknesses in this model, not least the absence of any feedback loops and the unwarranted disdain for certain kinds of knowledge. The absence of feedback loops meant that 'upstream' activities like R&D, for example, would have little or no opportunity for learning about their effects on user communities (i.e. customers), a recipe for disaster. The second weakness, which is still prevalent in the

West today, stems from an elitist conception of knowledge in which scientific knowledge is extolled, while 'lower' forms of knowledge (like engineering and production know-how) are undervalued (Rosenberg, 1976). There is now growing support for the view that innovation is an interactive process – between firms and the basic science infrastructure, between the different functions within the firm, between producers and users at the interfirm level and between firms and the wider institutional *milieu* – and that this process should be conceived as a process of *interactive learning* in which a wide array of institutional mechanisms can play a role (Lundvall, 1992; OECD, 1992).

The second proposition should be read in conjunction with the first, namely that *innovation is shaped by a variety of institutional routines and social conventions*. In recent years no one can fail to have noticed the growing interest within economics in the role and nature of social institutions, a welcome, if belated, reaction to the under-socialized conceptions of neoclassical economics (Hodgson, 1988, 1993). At the most abstract level the concept of an 'institution' in this literature refers to recurrent patterns of behaviour – habits, conventions and routines. For many of these writers the most elemental form of a business institution is a production routine, that is 'a habitual pattern of behaviour embodying knowledge that is often tacit and skill-like' (Langlois and Robertson, 1995). Conventions and routines may help to regulate economic life, by reducing uncertainty for example, but, being cultural artefacts, they are anything but uniform in character. Take trust, for example. In purely economic terms trust is an extremely valuable resource, not least because 'it saves a lot of trouble to have a fair degree of reliance on other people's word' (Arrow, 1974). But, as Arrow and others have argued, one cannot buy trust. Rather, trust has to be earned in and through repeated transactions. The significance of routines and conventions for innovation and economic development generally is summarized in the concept of *social capital*, which can be defined in the following way:

> By analogy with notions of physical capital and human capital – tools and training that enhance individual productivity – social capital refers to features of social organisation, such as networks, norms and trust, that facilitate coordination and cooperation for mutual benefit. Social capital enhances the benefits of investment in physical and human capital and is coming to be seen as a vital ingredient in economic development around the world. (Putnam, 1993)

Taken together, these two propositions have helped to stimulate an interesting, and highly significant, debate about the nature of capitalism as a *learning economy*. This debate owes a great deal to the Aalborg group of economists in Denmark and in particular to the work of Bengt-Åke

Lundvall, one of its leading theorists. Because there is no space to do justice to this work here, suffice it to say that one of the key arguments of this school is that contemporary capitalism has arrived at the point 'where knowledge is the most strategic resource and learning the most important process' (Lundvall, 1994). Because of the accelerating pace of innovation, Lundvall argues that know-how has become the key resource for firms to stay abreast of product and process innovation. Like trust, however, know-how cannot be entirely reduced to the status of a commodity because

> Parts of the know-how can be sold as patents and other parts as turn-key plants, but important parts remain tacit and cannot be removed from its human and social context. Therefore the labour market is the most important market for know-how and . . . important elements of tacit knowledge are collective rather than individual. (Ibid.)

These ideas resonate with the growing theoretical literature on the role of organizational innovation in the Japanese firm and, in particular, with the concept of the 'knowledge-creating company'. For example, some Japanese authors have argued that Japanese firms have a very different understanding of knowledge to that which prevails in the West. The argument here is that Japanese firms view formal, codified knowledge as merely the tip of the iceberg, because knowledge is felt to be primarily *tacit*, and tacit knowledge is highly personal, hence it is not easily codified and communicated. In the more extreme interpretations it is felt that 'the most precious knowledge can neither be taught nor passed on' (Nonaka and Takeuchi, 1994).

These arguments concerning know-how and tacit knowledge are part and parcel of a wider argument about the role of intangible or invisible factors in economic development (Doeringer and Terkla, 1990; Freeman, 1994). While there may be a growing disposition to accept the significance of such intangible assets – such as knowledge, competence, skill, organizational culture – these assets seem to defy precise measurement, a problem that continues to bedevil all forms of economic theory (Winter, 1987). Fortunately, we do not have to resign ourselves to cultural relativism because, patently, some organizational forms and social conventions are more conducive to fostering innovation and learning than others. Let us look at three examples drawn from different levels of aggregation.

At the *national* level there is a growing body of work on national innovation systems which suggests that the level of expenditure on science and technology, for example, is only one of the criteria for assessing the capacity of different national systems because the same inputs are often associated with very different outcomes. Equally important is the stock of social capital, which can, where it is well developed, facilitate collaboration between firms and the science base or between finance and industry, for example. In addition to the mainline institutions of the world of science and technology (for example, firms, universities, technical institutes), we should not forget the wide array of intermediate institutions (like trade associations, chambers of industry and the professional associations of engineers) which can function as learning laboratories for their respective firms and industries. This seems to be the case in Germany and Japan, where these intermediary organizations are strong, in contrast to the UK, where they are weak (Lundvall, 1992; Nelson, 1993).

At the *interfirm* level we know enough about the integrated supply chain systems of the leading Japanese firms to know that they delivered vastly-superior results relative to the arm's-length buyer–supplier relations which were, and possibly still are, typical in the West. The sweat-shop thesis about Japanese subcontractors cannot explain how these firms have enhanced their own innovative capacity over the past 30 years or so. The key feature of these integrated supply chains, from the leading customer down through a number of tiered suppliers, is their problem-solving capacity. Through a whole series of institutional innovations – like resident engineers based in the customer's plant, who were thus well placed to feed back information on the use of their products; supplier associations which disseminated 'best practice' among their members; and jointly agreed conventions to share the profits of interfirm collaboration – the leading Japanese firms were able to reap the benefits of an awesomely effective system of interactive learning. While the leading (customer) firms clearly gain most, the most authoritative study of the Japanese subcontracting system insists that '*both* purchasers and suppliers benefited from the synergistic effects that accrued from joint problem solving and continuous improvement in price, product quality, delivery, design and engineering' (Nishiguchi, 1994). It is also worth saying that this system of collaborative manufacturing is not so culturally embedded (as was once claimed) that it cannot work elsewhere, as we shall see later.

At the level of the *firm* there is widespread agreement that the innovative firm has a number of key features: among other things it has thick *horizontal* information flows between its R&D, manufacturing and marketing divisions; it sets a high premium on what we might call decentralized learning procedures and its routines are such that it is receptive to multiple channels of information, especially from customers, suppliers and competitors on the external side and, internally, from employees. Within the firm one of the key assets is the intangible asset of a workforce which feels a sense of 'belonging' to the firm. Where this exists, and where workers feel that they are not innovating themselves out of a job if they come up with creative solutions, we can say that this is a firm-specific asset that is difficult for competitors to emulate. All the evidence suggests that *kaizen*, the process of continuous improvement through interactive learning and problem-solving, a process that was pioneered by Japanese firms, presupposes a workforce that feels actively committed to the firm. It is in this social context that we should understand two of the key practices of the Japanese firm as an innovative institution, namely the practice of using the factory as a laboratory and the practice of decentralized learning (Freeman, 1988; Sabel, 1994).

All of this might seem far removed from the study of regional development. But in recent years there has been a growing convergence between students of economic geography and students of innovation; the former are becoming more interested in innovation capacity as a way of explaining uneven regional development, while the latter are no longer so impervious to spatial considerations in their work on technological change. Within economic geography a number of tentative efforts have been made to utilize some of the insights of evolutionary economic theory, especially with respect to learning, innovation and the role of institutions in regional development (Cooke and Morgan, 1990, 1994; Camagni, 1991; Amin and Thrift, 1995; Maskell and Malmberg, 1999). But the fullest and most sophisticated attempt to marry the two disciplines is to be found in the recent work of Michael Storper (Storper, 1992, 1994, 1995). Since it is not possible to do justice to the nuances of Storper's argument here, let me focus on one of the key issues.

Storper seeks to explain what he considers to be 'the principal dilemma' of contemporary economic geography: the resurgence of regional economies at a time when the forces of globalization (in transport, telematics and organizational techniques, for example) appear to have reduced the world to a 'placeless' mass. A key part of the explanation, he argues, is the disassociation between organizational and technological learning within agglomeration, which has two roots. The first concerns localized input–output relations, or traded interdependencies, which constitute webs of user–producer relations essential to information exchange. The second, and more important, factor concerns the role of *untraded* interdependencies (like labour markets, regional conventions, norms and values, public or semi-public institutions) which attach to the process of economic and organizational learning and co-ordination:

> Where these input–output relations or untraded interdependencies are localized, and this is quite frequent in cases of technological or organizational dynamism, then we can say that the region is a key, necessary element in the 'supply architecture' for learning and innovation. It can now be seen that theoretical predictions that globalization means the end to economics of proximity have been exaggerated by many analysts because they have deduced them only from input–output analysis. (Storper, 1995, p. 218)

On the basis of such reasoning Storper argues that the region has assumed a central theoretical status in the process of capitalist development and that (a part of) the explanation lies in its *untraded interdependencies*. This is an important development of Lundvall's argument that *tacit* knowledge is collective in nature and, because it is wedded to its human and social context, it is more territorially specific than is generally thought.

Storper's argument that regions (or, more accurately, that core regions) occupy such a pivotal role in the 'supply architecture' of the learning economy may seem provocative to the globalist school of thinking, which tends to the view that global forces, especially multinationals, are somehow impervious to spatial considerations. But we are now beginning to appreciate that globalization and localization, far from being mutually exclusive processes, are actually much more interwoven than is generally acknowledged because foreign direct investment is often attracted to, and has a reinforcing effect upon, 'innovation clusters' in the targeted country (Storper, 1992; De Vet, 1993).

Other authors argue that the globalization process has been exaggerated because the technological activities of the world's largest firms remain overwhelmingly concentrated in their home country. Why is this? Mainly because 'physical proximity facilitates the integration of multidisciplinary knowledge that is tacit and therefore "person-embodied" rather than "information-embodied" and it also facilitates the rapid decision-making needed to cope with uncertainty' (Patel and Pavitt, 1991, p. 18). Furthermore, since multinationals tend to tap into local fields of expertise for their technology intensive activities, 'globalization and national specialization are complementary parts of a common process' (Cantwell, 1995).

In the literature on foreign direct investment it is quite common to find that multinational firms are beginning to increase their R&D investments abroad and that these facilities are akin to 'listening posts', which is one way of tapping into foreign sources of learning and innovation. What is less common is to find that multinational firms can actually learn a great deal from their branch plants. These facilities are often engaged in more routine activities and, as such, they are perceived to be working with what Rosenberg (1976) called 'grubby and pedestrian forms of knowledge'. But, as Rosenberg argues, while these forms of knowledge – engineering, production and the like – often play a 'disconcertingly large role' in learning and innovation, they tend to be ignored by scholars and managers in the West.

We owe a debt to Erica Schoenberger for reminding us that learning, knowledge-acquisition and other transformative impulses flow in more than one direction, that they should *not* be seen as flowing in just one direction, from centre to periphery, from top to bottom, even if this is the dominant direction. In a series of corporate case studies she shows that large firms were imperilled by failing to appreciate that local innovations in their far-flung branches carried important lessons for the firm as a whole. As a result she rightly questions whether the branch plant should be treated as 'the passive creature of the centre' (Schoenberger, 1994). To the extent that branch plants are allowed to treat the factory as a laboratory, or to interact with sophisticated users, they may constitute an important laboratory for knowledge acquisition and the headquarters will ignore this at its peril.

These points about the potential learning capacity of branch plants need to be made because the main thrust of Storper's argument concerns the resilience of technology-intensive regional agglomerations, the 'motor' regions which are in the vanguard of learning and innovation. It is not difficult to accept that these robust regions enjoy strong 'untraded interdependencies', that their core activities, being sensitive to pockets of tacit knowledge, are not as locationally mobile as the less strategic investments that abound in other, more peripheral, regions. Here we come to one of the most difficult and challenging questions in economic development, namely to what extent, if at all, can peripheral regions innovate?

INNOVATION AND LEARNING IN LESS FAVOURED REGIONS: THE RTP EXERCISE

The broad contours of interregional inequalities in Europe are familiar enough, and the gap between the richest and poorest regions remains stubbornly large. As regards income per head, for example, the gap between the top 25 and bottom 25 regions was relatively unchanged between 1983 and 1993. On the unemployment front the 25 worst-affected regions had an unemployment rate averaging 22.4 per cent in 1995, nearly five times the average for the 25 least-affected regions (European Commission, 1996).

But low income per head and high unemployment are symptoms, the tip of the proverbial iceberg. Underlying these symptoms is a poor developmental capacity, which is a shorthand way to signal the relative absence of physical infrastructure (road, rail, telecommunications), qualified labour and research and technological development (RTD) activity, etc. But in addition to these conventional weaknesses we might add that less favoured regions (LFRs) seem to have little or no social capital on which they can draw, a point which turns the spotlight on factors such as the institutional capacity of the region, the calibre of the political establishment, the disposition to seek joint solutions to common problems. These factors – the invisible factors in economic development – are just as important as physical capital (Doeringer and Terkla, 1990; OECD, 1993).

The fact that EU regional policy is mainly addressed to fighting symptoms (like high unemployment) rather than causes (like low innovation potential) has caused concern for many years. Critics have rightly pointed to the fact that innovation support (in the shape of the EU Framework Programme) has been overwhelmingly directed towards existing centres of excellence, which are invariably to be found in the prosperous regions and more specifically in the so called 'islands of innovation', namely Greater London, Rotterdam/Amsterdam, Île-de-France, Frankfurt, Stuttgart, Munich, Lyon/Grenoble, Turin and Milan. By default rather than design, the Framework Programme serves to reproduce the gap between poor and prosperous regions (Morgan, 1992).

To its credit, the Regional Policy Directorate General (DG XVI) has fought long and hard with DGs XII and XIII to establish the principle that there ought to be closer integration of the Structural and Framework Funds. More concerned with the external threat from Japan and the USA, DGs XII and XIII are understandably keen to distribute innovation support to existing centres of excellence, a principle they do not wish to see diluted by the diversion of Framework Funds to what they see as inferior centres in less favoured regions. Forunately, there are signs – as in the RTP exercise, for example – that the DGs are now beginning to co-operate to a much greater extent than hitherto in the cause of promoting innovation in peripheral regions.

Generally speaking, the Structural Funds have not been utilized to promote RTD capacity, although the commitment to this field of activity varies widely even among less favoured regions themselves. Between 1989 and 1993, for example, Objective 1 regions as a whole devoted just 2.7 per cent of their Structural Funds budget to RTD-related activities, whereas the more developed Objective 2 regions devoted 9.3 per cent of their budget to this activity. For its part DG XVI has encouraged the regions to raise their RTD capacity and, to this end, it launched a number of RTD-related Community Initiatives during this period, in particular STRIDE, aimed at strengthening the research and technological capacity of less favoured regions, while PRISMA, ENVIREG, EUROFORM, VALOREN and TELEMATIQUE all had a strong regional innovation component (CEC, 1994a).

In the past, innovation was too narrowly equated with RTD activity and the latter was too often perceived as a supply-side phenomenon. In other words the first generation EU programmes could be criticized for not paying sufficient regard to the social, institutional and commercial dimensions of innovation. And, to the extent that low RTD activity was defined as a supply-side problem, the 'solution' sometimes ended up as a cathedral in the desert, i.e. a facility that was massively under-utilized by local firms in the region. Recognizing the need to link supply-side initiatives to local demand-side conditions, one of the seminal studies concluded by saying:

it is not simply the presence of units of RTD infrastructure, but of the degree of interaction between them which is the most significant factor in local innovation. The quality of the linkage and the presence of local synergy is the key element. Therefore a systems or network approach provides the best basis for understanding and promoting regional RTD-based innovation. (CEC, 1988)

This simple but fundamental point is now accepted as axiomatic in the design and delivery of innovation support policies for less favoured regions. Indeed, the diagnosis of the problem has now shifted to the extent that the Commission is now proposing that 'regional planners have to address not only a supply problem (the lack of RTD capacity and mechanisms for diffusing technology) but also – and probably most importantly in the first place – a problem of demand' (CEC, 1994a).

In many ways this problem of *receptivity* on the demand side is more difficult to resolve because it involves modifying internal routines within the firm so as to promote at least three types of competence. First, *technological* competence, the ability of an enterprise to master particular technologies that are relevant to its needs; second, *entrepreneurial* competence, the ability to integrate relevant technologies with the wider corporate strategy of the firm; and third, *learning* ability, which partly involves structuring a firm's organizational and management routines such that they can absorb information on changing markets, new technologies and innovative organizational structures. To address this problem of receptivity, the key point to recognize is that firms are most receptive to, and likely to learn most from, other firms, especially from customers, suppliers and competitors (Cooke and Morgan, 1990; Dankbaar, 1994). The design and delivery of innovation support services should therefore be predicated on this crucially important aspect of microeconomic reality.

Fortunately, this insight has been woven into the design of the Regional Technology Plan (RTP) exercise which the Commission launched in June 1994. Four regions were selected to pilot the RTP exercise – Limburg (Netherlands), Lorraine (France), Saxony (Germany) and Wales (UK) – and these have been joined by a second group of regions, namely, Norte (Portugal), Central Macedonia (Greece), Abruzzo (Italy) and Castilla y Leon (Spain). Despite its rather limited name the RTP

starts from the principle that brakes to innovation are not always linked directly to technology: these brakes can result from a lack of qualified personnel, an absence of investment, a lack of clear leadership. In this perspective the RTP initiative goes largely beyond the bounds of technology and becomes an integral part of the policies for regional economic development . . . over and above this, the exercise will open up new prospects for many actors. It will in fact provide an opportunity to break old habits and to create new openings. (Shotton and Miege, 1994)

The main objectives of the RTP exercise are twofold. In the first place it is designed to encourage LFRs to develop a regional innovation *process*, in which the regional stakeholders are enjoined to define a commonly agreed, bottom–up strategy which is attuned to the nuances of their regions. Second, it is hoped that the RTP will provide a framework in which the recipient regions and the Commission can jointly agree a more optimal strategy for future investments in RTD initiatives at the regional level, with the result that the RTP pilot regions may be in a stronger position to utilize RTD-related programmes in the future. For its part the Commission identified some 'best-practice' guidelines which should govern the design stage of the RTP exercise, and these are shown in Table 5.1.

Having outlined the main aims and objectives of the RTP, how should we evaluate this exercise? While it is far too early to reach a definitive

Table 5.1   Regional Technology Plan guidelines

- *A bottom–up approach:* they should be demand driven, with an emphasis on SMEs. In other words, each region must demonstrate a commitment to a demand-driven approach, based on strengthened dialogue between firms, regionally based capabilities for research for technology diffusion, and the public sector.
- *A regional approach:* they should have a specific territorial dimension which takes full account of the national and international context. And, perhaps more importantly, RTPs should aim at building a consensus at a regional level on priorities for action between the principal actors involved. The inclusion of different regional economic agents and public and private institutions in the elaboration process and management of the RTPs should therefore be mandatory.
- *A strategic approach:* they should apply a strategic planning approach to regional development in the field of technological development and innovation. They should plan for short and medium term actions that fit in with the long term objectives and priorities defined by the region.
- *An integrated approach:* they should try to link efforts from the public sector (local, regional, national and European) and the private sector towards the common goal of increasing regional productivity and competitiveness. They should try to maximize the economic impact of regional, national and Structural Funds actions.
- *An international approach:* they should keep an international perspective in terms of the analysis of global economic trends as well as on the need to co-operate nationally and internationally to be more effective in the field of RTD and innovation.

Source: CEC (1994b).

judgement, not least because the results will only show up in the longer term, it is clear that the RTP is not just another chapter in the subsidy saga. With just 500 000 Ecus per region, in which the maximum contribution from the Commission is 250 000 Ecus, the RTP exercise might be dismissed as regional policy on the cheap. But such a view misconstrues the novel nature of the exercise because, first and foremost, the RTP is designed to stimulate a *collective learning* process in less favoured regions. In other words it is an attempt to persuade the key regional actors – private firms, public agencies and a wide array of intermediary institutions in such fields as technology transfer and training provision – that the initial impetus for regional renewal must come from *within* the region and that, in practical terms, this turns, in part, on the region's networking capacity, i.e. the disposition to collaborate to achieve mutually beneficial ends. In short, the RTP exercise is about building a stock of social capital in regions where these invisible assets are thin on the ground. Compared to the traditional repertoires of regional policy – many of which were just glorified subsidy regimes to attract mobile capital – the RTP exercise is at least engaging with the right targets, namely the institutionalized inertia which characterizes so many less favoured regions.

Developing new routines – with respect to reciprocity, trust, formal interaction and informal know-how trading, etc. – requires time, resources and, equally important, a collective vision of regional renewal. To suggest that all LFRs are structurally condemned to their current status seems to foreclose all possibility for change, a truly paralysing prospect. On the other hand, to pretend that all LFRs are equally capable of renewing themselves, regardless of their institutional deficits, is utopian in the extreme. Whatever the future holds in this regard, it is nevertheless encouraging to see the beginnings of a serious debate on the institutional preconditions of the learning region (Abicht, 1994; Koch, 1994; Stahl, 1994).

It may be instructive to recall the findings of a major study of winners and losers in the EU, which came to the conclusion that the successful regions were those which set a high premium on 'consensus, collective success, long-term objectives and quasi-corporatist institutions' (Dunford, 1994). While this is the model for the RTP exercise, mere aspirations are not enough. Laudable though it is, the bottom–up emphasis of the exercise needs to be complemented by more supportive top–down initiatives at both the national and supranational level. In the absence of a more supportive macro-environment – with respect to investment, skills formation, technology transfer and regional governance structures, for example – it is difficult to see how the RTP dynamic can be sustained. Perhaps Gramsci's famous dictum, concerning optimism of the will, pessimism of the intellect, is the most appropriate interim verdict on the RTP exercise.

TOWARDS A LEARNING ECONOMY IN WALES: THE DEVELOPMENT AGENCY AS *ANIMATEUR*

Wales was invited to be one of the RTP pilot regions because, in the eyes of the European Commission, the regional authorities had demonstrated their resolve to upgrade the economic fabric through a collaborative effort between the public and private sectors. In the Commission's view the RTP approach would be most fruitful 'in areas where well-founded co-operation between the private and public sectors is – or can be – established' (CEC, 1994b). In this section the focus is not so much on the formal RTP process, but on a series of efforts designed to build a networking culture in Wales, efforts which correspond to the RTP goal of innovating by networking.

To understand the problems and possibilities in Wales, it is worth setting the context with respect to economic and institutional structures. On the economic front Wales has made the transition from a heavy dependence on coal and steel to a more diversified economy based on manufacturing and services. Unable to draw on the resources of a robust indigenous business class, the postwar modernization of the Welsh economy was developed through a combination of public sector investment in the nationalized coal and steel industries and foreign inward investment from the USA, Europe and Japan. With the subsequent decline of coal and steel, large swathes of the Welsh industrial economy were dominated by foreign-owned branch plants geared towards low-skill production activities (Morgan and Sayer, 1988). Relative to UK regions, Wales has done remarkably well in attracting foreign inward investment. Indeed it topped the UK regional league table in the decade to 1992 (Hill and Munday, 1994). Even so, Wales continues to suffer from major structural problems: it has the lowest GDP per capita in the UK, it remains at the bottom end of the UK regional wages league and it has one of the lowest regional economic activity rates in the country.

For all these problems Wales is not without assets. Being a nation, rather than a region, it has benefited from a large measure of institutional devolution in a state system which is still inordinately centralized in London. By the standards of the English regions, which are largely devoid of regional institutions, Wales has managed to develop something of a 'regional state' on which it can draw for economic development purposes (Rees and Morgan, 1991). At the heart of this 'regional state' are the Welsh Office, which is a multifunctional government department with an annual budget of some £7 billion, and the Welsh Development Agency (WDA). With an annual budget of some £170 million, and around 300 staff, the WDA is one of the largest and most experienced regional development agencies in the EU today (Morgan, 1997).

In contrast to regions like Baden-Württemberg (where locally based private capital plays a prominent role in regulating the regional economy, through collective institutions like chambers of commerce and sectoral associations), the business class in Wales has never played more than a muted role in civic and economic life. Historically, this can be explained by the fact that many of the coalowners were externally based; indeed such was their limited contribution to Welsh life that when they disappeared, with the nationalization of the industry in 1947, it was as if 'they had never been' (Williams, 1990).

Recent experience with a number of leading branch plants in Wales has triggered a debate which would have been unthinkable in the past, when the branch plant was perceived to be part of the problem in LFRs (Firn, 1976). At the heart of this debate lies the question as to whether *certain* types of branch plant can have an innovative vocation in *certain* types of regional economy because, in Wales at least, there are signs that this may be happening (Lawson and Morgan, 1991; Price et al., 1993). There is also evidence to suggest that this phenomenon is occurring in other regions (Amin et al., 1994). Clearly this question – of the 'embedded' branch plant – needs to be more rigorously researched because it is hardly a uniform phenomenon (Dicken et al., 1994).

Novel demands from branch plants in Wales were one of the key factors which persuaded the WDA that it should re-think its approach to regional development. Other pressures conspired to the same end, namely, the fact that UK regional aid, which had buttressed the economy since the 1930s, had been cut by some 70 per cent in the decade to 1992. Furthermore, the fact that foreign inward investment was becoming more and more difficult to obtain, on account of growing competition from other European regions, also made the WDA's strategy less sustainable. For all these reasons, therefore, the WDA set about revising its traditional three pillar strategy of land reclamation, advance factory building and inward investment. In contrast to this 'hard' infrastructure, the Agency began to set a higher premium on the 'soft' infrastructure of business support services, technology transfer, skills development and, most crucially of all, it began to pay far more attention to the needs of existing firms, both local small and medium sized enterprises (SMEs) and foreign-owned plants (Morgan, 1997).

The early generations of branch plants made few demands on the regional economy, which was not surprising when all they required was a pool of tractable, low-cost labour – prosaic requirements which could easily be met by the WDA's 'hard' competencies. Over the past decade, however, the more innovative branch plants have begun to make novel, and more exacting, demands on the regional infrastructure. Among other things they have shown themselves to be interested in the quality of technical skills, the calibre of local suppliers, the availability of digital telecommunication links and the aftercare service of the WDA. Taken together, these demands required a new set of competencies within the WDA, and a more innovative approach to the way it designed and delivered its core programmes. Let us look in more detail at how the WDA is trying to respond to novelty in the periphery, beginning with the changing nature of inward investment.

Like most regional agencies, the WDA has always set a high premium on attracting inward investment, especially in the form of greenfield projects. However, this type of project is no longer the most important form of inward investment in the UK. In the seven years to 1991, for example, new starts accounted for 37.6 per cent of all foreign direct investment projects, while expansions (i.e. reinvestment at the existing site) accounted for 45.6 per cent of projects (Morgan, 1997). The changing form of inward investment requires new procedures and new skills because the factors which are important for new starts, like the up-front grant package, for example, are less effective in securing expansion projects. To secure reinvestment, local managers need to convince themselves and their HQs that the region offers *sustainable* attractions.

These new trends have forced the Agency to develop an *aftercare* service for key branch plants. Here the Agency has recognized that aftercare covers such a wide spectrum of services that no single agency could possibly satisfy these needs. Consequently, the WDA has put together a network of organizations – called Team Wales – through which it hopes to deliver a wide array of aftercare services. In other words, the responsibility for aftercare extends a way behind the WDA itself, and this has forced the Agency into a network approach for the design and delivery of services.

One of the key parts of the Agency's aftercare repertoire is the *Source Wales* programme. Local sourcing schemes are nothing new, of course, but what differentiates the Source Wales service is that it is a supplier development programme first and a local sourcing scheme second. By working on behalf of the large firm, which is a potential customer, the Agency is able to secure the interest of local SMEs in supplier development services to a much greater extent than if it were acting on its own account. Taking its cue from the Japanese experience, which is directly at hand in the region through the presence of 50 Japanese firms, the WDA has sought to promote long-term partnerships between major buyers and local suppliers. One of the mechanisms through which this is prosecuted is the Supplier Association, a forum in which new skills and techniques are exchanged between buyers and their key suppliers, a forum in which the large customer acts as a tutor to less talented SMEs. Drawing on the most recent thinking in the field of materials management, the Source Wales programme seems to have stimulated more Supplier Associations in Wales than any other part of Europe and it has been acclaimed as an innovative and effective programme (Segal Quince Wicksteed, 1996).

Another category of business service is the *technology support* programme which aims to enhance the capacity for product, process and organizational innovation in the SME sector. One of the ways in which the Agency delivers this service is through on-site technology audits which identify the strengths and weaknesses of each firm. These audits, which are part-funded by the EU's STRIDE programme, have thus far assessed over 250 firms. Apart from working on a one-to-one basis, the Agency has also sought to enhance the technology-support infrastructure in the region by promoting a network of centres of excellence. This network, which embraces over 30 technical centres, is designed to offer specialized assistance to Welsh-based firms, especially to SMEs. Being largely university-based, one of the problems with these centres is that they need to develop a more professional approach to the marketing of their services because a supply-side strategy is simply not enough; if firms do not utilize their services, then these centres will become cathedrals in the desert (Cooke and Morgan, 1992).

The Agency is also learning that the best business support initiatives are those in which firms are helped to help themselves. As we saw earlier, firms are most receptive to, and learn most from, other firms, be they suppliers, customers or competitors. In an attempt to put these insights into practice, the Agency has promoted the concept of *technology clubs*, a sectorally based initiative it pioneered in the Welsh medical sector and which is now being extended to other sectors. The aim of these clubs is to network the disparate sources of expertise in each sector so as to create the conditions for collaborative learning, a process which is driven by the needs of the members (in this case, a combination of users, producers, researchers and regulators) and facilitated by the Agency.

No less importantly, the Agency is now paying far more attention to the *skills* formation process. Although it has no formal responsibility for training provision – where the Training and Enterprise Councils (TECs) and the Further Education (FE) colleges are the main delivery vehicles – the Agency has been drawn into this field because skills formulation is so critical to regional economic development. There are two ways in which the WDA has intervened in this field, but in both it plays the role of broker rather than of direct provider.

In the first place it has encouraged FE colleges to work in partnership with large branch plants to develop customized training packages for these firms. The WDA was late in recognizing the potential of FE colleges, though it was not alone in this: the FE colleges are the Cinderella of the UK's elitist education system, where vocational skills have been undervalued for the best part of a century. What really helped to raise the status of FE colleges in Wales was the way in which these colleges were treated as serious interlocutors by the Robert Bosch company, one of the most training-conscious firms in Europe. Because of the shallow base of intermediate technical skills in the UK (for example, technician and craft grades), Bosch decided to develop a close working partnership with a number of different colleges. While Bosch proved to be an exacting client, the FE colleges delivered everything that was asked of them. Limited as it was, this experience seems to have done wonders for the self-esteem of the FE staff; so much so that it has given them the confidence to design and deliver new customized training modules for other firms, some of which would not have considered the prosaic FE sector before it had received Bosch's seal of approval. On the basis of this experience the WDA is now trying to disseminate this partnership model to a wider population of firms, no easy task in a region which has specialized in low-skill tasks (Morgan and Rees, 1994).

The second way in which the WDA has involved itself with skills formation is in the SME sector. Here the challenge was even more daunting because there was no equivalent of a Bosch to play the role of tutor. Even so, the WDA, in tandem with the TECs and the FE colleges, set up a number of sector-based fora to ascertain the demand for collaborative training schemes. This led to a number of training consortia being formed to find joint solutions to common problems. By acting in concert, the SMEs felt that they could get cheaper, and more customized, services than if each acted on its own account. However, while the training packages were designed by the firms themselves, and while the costs were subsidized by the WDA, the courses were ill attended because the SMEs found it difficult to release key staff on the specified dates. In other words, here was a training scheme which was well designed and reasonably costed, yet which failed to meet its targets because of SMEs' internal problems. Fortunately, this scheme is being revamped to take account of certain design faults, like the problem of dealing with managers who were too junior to deliver on the agreement (Morgan and Rees, 1994).

While the Agency is beginning to address a genuine developmental agenda, instead of being just a glorified property developer, it needs to secure more autonomy from its political masters in the Welsh Office to promote this agenda. Having failed to regulate the WDA properly in the 1980s, when serious problems took root, the Conservative-controlled Welsh Office now seems intent on over-regulating the Agency to compensate for past failures (Morgan, 1997). While Wales enjoys a reasonable degree of institutional capacity by UK standards, this capacity has never been fully tapped. For this reason, among others, there is now growing pressure for a new constitutional settlement, including a Welsh Assembly empowered to design policies which are attuned to the needs of economy and society in Wales rather than policies which reflect the Whitehall template (Osmond, 1994).

CONCLUSIONS AND IMPLICATIONS

In this paper I have tried to advance three propositions. First, that the network paradigm helps to overcome the traditional antinomy between state and market by asserting the interdependence of public and private power and by highlighting the potential of devolved, intermediate institutions like regional development agencies. Second, that the growing confluence between economic geography and innovation studies creates a potentially significant research agenda with respect to the interactive model of innovation and the role of institutions and social conventions in economic development. Third, that recent regional development strategies, from the EU and the WDA, are striving to give practical expression to some of these theoretical ideas, not least by promoting the principle of innovating-by-networking and by exploring the potential of social capital (including trust and reciprocity) at the regional level. In this final section I shall try to spell out the implications of these new regional development strategies.

The RTP signals a decisive break from the traditional infrastructure-led approach of EU regional policy because it addresses the *process* of building a collective learning capacity in a bottom–up and interactive fashion – the most important goal of the exercise (Landabaso, 1995). In contrast to traditional regional policy, which did little to enhance institutional capacity, the RTP consciously aims to build 'capacities for action', where this is understood to mean 'mutually coherent sets of expectations, built into conventions, which underlie technological–economic spaces, permitting the actors involved to develop and coordinate necessary resources' (Storper, 1995, p. 193). Herein lies the significance of initiatives like the RTP.

In the case of the WDA I focused on those activities – like supplier development, aftercare, technology support and skills formation – which constitute the core of its emerging regional innovation strategy. In each of these activities the Agency is engaging with issues which lie at the very heart of the development process in peripheral regions. I would suggest that this is precisely what innovating in the periphery means: working with what exists, however inauspicious, in an effort to break the traditional institutional inertia in the public and private sectors, fostering interfirm networks which engage in interactive learning, nurturing trust and voice-based mechanisms which help to lubricate these networks and promoting a cultural disposition which sets a premium on finding joint solutions to common problems. It may be that trust, and other forms of social capital, are best developed at the regional level because this is the level at which regular interactions, one of the conditions for trust-building, can be sustained over time.

Learning, of course, is worth little if there are no opportunities to implement what has been learned. If the EU's regions are expected to do more for themselves, then they need to be empowered to design and deliver policies which are attuned to the nuances of their regional economies. This is why devolved institutional capacity is so important to the regional development agenda in the EU today. While devolution is not necessarily a progressive doctrine – witness the USA, where the Republican strategy aims to emasculate the Federal Government under the flag of devolution to the states – it needs to be championed in conjunction with a supportive central state, so that bottom–up initiatives can be complemented by top–down measures with respect to investment, training and technology transfer. A supportive central state is also necessary to compensate those LFRs which do not have the capacity to experiment with their own institutional resources (Amin and Thrift, 1995).

The significance of the new regional innovation strategies has been dismissed by critics, who argue that they offer little or no prospect of alleviating the key problems in LFRs, namely mass unemployment and social exclusion (Lovering, 1996). This criticism is valid but partial: valid because innovation policy cannot resolve these problems, partial because innovation policy is not designed to do so. The WDA's regional innovation strategy has thus far had a modest effect, not least because 70 years of economic decline cannot be reversed overnight. The interfirm networks which the Agency has promoted are as yet confined to a few key sectors, which is hardly surprising since this is an immensely time-consuming endeavour. Even so, the rationale for this strategy is sound; while it may not have created a vast number of new jobs, it helps to safeguard existing jobs, embed existing foreign plants, promote more robust linkages between these plants and indigenous firms, and helps to disseminate 'best practice' throughout the regional economy. This may not seem much, but I believe it is sufficient to justify the strategy.

However, if we are serious about addressing unemployment and social exclusion we need to recognize that conventional economic growth no longer offers a credible solution for the long term unemployed in our societies. Indeed, this problem requires more innovative *labour market* policies, like the 'socially useful third sector' (Lipietz, 1992; Rifkin, 1995), the 'sheltered economy' (Freeman and Soete, 1994) and the 'intermediate labour market' (Wise Group, 1994). The common thread running through these new labour market concepts is the idea of marrying idle hands with unmet social needs, an idea which is now being explored by the European Commission (EC, 1995). In the UK, the Glasgow-based Wise Group has demonstrated what an imaginative third-sector organization can achieve, despite a hostile political climate, in offering the long term unemployed a bridge back to work (Wise Group, 1995). If it is to operate on an EU-wide basis, however, this third-sector strategy will need to combine local knowledge of supply and demand with national and supranational political support, because it presupposes radical reform of the current tax and benefit system (Gregg, 1996).

The challenge facing LFRs in Europe today is twofold: to raise the innovative capacity of their regional economies; and to marry idle hands with unmet social needs. Rather than dismissing regional innovation policy for not addressing the problems of social exclusion, far better to think of a repertoire of policies which affords parity of esteem to economic renewal and social justice.

NOTE

1. At this point I ought to declare a personal interest: I am a member of the RTP Steering Committee in Wales.

REFERENCES

Abicht, L. (1994), *Considerations Concerning the Development of a Learning Region*, Institut für Strukturpolitik und Wirtschaftsforderung, Sachsen-Anhalt.

Amin, A., Bradley, D., Howells, J., Tomaney, J. and Gentle, C. (1994), 'Regional incentives and the quality of mobile investment in the less favoured regions of the EC', *Progr. Plann.*, **41** (1).

Amin, A. and Thrift, N. (1995), 'Institutional issues for the European regions: from markets and plans to socioeconomics and powers of association', *Economy and Society*, **24** (1), 41–66.

Arrow, K. (1974), *The Limits of Organization*, New York: Norton.

Camagni, R. (ed.) (1991), *Innovation Networks: Spatial Perspectives*, London: Belhaven.

Cantwell, J. (1995), 'The globalization of technology: what remains of the product cycle model?', *Cambridge Journal of Economics*, **19**, 155–74.

Commission of the European Communities (CEC) (1988), *Science and Technology for Regional Innovation and Development in Europe*, Brussels: CEC.

CEC (1993), *Growth, Competitiveness, Employment*, Brussels: CEC.

CEC (1994a), *Competitiveness and Cohesion: Trends in the Regions*, Brussels: CEC.

CEC (1994b), *The Regional Technology Plan Guidebook*, Brussels: CEC.

Cooke, P. and Morgan, K. (1990), *Learning through Networking: Regional Innovation and the Lessons of Baden-Württemberg*, RIR Report No. 5, University of Wales, Cardiff.

Cooke, P. and Morgan, K. (1992), *Regional Innovation Centres in Europe*, RIR Report No. 10, University of Wales, Cardiff.

Cooke, P. and Morgan, K. (1993), 'The network paradigm: new departures in corporate and regional development', *Environmental Planning D*, **11**, 543–64.

Cooke, P. and Morgan, K. (1994), 'The creative milieu: a regional perspective on innovation', in M. Dodgson and R. Rothwell (eds), *The Handbook of Industrial Innovation*, Aldershot: Edward Elgar, pp. 25–32.

Dankbaar, B. (1994), *Research and Technology Management in Enterprises: Issues for Community Policy*, Brussels: CEC–SAST.

De Vet, J. (1993), *Globalization and Local and Regional Competitiveness*, STI Review, No. 13, OECD, Paris.

Dicken, P., Forsgren, R. and Malmberg, A. (1994), 'The local embeddedness of transnational corporations', in A. Amin and N. Thrift (eds), *Globalization, Institutions and Regional Development in Europe*, Oxford: OUP, pp. 23–45.

Doeringer, P. and Terkla, D. (1990), 'How intangible factors contribute to economic development', *World Development*, **18** (1), 295–308.

Dosi, G., Freeman, C., Nelson, R., Silverberg, G. and Soete, L. (eds) (1988), *Technical Change and Economic Theory*, London: Pinter.

Dunford, M. (1994), 'Winners and losers: the new map of inequality in the European Union', *European Urban & Regional Studies*, **1** (2), 95–114.

European Commission (1995), *Local Development and Employment Initiatives*, Brussels: EC.

European Commission (1996), *First Cohesion Report*, Brussels: EC.

Firn, J. (1976), 'External control and regional policy', in G. Brown (ed.), *The Red Paper on Scotland*, Edinburgh: EUSPB.

Freeman, C., Clark, J. and Soete, L. (1982), *Unemployment and Technical Innovation*, London: Pinter.

Freeman, C. (1988), *Technology Policy and Economic Performance*, London: Pinter.

Freeman, C. (1994), 'Critical survey: the economics of technical change', *Cambridge Journal of Economics*, **18**, 463–512.

Freeman, C. and Soete, L. (1994), *Work for All or Mass Unemployment*, London: Pinter.

Grabher, G. (1993), *The Embedded Firm*, London: Routledge.

Gregg, P. (1996), *Jobs, Wages and Poverty*, London School of Economics: Centre for Economic Performance.

Hill, S. and Munday, M. (1994), *The Regional Distribution of Foreign Manufacturing Investment in the UK*, London: Macmillan.

Hodgson, G. (1988), *Economics and Institutions*, Cambridge: Polity Press.

Hodgson, G. (1993), *Economics and Evolution*, Cambridge: Polity Press.

Illeris, S. and Jakobsen, L. (1990), *Networks and Regional Development*, Copenhagen: University Press.

Koch, J. (1994), 'The learning region: a model on how to surmount technological and economic change', in *Lernende Region*, Brussels: Eurotecnet, pp. 214–22.

Landabaso, M. (1995), 'The promotion of innovation in regional community policy: lessons and proposals for a regional innovation strategy', paper at the International Workshop on Regional Science and Technology Policy, February, Himeji, Japan.

Langlois, R. and Robertson, P. (1995), *Firms, Markets and Economic Change: A Dynamic Theory of Business Institutions*, London: Routledge.

Lawson, G. and Morgan, K. (1991), *Employment Trends in the British Engineering Industry: A Review of Change by Sector, Occupation, Region and Gender*, Watford: Engineering Industry Training Board.

Lipietz, A. (1992), *Towards a New Economic Order*, Cambridge: Polity Press.

Lovering, J. (1996), 'New myths of the Welsh economy', *Planet*, **116**, 6–16.

Lundvall, B.-Å. (ed.) (1992), *National Systems of Innovation: Towards a Theory of Innovation and Interactive Learning*, London: Pinter.

Lundvall, B.-Å. (1994), 'The learning economy: challenges to economic theory and policy', paper at the EAEPE Conference, October, Copenhagen.

Maskell, P. and Malmberg, A. (1999), 'Localised learning and industrial competitiveness', *Cambridge Journal of Economics*, **23** (2), 167–85.

Marx, K. (1976), *Capital*, vol. 1, London: Penguin Books.

Morgan, K. (1992), 'Innovating by networking: new models of corporate and regional development', in M. Dunford and G. Kafkalis (eds), *Cities and regions in the New Europe*, London: Belhaven, pp. 150–69.

Morgan, K. (1997), 'The regional animateur: taking stock of the Welsh Development Agency', *Regional & Federal Studies*, **7** (2), 70–94.

Morgan, K. and Rees, G. (1994), 'Vocational skills and economic development: building a robust training system in Wales', Occasional Papers, Department of City and Regional Planning, University of Wales, Cardiff.

Morgan, K. and Sayer, A. (1988), *Microcircuits of Capital: Sunrise Industry and Uneven Development*, Cambridge: Polity Press.

Nelson, R. (ed.) (1993), *National Innovation Systems*. Oxford: Oxford University Press.

Nishiguchi, T. (1994), *Strategic Industrial Sourcing: The Japanese Advantage*, Oxford: Oxford University Press.

Nonake, I. and Takeuchi, H. (1994), 'A theory of the firm's knowledge creation dynamics', The Prince Bertil Symposium, June, Stockholm.

OECD (1992), *Technology and the Economy: The Key Relationships*, Paris: OECD.

OECD (1993), *Territorial Development and Structural Change: A New Perspective on Adjustment and Reform*, Paris: OECD.

Osmond, J. (ed.) (1994), *A Parliament for Wales*, Llandysul: Gomer.

Patel, P. and Pavitt, K. (1991), 'Large firms in the production of the world's technology: an important case of "non-globalisation"', *Journal of International Business Studies*, **22** (1), 1–21.

Powell, W. (1990), 'Neither market nor hierarchy: network forms of organisation, *Research into Organisational Behaviour*, **12**, 295–336.

Price, A., Morgan, K. and Cooke, P. (1993), *The Welsh Renaissance: Inward Investment and Innovation*, RIR Report No. 14, Cardiff: University of Wales.

Putnam, R. (1993), 'The prosperous community: social capital and public life', *American Prospect*, **13**, 35–42.

Rees, G. and Morgan, K. (1991), 'Industrial restructuring, innovation systems in the regional state', in G. Day and G. Rees (eds), *Regions, Nations and Europe: Remaking the Celtic Periphery*, Cardiff: University of Wales Press.

Rifkin, J. (1995), *The End of Work*, New York: Putnams.

Rosenberg, N. (1976), *Perspectives on Technology*, Cambridge: Cambridge University Press.

Sabel, C. (1992), 'Studied trust: building new forms of co-operation in a volatile economy', in F. Pyke and W. Sengenberger (eds), *Industrial Districts and Local Economic Regeneration*, Geneva: International Institute for Labour Studies, pp. 215–50.

Sabel, C. (1994), 'Learning by monitoring: the institutions of economic development', in N. Smelser and R. Swedberg (eds), *Handbook of Economic Sociology*, Princeton, NJ: Princeton University Press, pp. 137–75.

Schoenberger, E. (1994), 'The firm in the region and the region in the firm', paper at the conference Regions, Institutions and Technology: Reorganizing Economic Geography in Canada and the Anglo-American World, September, Toronto.

Schumpeter, J. (1943), *Capitalism, Socialism and Democracy*, London: Allen & Unwin.

Segal Quince Wicksteed (1996), *Evaluation of Source Wales*, Cambridge: SQW.

Shotton, R. and Miege, R. (1994), 'The Regional Technology Plan: why and how?', RTP Newsletter No. 1, November, Brussels.

Stahl, T. (1994), 'En route to the learning region', in *Lernende Region*, Brussels: Eurotecnet, pp. 196–209.

Stohr, W. (ed.) (1990), *Global Challenge and Local Response*, London: Mansell.

Storper, M. (1992), 'The limits to globalization: technology districts and international trade', *Economic Geography*, **68**, 60–93.

Storper, M. (1994), 'Institutions of the learning economy', paper presented to the conference on Employment and Growth in the Knowledge-based Economy, November, Copenhagen.

Storper, M. (1995), 'The resurgence of regional economics, ten years later: the region as a nexus of untraded interdependencies', *European Urban & Regional Studies*, **2**, 191–221.

Williams, J. (1990), 'The coalowners', in D. Smith (ed.) *A People and A Proletariat: Essays in the History of Wales*, London: Pluto Press, pp. 94–113.

Winter, S. (1987), 'Knowledge and competence as strategic assets', in D. Teece (ed.), *The Competitive Challenge: Strategies for Industrial Innovation and Renewal*, Cambridge, MA: Ballinger, pp. 159–83.

Wise Group (1994), *Annual Review*, Glasgow: Wise Group.

Wise Group (1995), *Annual Review*, Glasgow: Wise Group.

PART II

State of the Art

6. The learning region: a conceptual anatomy

Roel Rutten and Frans Boekema

Underlying the learning region is a multitude of concepts, many of them interlinked. Although, from their own perspective, the four authors in the foundation section have each discussed several concepts, the results of these four efforts do not amount to a clear conceptualization of the learning region. However, such a conceptualization is necessary as a basis for discussion and elaboration of the learning region in this part of the book. The aim of this chapter, then, is to discuss the four articles from the foundation section and identify from them the key concept used by each author. These concepts are the theoretical building blocks for the learning region and will be identified and brought together in one conceptual framework at the end of this chapter. They will not all be nicely chiselled blocks, nor could they be, as the learning region is not yet a mature concept. Therefore the framework is not a conceptual model in the strict sense; instead, it provides a logical ordering of the various concepts that together form the higher-level concept of the learning region. The framework is, as it were, the conceptual anatomy of the learning region. The next chapters in this part will each explore several of the key concepts identified in this chapter. This chapter therefore forms the logical connection between the conceptual foundations of the learning region and the subsequent discussion of the key concepts in the subsequent chapters.

STORPER: 'WORLDS OF PRODUCTION'

In his 1993 article for *Regional Studies*, Michael Storper's main concern was forms of production organization. Like many of his contemporaries, among them Piore and Sabel (1984) and Best (1990), Storper observed a growing influence of new technology development on the economy. Companies had to find different ways to organize their production in order to deal with this development. In a series of case studies in his article, Storper showed that a successful new form of production organization was one that paired vertical disintegration with geographical concentration. The former gave firms the necessary flexibility to cope with technological dynamism; the latter yielded economies of scale that made vertical disintegration economically feasible. Moreover, vertical disintegration went hand in hand with production in networks, as it enabled flexible interfirm division of labour. In terms of organization, the technologically dynamic form of production is thus far more complex than traditional markets or hierarchies. Although Storper does not use the concepts of 'market' and 'hierarchy', a clear transaction-cost logic is visible in his article. Spatial clustering of activities, in this line of thinking, follows from the desire on the part of companies to minimize the costs and time of transactions that result from vertical disintegration and the accompanying division of labour. However, Storper made two critical reservations regarding transaction-cost logic. In the first place, he argued that 'a given transactional relationship in the presence of learning tends to be qualitatively denser than in the case of simple market fluctuations'(Storper, 1993: 434) because it involves tacit, undeveloped knowledge. Ingrained in this statement is the conceptualization of learning, or knowledge creation, as an inherently social process (e.g. Rutten, 2004). Learning as a social process, transcending traditional transactional relations between companies, is central to the concept of the learning region. Second, Storper discussed the concept of 'untraded' interdependencies, which 'emphasize the behavioural basis for [interfirm relations] that lead to learning, arguing that rules, institutions and practices of key collective agents enable local technological learning' (Storper, 1993: 434). Again, Storper stressed the importance of the social context of technological learning. The implication of this statement is that actors can no longer be seen as individual decision makers, as their decisions are influenced by the 'conventions' (Storper's word) of the local network that they are part of. Moreover, these conventions pertain to specific networks and locations and differ between them; hence they are 'untraded'. By referring to Granovetter's 1985 article on embeddedness, Storper further underlined his reservations regarding the ability of transaction-cost economics to deal with something as inherently social as learning. Storper recognized the importance of informal institutions, which was a relatively new element in economic geography at the time.

The exact point where this division occurred is difficult to identify, but in economic geography this article was instrumental in separating a branch from the mainstream that demands centre stage for social processes. Mainstream economic geography kept its focus on transaction-cost economics and would develop into what is now known as 'new economic geography' (e.g. Krugman, 1998). The origins of the learning region can thus be traced back to Michael Storper explaining in his 1993 article the limitations of transaction-cost economics in conceptualizing learning.

Another important insight from Storper's 1993 article is the difference between regional learning and the learning region (cf. Boekema et al., 2000). The fact that technological learning very often takes place in geographically concentrated networks is not a statement about space but about learning. Storper argued that geographical concentration may facilitate learning as it reduces transaction costs. Put differently, this is what can be described as regional learning. However, technological learning is affected by the rules, institutions and practices – that is, the conventions – of the actors involved. These conventions are 'wedded' to specific actors in specific geographical locations. They can differ from location to location. That is why Storper argued that technology districts, i.e. regions where technological learning takes place within regional networks wherein the behaviour of actors is affected by regional conventions, are in effect separate 'worlds of production'. The conceptual coupling of regional learning with region-specific conventions is another key element of the learning region.

Finally, Storper keenly understood one of the key weaknesses of the learning region. The empirically very rich case studies in his article showed him that, although the technology districts in his study shared basic organizational characteristics, they had all followed quite different routes to the same result. In Storper's words, this 'analytical paradox' is probably one of the main reasons why the learning region has thus far eluded rigorous empirical testing (e.g. Hassink, 2001). As scientific journals show an increasing bias towards quantitative empirical studies and modelling, good case studies are fewer and further between. This constitutes a problem for a concept that is still in the process of establishing its legitimacy in the eyes of mainstream economic geography.

Searching Storper's 1993 article for key concepts underlying the learning region produced the following:

- Networks are identified as key organizational forms within which learning takes place.
- Learning is a social process, which transcends transaction-cost logic.
- The functioning of networks is subject to conventions, i.e. untraded interdependences.
- Geographical concentration of activities has two theoretical rationales: first, the fact that geographical concentration yields economies of scale and facilitates learning; and, second, the fact that conventions are wedded to specific geographical locations.

FLORIDA: 'TOWARD THE LEARNING REGION'

By the mid-1990s, when Richard Florida published his article on the learning region (1995), the idea of the capitalist economy having transitioned into a knowledge-based economy had gained wide acceptance (e.g. European Commission, 1995). Like Storper, Florida was interested in the implications of this transition for the organization of production. He entertained very similar ideas, in particular with regard to the role of networks as the dominant organizational mode. Florida was probably the first to coin the term 'learning region', using it to refer to regional infrastructures that must support learning. In Florida's view, knowledge-based capitalism would see the rise of global networks of companies. However, these companies would be dependent on their home regions because regions 'function as collectors and repositories of knowledge and ideas and provide an underlying environment or infrastructure which facilitates the flow of knowledge, ideas and learning' (Florida, 1995: 528). So, in Florida's view, globalization and regionalization went hand in hand – an uncharacteristic statement for a time when the belief had taken hold that new, electronic forms of communication would erase distance as a factor in economic transactions (e.g. Brunn and Leinbach, 1991). The 'infrastructure' that Florida talked about consisted of four elements:

- the manufacturing infrastructure, or companies and, in particular, networks of co-dependent end users and suppliers;
- the human infrastructure, or the presence of sufficient and sufficiently skilled knowledge workers;
- the physical and communications infrastructure, which should be geared not to supporting physical assets but to knowledge assets;
- industrial governance, a concept very similar to Storper's 'conventions'.

Florida's article brings to light the fundamental problem of the learning region as a concept. Since the name of the concept refers to regions, one might expect that regions, too, are the analytical focus of this concept, i.e. that they are the level of analysis. In an important way, they are. From Florida's discussion of infrastructure it follows that this infrastructure may be different from one region to another. Consequently, one of the explanations for the fact that some regions fare better in the global economy than others may be the difference in the (performance or functioning of their) infrastructures. However, explaining the performance of regions was the objective of neither Florida nor Storper. Their focus was on the performance of companies and on how companies organized their production function in response to the demands of the knowledge-based economy.

This, of course, implies that the level of analysis is the company and not the region. This analytical schizophrenia of the learning region, understandably, has given rise to criticism (e.g. Oinas and Virkkala, 1997). Yet, taking a closer look at Florida's 1995 article could solve this analytical problem. In Florida's own words, regions are the environments that facilitate the flow of knowledge, ideas and learning. From this statement it follows that companies, not regions, learn. Regions support the process of learning, particularly as it takes place within networks of companies. Therefore the analytical focus is neither on companies nor on regions; instead, it is on the process of learning in networks. So the concept of the learning region is not interested in particular regions, but in regions as an environment for learning in networks. Put differently, 'the region is a process or, more accurately, a nexus of processes rather than a thing' (Cooke and Morgan, 1998: 63). In sum, if the process of learning is to be understood, it is important to consider the contexts within which this process is embedded. These contexts are both networks of companies and regions. Crucially, the learning-region argument goes, it is regional networks in particular that merit attention, as regional networks provide a unique, non-transferable (untraded) environment for firms to learn. This focus on process clearly separates the learning region from mainstream economic geography, which focuses on transactions and firms (new economic geography) or on regions (spillover theory).

The key concepts to remember from Florida's article, then, are the following:

- The analytical focus of the learning region is the process of learning in networks, as networks are the favoured organizational mode in the knowledge-based economy.
- Learning in networks is dependent on both the characteristics of these networks themselves and on the characteristics of the regions in which these networks are embedded.
- Regional embeddedness of networks implies that interaction within these networks is subject to the 'conventions' of the regions in question.

ASHEIM: 'INDUSTRIAL DISTRICTS AS "LEARNING REGIONS"'

As with the previous two authors, Asheim's main concern was new forms of organization. More specifically, he asked himself which organizational forms would be most conducive to learning. Answering that question, he developed a conceptualization of learning that became a cornerstone of the learning region. Asheim was by no means the only person to work on this conceptualization, nor was his 1996 article recognized as instrumental in developing that conceptualization. Nevertheless, he neatly outlined the essence of the learning region's conceptualization of knowledge as 'a technical as well as a social process' and an interactive, rather than a linear, process (Asheim, 1996: 385). This conceptualization was opposed to mainstream thinking on learning. For example, Williamson (1999) still looked at learning as something pertaining to transactions; that is, as pertaining to the individual decision-making *homo economicus*. Instead, Asheim argued that learning, given its social and interactive nature, can only be understood within its institutional and cultural context (Asheim, 1996: 385). In his own words, Asheim explained that Storperian 'conventions' are the context within which learning must be understood. In correspondence with the dual analytical focus of the learning region, Asheim explored two important themes in his article: networks as the desired organizational form for learning and the advantages of agglomeration with regard to learning.

With regard to networks, Asheim argued in favour of quasi-integrated networks as the best organizational form to support learning. Being flat, flexible and egalitarian, they provided the best trigger for employees to engage in interactive learning. As opposed to integrated networks of the former 'industrial economy', quasi-integrated networks were loosely coupled and could, thus, more easily escape the so-called lock-in effects that blind network partners to new developments. Moreover, learning worked best in geographically concentrated networks – although Asheim does not give an elaborate explanation of this assertion. So, in fact, Asheim argued in favour of quasi-integrated regional networks as the best organizational context for (interactive) learning. Trying to describe what those networks look like, the conclusion may be that they are composed of a number of firms that periodically engage in both vertical and horizontal collaboration. These firms collaborate in networks all of the time but do not always do so with the same partners. They change partners, for example, depending on the needs of a particular client. In order to do this, firms would have to know each other; that is, they would have to belong to the same 'social network' all of the time, but they would not have to maintain actual economic or learning relations all of the time. Empirical evidence of such networks does exist and speaks in their favour (e.g. Best, 1990; Cooke and Morgan, 1998; Rutten, 2003; Storper, 1993; Uzzi, 1997). Of course, these quasi-integrated networks would need a different mode of control than traditional, formalized and hierarchical control (e.g. Williamson, 1999). Asheim's solution was to suggest trust as a control mechanism in these networks. In a broader view, trust can be seen as a 'social characteristic' of networks, the importance of which had also been stressed by Storper (1993, conventions), for example, and Granovetter (1985, embeddedness). This emphasis on social characteristics with respect to explaining learning in networks is an important difference between the learning region and main-stream economic geography (e.g. Rutten, 2004).

His discussion on agglomeration advantages provided Asheim with a definition of learning regions. Although economists had long recognized the advantage of agglomeration in terms of economies of scale and more efficient transaction, a more important kind of agglomeration advantage, according to Asheim, was connected to the institutional set-up of a region. This he understood in two ways. On the one hand, the institutional set-up concerns the now familiar notions of conventions, untraded interdepend-encies (Storper, 1993) and industrial governance (Florida, 1995). On the other hand, Asheim's institutional set-up included a region's innovation policy and innovation support organizations (Asheim, 1996: 393). It was this second characteristic of the institutional set-up that, according to Asheim, distinguished learning regions from industrial districts. Industrial districts are beneficial to firms in that they provide agglomeration advan-tages and solidify collaboration in networks through conventions, but they do not necessarily facilitate learning. A learning region functions as a regional innovation system. In a learning region, geographically concen-trated learning networks, territorially embedded conventions, regional innovation policy and regional innovation support organizations depend on each other and reinforce each other. They work together as if they were part of a coherent system. This constituted an important step forward in conceptualizing the learning region, but it also created a problem: how to distinguish the learning region from regional innovation systems.

The key concepts that follow from Asheim's article can summarized as follows:

- In order for learning networks to actually enable learning, they should be flat and flexible; that is, they should be quasi-integrated networks.
- Geographical concentration of learning networks yields agglomera-tion advantages.
- The most relevant agglomeration advantages pertain to territorially embedded conventions.
- These territorially embedded conventions, together with regional innovation policy and regional innovation support organizations, constitute the institutional set-up of a region.
- If geographically concentrated learning networks and the institu-tional set-up function as a system, regions can become learning regions.

MORGAN: 'INSTITUTIONS, INNOVATION AND REGIONAL RENEWAL'

Contrary to the previous authors, Morgan's initial concern was of a social rather than a theoretical nature. He argued that neither the state nor the market could adequately provide for social welfare. Instead, relief should come from a shift towards the network, or associational paradigm – the essence of which was explained previously. Morgan explicitly linked innovation to economic development and saw it as an instrument to further social welfare. He thus gave the learning region a social agenda in addition to its theoretical one. In Morgan's view, the learning region constituted an attempt to marry two disciplines (economic geography and innovation) and should be concerned with the spatial implications of learning in networks (the associational paradigm) and with the institutional capacity of regions to support this learning. The need for such a new attempt at conceptualizing regional renewal followed from the inability of the European Union to close the gap between rich and poor regions on the basis of traditional economic policy – be that a neoclassical, market-led policy or neo-Keynesian, state-led one. Following evolutionary economic theory, Morgan conceptualized innovation as 'an interactive process . . . [that] is shaped by a variety of institutional routines and social conventions' (Morgan, 1997: 493). This emphasis on the social characteristics of learning puts Morgan very much in line with the above authors. Around that time, a new concept to grasp the 'social' entered the vocabulary of economic geographers: social capital. Borrowing from Putnam, Morgan defined it as 'features of social organisation, such as networks, norms and trust that facilitate coordination and cooperation for mutual benefit' (Putnam, 1993, in Morgan, 1997: 493). Although Putnam's definition leaves open the possibility of social capital pertaining to interfirm relations, a way in which it is often used in contemporary literature (e.g. Field, 2003), Morgan sees social capital as something pertaining explicitly to regions. A region's stock of social capital, or lack thereof, according to Morgan, was an important factor in explaining the difference between economically successful regions and less favoured regions (LFRs). The key, then, to regional renewal and social welfare lay in strengthening a region's social capital and institutional capacity to support learning.

Building social capital had a very practical tone in Morgan's article. For example, he pointed to the important role of regional knowledge infrastructures with regard to innovation. In line with his interactive conceptualization of innovation, intermediary organizations, such as regional development agencies rather than research centres, should be seen as the principal agents in the knowledge infrastructure. Intermediary organizations, when functioning as regional 'animators', facilitated the establishing of linkages between firms and knowledge centres in order to achieve regional learning. On a theoretical level Morgan grasped the essence of why the region merits a central theoretical status with regard to learning and innovation. One the one hand, he argued that physical proximity facilitates integration of tacit, person-embedded knowledge (Morgan, 1997: 495). Storper (1997) labelled this phenomenon 'the geography of knowledge', arguing that codified knowledge can be exchanged globally with relative ease, but that spatial proximity between partners is a major factor in facilitating the exchange of tacit knowledge. On the other hand, Morgan argued that social capital is 'best developed at the regional level because this is the level where regular interactions, one of the conditions for trust-building, can be sustained over time' (Morgan, 1997: 501). Put differently, the regional level best acknowledged the human and social context of knowledge, from which it cannot be removed.

Morgan's views on regional renewal can also be found in the European Union's regional development policy, as it emerged from the mid-1990s in the form of Regional Technology Plans (RTPs). This is not entirely surprising, as Morgan himself was involved in the RTP for his home region of Wales.[1] The RTP Wales was a pilot project for the European Union (see Morgan, 1997), the lessons of which were in incorporated in follow-up initiatives that still run today. In Morgan's view, the concept of the learning region provided LFRs a way out of their troubles. Acknowledging that the 'impetus for regional renewal must come from within' (Morgan, 1997: 497), Morgan, argued that LFRs should build institutional capacity from what little innovation support infrastructure they had. Using intermediary organizations as 'animators' and exploiting their social capital LFRs should trigger innovation and thus initiate regional renewal. As argued, the European Union, not unsuccessfully, put into practice some of Morgan's ideas (e.g. Landabaso, 2000). This intimate connection between the learning region and (European) regional development policy has led several authors to the false conclusion that the learning region is only about regional innovation policy (e.g. Hassink, 2001). To Morgan's credit, he is realistic about the limitations of the learning region. Regions cannot take the place of the central state, because a 'supportive central state is also necessary to compensate those LFRs which do not have the capacity to experiment with their own institutional resources' (Morgan, 1997: 501). Nor is innovation policy a sufficient condition to solve the problem of mass unemployment and social exclusion. Morgan aimed to attribute to the (learning) region a crucial place in modern knowledge-based capitalism, a claim that still stands today.

The key concepts from Morgan are as follows:

- The network or associational paradigm is central in marrying the disciplines of economic geography and innovation.
- Social capital pertains to networks as well as regions, but on the regional level it constitutes the institutional capacity of a region.
- Strengthening institutional capacity is the key to regional renewal and it should be the aim of regional innovation policy.
- The region merits a central, theoretical status in the knowledge-based economy as the nexus of learning processes and as the social capital carrying these processes.

TOWARDS A CONCEPTUALIZATION OF THE LEARNING REGION

Although all of the above authors have their own emphases, a good deal of overlap between them is clearly visible. A tentative definition of the learning region may be deduced from the above and could be phrased as follows:

> In a learning region, regional actors engage in collaboration and coordination for mutual benefit, resulting in a process of regional learning. Regional characteristics affect the degree to which the process of regional learning leads to regional renewal.

This definition carefully avoids using a concept such as transactions, so as to stress the fact that the learning region is not part of mainstream economic geography. Regional learning is, of course, the key to the whole concept. It pertains to the transfer, creation, absorption and implementation of knowledge among regional partners, which, in turn, triggers innovation and regional renewal. The latter can be understood both in economic terms (regional development) and in institutional terms. If a region truly is a learning region, it must achieve two things. First, mutually beneficial collaboration and coordination between regional actors must function as a coherent system. Second, the regional renewal must lead to changes for the better in the regional context. Arguably, this definition allows identifying real regions as learning regions. Note, however, that this definition does not say anything about the size of a learning region. Following the above authors, regions such as Silicon Valley may qualify as learning regions, but also, for example, Manhattan, as in the case of the New York fashion industry (Uzzi, 1997). Functioning as a system is more important than size. The system defines the boundaries of a learning region, not administrative or geographical features. Or, as Morgan (1997) put it, a region must be understood as a nexus of processes.

As a next step towards a conceptualization of the learning region, it would be helpful to distinguish between groups of variables that should make up such a conceptualization. Ultimately, the learning region should promote regional development by facilitating regional companies to bring about product and process innovations. These can be considered outcome variables. Interestingly, very little attention is paid to how product and process innovations actually happen in companies and how this leads to regional development. Of course, this is perfectly in line with the observation that the real focus of the learning region, i.e. its level of analysis, is the process of regional learning. This leads to the identification of a second group of variables, process variables – exactly how the process of regional learning produces outcomes in terms of product and process innovation is assumed rather than explained within the concept of the learning region. This is neither an omission nor a weakness. The link from learning to innovation to (economic) development has been made in various publications, from which the learning region borrows. Leaving the outcomes to other theories allows the learning region to place its own focus, i.e. regional learning. After all, the objective of the learning region (as a concept) is to 'marry' innovation theory with regional development theory, not to copy them. Deducing from the above authors, the learning region sees the best opportunities for a fruitful marriage in the process of regional learning. The next step in the conceptualization is to recognize that the effectiveness of the process of regional learning depends on the regional context in which it takes place. Therefore the regional context constitutes the third group of variables. After all, it is sufficiently clear that some regions provide a better 'milieu' for regional learning than others.

Taking a closer look at the three groups of variables – outcomes, process and regional context – the first conclusion is that the outcome variables do not need further elaboration. Next, in the process group, two variables can be distinguished, regional learning and innovation policy. Regional learning, of course, is obvious: it is the key process in the concept of the learning region. Regional innovation policy, too, is a process in this conceptualization. It is what regional authorities do (or fail to do) to facilitate the process of regional learning. Therefore regional innovation policy should be seen as a process, an activity, rather than as a collection of good intentions and patient documents. As the article by Morgan, in particular, showed, regional authorities can have an important effect on collaboration and coordination in a region. Turning to the regional-context variables, at least three such variables can be identified: spatial proximity, regional interfirm networks and the institutional set-up of a region.

- *Spatial proximity* can facilitate regional learning in either of two ways. On the one hand, 'traditional' agglomeration advantages yield economies of scale with regard to labour market and transactions, for example. On the other hand, spatial proximity facilitates the exchange of tacit knowledge, the mechanism that has been referred to as the geography of knowledge.
- From a conceptual perspective, organization studies contributed *regional interfirm networks* to the learning region. Such networks are the key instruments through which regional learning is brought about. That is, regional learning, largely, takes place within regional interfirm networks. These networks bring about innovations. What is important, though, are the characteristics of these networks, as not all networks are equally conducive to learning. According to the literature discussed above, networks should have flat, flexible organizational structures. Moreover, it helps if network partners have a mutual range of economic and social relations, even when they are not actually engaged in networking at any given time. Put differently, a substantial degree of embeddedness among regional firms is believed to be a favourable network characteristic (cf. Granovetter, 1985).
- The *institutional set-up of a region* is the most visible feature of the regional context affecting regional learning. The presence of knowledge centres (public or private) in a region can be of great help in fostering regional learning, although it is by no means sufficient (see Morgan, 1997). More important is the presence of regional 'animators'. If regional knowledge centres and 'animators' are strongly connected to the regional business community – and if they play an active role in the development and dissemination of knowledge – then the collection of regional actors starts to function as a regional innovation system. Finally, the institutional set-up of a region, of course, is subject to influence from regional innovation policy.

A final variable that must be part of a conceptualization of the learning region is *social capital*. Whether social capital is a characteristic of a region, of relations, or both, its proper place in a conceptual framework is probably not as part of the regional context. Social capital pertains to the regional institutional capacity, that is, the region's networking capability and regionally embedded conventions. As such, social capital affects both the process of regional learning and the regional context. Social capital can smooth the process of regional learning, i.e. the communication and interaction between regional partners. But social capital also underpins regional, interfirm networks and the (smooth) functioning of the regional institutional set-up. Therefore social capital should be seen as a moderating variable in the conceptual framework of the learning region.

A final observation regarding the learning region is its neglect of the national and international context of regions. Although paying lip service to it, the learning region does not provide for a conceptual embedding of the national and international context. Nor is that a problem. The learning region is a concept of endogenous regional development; that is, it puts the spotlight on processes within regions (i.e. learning and networking) and on how regional context factors affect these processes. Because some regions obviously fare better than others, even in our globalized economy, this is an altogether valid approach. Moreover, having regional networks that are linked to national and international networks can be an important regional characteristic (see Florida, 1995). Seen in this way, the proposed conceptualization of the learning region, to some degree, does account for the national and international context. Finally, if a good conceptualization necessitates having a clear focus, then omitting the national and international context may be seen as a strength rather than a weakness of the learning region – as long as it is appreciated that endogenous developments do not explain all regional outcomes and that they may not even explain everything of some regional outcomes. However, this reservation applies to conceptualizations in general, not to the learning region in particular.

The above conceptualization is visualized in Figure 6.1. Of course, it is not a perfect conceptualization, nor could it be, as it is based only on the four foundation papers. The purpose of this conceptualization is to provide a starting point for the next chapters, the state of the art. The way in which this is done is also visualized in Figure 6.1. Each of the next chapters in this part discusses a variable from the conceptual framework and explores how this variable affects the process of regional learning – except for the chapter on social capital, which discusses how social capital, being a moderating variable in this conceptual framework, affects both the process and the regional context of the learning region. The final chapter in this part, Chapter 12, does not discuss any particular variable form of the conceptual framework. Instead, it takes a critical look at the whole concept in an attempt to identify its flaws and weaknesses. Together, the discussion, exploration and criticism will be the input for the final part of this book: the future of the learning region.

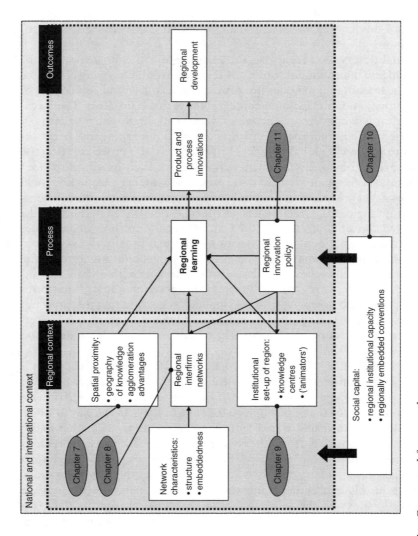

Figure 6.1   Conceptual framework

NOTE

1. Incidentally, two other contributors to this volume were involved in the first batch of RTP projects in 1994 as well. Michael Landabaso, as a representative of the European Commission, was involved in conceiving and managing the RTP effort, and Roel Rutten was a consultant for one of the participating regions (the Dutch province of Limburg).

REFERENCES

Asheim, B. (1996), 'Industrial districts as "learning regions"': a condition for prosperity', *European Planning Studies*, **4** (4), 379–400.
Best, M. (1990), *The New Competition: Institutions of Industrial Restructuring*, Cambridge: Polity Press.
Boekema, F., Morgan, K., Bakkers, S. and Rutten, R. (eds) (2000), *Knowledge, Innovation and Economic Growth: The Theory and Practice of Learning Regions*, Cheltenham, UK and Northampton, MA, USA: Edward Elgar.
Brunn, S. and Leinbach, T. (eds) (1991), *Collapsing Space and Time: Geographical Aspects of Communications and Information*, London: HarperCollins Academic.
Cooke, P. and Morgan, K. (1998), *The Associational Economy: Firms, Regions, and Innovation*, Oxford: Oxford University Press.
European Commission (1995), *The Green Paper on Innovation*, Brussels: European Commission.
Field, J. (2003), *Social Capital*, London: Routledge.
Florida, R. (1995), 'Toward the learning region', *Futures*, **27** (5), 527–36.
Granovetter, M. (1985), 'Economic action and social structures: the problem of embeddedness', *American Journal of Sociology*, **91** (3), 481–510.
Hassink, R. (2001), 'The learning region: a fuzzy concept or a sound theoretical basis for modern regional innovation policies?', *Zeitschrift für Wirtschaftsgeographie*, **45** (3–4), 219–30.
Krugman, P. (1998), 'What is new about the new economic geography?', *Oxford Review of Economic Policy*, **14** (2), 7–17.
Landabaso, M. (2000), 'Innovation and regional development policy', in F. Boekema et al. (eds), *Knowlege, Innovation and Economic Growth: The Theory and Practice of Learning Regions*, Cheltenham, UK and Northampton, MA, USA: Edward Elgar, pp. 73–94.
Morgan, K. (1997), 'The learning region: institutions, innovation and regional renewal', *Regional Studies*, **31** (5), 491–503.
Oinas, P. and Virkkala, S. (1997), 'Learning, competitiveness and development: reflections on the contemporary discourse on "learning regions"', in E. Eskelinnen (ed.), *Regional Specialisation and Local Environment: Learning and Competitiveness*, NordREFO 1997-1, pp. 263–77.
Piore, M. and Sabel, C. (1984), *The Second Industrial Divide*, New York: Basic Books.
Rutten, R. (2003), *Knowledge and Innovation in Regional Industry: An Entrepreneurial Coalition*, London: Routledge.
Rutten, R. (2004), 'Inter-firm knowledge creation: A re-appreciation of embeddedness from a relational perspective', *European Planning Studies*, **12** (5), 659–74.

Storper, M. (1993), 'Regional "worlds" of production: learning and innovation in the technology districts of France, Italy and the USA', *Regional Studies*, **27** (5), 433–55.
Storper, M. (1997), *The Regional World: Territorial Development in a Global Economy*, New York: The Guilford Press.
Uzzi, B. (1997), 'Social structure and competition in interfirm networks: the paradox of embeddedness', *Administrative Science Quarterly*, **42** (1), 35–67.
Williamson, O. (1999), 'Strategy research: governance and competence perspectives', *Strategic Management Journal*, **20** (12), 1087–108.

7. Knowledge and the competitiveness of places

Ed Malecki and Gert-Jan Hospers

Generally speaking, knowledge created and shared forms the basis of competitive areas. The competitiveness of places – localities, regions and nations – refers to the ability of the local economy and society to provide a rising standard of living for its inhabitants. Rarely is this possible by relying upon external investment such as branch plants, whose principal orientation and organizational links are external to the region. Rather, the strength of an economy is dependent on the degree to which knowledge is created, used and shared. Places are better off when they promote shared or public knowledge from which many firms and other organizations can benefit. It is difficult to create sufficient knowledge that could serve as a basis for local competitiveness. It is even more difficult to sustain it, however, because of the continuous emergence of competitor regions (Malecki, 1997; Hospers, 2005).

This chapter deals with the link between knowledge and the competitiveness of places. In particular, it examines the link between creativity, knowledge, competence, learning and their role in creating and sustaining regional economic development. The chapter begins by defining knowledge and identifying the various forms that knowledge takes in the economic geography of places. Next, knowledge as input to economic growth and the transfer of knowledge are discussed, including a consideration of how local knowledge has become central to understanding firms. The focus of the chapter then shifts to the culture of knowledge, which is not only localized but also able to use non-local networks or to take advantage of global trends. The chapter ends with a brief conclusion.

KNOWLEDGE, CREATIVITY AND THE SPATIAL CONTEXT

What is knowledge? Knowledge can be seen as the third step in a hierarchical ordering that progresses from data as the lowest-order unit and progresses to wisdom or nirvana as the highest-order capability (Table 7.1).

Table 7.1   Levels of knowledge-related concepts

Concept	Characteristics
Wisdom or nirvana	Complete knowledge
Creativity	Creativity presumes a capacity to order and reorder information with the aid of a knowledge system
Competence	Embodied knowledge, being one of three types: (1) instrument-oriented competence, (2) sector-specific competence, and (3) regional-specific competence
Knowledge	Structurally ordered information, including reflection, synthesis, and context
	Information laden with experience, truth, judgement, intuition and values
	Concepts, ideas and patterns are subsets of knowledge
	Often tacit, hard to transfer
Information	Data endowed with relevance and purpose
Data	Simple observations of states of the world; easily structured, easily captured on machines, easily transferred

Source: Adapted from Andersson (1985: 13), Davenport (1997) and Huseman and Goodman (1999).

Andersson (1985: 13) suggests that 'one can view information as variables, whereas knowledge is a set of equations containing these variables'. Competence and creativity reflect a further refinement and application of knowledge as we move higher on the path toward wisdom. Huseman and Goodman (1999) skip these intermediate steps, saying that 'wisdom arises from the processing of knowledge' (p. 211). At a less abstract level, knowledge includes the skills of workers, the experience of managers and owners, and the 'pulse' of customers' needs and demands. The accumulation of skills and knowledge in particular places, long recognized as a phenomenon in the location of economic activity, arguably has increased in importance in recent years. This phenomenon includes two dimensions. First, firms and industries depend on localized knowledge. Second, knowledge is not limited to a few high-technology or knowledge-based sectors; the innovative or knowledge activities of all sectors can be called activities with a knowledge-based character. At the risk of focusing on a single dimension of a multidimensional phenomenon, let us look at the creativity aspect of knowledge in a regional context (Amin and Graham, 1997).

Andersson (1985: 19) has suggested that creativity develops in regions that are characterized by five criteria:

1. high levels of competence (and its embodiment of knowledge);
2. many fields of academic and cultural activity (diversity);
3. excellent opportunities for internal and external communication;
4. widely shared perceptions of unsatisfied needs; and
5. a general situation of structural instability facilitating a synergetic development.

Andersson's five conditions for regional creativity can be combined into three familiar policy variables: (1) the presence of professional and technical labor (representing competence); (2) urban agglomeration, or a threshold size of place where cultural activity and communication will be heightened; and (3) conditions that promote synergy or instability.[1] The first two elements of these are relatively easy to analyze and data are readily available. The third element is more difficult to identify, even when it is present, but it is related to the local environment or entrepreneurial climate of a place, as seen in its degree of networking, the presence of venture capital and local supporting institutions (Malecki, 1997). Silicon Valley, perhaps the model of regional creativity, has been analyzed more than most places. Micklethwait (1997: 7), in a survey of Silicon Valley titled 'Future perfect?', summarizes his conclusion: 'culture, irritatingly vague though it may sound, is more important to Silicon Valley's success than economic or technological factors'. He concludes, following Saxenian (1994), that more than anywhere else in the world Silicon Valley has some unique local conventions, such as tolerance of failure, risk-seeking, reinvestment in the community, enthusiasm for change and rapid response to technological change, a climate for collaboration, promotion on merit and openness to immigrants and women and an obsession with the product and a technologically 'cool idea'.

Most of these items are 'untraded interdependencies' (Storper, 1995) and thus difficult to transplant to other places. Let us examine a few of these cultural aspects in Silicon Valley in the context of regional knowledge. First, the region has a strong tradition in the field of venture capital, which Micklethwait (1997) includes as 'reinvestment in the community'. Interestingly, the 'angels' and formal venture capitalists are very concentrated, only within a small (80 km) radius (Zook, 2004). Second, the Valley comprises an 'ecosystem' within which firms form and re-form through continual entrepreneurship. Networks of interpersonal relationships support entrepreneurship, links among enterprises (large and small alike), and innovative activity (Saxenian, 1994). Networks thus provide the 'soft' bonds that link the 'hard' qualities of Silicon Valley, which take the form primarily of high levels of state-of-the-art R&D. Imitation of the 'hardware' of Silicon Valley through the creation of science or research parks has not been effective and has merely led to the next 'Silicon Somewhere' (Hospers, 2005). Something else is needed, which can be thought of as the 'software' of a region: the presence of social structures of sociability, trust and an industrial structure that demands interaction among firms (for example highly linked industries making flexibly changing products). Third, Silicon Valley stands out for its set of institutional factors that influence the production of synergy in regional clusters. Firms must cooperate, share information and resources, and tackle problems jointly. In ideal settings, firms are supported by strong local government and non-governmental institutions, along with the provision of a wide range of social services (Cooke and Morgan, 1998).

Perhaps the premier European examples of such positive 'soft' regional development trajectories, based on institutions, conventions and culture, are Baden-Württemberg and Emilia-Romagna (Cooke and Morgan, 1998). The German region Baden-Württemberg is presented as a model region, one which has cooperation at the core of a comprehensive and multi-layered 'enterprise and innovation support system' (Cooke and Morgan, 1998: 94). Emilia-Romagna is another model of associationalism, centered on regional service centers and other intermediaries that support the networks of small firms in Italy's industrial districts. Cooke and Morgan conclude that 'co-operative yet still competitive systems such as that in Emilia-Romagna will learn, adjust, and evolve' to globalized markets and production, a more uncertain prospect than that for Baden-Württemberg. Cooke and Morgan (1998) conclude that successful regional economies are associational economies, i.e. places with a high degree of interfirm and firm–agency interaction. The associational model is a 'third way', between state-led and market-led development, demanding a more collaborative mode of operation in the form of network relationships. Social and economic success, then, seems to be based to a considerable degree on regional capability in place-specific relationships of trust and learning as well as on regional network competence.

KNOWLEDGE, COMPETENCE AND LEARNING PROCESSES

Let us return to the first of Andersson's criteria for regional creativity: competence. Competence refers to the knowledge embodied in the labor force. In general, localization or concentration of competence in a certain place benefits both workers and employers. High-technology (or high-value-added) industries are notable for their geographical concentration, which is due in large part to labor market considerations (Malecki, 2000a). Again, Silicon Valley is a good example of this. Almeida and Kogut (1999), examining in detail the mobility of engineers in the semiconductor industry, find that Silicon Valley has an unusually high degree of interfirm mobility, which affects technology transfer between firms. Not only in Silicon Valley, but also in other places across the world, high-technology industries tend to be geographically concentrated. Those industries employ high-skilled workers and have a high research and development (R&D) intensity: aerospace, pharmaceuticals, computers and office equipment, communications equipment and semiconductors, scientific instruments and electrical machinery are commonly concentrated within all countries where they are found (OECD, 1995). In addition to high-tech manufacturing sectors, a large number of producer services – those services for which firms are the principal customers – are knowledge-intensive and information-intensive, such as financial and legal services, marketing and R&D (Teece, 1998). The concentration of highly educated 'white-collar' professionals in these jobs, whose work includes problem-solving, problem-identifying and strategic-brokering activities, often require face-to-face contact and collaboration as they have to customize their service to specific clients (von Ginlow, 1988). Also these economic activities are not evenly spread across the landscape: like high-technology sectors, producer service activities are located disproportionately in the largest cities (Cooke, 2002; Porter, 1998).

The agglomeration of knowledge allows firms both to minimize transaction costs and to specialize within a spatial division of labor (Storper, 1995). Traditional, static agglomeration economies and traded interfirm interdependencies resulting from geographical concentration do not, however, explain agglomeration entirely. More important are 'untraded interdependencies', which take the form of conventions, informal rules and habits that coordinate economic actors under conditions of uncertainty (Storper, 1995). These untraded interdependencies are the basis of dynamic agglomeration economies, which enhance opportunities for technological learning, as opposed to simply reductions in the unit costs of production with a given technology. By means of these interdependencies, knowledge can be exchanged, created, improved and sustained on a regional level. Lawson (1999) uses this idea to propose that regional competence – region-specific knowledge shared by a group of firms and based on their interaction – is produced in a regional system with higher-order capabilities (i.e. capabilities that cannot be reached individually, but only collectively) that are distinct from the capabilities of individual firms. The idea of regional competence is based on the competence theory of the firm. We will dwell on this theory briefly to clarify the idea of 'regional competence'. The competence theory of the firm is a distinct alternative to both neoclassical economics and transaction-cost economics. In the competence perspective, the firm is a repository of skill, experience and knowledge, rather than merely a set of responses to information or transaction costs (Carlsson and Eliasson, 1994; Knudsen, 1996). For firms, knowledge is both a product or output and a factor of production. As a product, knowledge is embodied in new products and services. As an input to production, knowledge also is embodied in people and in organizational routines. The resultant knowledge is greater than the sum of the individual knowledge possessed by a firm's employees. Knowledge thus leads to competence, which is a 'strategic asset' favoring a firm's competitiveness (Cooke, 2002).

From a competence perspective the process of 'learning' is recognized as the highest-level capability, which allows firms to adapt to changed circumstances in its competitive environment. Learning received little attention within the studies of firms until Nelson and Winter's (1982) work, and was given new significance by the work of Cohen and Levinthal (1990), who expanded the conventional concept of R&D to include its 'two faces': innovation and learning. More influential was their proposed concept of 'absorptive capacity' for learning: a firm's ability to evaluate, assimilate and apply potential knowledge. Further refinement proposed that 'the prepared firm' is one that does R&D as much to accumulate related knowledge as to accomplish a specific technological objective (Cohen and Levinthal, 1990). One firm's knowledge can be purchased or it can be acquired through interpersonal contacts, which are most easily accomplished in geographic proximity. It is easier to transfer codified knowledge – that which is tangible in some way, usually in printed form, as in books, patent applications and scientific papers. Eventually, however, through the transfer and replication of codified knowledge, it can become ubiquitous and thus of little competitive advantage. After all, competitiveness is about making a difference (Maskell, 1999; Hospers, 2005). Tacit knowledge generally is embodied in people, rather than in written form or in objects. It is privately held and often builds on a long period of (shared) experience. Tacit knowledge can be acquired through hiring, R&D and interpersonal networking (Nonaka and Konno, 1998). However, it is seldom easy to transfer complex knowledge from one person to another. On-the-job training, on-site engineering and other means of learning have been central to the process of technology transfer, but few attempts have been made to translate these mechanisms to more general situations. In an important contribution, Nonaka and Konno (1998) propose the Japanese concept of 'ba', or shared space, as the key to the relationships of knowledge creation and learning. Knowledge is created through a spiraling process of interactions between explicit (or codified) and tacit knowledge: socialization (sharing tacit knowledge), externalization (expression of tacit knowledge to transmit to others), combination (conversion of explicit knowledge into more complex explicit knowledge) and internalization (conversion of newly created knowledge into the organization's tacit knowledge). There are four types of shared space ('ba'), including face-to-face, peer-to-peer, group-to-group and on-site interaction. The need to shift from individual knowledge to group knowledge understood by a larger group, and vice versa, seems to be the central feature of the 'ba' concept and the spiraling process. Group and individual knowledge generally are distinct in accounts of tacit knowledge, as illustrated in Table 7.2.

Nonaka and Konno's spiraling process of interactions and learning processes is significant for several reasons. First, it explicitly recognizes knowledge creation and learning as continual, ongoing processes in Japanese companies (Malecki, 2000a). Moreover, there is no one-way path from tacit to explicit knowledge; instead, explicit knowledge is internalized and used to develop new tacit knowledge. Second, several different 'shared spaces' are involved in knowledge creation. Some of these are internal to the firm; others are external. Some can be local; others rely on organizational rather than geographic proximity (Rallet and Torre, 1998). Time, space and infrastructure must be available for seeking, generating and exchanging, irrespective of whether they are based on geographic or organizational proximity. Often, this is best done by urban institutions that can provide the shared space for many different groups (Maillat, 1998). Third, as tacit knowledge becomes more diffused and shared, imitation becomes more difficult. If firms are to be 'learning organizations', then the firm's employees must be able to learn to 'gain knowledge' from many sources (Teece, 1998). The experience of multinational firms suggests that in order to exploit geographically dispersed knowledge a firm must become a 'local' in several locales simultaneously and integrate knowledge from various

Table 7.2   Where to find tacit and explicit knowledge

Types of knowledge	Individual	Group
Explicit	Job skills	Best practices
	Design rules	Stories
	Procedures	Work processes
Tacit	Intuition	Rules of thumb
	Know-how	Traditions
	Common sense	Sources of information
	Judgment	Requirements for survival

Source: Davenport (1999: 149).

sources (Amin and Cohendet, 2004). Because tacit and idiosyncratic knowledge are decentralized, co-location is required at several locations; the necessary knowledge cannot be centralized in a single point. The importance of 'being there', not just being linked remotely, has become recognized as critical (Gertler, 1995; Maskell, 1999). It has become apparent that telecommunication applications, such as e-mail and the Internet, provide access to knowledge but do not necessarily facilitate its understanding and implementation. The reason is that tacit knowledge, on which localized capabilities are based, is 'sticky' and difficult to transfer within or between organizations (von Hippel, 1998; Teece, 1998). In essence, as firms attempt to become closer to their customers in a world of short product cycles, the locus of problem-solving tends toward users because of sticky local information that must be transferred a number of times (von Hippel, 1998). These transfers of knowledge represent the externalization or transformation of tacit knowledge into codified knowledge to transmit it elsewhere within the firm. This externalization complements local knowledge but does not replace it. User–producer interaction is a key mechanism for obtaining, understanding and incorporating outside knowledge and technologies. In addition, it is essential that the recipient have sufficient absorptive capacity for knowledge transfer to occur, even between units within a firm. Technology transfer requires technical competence – absorptive capacity – in both the provider and the recipient. In most cases, such producer–user links are emphasized in modern concepts in the economic geography literature, such as 'regional innovation systems' (Cooke, 2002) and 'regional clusters' (Porter, 1998). We only briefly mention these well-known concepts here, as they are elaborated upon in other chapters of this book.

REGIONAL KNOWLEDGE AND COMPETITIVENESS

The interplay of knowledge, competence and learning processes of individual firms in a region-specific setting may result in a distinctive competence of a region. A place only begins to be competitive through the presence of localized, place-specific knowledge. It also requires the sharing of that knowledge among the regional actors and its comparison to benchmarks elsewhere. Regional competitiveness finally requires a process of continuous improvement based on the awareness of local and global competitors as well as complementary partners. A distinctive regional competence is likely to be based initially on advanced factors, including knowledge resources (represented by highly educated personnel and university research institutes) and infrastructure, which go beyond the neoclassical or basic factors of production: physical, capital and human resources (Porter,

1998). The spectrum of complementary assets, which encompasses a range of capabilities that support and sustain the development and enhancement of technology, also makes some places better in many ways for knowledge-based efforts. Some systems of interaction are better than others, whether for exchanging internal knowledge or accessing external knowledge. A region with such 'thick' or 'deep' competences can add to the competences of its individual firms (Lawson, 1999).

The region or territory has an internalness to it as well. In effect, the local culture of some regions operates as 'internal' and facilitates knowledge creation and widespread learning. Learned skills become partially embedded in habits, which grow into routines or customs – or conventions – and become a common part of a social culture (Storper, 1995). Institutions, in turn, are durable and integrated complexes of routines and customs. Thus habits, conventions and routines preserve knowledge, particularly tacit knowledge in relation to skills, and institutions act as a transmission belt. The tacit nature of new or innovative knowledge and the localness of much tacit knowledge make knowledge difficult to tap from a distance or to transfer to other places. The 'stickiness' of regional knowledge is a result not only of learning (organizational as well as collective) and its support systems, discussed above. Stickiness also is a result of trust and mutual understanding, which reinforce local interfirm cooperation that is embedded in the business culture of an area, making it even more difficult for outsiders to imitate. The development of specialized skill depends on accumulated experience and a variety of experience found in a local area, but that variety can only be encompassed within a network of connections. The collective nature of a territory can be seen in the presence of its collective entrepreneurs: not only firms, but also interfirm associations, worker organizations, financial institutions and governmental agencies. They represent the social capital that firms are able to build and draw upon through their ties within the regional institutional environment. In addition, vertical links to other regions and the presence of gatekeepers are significant (Flora et al., 1997). Flows and linkages to the outside need to be balanced: to include not only flows (such as exports) out but also receptivity to new ideas coming from other places. External connections do not 'just happen'; they rely on intermediaries, especially wholesalers, who buy and sell outside the region, bringing new information and competing products back to the region. Other key individuals in wholesaling, producer services and financial services act as bridges that cross industry lines.

Some places are able to create, attract and keep economic activity – to maintain their competitiveness in a world of increasingly global competition. They do so because people in those places 'make connections' with other places, retaining close network links with other local systems and with global knowledge (Amin and Thrift, 1992; Becattini and Rullani, 1996). Such an innovative milieu is the seat of permanent processes of adjustments and transformations to external changes, such as competition and technological discontinuities. These adjustments can occur when interaction and cooperation are the social norm, and where learning and innovation are able to respond to and incorporate new knowledge. These are externalities of proximity, variety and accessibility that are usually found in larger cities (Maillat, 1998). In order to be competitive, firms need a web of interactions and information flows within and into the region, including high-tech knowledge that is translated to make it applicable to the industry. A focus on learning removes the artificial distinction that has been placed in the literature between high-tech and low-tech sectors and between innovative and non-innovative firms (Maskell, 1999). R&D by firms still is important, however, because it represents an 'active' outlook, an absorptive capacity, a level of technological progressiveness and an 'open mind', reaching out for – and being receptive to – new information. Technically progressive firms take part in information exchange, they continually search for information, and they maintain internal communication. Small firms (SMEs) have great difficulty in being progressive, but we must not think of small firms as homogeneous. SMEs vary greatly in their information-seeking and learning behavior.

By way of example, think of the associational model as found in Baden-Württemberg and Emilia-Romagna. The competitiveness of these regions can be related largely to the existence of effective network associations at the regional level. Besides the examples of Baden-Württemberg and Emilia-Romagna, some other regions also stand out for their thick regional competence. Known as an 'innovative milieu', the Swiss Jura d'Arc region is an example of this. Milieux such as the Jura d'Arc have been the subject of a series of studies both by GREMI (Groupe de Recherche Européen sur les Milieux Innovateurs) and others (Bramanti and Ratti, 1997). Learning is identified as only one of a group of conditions that remain through structural changes. The others are the interlinked industrial production system, governance structures and 'support space' relationships between enterprises and local institutions. These are seen as crucial to the creation of a proper mix of, on the one hand, connections internal to the milieu and its internal synergy and, on the other hand, external networks and openness to outside knowledge (Bramanti and Ratti, 1997). An innovative milieu combines learning (from both local and non-local sources of knowledge) and interaction, or cooperation with respect to innovation (Maillat, 1998). Likewise, Pinch and Henry's (1999) account of Britain's Motor Sport Valley includes close connections between the region's aerospace and automotive industries. Such an environment, which may not be restricted to innovative milieux, promotes entrepreneurship and innovations and the development of dynamic learning externalities and technological spillover. In other words, firms become – and remain – competitive by conceiving and implementing strategies that utilize – directly or indirectly – the valuable traits of their location. These traits enable those firms to earn a profit despite being otherwise similar competitors located in other places (Cooke, 2002; Maskell, 1999).

THE IMPORTANCE OF NON-LOCAL LINKS

Regional competitiveness, however, cannot be built solely on local know-ledge and competences. Typically, successful regions show how important it is to have links with the non-local, outside world as well (see Table 7.3). Silicon Valley and Cambridge are examples of regions with such global–local connections (Amin and Thrift, 1992). High-tech and R&D activities can be a linking pin between the local and the non-local. After all, state-of-the-art research activities ask for an 'active' outlook, an absorptive capacity, a level of technological progressiveness and an 'open mind', reaching out for – and being receptive to – new information. Technically progressive firms take part in information exchange; they continually search for information, often at a global level. In developing global–local links, connections to other regions and the presence of gatekeepers can be significant as well (Flora et al., 1997). Flows and linkages to the outside need to be balanced, to include not only flows (such as exports) out but also receptivity to new ideas coming from other places. External connections do not 'just happen'; they rely on intermediaries, especially wholesalers, who buy and sell local products outside the region, bringing new information and competing products back to the region. Other key individuals in whole-saling, producer services and financial services act as bridges that cross industry lines, serving as community entrepreneurs. In this way, some places are able to create, attract, and keep economic activity, and thus to

Table 7.3   Result of interaction between firm personality and regional characteristics for firm performance

	Introverted firm	Extroverted firm
Sparse regional environment	Few local or non-local links	Firms make many non-local links
Innovative milieu	Many local links	Both local and non-local links are numerous

maintain their competitiveness in a world of increasingly global competition. People in those places are able to 'make connections' with other
places, retaining close network links with other local systems and with
global knowledge (Amin and Thrift, 1992). However, the identification of
these local and non-local links is no easy task. This task is commonly by-
passed in favor of the easier filtering of input–output relationships. Porter
(1998), for example, stresses that clusters cannot be identified in this way.
What is needed is a meticulous identification of links and relationships that
are critical to an industry and its technologies. These links and relationships
are the intangible essence of the competitive firm and the competitive
region. Some of these links and networks are within the local agglomeration, while others exhibit awareness of, and close ties to, centers of excellence in other places in the world. Where does this take us beyond '(neo)
Marshallian nodes in global networks'? In that work, Amin and Thrift
(1992) stressed the local: that local places need a critical mass of know-how,
skills and finance, a 'thick' institutional infrastructure and entrepreneurial
traditions.

There are several examples of regions whose competitiveness is due to
well-developed global–local connections (Maskell, 1999; Hospers, 2005).
Table 7.1 lists a few 'success stories' from Europe (see Hospers, 2004 and
2005 for more illustrations). As the table shows, in some places traditional
industrial crafts have been rejuvenated by fostering the introduction of high
technology in design, production and marketing on a global scale. With
such a 'glocal' (the global combined with the local) strategy 'new combinations' have been realized in Swiss watch making (Swatch!), Italian textiles
and Danish furniture. Other cases show how the expertise of a declining
sector may be exploited for emerging global trends. The pop music and art
cluster in Manchester (UK) and the multimedia cluster in Baden-
Württemberg (Germany) can be traced back to the prior existence of
industries whose know-how on advanced materials proved to be useful for
the new businesses. Other areas have taken advantage of the rising trend in
demand for consumer services. In North Pas-de-Calais (France) several
textile factories have been transformed into mail order firms specialized
in clothing, while in the Ruhr Area (Germany) former mines and steel
factories are used for tourist-related purposes ('industrial culture').
Relevant examples of such 'global trends through local tradition' in Central
and Eastern Europe are modern health resorts around Hungarian spas
and high-tech restoration services in the Polish construction cluster. In an
attempt to explain the strong performance of these global–local interfaces,
two points stand out. In the first place, the examples suggest that successful
global–local connections almost always have their basis in present
economic structure. The centuries-old tradition of watch making in

Switzerland, coal and steel in the Ruhr Area and spas in Hungary, to high-light just a few examples, have laid the foundations for modern clusters in these areas. Apparently, where areas are headed still depends on where they are coming from (Cooke and Morgan, 1998). Even if it may be a trivial statement, the economic perspectives of an area cannot but be somehow connected to its past. Thus these examples are not 'best practices' but rather 'unique practices', demonstrating only that it is always an area's uniqueness that counts for regional competitiveness. In the second place, unlike an approach of 'backing losers', building on the past only makes sense when a cluster's traditions are connected to global trends. In fact, successful clusters are always 'new combinations' of local traditions and global trends (Cooke, 2002; Porter, 1998). As the table shows, such global–local interfaces with opportunities for growth may come from joining existing economic activities in an area, upgrading traditional industries for the new economy or making use of old industrial knowledge for novel purposes, as dictated by economy-wide, structural developments on a global scale.

Let us take a look at the government role in raising the competitiveness of the regions reviewed in Table 7.4 (Hospers, 2005). In some areas public authorities have been largely absent in the process of linking regional knowledge to global trends. This was the case in Manchester, North Pas-de-Calais, Dunakanyar and the Krakow Region. To be sure, the governments of these regions brand their areas now for tourist-related and business purposes by highlighting their strong regional clusters – but only after the clusters emerged spontaneously. In Emilia-Romagna, Baden-Württemberg and Jutland, governments have enabled the creation of business support and technology transfer centers providing 'real services' (e.g. technological advice and networking events) to the clusters. Governments did not interfere in the cluster, but only offered information and contacts at the request of the business community. In other places governments have entered the scene predominantly in the marketing of the cluster. In the Jura d'Arc, Baden-Württemberg and the Ruhr Area, it was the local business community that decided to join forces and develop clusters in the field of watch making (Swatch), industrial culture and multimedia technology. When the resulting clusters turned out to be a success, governments joined in and took care of the marketing (branding) of the clustering in the outside world. Thus the regions have been promoted as 'places to be' for parties (investors, tourists) interested in the activities of the clusters. In general, 'public marketing' can help to attract the attention of new investors or clients contributing to the continuation of unique regional competences. The motto 'be good and let it be known' also applies to regions. Again, these global–local interfaces in a regional setting should be viewed as nothing more than sources of inspiration. They demonstrate that

Table 7.4   Examples of regions combining global trends and local traditions

European region	Local tradition	Global trend	New combination
Jura d'Arc	Watch making	Marketing and lifestyle	Swatch watches
Emilia-Romagna	Textiles industry	High-tech production	Trendy fashion
Baden-Württemberg	Machine tools	Growing digitalization	Multimedia devices
Jutland	Furniture	Quality and lifestyle	Design furniture
Manchester	Heavy industries	Pop music/ pop art	Cultural industries
North Pas-de-Calais	Clothing sector	Need for convenience	Mail order services
Ruhr Area	Heavy industries	Experience economy	Industrial culture
Dunakanyar	Bathing culture	Ageing and wellness	Health resorts
Krakow Region	Building and painting	Need for maintenance	Restoration services

Source: Hospers (2004, 2005).

an approach aimed at regional uniqueness rather than regional ubiquities is the most feasible way to proceed.

CONCLUSION AND DISCUSSION

Knowledge has become a central concept for those concerned with regional economic development. This chapter has traced the role of knowledge to the competence of firms, learning processes and, finally, local and non-local networks of knowledge exchange. Going well beyond the concern for the high technology of the 1970s and for the flexibility of the 1980s, knowledge, competence and learning have become means to understanding regional competitiveness. Local knowledge, rooted in the regional culture and its intrinsically human characteristics, is fundamental to understanding the spatial concentration of economic activity and the ability of places to develop competitiveness – especially regions that are able to connect this local knowledge with global networks and trends face a favorable economic future.

It is evident, however, that these conditions for learning do not exist – and probably cannot be created – in all places. Moreover, there is more needed than knowledge alone: the growing consensus on competitiveness seems to demand advanced infrastructure, government and institutions that not only accept but embrace change and disequilibrium. Such a culture is relatively new outside private companies, and is resisted by most bureaucrats and politicians. Conditions for learning can develop where knowledge takes center stage in the culture and, consequently, in policies and in the actions of the region's firms and institutions. The challenge for all regions in our competitive times is to incorporate this change-oriented and knowledge-based culture in their strategies.

ACKNOWLEDGEMENT

This chapter draws on Malecki (2000b) but was substantially rewritten for this volume by Gert-Jan Hospers.

NOTE

1. Note that we focus here on the link between human creativity and places in general and not on the 'creative class' (knowledge workers in creative professions like arts, design and science) and their location preferences as stressed in Florida's recent work on cities (Florida, 2002).

REFERENCES

Almeida, P. and Kogut, B. (1999), 'Localization of knowledge and the mobility of engineers in regional networks', *Management Science*, **45**, 905–17.

Amin, A. and Cohendet, P. (2004), *Architectures of Knowledge*, Oxford: Oxford University Press.

Amin, A. and Graham, S. (1997), 'The ordinary city', *Transactions of the Institute of British Geographers*, **22**, 411–29.

Amin, A. and Thrift, N. (1992), 'Neo-Marshallian nodes in global networks', *International Journal of Urban and Regional Research*, **16**, 571–87.

Andersson, A.E. (1985), 'Creativity and regional development', *Papers of the Regional Science Association*, **56**, 5–20.

Becattini, G. and Rullani, E. (1996), 'Local systems and global connections: the role of knowledge', in F. Cossentino, F. Pyke and W. Sengenberger (eds), *Local and Regional Response to Global Pressure: The Case of Italy and Its Industrial Districts*, Geneva: ILO, pp. 159–74.

Bramanti, A. and Ratti, R. (1997), 'The multi-faced dimensions of local development', in R. Ratti, A. Bramanti and R. Gordon (eds), *The Dynamics of Innovative Regions: The GREMI Approach*, Aldershot: Ashgate, pp. 3–44.

Carlsson, B. and Eliasson, G. (1994), 'The nature and importance of economic competence', *Industrial and Corporate Change*, **3**, 697–711.

Cohen, W.M. and Levinthal, D.A. (1990), 'Absorptive capacity: a new perspective on learning and innovation', *Administrative Science Quarterly*, **35**, 128–52.

Cooke, P. (2002), *Knowledge Economies: Clusters, Learning and Cooperative Advantage*, London: Routledge.

Cooke, P. and Morgan, K. (1998), *The Associational Economy: Firms, Regions, and Innovation*, Oxford: Oxford University Press.

Davenport, T.H. (1997), *Information Ecology: Mastering the Information and Knowledge Environment*, Oxford: Oxford University Press.

Davenport, T.O. (1999), *Human Capital: What It Is and Why People Invest In It*, San Francisco, CA: Jossey Bass.

Flora, J.L., Sharp, J., Flora, C.B. and Newlon, C. (1997), 'Entrepreneurial social infrastructure and locally initiated economic development in the nonmetropolitan United States', *Sociological Quarterly*, **38**, 623–45.

Florida, R. (2002), *The Rise of the Creative Class: And How It's Transforming Work, Leisure, Community and Everyday Life*, New York: Basic Books.

Gertler, M.S. (1995), '"Being there": proximity, organization, and culture in the development and adoption of advanced manufacturing technologies', *Economic Geography*, **71**, 1–26.

Hospers, G.J. (2005), '"Best practices" and the dilemma of regional cluster policy', *Tijdschrift voor Economische en Sociale Geografie*, **96** (4), 336–41.

Howitt, P. (1997), 'On some problems in measuring knowledge-based growth', in P. Howitt (ed.), *The Implications of Knowledge-Based Growth for Micro-Economic Policies*, Calgary: The University of Calgary Press, pp. 9–29.

Huseman, R.C. and Goodman, J.P. (1999), *Leading with Knowledge*, Thousand Oaks, CA: Sage.

Knudsen, C. (1996), 'The competence perspective: a historical view', in N.J. Foss and C. Knudsen (eds), *Towards a Competence Theory of the Firm*, London: Routledge, pp. 13–37.

Lawson, C. (1999), 'Towards a competence theory of the region', *Cambridge Journal of Economics*, **23**, 151–66.

Maillat, D. (1998), 'Interactions between urban systems and localized productive systems: an approach to endogenous regional development in terms of innovative milieu', *European Planning Studies*, **6**, 117–29.

Malecki, E.J. (1997), *Technology and Economic Development*, 2nd edn, London: Addison Wesley Longman.

Malecki, E.J. (2000a), 'Network models for technology-based growth', in Z. Acs (ed.), *Regional Innovation, Knowledge and Global Change*, London: Pinter, pp. 187–204.

Malecki, E.J. (2000b), 'Knowledge and regional competitiveness', *Erdkunde*, **54**, 334–51.

Maskell, P. (1999), 'Globalisation and industrial competitiveness: the process and consequences of ubiquitification', in E.J. Malecki and P. Oinas (eds), *Making Connections: Technological Learning and Regional Economic Change*, Aldershot: Ashgate, pp. 35–59.

Micklethwait, J. (1997), 'Future perfect? A survey of Silicon Valley', *The Economist*, 29 March.

Nelson, R.R. and Winter, S.G. (1982), *An Evolutionary Theory of Economic Change*, Cambridge, MA: Belknap Press.

Nonaka, I. and Konno, N. (1998), 'The concept of "ba": building a foundation for knowledge creation', *California Management Review*, **40**, 40–54.

OECD (1995), *Industry and Technology: Scoreboard of Indicators 1995*, Paris: Organisation for Economic Co-operation and Development.

Pinch, S. and Henry, N. (1999), 'Discursive aspects of technological innovation: the case of the British motor-sport industry', *Environment and Planning A*, **31**, 665–82.

Porter, M.E. (1998), 'Clusters and competition: new agendas for companies, governments, and institutions', in M.E. Porter, *On Competition*, Boston, MA: Harvard Business School Press, pp. 197–287.

Rallet, A. and Torre, A. (1998), 'On geography and technology: proximity relations in localized innovation networks', in M. Steiner (ed.), *Clusters and Regional Specialisation: On Geography, Technology and Networks*, London: Pion, pp. 41–56.

Saxenian, A. (1994), *Regional Advantage: Culture and Competition in Silicon Valley and Route 128*, Cambridge, MA: Harvard University Press.

Storper, M. (1995), 'The resurgence of regional economies, ten years later: the region as a nexus of untraded interdependencies', *European Urban and Regional Studies*, **2**, 191–221.

Teece, D.J. (1998), 'Capturing value from knowledge assets: the new economy, markets for knowhow, and intangible assets', *California Management Review*, **40**, 55–79.

von Ginlow, M.A. (1988), *The New Professionals: Managing Today's High-Tech Employees*, Cambridge, MA: Ballinger Publishing Co.

von Hippel, E. (1998), 'Economics of product development by users: the impact of "sticky" local information', *Management Science*, **44**, 629–44.

Zook, M.A. (2004), 'The knowledge brokers: venture capitalists, tacit knowledge and regional development', *International Journal of Urban and Regional Research*, **28**, 621–41.

8. Regional innovation networks

Leon Oerlemans, Marius Meeus and Patrick Kenis

INTRODUCTION

Over the last 20 years, several new theoretical approaches have been developed to understand the determinants of successful regional development and policy in an economic environment that has become increasingly competitive and global. As argued by Mouleart and Sekia (2003), this search for a 'new' model of regional development was partially a result of the ambiguous results of regional policies implemented in the period after the Second World War. The larger part of regional policies in this period encompassed relative price incentive structures aimed at attracting employment to traditional manufacturing regions, building new infrastructures and the encouragement of production investments in lagging regions. Although these measures stimulated job creation in local firms and attracted external direct investments to these regions, these policies often suffered from a lack of structural embeddedness within regions.

From the early 1980s onwards, several scholars (Lundvall and Borras, 1999; Asheim, 1999) observed a qualitative and structural change in the development of capitalist economies, that is, a transition from Fordism to post-Fordism leading to a so-called learning economy. Combined with an ongoing globalization, innovation and learning are regarded as core processes for maintaining and improving organizational competitiveness. Moreover, in this different context the nature of the innovation process has changed considerably. The linear model of innovation, in which innovation activities are sequentially conducted in the absence of feedback loops, is succeeded by the view that innovation is an interactive, cumulative and path-dependent process, following specific technological trajectories (Tödtling, 1999).

Starting in the early 1980s, the outlined regional policy and structural developments resulted in a growing attention to theoretical perspectives and policy strategies that stimulated the innovative capabilities of regions. A regional endogenous development approach emerged in which elements such as human capital, regional institutions, infrastructure, educational and regulatory institutes, quality of production factors and systems, innovation and learning were the main ingredients (Moulaert and Sekia, 2003). These elements were cemented together by regional (innovation) networks in which regional actors were linked by informal and formal social, economic and political relationships.

In this chapter, the focus will be on these regional (innovation) networks. Two related questions will be answered. First, why would firms organize parts of their activities in (innovation) networks and, second, why should these innovation networks be regional? To answer the first question, insights derived mainly from organization science will be used. To answer the second question, a brief overview of the literature on territorial innovation models will be presented. The main aim of this overview is to analyse and evaluate the ways in which the proximity–network relationship is conceptualized in these models. These insights will be used to propose some alternative theoretical and empirical directions that will enable researchers to study the importance of proximity in a more fine-grained way.

At the end of this section, it is important to note that, in the literature, innovation can have at least two meanings. On the one hand, innovation is defined as an outcome, indicated by the number of patents an organization has filed or the number of new product announcements it has made. On the other hand, innovation is conceptualized as a process pointing to the generation and introduction into the market (economic or social) of new or improved processes, products and services. Where possible, we will indicate which definition of innovation is applicable to avoid confusion and misinterpretation of the literature discussed in this chapter.

WHY PARTICIPATE IN INNOVATION NETWORKS?

Fortunately, there exists a large body of earlier research on networks specifying what motivates organizations to cluster in networks (see, e.g., Oliver, 1990; Alter and Hage, 1993; Ebers and Jarillo, 1998). Research has found several important causes for networking between for-profit business organizations, such as technology development, increased (market) power, market development, uncertainty reduction and cost savings, among others. In her seminal paper, Oliver (1990) provided a general set of reasons for inter-organizational network and relationship formation:

- *Necessity*: linkages are established to meet necessary legal or regulatory requirements or to supplement internal resource deficits.

- *Asymmetry*: ties are formed in order to exercise power or control over other organizations or their resources.
- *Reciprocity*: tie formation is motivated by reciprocity; that is, the willingness to cooperate, collaborate and coordinate for the purpose of pursuing mutual beneficial goals or interests.
- *Efficiency*: organizations link with other organizations to improve their internal input–output ratios. For instance, by networking, organizations want to increase return on assets, and reduce unit or transaction costs.
- *Stability*: many organizations are confronted with environmental uncertainty. As an adaptive response to this uncertainty, organizations establish relationships to achieve stable and predictable resource flows and exchanges.
- *Legitimacy*: by linking to other, specific organizations, an organization can improve its reputation or image, or show congruence with dominant norms in its institutional environment.

When dealing with technological innovation processes and networks, two groups of motives can be distinguished (Pyka, 2002). A first group can be labelled incentive-based approaches to networking; it comprises motives such as cost sharing, putting in place pre-emption strategies or reducing time to market. This group of motives uses a marginalist perspective by comparing the marginal costs and benefits of different organizational modes and has found a powerful application in transaction cost economic theory.

A second group of motives reflects so-called knowledge-based approaches. Important motives in this group are the exploration of new markets and market niches, technology transfer, profiting from technological complementarities, and monitoring technological developments and opportunities. The view on the innovation process changes from an optimal cost–benefit analysis to a collective, experimental and problem-solving process. Knowledge in general, and new technological knowledge in particular, is no longer considered freely available, but as specific, tacit, and complex. To understand and utilize this knowledge, firms have to develop specific competences, absorptive capacity and receiver competence, the development of which takes time. Moreover, due to the increased complexity of modern innovation processes, firms have to master multiple knowledge fields, which is a difficult task. Therefore, the probability that firms are successful in these complex technological environments with strategies that focus on their own R&D effort only, has lowered considerably. Innovation networks are viewed as flexible organizational devices to overcome these difficulties (Teece, 1986: 416).

In sum, networks perform three important general functions for innovation (Osborn and Hagedoorn, 1997; Kraatz, 1998; Pyka, 2002). First, they are a coordinating device enabling and facilitating interfirm learning and the diffusion of new technological know-how. Second, they facilitate exploitation of and access to technological complementary assets. Third, they provide an organizational platform to combine different technological competences, which is an important feature since mastering technological complexity and multiple knowledge fields are important necessities in modern innovation processes.

The literature distinguishes two approaches in which networks perform these functions: a structural and a relational account (Borgatti and Foster, 2003). The structural account focuses on the impact of structural or topological (e.g. centrality, density or betweenness) aspects of (whole) network structures on knowledge flows and innovation outcomes. However, a debate has arisen about the form of network structure that is (most) beneficial for innovation outcomes. One view advocates that densely embedded networks with many interconnections between actors are advantageous (Coleman, 1988). In such 'closed networks', the extensive relations between partners foster the development of trust, shared norms of behaviour and inter-organizational, knowledge-sharing routines. Moreover, dense networks stimulate relation-specific investments that help to utilize the yields of collaboration and facilitate fine-grained transfer of information and joint problem solving. Further, dense networks are also helpful in minimizing opportunistic behaviour because information about an actor's opportunistic actions diffuses quickly to other actors in the network, resulting in a loss of reputation.

According to an alternative view within the structural account (Burt, 1992), advantages arise from brokerage opportunities created by so-called open networks. Open networks contain many structural holes. Structural holes are gaps in information flows between actors linked to the same actor (the broker), but not linked to each other. As a result, actors on either side of the structural hole have access to different flows of knowledge and information. Therefore, innovating actors can benefit from open networks since they produce low levels of redundant information and knowledge. This diversity and variety is beneficial for innovation outcomes because innovation is regarded as combining new knowledge and information or recombining existing knowledge and information in new ways. Since innovation depends on the level of newness of knowledge and information, open networks are usable devices.

Mainstream network research focuses heavily on the structural features of networks, paying less attention to *relational* characteristics. However, little is known about the ways in which different types of network relationships condition information flows and learning in networks (Borgatti and Cross, 2003). Here, the relational account could be helpful. Several network researchers have investigated the role of strong and weak ties in the acquisition of new information. Granovetter (1973) argued that weak ties are more likely than strong ties to be bridges to different, low interconnected parts of a network and, therefore, new information. Subsequent research on the importance of weak ties has revealed that this type of relationship can be helpful to finding a job (Lin, 1988), individual advancement (Burt, 2000) and the diffusion of ideas (Rogers, 1995). More recently, however, the role of strong ties has been emphasized more often. Jack et al. (2004), for example, pointed to the importance of strong ties in entrepreneurial networks for the performance of the enterprise, whereas Hansen (1999) argued that strong ties promote the transfer of complex knowledge, while weak ties facilitate the transfer of simple knowledge and information. Recently, Nooteboom and Gilsing (2006) argued that in networks for exploration (i.e. for more radical innovation) higher levels of density and stronger ties are more beneficial to innovators, since both facilitate competence (for the transfer of tacit knowledge) and governance (for the management of risk and opportunism).

However, this literature does not answer the question as to which precise mechanisms are at work when actors search for external information in order to learn and innovate. Recently, Borgatti and Cross (2003) proposed an argument that takes relational aspects into account. In their view, the process of information seeking – who seeks whom for information and knowledge – is dependent on what they label as 'learned relational characteristics'. They argue that an intentional search for information and knowledge in an organizational setting can be viewed as a dynamic choice process. The decision to seek informational resources from other specific actors, in their view, depends on the characteristics of the relationship between the knowledge seeker and a set of other actors that serve as information sources. In turn, interactions between these actors update the seeker's perception of other actors with respect to these features. More specifically, they propose that knowledge and information seeking is a function of (1) the extent to which an actor knows and values the expertise of another actor, (2) the accessibility of this actor and (3) the potential costs incurred in seeking information from this actor (Borgatti and Cross, 2003: 434). As far as 'knowledge about the other' is concerned, they draw on work in transactive memory and distributed knowledge, in which a baseline condition for approaching a given actor for information is the awareness of that actor as a possible source in light of a current problem or opportunity. Moreover, it is also important that a knowledge seeker positively evaluates the knowledge and skills embodied in the other actor. Although an actor positively evaluates the expertise of another actor, their knowledge is valuable only if they are accessible. Actors' accessibility can be viewed as a function of timeliness, engagement, information-processing capabilities, culture, and power distance. Therefore, the decision to seek information from a given actor depends on an actor's perception of the accessibility of other actors. Lastly, information seeking is not without cost. These costs concern interpersonal risks and obligations (e.g. norms of reciprocity), for example. On the basis of their empirical research, Borgatti and Cross found that knowledge, value and access predict information-seeking behaviour in networks, whereas cost does not. Therefore, this study shows that so-called learned relational characteristics facilitate information-seeking behaviour.

In this section, the question 'why do organizations participate in innovation networks?' was answered by (1) looking at the motives organizations can have to do so, (2) discussing the functions networks have for innovating and learning organizations and (3) studying the determinants of knowledge and information-seeking behaviour in networks. As far as the first point is concerned, it was found that two groups of motives for technological collaboration could be discerned. On the one hand, so-called incentive-based motives, such as cost sharing or reducing time to market and, on the other hand, knowledge-based motives such as technology transfer or monitoring external technological developments. The functions of networks (the second point) for innovation are threefold. Networks function as a coordinating device facilitating learning; they help to exploit and provide access to technological complementary assets; and networks serve as platforms for technological combination. The behaviour of actors seeking knowledge and information (the third point) turned out to be determined by the knowledge about other actors in the network, the accessibility of the actors, and search costs.

At this point in our discussion, it is important to note that a vast majority of studies dealing with networks, inter-organizational relationships and innovation in the field of organization studies take a structural approach to the issue. However, since innovation is highly dependent on flows of knowledge and information between actors, one could argue that the structural approach is missing the point. In other words, by mainly focusing at the topological features of networks and relating these to innovation outcomes, interactions and flows between actors are only assumed (in a later section, we will see that the knowledge spillover literature in economics has the same problem), but not measured. This does not mean that we would like to downplay the merits of the structural account of networks, but we argue for an approach balancing the two accounts.

Up to now the spatial dimension of innovation in networks has not been discussed. This issue will be addressed in the next section.

WHY DO ORGANIZATIONS PARTICIPATE IN REGIONAL INNOVATION NETWORKS?

The question raised in the title of this section is basically a specification of the first research question. To answer this question, two bodies of literature have to be discussed. On the one hand, there is the 'geography of innovation' literature (e.g. Feldman, Audretsch) that tries to answer the question to what extent and why unintended knowledge flows (knowledge spillovers) are geographically bounded. This literature is strongly rooted in the economics of technology and innovation, and mainly takes an empirical approach to the issue. On the other hand, there is a group of approaches that we label 'spatial interaction' literature. Examples of this group are the innovative milieu approach (Maillat), the new industrial spaces approach (Storper), or the industrial district approach (Becattini). In contrast to knowledge spillover literature, which *assumes* interaction between actors in geographical space, these approaches study *actual interaction between spatially concentrated actors*, often organized in localized networks of inter-organizational relationships.

Knowledge Spillovers

The last two decades have witnessed the growth of (mainly empirical) literature on the 'geography of innovation' that tries to evaluate whether knowledge spillovers exist and are geographically bounded. The starting point of these studies is the observation that innovative activities are strongly concentrated in geographic space and that firms located in certain areas are systematically more productive than firms located in other geographical regions. Due to the assumed non-rival nature of knowledge, spillovers are conceptualized as externalities. Put differently, a small group of actors investing in research or technology development will end up facilitating the innovation efforts of other organizations, thus stimulating (regional) economic growth. In this literature, it is proposed that information about novelties and innovation flows more easily among actors located within the same spatial area. Social bonds that foster reciprocal trust and frequent face-to-face communication are assumed to facilitate these flows. More specifically, this line of reasoning can be broken down into a three-step logical chain (Breschi and Lissoni, 2001: 980):

- knowledge produced by innovative firms and universities is transferred to other organizations;
- knowledge that spills over is a collective good, which is freely available to those who want to invest in searching for it (non-excludability),

and can be utilized by other organizations at the same time (non-rivalry);

- despite the above, knowledge that flows is mainly 'tacit' in nature, which means that it is highly contextual and difficult to codify, and is thus more easily transferred by face-to-face communication and personal relationships that require spatial proximity. This implies that knowledge is a public good, but a local one.

Therefore, from the point of view of the spillover literature, it is beneficial for innovating firms to be located in regions in which networks exist with high flows or stocks of both private and public R&D and academic research. As a result of leakages in these networks, these organizations are more likely to be innovative, compared to firms located in regions characterized by less resourceful networks. The reason that spatial distance matters for these knowledge spillover networks is found in the distinction between 'tacit' knowledge and information, the latter often being labelled 'codified' knowledge. As Audretsch (1998: 23) argues, 'the propensity for innovative activity to cluster spatially will be the greatest in industries where tacit knowledge plays an important role, . . . [I]t is tacit knowledge, as opposed to information, which can only be transmitted informally and typically demands direct and repeated contacts.' This quotation illustrates that the localized knowledge spillover literature combines the tacit/codified dichotomy with the use of a knowledge production function in which R&D and other innovative inputs are related to innovation output. As a consequence, local (i.e. outside the innovating organization, but within its geographical region) and distant external innovation inputs (inputs located outside the organization and outside its region of location) are distinguished. Statistically significant differences between the model parameters of the two kinds of R&D are then interpreted as evidence of the existence and the localization of knowledge spillovers. The approaches developed in the R&D spillover literature encountered severe criticism (see the Breschi and Lissoni, 2001 paper for an extensive overview). Here, we list the most important points. First, administrative boundaries are very poor proxies for the geographical levels at which different knowledge flows operate. Second, the assumption that within these geographical units common cultural backgrounds exist promoting the development of trust and the reduction of transaction costs does not hold, since no empirical evidence for it is provided. Third, the measures used to indicate innovation outcomes, such as patent counts or innovation counts, have severe flaws (e.g. firms in some sectors have a lower propensity to patent and prefer a secrecy strategy), often leading to an underestimation of regional innovative activity or a bias towards large innovating firms, underestimating the innovative performance of small firms. Fourth, this literature neglects the fact that knowledge is not only tacit, but also highly specific, which implies that a specific vocabulary is needed to communicate and transfer knowledge. As a consequence, spatial proximity might be less important and organizational proximity (e.g. epistemic communities) might be more important for the innovation process. Fifth and lastly, the R&D spillover literature basically does not study the ways in which knowledge is transferred among actors located in the same geographic unit, a characteristic they share with the structuralistic approach in network studies.

Spatial Interaction Literature

During the 1980s, the discussion in the spatial sciences about the relationship between innovation and proximity was strongly influenced by insights from other scientific disciplines, such as the theory of industrial organization, sociology, and the (economic) network approach. The introduction of concepts such as 'transaction costs', governance structures, embeddedness, clusters and networks are cases in point. In addition, the relationship between innovation, networks and spatial economic development is given a far more prominent place on the agenda. In this context, a number of alternative theoretical perspectives have emerged.

Before discussing these perspectives in greater depth, it should be noted that much of the research conducted within this area uses different theoretical and methodological models and techniques, compared to the R&D spillover literature, which uses macro- and meso-theoretical frameworks, formal models, econometric techniques and large data sets of a quantitative nature to arrive at their conclusions. Contrary to this, with notable exceptions, the spatial interaction literature uses less formalized, micro-theoretical models, case-study approaches in which qualitative data are analysed. As a result of this, the spatial interaction literature is less mainstream and generally accepted in the broader scientific community of the regional sciences.

Below, the main characteristics of these 'new' approaches will be discussed with a special focus on the role of regional or localized innovation networks. At the end of the section, the various dimensions of these views will be compared.

The Innovative Milieu

In order to develop better theoretical and empirical insight into the effects of technological innovation and the rise of high-tech industries for local and regional economic development, a group of European researchers united in GREMI has introduced the concept of the innovative milieu.

In this approach, the firm is not an isolated innovative actor, but placed in its spatial context. The central idea is to understand what external conditions contribute to the emergence of new firms or the adoption of innovations by existing enterprises. Innovative environments are seen as the breeding grounds of innovation and innovative enterprises. Access to technological know-how, the availability of local linkages and inputs, the proximity of markets, and the presence of qualified labour are seen as factors determining the innovativeness of an area. It is therefore not surprising that the central hypothesis of the innovative milieu approach is as follows: 'it is often the local environment which is, in effect, the entrepreneur or innovator, rather than the firm . . . ' (Aydalot and Keeble, 1988: 9). The approach distinguishes three functional spaces for the organization: the production; the market; and the support space. The last space is based on three types of relationships: (a) preferred relations as to the organization of production factors; (b) strategic relations between the organization, its partners, suppliers and clients; (c) strategic relations with actors that are part of the territorial environment. It is especially the support space that qualifies the nature of innovative milieu, because it facilitates the transfer of resources important to (innovating) organizations.

Although the above may have given the impression that the innovative capabilities of firms are exclusively determined by the environment in which the firms operates, several authors also take the *characteristics* of the innovating firm into account. The nature of the production, the strategy used, intensity of R&D, or the nature of the innovation process may be mentioned in this context (Aydalot and Keeble, 1988: 12–14; Maillat, 1991: 110–13; Saxenian, 1994: 7–9).

Networks and inter-organizational interaction in tandem with the idea of apprenticeship are the core elements of the innovative milieu approach. Networks are seen as strategic devices that help regional actors to monitor environmental developments and change, enabling them to adjust behaviours. Moreover, necessary resources flow to innovating firms through localized networks. The emphasis is on relational characteristics (trust, reciprocity), whereas structural features of networks are hardly studied.

'Industrial District'

The concept 'industrial district' originates from the English economist Marshall. In his book, *Principles of Economics* (1890), two types of 'economies' are distinguished: *internal economies*, i.e. the efficiency of the production organization of an individual enterprise; and *external economies*, which refer to the cost benefits resulting from the distribution of work among enterprises. The 'external economies', according to Marshall, can be achieved by the spatial concentration of small companies. Adding qualitative elements such as mutual trust among parties, 'atmosphere', and 'skills and knowledge', the most important component parts of an industrial district are put in place.

Hence industrial districts can be regarded as a special form of agglomeration. They are characterized by 'a local "thickening" of inter-industrial relationships, which is reasonably stable over time . . . ' (Becattini, 1989: 132). Small specialized and innovative firms operating on national and international competitive markets populate the districts. The inter-organizational relationships among enterprises in industrial districts are based on different kinds of social interaction among actors, such as cooperation, mutual dependence, and trust. These relations stimulate innovation, with ties of kinship among entrepreneurs often facilitating the spread of information. In short, the building blocks of the industrial district are the *social* links and networks among actors.

In the literature, a number of examples of successful 'districts' such as the 'Third Italy' (Benetton), Central Portugal (wooden and metal furniture) and the Japanese Sakari district are mentioned. However, Zeitlin (1992) concludes that these examples are the exception rather than the rule. Firms in these successful regions manage to apply 'best-practice' technology, which in addition to the socio-cultural circumstances in these regions are such that they foster innovation. Moreover, the emergence of this type of local production system in Emilia-Romagna, the heart of the 'Third Italy', is the result of very specific local developments originating in sixteenth-century silk production in this region (Malecki, 1991: 223). In other words, the district approach puts too strong an emphasis on the significance of successful small-scale, localized production systems in specific sectors that have developed under special historical circumstances. It very much remains to be seen whether such developments can automatically be predicted for other regions (see Hadjimichalis and Papamichos, 1991: 145–9).

In more than one sense, the industrial district approach is close to the innovative milieu line of thinking. Both stress the role of the local social–economic community, based on cooperative efforts and complementarities among functionally specialized firms. Both also put much emphasis on the relational aspects of networking. Reciprocity, trust, social and family bonds, along with knowledge and information exchange between actors, create a coordination system that outperforms other coordination mechanisms such as the market, creating a regional environment that facilitates and eases innovation. Structural network features such as centrality or density of networks are hardly taken into account.

New Industrial Spaces

During the 1980s, an approach was developed that was to exert a powerful influence on the spatial sciences: new industrial spaces (NIS). The core of the approach, which is strongly inspired by transaction costs theory, is formed by the assumed reciprocal relationship between vertical disintegration and the spatial organization of production (Scott and Storper, 1992: 8). On the one hand, there is the emergence of a disintegrated network economy causing agglomeration of economic activities in certain regions. On the other hand, these territorial production systems facilitate a further disintegration of production and a further distribution of labour.

As regards the relationship between (technological) innovation, networks and space, it is pointed out that technological innovation is often restricted to a particular area. Here, reference is made to two geographic dimensions of the innovation process. In highly innovative sectors, the knowledge bases are commonly embodied in specialized workers, who often show a strong spatial concentration and little geographical mobility. In addition, localized inter-organizational network relations in these sectors are channels through which knowledge is spread.

In the NIS framework, the relationship between innovation, network and proximity is established as follows. External economies of scale and scope are caused by production flexibility. Although there are various ways to achieve this flexibility, network production is considered to be of crucial importance. Through adaptation of inter-organizational relations, it is possible to introduce changes in the quality and the quantity of the output. More than elsewhere, spatially concentrated networks play an important role in innovation because the (tacit) knowledge necessary for innovation can be disseminated. Since in these relations there is often unstandardized and dynamic exchange causing higher transaction costs, the tendency of innovative production units towards localized networking is strong.

The NIS is criticized for its inadequate conception of the behaviour of economic actors (economic and technological determinism) and its neglect of the social dimensions of inter-organizational relations (strong focus on 'traded interdependencies'). These shortcomings, incidentally, have been recognized in more recent NIS publications. Storper (1995, 1997), for example, now makes a distinction between 'traded' and 'untraded interdependencies', the former being the input–output relations (localized or not) that together form a web of user–producer relations, which are extremely important for the exchange of information. The latter are, among other things, (regional) labour markets and conventions, norms and values and (semi-)public institutions that are connected with economic and organizational learning and coordination processes. In this line of argument, innovation and proximity are again related. As Storper (1995: 897) puts it: 'Where these input–output relations or untraded interdependencies are localized, and this is quite frequent in cases of technological or organizational dynamism, then we can say that the region is the key, necessary element in the "supply architecture" for learning and innovation.'

Initially, NIS takes a transaction costs theory approach to (regional) networks and innovation. Innovating firms can profit from these networks because they provide opportunities to reduce the spatially dependent costs of external transactions. Thus networks are viewed as devices to increase efficiency. Localization forces are further strengthened in cases where inter-organizational relationships encompass frequent transactions, just-in-time processing, idiosyncratic and variable forms of inter-organizational transacting, and small-scale linkages with high unit costs are present. Since innovation relationships often have these characteristics, regional innovation networks can serve as efficient governance mechanisms.

Regional Innovation Systems

The central idea behind the concept of (regional) innovation systems (RIS) is that the innovative performance of an (regional) economy does not exclusively depend on the individual innovative performance of organizations alone, but is dependent on interactions with other actors. Innovative firms function in a shared, institutional context. They are dependent on, contribute to, and make use of a joint knowledge infrastructure, which is a system that creates and distributes knowledge, uses this knowledge to achieve innovation, thus generating economic value (Gregersen and Johnson, 1997: 482). Therefore, the emphasis is on collective learning processes, which are facilitated by strong cooperative relationships between system members.

Within this approach, various systems emerge. Innovation systems are defined for particular sectors or specific technologies or on the basis of (geographical) proximity. Within the (geographical) innovation systems, the concept of 'interactive learning' is central. Learning is conceived as a process in which all kinds of knowledge are (re)combined. The interactivity of this learning refers to learning that is co-dependent on the communication between people or organizations that possess different knowledge bases.

As innovations are the result of cumulative learning processes (Lundvall, 1992: 8), the performance of territorial innovation systems depends on the relations between a diversity of sources of knowledge and proximity. To formulate it simply: 'A larger territorial space may contain more diversity, but this will not lead to innovation if there is not enough proximity to support communication . . . ' (Gregersen and Johnson, 1997: 482). Besides spatial proximity, other dimensions of proximity exist, such as, for example, economic, organizational, and cultural proximity (Lundvall, 1992; Boschma, 2005). The central idea is that interactive learning and innovation will be restrained if these distances become too great. Therefore, (geographical) proximity facilitates the innovation process.

Within the RIS framework, Lundvall (1992) developed an argument for the relation between innovation, networks and spatial proximity. Lundvall studied the relationship between the radicalness of technological change and spatial interaction. It is argued that the more radical the process of technological innovation, the less codified knowledge is. The more tacit the knowledge communicated, the more important spatial proximity between user and producer is. So a positive relationship between the level of tacitness of knowledge and the importance of spatial proximity is assumed.

In sum, in the RIS approach, innovative networks are the channels through which (new) knowledge is generated and transmitted. Moreover, network relationships are the stage on which interactive learning processes between actors in the system take place. Firms can profit from regional innovation networks because these types of networks enable the transfer of tacit knowledge. Tacit knowledge is difficult to imitate and, as a result, organizations in regional innovation networks can develop competitive advantages.

The Learning Region

The learning region approach can be viewed as an intermediate synthesis in the models on territorial innovation, since it combines several theoretical bodies of literature (Moulaert and Sekia, 2003). As Morgan (1997: 492) puts it, the purpose of the learning region approach is to 'connect the concepts of the network (or associational) paradigm – like interactive innovation and social capital – to the problems of regional development'. The approach takes the premise that knowledge is the most important resource in an economy, whereas learning is the most important process. Moreover, innovation is conceptualized as an interactive process and shaped by a variety of institutional routines and social conventions. As in the regional innovation systems approach, ties between actors in a regional innovation network facilitate the exchange of knowledge and the building of social capital. Basically, the learning region approach uses the reasoning of the new industrial spaces approach on localization; that is, where traded and untraded interdependencies are localized, the region is a key element in the 'supply architecture' of learning and innovation. Also in this approach, the transfer of tacit knowledge and spatial proximity are closely connected. As Morgan stated (1997: 495), 'tacit knowledge is collective in nature and, because it is wedded to its human and social context, it is more territorially-specific than is generally thought'.

After this discussion of different perspectives that are part of the spatial interaction literature, we can summarize them by highlighting those elements that are central to the understanding of the regional innovation networks (see Table 8.1). The following dimensions are taken into account:

- *The core of innovation.* Since innovation is the core of regional innovation networks, the question is asked how innovation is conceptualized (e.g. as an outcome or a process).
- *The role of institutions.* Institutions, such as rules and norms, enable and constrain organizational and social behaviour in general and innovative behaviour and interaction in networks in particular. Therefore, they are an important ingredient of innovation networks.
- *The type of relations and networks.* This refers to the organizational dimension of regional innovation networks. The question is asked how inter-organizational relations and networks are conceptualized. Are they a mode of social regulation or a coordination device?
- *The relation between innovation and proximity.* This and the next dimension describe the core of regional innovation networks. As far as this item is concerned, we look at how innovation and geographical space are related.
- *The proximity mechanism.* The last dimension is about how the interaction between innovation and geographical space is conceptualized.

Most of the above approaches, as in spillover literature, assume a negative elasticity as to the transfer of (technological) knowledge in space. The level of codification matters here since spatial proximity is important, especially if tacit knowledge has to be exchanged. Moreover, in contrast to regional spillover literature, it is intended interaction between economic actors that is functioning as the mechanism of knowledge transfer. Although the approaches are heterogeneous because of their variety of concepts and perspectives, the importance of interpersonal links, of a common institutional culture among workers, entrepreneurs and politicians, and of a positive attitude towards collaboration, all facilitated by spatial proximity, stimulate interactions between actors in general and the flow of knowledge and information in geographical space in particular. They all assume that firms that tap into tacit regional knowledge flows will acquire necessary resources more easily and will therefore able to perform better or be more competitive.

Recently, however, several scholars have challenged the received wisdom on the relation between tacitness and spatial proximity. Asheim (1999: 348)

Table 8.1 Views on regional innovation networks

Features	Theoretical approach				
	Innovative milieu	Industrial district	Regional innovation systems (RIS)	New industrial spaces (NIS)	Learning region
Core of innovation	Capacity of firms to innovate through relationships with agents of the same milieu	Capacity of actors to implement innovation in a system of common values	Innovation as an interactive, cumulative and specific process (path dependency)	Innovation is a result of R&D and its implementation; application of new production technologies	As for RIS, but stressing co-evaluation of technology and institutions
Role of institutions	Very important role of institutions in the research process	Institutions are 'agents', enabling social regulation, fostering innovation and development	Institutions lead to a regulation of behaviour, both inside and outside organizations	Social regulation for the coordination of interfirm transactions and the dynamics of entrepreneurial activity	As in RIS, with a stronger focus on the role of institutions
Type of relations/ networks	Role of support space: strategic relations between the firm, its partners, suppliers and clients	The network is a social regulation mode and a source of discipline. It enables both cooperation and competition	The network is an organizational mode of interactive and collective learning	Interfirm transactions	Networks of embedded actors

Table 8.1 (continued)

Features	Theoretical approach					
	Innovative milieu	Industrial district	Regional innovation systems (RIS)	New industrial spaces (NIS)	Learning region
Relation between innovation and proximity	Depending on the nature of innovations and technology strategies of actors, the environment is a supplier of resources or a supporting production system	Through social links and networks of actors, information, knowledge, standards, etc. are communicated and distributed	Institutions, proximity and diversity of resources stimulate or restrict interactive communication, learning, and innovation in regions	Localized knowledge (labour) is an immobile resource; exchange relations with other actors are resources for innovation	As in NIS
Proximity mechanism at work	Innovative milieux are an effect of capacities of certain regions to improve organization of collective learning processes and to realize lower information costs	Districts are a way in which a production organization can compete internationally (think global, act local). Proximity eases exchange of resources	Spatial proximity stimulates interactive learning and the transmission of tacit knowledge	Vertical disintegration and characteristics of transactions between organizations generate spatial concentration. Proximity facilitates the exchange of tacit knowledge	Proximity facilitates the exchange of tacit knowledge

Sources: Oerlemans et al. (2000); Moulaert and Sekia (2003).

argues that 'localised learning is not only based on tacit knowledge, as we argue that contextual knowledge also is constituted by "sticky", codified knowledge'. This latter type of so-called disembodied knowledge is based on individual skills and experience, a collective technical culture and a well-developed institutional framework, which are all highly spatially immobile.

Torre and Gilly (2000) state that there is a frequent combination of tacit and codified within firms and networks. Lundvall and Johnson (1994) maintain that the growth of knowledge-based networks and teams may be seen as an expression of the increasing importance of knowledge, which is codified in local rather than universal codes. The skills necessary to understand and use these codes will often be developed by those actors allowed to join the network and be a part of interactive learning processes. Therefore, a social network perspective in which processes of inclusion and exclusion are important is added to the discussion.

Breschi and Lissoni (2001) develop this argument further by pointing to the existence of epistemic communities in which specific language for the exchange of technical and scientific messages is used. A lack of disclosure of these codes may function as a strong device of exclusion, even for actors in the same region. Since tacitness and codification are mutually compatible, tacit knowledge can be communicated over even large geographical distances by means of different media. The implication is that innovating firms have to tap into networks at different geographical levels in which both tacit and codified information and knowledge are transferred. Asheim (1999), Lundvall and Borras (1999), Dicken and Malmberg (2001), and Sternberg and Arndt (2001) developed comparable lines of thought.

What this all boils down to is that a majority of scholars studying regional innovation networks tends to take a somewhat simplistic approach to the proximity issue. The knowledge and information interaction processes in (regional) networks are studied through the one-dimensional lens of tacit–codified dichotomy. However, interaction in (regional) innovation networks is far more complex, as several of the authors discussed in the last part of this section have argued. This calls for an approach in which the multidimensional nature of inter-organizational relationships is recognized. In the next section, we will discuss some of the implications of this observation.

CONCLUSIONS AND DISCUSSION

In this chapter, we have tried to answer two questions: (1) why do organizations participate in innovation networks and (2) why do organizations participate in regional innovation networks?

The former question was answered by first discussing the general motives for network participation (e.g. necessity, efficiency, reciprocity). Second, we looked into motives found in the literature for participating in innovation networks. Two groups of motives could be discerned:

- incentive-based (e.g. sharing costs, reducing risks, shorter product development cycles);
- knowledge-based motives (e.g. transfer of knowledge, monitoring technology developments and opportunities).

If we compare the motives for entering innovation networks with those proposed by Oliver (1990), it can be concluded that the former sets of motives can be grouped into two 'general' motives, namely efficiency (incentive-based) and reciprocity (collective-knowledge-based). Third, the functions of networks for innovation were discussed. Innovation networks are a coordination device enabling and facilitating interfirm learning and the diffusion of new technological know-how. Moreover, these networks facilitate the exploitation and access to technological complementary assets and provide an organizational platform to combine different technological competences.

In general, there seems to be a network bias; that is, most scholars and approaches tend to emphasize the positive elements of network participation. Negative effects of participation in (innovation) networks receive far less attention in the literature. For example, negative lock-in effects, network failure and its causes, and the effects of power asymmetries are understudied topics. It can be concluded that more empirical research on these topics is needed. For instance, one could investigate to what extent the duration of ties in a (regional) network affects its ability to generate new knowledge.

The structural account dominates the research agenda in the a-spatial network studies on innovation. However, innovation is not only the production of artefacts (products or patents), but also a process. From this process perspective:

- more attention could be paid to relational and process aspects of (innovation) networks in organization studies, as some scholars in the field seem to realize;
- a process view on networks and innovation also points to the need for longitudinal research designs that will help us to come to a deeper understanding of the co-evolution of network development and innovation. An interesting research question could be how network composition and exchange patterns change while the innovation process unfolds.

Many network studies emphasize the importance of structural holes for innovation. However, an open network is not only a potential for the formation of relations; it also represents a culture in which the probability of opportunistic behaviour is higher, resulting in greater concerns for the misuse of acquired knowledge, exactly because network actors are less densely interconnected. These concerns call for countermeasures and safeguarding behaviour, causing more hierarchical governance and higher organization costs. This eventually indicates that collaboration is 'not done'. If this argument holds, the structural holes in a network can be pitfalls instead of brokerage opportunities. Moreover, organizations do not have the choice of being part of a complete network with structural holes (or a dense network). An organization is or is not part of it. This implies that a managerial view in which whole networks, including structural holes, are purposely built, does not apply. In other words, the network formation process is more 'random' than many scholars would like to admit.

The functions of networks for innovating organizations are even strengthened in a regional context. Scholars in regional economics and economic geography came up with a variety of approaches that all are combinations of three dimensions (Crevoisier, 2004):

- a technological dimension stressing innovation, learning and know-how as the most important competitive advantages of organizations;
- an organizational dimension stressing the role of networks, collaboration and competition, the rules and norms of collaboration, as well as relational and social capital;
- territory, which accounts for the role of proximity and distance and stresses the idea that competition occurs between regions.

The dominant view on the role of the region or of proximity for innovation is either that the region is a context from which innovative organization can mobilize valuable resources or that proximity eases the transmission of especially tacit knowledge. Exactly this type of knowledge is an important building block for the competitive position of organizations in general and the innovative performance of firms in particular.

In a previous section, it was argued that our second research question basically is a (spatial) specification of the first research question. Yet this specification can be done at several levels of analysis (see also Morgan, 2004):

1. The complete network level, which raises the question of which parts of the network are local or regional and which parts are national or international. This raises a related issue: how to define local versus non-local boundaries?

2. The dyad level and especially the relational features such as, for example, trust, knowledge exchange and tie strength.
3. The level of the individual network actor is also of importance. At this level, partner features or so-called attribute variables come into play.

Although the literature discussed in this paper hints at the importance of these levels of analysis for the innovative outcomes of networks, systematic theorizing on the interplay of these levels is lacking. Moreover, taking different levels of analysis into account opens up the possibility of applying multi-level analysis to empirical research on (regional) innovation networks and test theoretical models. This would result in an interesting new research direction. An example of such a study could be to assess the impact of the mobility of engineers (attribute variable) on the level of knowledge exchange (relational feature) in the innovativeness of a network (network level).

To answer the two questions posed in this chapter, we tapped into two bodies of literature: organization studies on the one hand and regional science on the other. Some interesting conclusions can be drawn when comparing this literature:

1. The network studies performed in the field of organization studies tend to have a structural approach to networks, whereas relational aspects are understudied. For the approaches developed in the regional sciences, the opposite is true. Much attention is paid to relational aspects of networks (such as social bonds, family ties, interactive and collective learning), while structural aspects of networks are often neglected.
2. Empirical and theoretical studies in both fields seem to indicate some convergence. As we have pointed out, in organization studies the relational account is emerging in an effort to get more insight in the relational determinants of network flows, whereas the discussion in regional studies on the tacit–codified knowledge dichotomy led to the understanding that innovating organizations have to be connected to networks populated by a diverse set of localized and non-localized actors, which brings us in the realm of the structural network account, studying whole network studies and applying its related analytical tools.

These conclusions point to an interesting research avenue for the regional sciences; that is, to include both relational and structural accounts in the study of regional innovation networks. Network population size is an important issue in analysing networks, because most network measures are using this as a parameter for centrality or density, for example. This could especially be applied in regional networks, because this allows the inclusion of regional features in network analysis, whereas they are now completely out of sight. Other interesting examples of a similar approach can be found in the recent work of Reagans and McEvily (2003) and Owen-Smith and Powell (2004). The work of the latter authors is especially important, as they contend that integrating considerations of geographic proximity of network structures and the institutional demography of network nodes offer new insights in the relationship between structural network positions and organization-level outcomes. Within regional economies, linkages among spatial proximate partners stand for relatively transparent channels for knowledge transfer because they are embedded in an ecology rich in formal, informal and labour market transfer mechanisms. When the central nodes in innovation networks have institutional features (norms and values) stimulating open regimes of knowledge disclosure, the entire network structure is characterized by less tightly monitored ties, resulting in a freer flow of knowledge that could impact positively on organizational outcomes.

In sum, in this chapter we have argued that a further integration of the insights of regional and organization studies is very helpful in deepening our knowledge and understanding of (regional) innovation networks.

REFERENCES

Alter, C. and Hage, J. (1993), *Organizations Working Together*, Newbury Park, CA: Sage.

Asheim, B.T. (1999), 'Interactive learning and localised knowledge in globalising learning economies', *GeoJournal*, **49** (4), 345–52.

Audretsch, D.B. (1998), 'Agglomeration and the location of innovative activity', *Oxford Review of Economic Policy*, **14** (2), 18–29.

Aydalot, P. and Keeble, D. (1988), *High Technology Industry and Innovative Environments: the European Experience*, London: Croom Helm.

Becattini, G. (1989), 'Sectors and/or districts: some remarks on the conceptual foundations of industrial economics', in E. Goodman and J. Bamford (eds), *Small Firms and Industrial Districts in Italy*, London and New York: Routledge.

Borgatti, S. and Cross, R. (2003), 'A relational view of information seeking and learning in social networks', *Management Science*, **49** (4), 432–45.

Borgatti, S. and Foster, P. (2003), 'The network paradigm in organizational research: a review of typology', *Journal of Management*, **29** (6), 991–1013.

Boschma, R.A. (2005), 'Role of proximity in interaction and performance: conceptual and empirical challenges', *Regional Studies*, **39** (1), 41–5.

Breschi, S. and Lissoni, F. (2001), 'Knowledge spillovers and local innovation systems: a critical survey', *Industrial and Corporate Change*, **10** (4), 975–1005.

Burt, R. (1992), *Structural Holes*, Cambridge, MA: Harvard University Press.

Burt, R. (2000), 'The network structure of social capital', in B. Staw and R. Sutton (eds), *Research in Organizational Behavior*, vol. 22, Greenwich, CT: JAI Press.

Coleman, J. (1988), 'Social capital in the creation of human capital', *American Journal of Sociology*, **94**, S95–S120.

Crevoisier, O. (2004), 'The innovative milieus approach: toward a territorialized understanding of the economy?' *Economic Geography*, **80** (4), 367–79.

Dicken, P. and Malmberg, A. (2001), 'Firms in territories: a relational perspective', *Economic Geography*, **77** (4), 345–63.

Ebers, M. and Jarillo, J.C. (1998), 'The construction, forms, and consequences of industry networks', *International Studies of Management & Organization*, **27**, 3–21.

Granovetter, M. (1973), 'The strength of weak ties', *American Journal of Sociology*, **78**, 1360–80.

Gregersen, B. and Johnson, B. (1997), 'Learning economies, innovation systems and European integration', *Regional Studies*, **31** (5), 479–90.

Hadjimichalis, C. and Papamichos, N. (1991), ' "Local" development in Southern Europe: myths and realities', in E. Bergman, G. Maier and F. Tödtling (eds), *Regions Reconsidered: Economic Networks, Innovation, and Local Development in Industrialized Countries*, London/New York: Mansell, pp. 141–64.

Hanssen, M. (1999), 'The search–transfer problem: the role of weak ties in sharing knowledge across organization subunits', *Administrative Science Quarterly*, **44**, 82–111.

Jack, S.L., Dodd, S. and Anderson, A. (2004), 'Social structure and entrepreneurial networks: the strength of strong ties', *International Journal of Entrepreneurship and Innovation*, **5** (2), 171–89.

Kraatz, M.S. (1998), 'Learning by association? Interorganizational networks and adaptation to environmental change', *Academy of Management Journal*, **21**, 621–43.

Lin, N. (1988), 'Social resources and social mobility', in R. Breiger (ed.), *Social Mobility and Social Structure*, Cambridge, UK: Cambridge University Press.

Lundvall, B.-Å. (1992), *National Systems of Innovation: Towards a Theory of Innovation and Interactive Learning*, London: Pinter Publishers.

Lundvall, B.-Å. and Johnson, B. (1994), 'The learning economy', *Journal of Industry Studies*, **1** (1), 23–42.

Lundvall, B.-Å. and Borras, S. (1999), *The Globalising Learning Economy: Implications for Innovation Policy*, Luxembourg: Office for Official Publications of the European Communities.

Maillat, D. (1991), 'The innovation process and the role of the milieu', in E. Bergman, G. Maier and F. Tödtling (eds), *Regions Reconsidered: Economic Networks, Innovation and Local Development in Industrialized Countries*, London/New York: Mansell, pp. 103–17.

Malecki, E.J. (1991), *Technology and Economic Development: the Dynamics of Local, Regional, and National Change*, Harlow/New York: Longman Scientific & Technical; Wiley.

Marshall, A. (1920), *The Principles of Economics*, London: Macmillan.

Morgan, K. (1997), 'The learning region: institutions, innovation and regional renewal', *Regional Studies*, **31** (5), 491–503.

Morgan, K. (2004), 'The exaggerated death of geography: learning, proximity and territorial innovation systems', *Journal of Economic Geography*, **4** (1), 3–21.

Moulaert, F. and Sekia, F. (2003), 'Territorial innovation models: a critical survey', *Regional Studies*, **37** (3), 289–302.

Nooteboom, B. and Gilsing, V. (2006), 'Exploration and exploitation in innovation networks: the case of pharmaceutical biotechnology', *Research Policy*, **35** (1), 1–23.

Oerlemans, L., Meeus, M. and Boekema, F. (2000), 'Innovation and proximity: theoretical perspectives', in M. Green and R. McNoughton (eds), *Industrial Networks and Proximity*, Aldershot: Ashgate, pp. 17–46.

Oliver, C. (1990), 'Determinants of interorganizational relationships: integration and future directions', *Academy of Management Review*, **15**, 241–65.

Osborn, R.N. and Hagedoorn, J. (1997), 'The institutionalisation and evolutionary dynamics of interorganizational alliances and networks', *Academy of Management Journal*, **40**, 261–78.

Owen-Smith, J. and Powell, W.W. (2004), 'Knowledge networks as channels and conduits: The effects of spillovers in the Boston biotechnology community', *Organization Science*, **15** (1), 5–21.

Pyka, A. (2002), 'Innovation networks in economics: from the incentive-based to the knowledge-based approaches', *European Journal of Innovation Management*, **5** (3), 152–63.

Reagans, R. and McEvily, B. (2003), 'Network structure and knowledge transfer: the effects of cohesion and range', *Administrative Science Quarterly*, **48**, 240–67.

Rogers, E. (1995), *The Diffusion of Innovations*, New York: Free Press.

Saxenian, A. (1994), *Regional Advantage. Culture and Competition in Silicon Valley and Route 128*, Cambridge, MA: Harvard University Press.

Scott, A.J. and Storper, M. (1992), 'Regional development reconsidered', in H. Ernste and V. Meier (eds), *Regional Development and Contemporary Industrial Response. Extending Flexible Specialisation*, London: Belhaven Press, pp. 3–24.

Sternberg, R. and Arndt, O. (2001), 'The firm or the region: what determines the innovation behaviour of European firms?', *Economic Geography*, **77** (4), 364–82.

Storper, M. (1995), 'Regional technology coalitions: an essential dimension of national technology policy', *Research Policy*, **24** (6), 859–911.

Storper, M. (1997), *The Regional World: Territorial Development in a Global Economy*, New York and London: Guilford Press.

Teece, D.J. (1986), 'Profiting from technological innovation: implications for integration, collaboration, licensing and public policy', *Research Policy*, **15**, 285–305.

Tödtling, F. (1999), 'Innovation networks, collective learning, and industrial policy in regions of Europe', *European Planning Studies*, **7** (6), 693–7.

Torre, A. and Gilly, J.-P. (2000), 'Debates and surveys: on the analytical dimension of proximity dynamics', *Regional Studies*, **34** (2), 169–80.

Zeitlin, J. (1992), 'Industrial districts and local economic regeneration: overview and comment', in F. Pyke and W. Sengenberger (eds), *Industrial Districts and Local Economic Regeneration*, Geneva: International Institute for Labour Studies.

9. Regional innovation systems, asymmetric knowledge and the legacies of learning

Philip Cooke

1. INTRODUCTION

In this chapter the aim is to achieve three main objectives. The first is to understand why *learning* discourses have failed. The second aim is to explain this in terms of the new imperatives of *knowledge* for innovation in a new phase of knowledge-driven globalization. Finally, we will attempt to show how the problem of regional and institutional lags is one of *asymmetric knowledge*. We ask what the main reasons are that the promise of learning – and particularly in this context – 'learning regions' has waxed and then waned so swiftly? Institutional learning has a respectable pedigree going back at least to Argyris (1962) and his efficiency question as to whether organizational hierarchy or heterarchy best nurtured it. Simultaneously, Arrow (1962) asked about the productivity implications of learning to a neoclassical economics community that had hitherto largely ignored it. Following Lundvall's (1994) exposition of the idea 'that what will matter is how well one succeeds in developing organisations, which promote learning and the wise use of knowledge . . .', 'learning' became an injunction that was increasingly the first item on a wider developmental wish list. However, its initial impulse as a quest for organizational efficiency inside the large corporation became submerged (Argyris and Schon, 1978).

Although 'the myopia of learning' has been condemned since at least Levinthal and March (1993), the most devastating recent critique of this comes from two sources. The first comes from work at Harvard Business School by Hansen (2002), who showed the failure of organizational learning wrapped in the language of 'knowledge management' to lie in failure to develop the organization. The second comes from Aalborg University, Denmark, where Dirckinck-Holmfeld (2002) showed how e-learning failed when no change was made to the traditional lecture-based pedagogy of traditional learning. Third, an organization or person that becomes accustomed to learning, presumably from elsewhere in the form of pre-existing (pre-digested) information, cannot cope with novelty any more than corn-fed geese confronted with *foie gras*. Desultory regional economies and their learning organizations are condemned to a treadmill of having to absorb old information. After trying to learn its lessons, it may possibly implement them in time to discover that superior intelligence from elsewhere has already set new standards. Learning and innovation are opposites, and innovation requires organizational change.

A complex organizational change that numerous regions effected in the 1990s and into the 2000s concerns innovation systems, specifically *regional* innovation systems. Although in the EU over one hundred regions have been exposed to regional innovation *strategies* since 1994 (Oughton et al., 2002), Carlsson (forthcoming) has tracked over two hundred regional inno-vation-system *studies* between 1987 and 2002, half of them products of empirical research. These show leading and lagging regions improving innovative performance by redesigning their boundary-crossing mechanisms or 'bridging social capital' (Putnam, 1999) between research (*explor-ation* knowledge) and commercialization (*exploitation* knowledge; March, 1991). Moreover, in Cooke et al. (2004) the evolution of regional innov-ation systems worldwide in the face of economic downturn and globaliza-tion effects was delineated. These now transcend simplistic knowledge transfer notions such as the 'Triple Helix' (Etzkowitz and Leydesdorff, 1997), which presents the institutional clash of 'epistemic communities' (Haas, 1992) among government, industry and universities as akin to a Holy Trinity. The disequilibrating impulses of the 'knowledge economy' have prompted innovative thinking in lagging regions, whereby the Holy Trinity is eschewed and, even the 'holiest of holies', the *university*, is looked upon askance in the quest for regional *constructed advantage* (Foray and Freeman, 1993). Solutions arising from these more nuanced, research-focused approaches will be presented in the chapter as a sequel to a modest critique of 'learning regions', along lines mapped out in the foregoing account. But, importantly, the superiority of the 'innovation systems' toolkit will be underlined and explained in simple but effective terms that bring to the fore the problem of 'asymmetric knowledge'.

2. KNOWLEDGE, INNOVATION AND LEARNING: SOME KEY DISTINCTIONS

The regional innovation systems approach is not particularly predicated on *learning*, not even referencing such literature at the outset (Cooke, 1992), but rather on *knowledge* and *innovation*. Conceptually speaking, it began with a recognition that what Triple Helix advocates see as easy is, in fact, exceptionally problematic. That is, there are major institutional barriers among industry, research universities and governments. The regional innovation systems work recognizes internal and external interactions involving two sub-systems, one that engages in knowledge exploration or generation and one that engages in knowledge exploitation. About the same time as Cooke (1992), James March (1991) had written influentially on knowledge *exploration* and *exploitation* as strategic choices in organizations, though this was unknown to the present author until much later. Hence, in regional innovation systems, work innovation is the focus but knowledge, especially from research, is the key driver. For these purposes, training derived from research-based learning, as in universities, is a sub-set of knowledge exploration. Academic entrepreneurship is a sub-set of knowledge exploitation.

Successful regional innovation systems have organizations that conduct research (including accessing results from elsewhere) that generates new knowledge in appropriate institutional settings. And *crucially*, other appropriate organizations, mostly firms, commercialize this knowledge as globally consumable innovations in the market, or for public organizations such as healthcare, educational or military establishments. In other words, Triple Helix chasms between research, markets and policies are successfully crossed; epistemic communities find transaction spaces where implicit knowledge gets made explicit and communities of intermediation practice operate these institutional bridges. These third parties deal in *complicit* knowledge since they can master the hybrid skills and languages needed to communicate between Wittgensteinian 'language worlds'. Finally, Cooke et al. (2004) showed that in general these bridging mechanisms are either *entrepreneurial* (*ERIS*) or *institutional* (*IRIS*), rather as Sidney Winter (1984) argued regarding technological regimes, another paper I discovered only much later. Silicon Valley is an example of an ERIS, while Baden-Württemberg is an IRIS. Both have problems as well as past successes: the first tends to 'crash and burn', costing 400 000 jobs 2000–2003; the second stagnates in labour market terms but continually exports luxury products in demand worldwide.

Unsuccessful regional innovation systems suffer from three asymmetric knowledge problems. The first, after Akerlof (1970), is quality of information, as when a consumer must trust that a product is safe, something of which the producer usually has superior knowledge. This actually introduces a third, intervening knowledge category of relevance to innovation systems thinking, namely *examination* knowledge, which is what institutional laggards also lack. This is not least, as we shall see, due to what March et al. (1991) call 'learning from samples of one' type problems common in so-called 'learning regions' that seek to emulate policy exemplars such as Silicon

Valley. Second, their knowledge institutions are not research- but learning-oriented; hence little research is produced and even less that is of interest for innovation. This is a common problem in university systems that do not co-evolve with socio-economic trajectories (Tavoletti, 2004). Finally, a common problem is that one or other of the main Triple Helix 'partners' dominates knowledge and innovation practice asymmetrically. It may be hierarchic public governance that is communicatively dissonant with industry and university language worlds (Wittgenstein, 1958). It may be an industry-dominated, corporately 'governed' region with no use for disruptive knowledge or government intervention. Or it might be a strong university and research region with few firms with which to interact, and weak regional governance.

Moving to a deeper analysis of knowledge and innovation, of pressing need are clear definitions and distinctions regarding types of *research* and knowledge, notably *abstract* (science), *synthetic* (technical) and *symbolic* (creative). What we mean here is that unlike some views (e.g. Amin and Cohendet, 2003) that present knowledge as uniform and architectonic, we recognize both the traditional categorization denoted above, and its elaboration along a second dimension spanning *exploration, examination and exploitation* knowledge – the distinction begun as a binary juxtaposition of 'exploration' and 'exploitation' by March (1991), to which we add the important knowledge prototyping, testing or trialling category of 'examination' knowledge. In Table 9.1, these are arranged to enable conceptual work directly relevant to a hypothesis-testing empirical framework.

What Table 9.1 shows is that all innovative knowledge of utility, by definition meaning new knowledge commercialized, must pass iteratively through similar stages of production from 'discovery' through invention or realization of the hitherto unrealized experimental form, to a testing process that establishes its reliability and validity, to a state where it has created demand, either market or social. The key thing to note here is that discovery involves not so much 'learning' as 'unlearning', by stepping beyond what can be learned as codified knowledge into the

Table 9.1   Forms and stages of knowledge production

	Abstract	Synthetic	Symbolic
Exploration	Mathematical reasoning	E.g. gene therapy	Experimental art work
Examination	Theorems to test	Clinical trials	Art exhibition
Exploitation	E.g. Penrose tiles/ patterns	Therapeutic treatment	Gallery sale

'unknown' creative space where cognition is tacit but interactive with reality and methodology. In a trivial sense 'methodology' may have been 'learned' but it may have to be transcended or even negated in the act of discovery. This often happened in mathematics where new process methodologies such as calculus had to be invented to solve some intractable problem. Similarly in art, Cubism required the unlearning of classic figurative art, even to the extent of appreciation of and experimentation with primitive or child art forms as process methodologies, to escape into 'the new'.

Learning as such is, by definition, a second-order process compared to innovation. It is cognate with Latour's (1998) distinction between 'science' and 'research': the former being certain, cold, straight, detached, settled and objective, while the latter is uncertain, warm, involving, risky, controversial and passionate. Science entails codified bodies of knowledge to be learned while research transforms them into objects of inquiry. Hence the contemporary economy finds new value from research more than from science, since innovation is, by definition, the commercialization not of old but new knowledge. Learning old knowledge is fatal for would-be innovators because, as even Chicago-school rational choice theory recognizes, the object or idea with which you are presented cannot be new since if it were, someone would already have exploited it. Taken to the bizarre extreme, it underpins the joke where the economist contradicts his wife who spotted a ten-dollar bill on the pavement by denying its existence since, if it were really a ten-dollar bill, someone would have already picked it up. Happily, his chapter does not offer such questionable advice. Rather, it queries the validity of a learning argument that posits it as a regional renewal strategy that, paradoxically, relies on non-innovative, second-hand knowledge to meet that end.

Finally, the chapter mobilizes evidence that suggests that, in what is increasingly referred to as the contemporary knowledge economy, there has been an economic geography and industry organization reversal, which means that large *scale* in corporate organization no longer determines what *magnetizes* economic development. Rather, in an approach that owes much to Penrose's (1959/1995) observation regarding knowledge networks *metamorphosing* industry organization (Quéré, 2003; Cooke, 2003, 2004a), we advance along lines identified in Cooke (2004b, c) towards a *regional knowledge capabilities* theory of economic geography and regional innovation that underpins the ways *globalization* proceeds. This is labelled 'Globalization 2' a theory that also postulates an *economic geography* of the spatially unexplored but suggestive findings of Chesbrough (2003) on the transformational impact on knowledge production of 'open innovation'.

3.   RESEARCH AND KNOWLEDGE: SPATIAL SHIFTS

In definitional terms, a *knowledge economy* is one in which several economic indicators, such as the ratio of intangible to tangible goods produced, the levels of tertiary education, the levels of R&D expenditure and patenting, and the use by economic organizations of all kinds of formal, scientific, creative or research-based knowledge rather than 'rules of thumb', are high and rising. According to statistics on such indicators published by OECD (2004b), such profiles are not only common among its members but prevalent in such non-OECD economies as Brazil, China and India. An elaboration on this of relevance to the regional question, where data are not so abundant, is that regions may be denoted as *knowledge economies* when they score high, at least 40 per cent, on defined sectoral employment indicators in high-technology manufacturing and knowledge-intensive services (OECD, 1996).

So what defines successful or promising 'knowledge economy' regions and where are they?

For the moment we may take bioregions, i.e. those with high location quotients in bioscientific research and production as our exemplar; but later we shall underpin this with reference to other industries. The simple answers to the questions raised are that *scale* is the normal ranking device among relevant variables like numbers of dedicated biotechnology firms (DBFs), size of research budgets, investment finance or number of life scientists. On such counts and in regard to bioregions, the answer to the question of *location* is North America, primarily the USA. But there are obvious weaknesses in taking scale at face value.

Thus, what may be controversial is the argument that in knowledge-based industry, generating and commercializing *abstract, synthetic* and *symbolic* knowledge derived from *research* is increasingly to be found outside the corporate sector and inside knowledge-intensive research institutes, consultancies and modestly sized but regionally agglomerated firms.

There are exceptions, as always, to an emergent trend, as Valentin and Lund-Jensen (2003) show for the food industry, something also argued from a different perspective by Smith (2001). This in turn, however, is a product of the *knowledge capabilities* of the agro-food sector, in which biology, not chemistry, as with pharmaceuticals, is a core research competence. Hence pharmaceuticals companies subcontract much R&D to dedicated biotechnology firms (DBFs) and university or research institute laboratories. But even in this regard, large corporates like Monsanto and Bayer show certain incapabilities, notably misjudgements of the nature and extent of the genetically modified organism (GMO) market for crops. Such knowledge management weaknesses have appeared in the form of low discovery rates in *research* and, nowadays even weaknesses in *development* activities such as combinatorial chemistry among large pharmaceuticals firms. Hence, even the hitherto relatively self-sufficient research capabilities of the agro-food, bioscience industry are now spawning more specialist DBFs than hitherto.[1]

In brief, in a knowledge economy in which mastery of scientific advance is demonstrated along with industry capability to commercialize it, regions displaying such accomplishments are relatively advantaged economically. Theoretically speaking, having composed this kind of 'constructed advantage' to generate and commercialize new knowledge equates to the traditional (e.g. Myrdal, 1957; Hirschman, 1958) definition of a successful economic region. This is that it possesses all or most of the key value-adding functions of a specific sector as well as reasonable diversification of the economic base into other separate or connected sectors. It thus combines depth and breadth in its economic capabilities. The role of *knowledge spillovers*, especially those having the quality of non-pecuniary externalities, seems to be important here. Why would firms cluster geographically, for example, in bioregions if there were little or no functional advantage when, according to normal supply and demand rules, overhead costs would be higher than if agglomeration had not occurred? Why, in contrast, locate in isolation and eschew the possible benefits of 'open science' or even 'open innovation'? The simple answer is that agglomerators gain advantage from the knowledge network capabilities that bioregions and other knowledge economies contain. These exist in the human capital 'talent' trained in local research institutes and university laboratories; the presence of 'star' scientists and their research teams; the possibilities for collaboration with like-minded research teams or other DBFs; and the presence of understanding financial investors also attracted to the 'ideas market' that a bioregion represents.[2]

Clearly, for innovation, the commercialization dimension is also crucial – the advantages of proximity to firms that 'make it happen' – i.e. help turn a scientific finding into, for example, a firm that commercializes a drug, treatment or diagnostic test. These are venture capitalists, specialist lawyers and consultants, and there is econometric and case study evidence that these knowledge demands cause them to locate their investment a mean distance of one hour's driving time from their office base, for the most part.[3] These are 'pipeline' type relationships, sealed from prying eyes and ears. This 'market' perspective focuses specifically on those contractual relationships where exacting transactions involve potentially large returns to partners from academe and enterprise. But the alternative, 'social' position observes, albeit with social anthropological data, a different characterization of the successful or potentially successful bioregion. That success is based on the practice of 'open science', transformed into a cluster convention of knowledge sharing rather than secreting. These authors examined the Boston bioregion and highlighted the following as key processes by which dynamic place-based capabilities are expressed in research, knowledge transfer, and commercialization of bioscience.

- The difference between 'channels' (open) and 'pipelines' (closed). The former offer more opportunity for knowledge capability enhancement since they are more 'leaky' and 'irrigate' more, albeit proximate, incumbents. Pipelines offer more capable means of proprietary knowledge transfer over great geographical distances based on contractual agreements, which are less 'leaky' because they are closed rather than open.
- Public research organizations (PROs) are a primary magnet for profit-seeking DBFs and large pharmaceuticals firms because they operate an 'open science' policy, which in the knowledge economy era promises innovation opportunities. These are widely considered to be the source of productivity improvement, greater firm competitiveness and, accordingly, economic growth.

Over time the PRO 'conventions' of 'open science' influence DBFs in their network interactions with other DBFs. Although PROs may not remain the main intermediaries among DBFs, as the latter grow in number and engage in commercialization of exploration knowledge and exploitation of such knowledge through patenting, they experience greater gains through the combination of proximity and conventions than through either proximity alone or conventions alone. This is dynamic knowledge networking capability transformed into a regional capability, which in turn attracts large pharma firms seeking membership in the 'community'.

These propositions each receive strong support from statistical analyses of research and patenting practices in the Boston bioregion. Thus:

> Transparent modes of information transfer will trump more opaque or sealed mechanisms when a significant proportion of participants exhibit limited concern with policing the accessibility of network pipelines . . . closed conduits offer reliable and excludable information transfer at the cost of fixity and thus are more appropriate to a stable environment. In contrast, permeable channels rich in spillovers are responsive and may be more suitable for variable environments. In a stable world, or one where change is largely incremental, such channels represent excess capacity. (Owen-Smith and Powell, 2004)

Finally, though, leaky channels rather than closed pipelines also represent an opportunity for unscrupulous convention-breakers to sow misinformation among competitors. However, the strength of the 'open science' convention means that, as long as PROs remain a presence, as they must in science-driven contexts, such 'negative social capital' practices are punishable by exclusion from PRO interaction, reputational degrading or even, at the extreme, convention shift, in rare occurrences, towards more confidentiality agreements and spillover-limiting, 'pipeline' legal contracts.

We therefore constructed a matrix (Table 9.2) from this analysis of two sets of competing explanations of successful bioregions. First, with regard to the *specialization* versus *diversification* debate on knowledge spillovers, this was concluded by observing the time difference in the prominence of one over the other in the evolution of the cluster, so we conclude that transactions are 'pipelines' when legally binding, confidential, contractual business is being transacted but are otherwise subject to 'open science' conventions. Table 9.2 also suggests that in the early stage (1) of a technology, there will be few firms or academics with the requisite combination of scientific and commercialization expertise for technology exploitation. However, when the two come together and the market potential of what has been discovered is realized, there will be a 'pipeline' type transaction to patent, arrange investment and create a firm. This was exactly the history of Genentech after Recombinant DNA Nobel Laureate, Herb Boyer, and partner Stanley Cohen met Robert Swanson, a venture capitalist with Kleiner, Perkins, Caufield & Byers in 1976, before any cluster existed in San Francisco. Thereafter (stage 2), more DBFs formed as scientific research evolved and new DBFs sought to emulate Genentech's success. These included Biogen in Cambridge, Massachusetts, and Hybritech in San Diego in the 1970s and early 1980s.[4] Once this process begins, the sector remains specialized. However, more DBFs and their employees who retain, as do founders, close affiliation with their host university, open 'channels' and knowledge spillovers are accessed to create a highly innovative environment around 'open science' conventions. The third stage is reached when diversification begins and specialist suppliers, on the one hand, but more importantly, new technology research lines and DBFs form linkages, for example, after a breakthrough such as decoding the human genome, on the other. Large research budgets are by now attracted to leading centres and

Table 9.2   Characterization of successful and potentially successful bioregions

	Specialization		Diversification	
Pipeline	1.	Embryonic	4.	High success
Open science	2.	Innovative	3.	High potential

this stimulates further 'open science' communication, cross-fertilization through knowledge spillovers and further DBF formation. Fourth, after this, many serious entrepreneurial transactions occurring through 'pipeline' relations with big pharmaceuticals take place, trialling proves successful and licensing deals for marketing a healthcare product are regularly struck between big pharmaceuticals and DBFs. Then, regarding further R&D, big pharmaceuticals with public-funded leading research institutes is further engaged and a potentially successful bioregion can be said to have become a highly successful one.

This explanatory model clearly works for the iterative process of taking exploration knowledge through its examination phases to ultimate exploitation as a commercial product, in the Genentech case, human insulin via academic entrepreneurship and 'big pharma' funding. But is it generic? In other words, does it also apply to knowledge-to-product processing in the completely different context of a project inside the firm? If so, we have an explanation of the modern innovation process that satisfies both the exigencies of markets and conventions of 'open innovation'. To test this, let us briefly take a further case from bioscience, as reported by Chesbrough (2003), before broadening the project model of 'open innovation', as he does, to other industries.

The first case in question is that of Millennium Pharmaceuticals. This company was founded in 1993 and by 2000 was valued at some $11 billion and employed 1530 people. To that point Millennium was a classic knowledge business, not selling a product as such but rather its methodology for analysing biological compounds. In its early years, Millennium formed 20 strategic alliances with leading pharmaceutical and biotechnology companies (e.g. Eli Lilly, Bayer, Roche, AstraZeneca and Wyeth) to exploit its expertise in drug-target discovery, using DNA sequencing technology. Unlike other project-based contract research organizations (CROs), Millennium observed that discovering new drug targets was only one step along the path towards its ultimate goal of discovering innovative therapeutic products for patient healthcare. So Millennium retained IPR (intellectual property rights) for the therapeutic targets it discovered that were beyond the specific interest of its customer. Hence it had a 'pipeline' relationship with its client for contractually agreed, genetically based diseases identified by its examination technology, but an 'open-innovation-channel' capability regarding discoveries outside the agreed targets. Millennium naturally also retained IPR over its core examination technology.

One of the aforementioned clients, Eli Lilly, then expressed interest in licensing the 'crown jewels', the core DNA sequencing technology platform. Later, Monsanto made a similar approach from the agro-food sector. Careful reflection upon its core capabilities and company vision led the board to agree to these out-licensing deals, the income from which enabled Millennium to become a therapeutics firm and to innovate its technology incrementally.

A 'transformational' merger with LeukoSite in 1999 resulted in the firm's first oncology drug coming to market, along with others in clinical trials. In 2000, a merger with Cambridge Discovery Chemistry brought Millennium a significant presence in the UK, adding 100 chemists to the firm. In 2002, a merger with COR Therapeutics further strengthened the company's standing as a leading DBF, adding cardiovascular research and a market-leading, intravenous cardiovascular drug into its portfolio. On its tenth anniversary in 2003, a treatment for patients with multiple myeloma, a cancer of the blood, received FDA (Food and Drugs Administration) approval. Hence, as Chesbrough (2003) notes, an 'open innovation' posture opened up avenues for innovative transformation and growth that would not have been thinkable had a traditional 'closed innovation' approach been adopted.

Finally, a case from a different industry that captures the fundamentals of the model in Table 9.2 concerns Procter & Gamble which, in 1999, established a director of external innovation under a programme called 'Connect & Develop'. Internal research by the firm's nearly 9000 scientists continues but, if the research results are not utilized after three years, they will be made available to other firms, including direct competitors. 'P&G's R&D department used to be like the Kremlin. Now we're more like the Acropolis – all ideas are welcome and get a fair hearing', according to Nabil Sakkab, Senior Vice President of Research and Development in Procter & Gamble's Fabric and Home Care division, describing the way P&G's R&D department has transformed itself into an externally focused 'Connect & Develop' – C&D (rather than R&D) organization. Although retaining significant R&D capability, with approximately $2 billion invested annually, the company has created some 20 different global 'communities of practice' that bring distinctive scientific capabilities together, encouraging and rewarding knowledge transfer from one business area to another. P&G leads in the reapplication of technologies, products and business models from suppliers, universities, entrepreneurs and institutes. 'C&D is about shared risk and interdependence', explains Sakkab, 'we'll licence, we'll collaborate where it makes sense.'[5] Such was the success of this strategy that the firm made sufficient profit to acquire the Gillette Corporation in 2005 for $57 billion, making Procter & Gamble the largest consumer products firm in the world, pushing Unilever into second place.

Clearly, there are two kinds of 'regional' innovation occurring in these examples. The first is geographically proximate; the second is functionally proximate. Thus Millennium's key customers are not all present in

Cambridge, Massachusetts, although AstraZeneca, Wyeth and Bayer (formerly) have R&D laboratories in proximity. However, LeukoSite was a Cambridge firm while COR Therapeutics was from San Francisco. Nevertheless, as demonstrated by, *inter alia*, Cortright and Mayer (2002), Zeller (2002) and Cooke (2004c), the two Cambridges and San Francisco are among the world's leading bioscientific *exploration* and *exploitation* knowledge complexes. Hence we also see a paradigm case of functional integration among highly capable knowledge clusters, animated in this case by companies but in others, for example, by academe, through co-publication by 'star' scientists and their institutional colleagues involving these same clusters. In other words, we see very clearly the process of 'globalisation of bioregions' proposed by Cooke (2004a). In the case of P&G, the key clue lies in reference to the 'communities of practice' bringing specific scientific capabilities together in 20 distinctive, but functionally related, global locations. These too are knitted together globally at the behest of P&G, practising 'open innovation' in conjunction with scientific communities possessing appropriate localized knowledge capabilities.

Finally, theoretical work by Lorenzen and Maskell (2004) and empirical research by Audretsch and Dohse (2004) lend support to the basic theory of *regional knowledge capabilities*. The latter deploy a model estimate using a dataset identifying the growth performance of small technology-based firms. Firm performance, as measured by employment growth, is influenced by locational characteristics as well as characteristics specific to the firm and the industry. In particular, the empirical evidence suggests that being located in an agglomeration rich in knowledge resources is more conducive to firm growth than being located in a region that is less endowed with knowledge resources. A supportive elaboration of that conclusion is supplied by Rosenthal and Strange (2003), who show the premium from own-industry agglomeration by small firms is 90 per cent regarding new firm births and 60 per cent for new firm employment compared to that for medium or large firms. With respect to the geographic scale of these effects, increasing returns to localization declined precipitously at the one-mile radius point. The key explanatory variable is knowledge spillovers.

These results strongly underline the economic value of co-location as a conduit for *prompt* accessing of external knowledge resources relevant to innovation, which in turn manifests itself in higher rates of regional growth. They provide support for the thesis that the 1990s saw a transition in globalization from the stage when multinationals created its economic geography to one where knowledge and research in knowledge-capable regions often clusters, causing multinationals to engage with and often within such knowledge concentrations. This outsourcing, particularly

R&D outsourcing,[6] aspect of globalization is what causes it to warrant the designation 'Globalization 2'.

4. ASYMMETRIC KNOWLEDGE AND REGIONAL KNOWLEDGE CAPABILITIES

As already noted, this chapter finds strong arguments to reject the fundamentally normative 'learning regions' view of regional development. It reasserts the relevance of the 'regional' as denoted and against advocates of the 'scalar envelope' that globalization wraps around everything, denying agency against linear and deterministic 'scale' processes (Bathelt, 2003; Brenner, 2001; Bunnell and Coe, 2001). On the contrary, at global and even national levels it is impossible effectively to study innovation and processes along the knowledge value chain involving knowledge exploration and production. Ironically, it is also impossible to understand transformations occurring in globalization itself without recognizing innovation as an expression of *regional knowledge capabilities.*

There is a clear connection here to literature recognizing interdisciplinary interaction as a key feature perceived to characterize emergent 'Mode 2' knowledge production (Gibbons et al., 1994). Traditional scholastic disciplines rooted in large-scale teaching departments of universities (Mode 1) were observed to be breaking down with the growth of funded academic research. Diversification of knowledge production in specialist research centres, or centres of excellence, that were at arm's length from normal pedagogic activity, capable of bridging industry–academe boundaries, as occurred most fully in the Stanford University model described by Gibbons (2000), but also closely in touch with problem-focused researchers from other disciplines, characterized Mode 2 as 'transdisciplinarity'. Further ingredients also included reflexivity, and networking to tackle knowledge 'heterogeneity'. This influential and somewhat prescient perspective was criticized later, not least by some of its authors (in Nowotny et al., 2001), because it remained rather lofty and science-centric, whereas socio-economic context is rather seen to be causing science and society to 'co-evolve' in their development.

This opens up a key question regarding such transaction spaces or milieux. Does the relational space in which such actors and others in a putative innovation system combine to create the knowledge surpluses that arise from 'localized knowledge spillovers'? Or do firms displaying capabilities in regard to the exploitation of localized knowledge spillovers cluster in proximity to gain from this 'constructed advantage'? This is the subject of work by Lorenzen and Maskell (2004). Basically two positions have emerged, represented to a considerable degree in the relevant literature. The first and strongest is that of Jaffe et al. (1993), Audretsch and Feldman (1996) and Malmberg and Maskell (2002), who argue in favour of the power of localized knowledge spillovers as drivers of innovation, especially in knowledge-based clusters. Breschi and Lissoni (2001) have argued that there is no convincing evidence that non-pecuniary spillovers have displaced Marshallian pecuniary (market) advantages. Interestingly, both sides argue their cases in respect of the meso-level of analysis (Caniëls and Romijn, 2005).

However, to come full circle back to the main critique of such notions as 'learning organizations' or 'learning regions', it is important to demonstrate that this is not fundamentally about pejorative connotations concerning 'myopia' or 'legacies' that the regional knowledge capabilities perspective recognizes in ways that even the 'rethinking science' perspective still fails to do, that knowledge is neither uniform nor ubiquitous. Rather, to reaffirm the insight of Akerlof (1970), knowledge is asymmetric. The researching firm or organization will, as Latour (1998) argues, be a source of disruptive innovation as well as more modest incremental discovery. It will destabilize the calm pedagogy of science that to be learned has to be taught, as a homogeneous narrative. Following Rosenthal and Strange (2003) and Audretsch and Dohse (2004), we see agglomerations of small firms (< 25 employees) outperforming both larger firms as sources of new firms and employment, benefiting from *prompt* access to localized tacit knowledge spillovers.

Where Akerlof's (1970) perspective adds to the analysis presented here is in its recognition of the non-uniformity, non-universality, non-ubiquity and sheer 'stickiness' of the kind of knowledge routinely valuable in research (as exploration and examination knowledge) and innovation (as exploitation knowledge). As noted, we are not in the stale atmosphere of the lecture hall receiving stable, homogeneous and settled scientific narratives; rather we are in Latour's (1998) universe in which research creates uncertainty, instability and disruption that are the characteristics from which innovation gains its value-creating knowledge capability. In Akerlof's terms, the learning region finds itself in a world of potential 'lemons'. The argument of relevance here is in the three points that follow:

- A producer, seller or investor in a specific professional field will generally have significantly greater knowledge of that field than a consumer of the product or service in question. In Akerlof's famous case of the used-car industry, the consumer, with only partial, amateur knowledge always faces the *risk* of purchasing a 'lemon'. The importance of the insight is that it provides a fundamental reason why markets are imperfect and, indeed, points to a basic cause of market failure. In our context, a 'learning organization' or 'learning region' faces an even bigger risk in borrowing either bespoke designed or generic policies from accomplished locations. The chances of a different region's bespoke approach working successfully elsewhere are, almost by definition, miniscule. If generic 'policy learning' is adopted, as with consultancy advice on clustering, for example, a quadruple risk arises from the fact that 'competitors' are likely already to have purchased the 'lesson'. In any case, it is not new, may not be adapted to regional conditions or even be adaptable, and there is the significant risk that it will not work anyway. Of course, this risk is one shared with the 'competition', a factor that probably explains the mysterious success of the consultancy business.

- Time economies play an important part in knowledge transfer. Thus, for a 'policy model' or even specific, successful policy instruments or measures to emerge in terms of concrete results is a process that may have begun five to ten years previously. If it is a set of practices involving leadership from private actors operating through market or quasi-market transactions, outcomes may be swifter in appearing, but will also have taken time to materialize and will have been embedded in a specific business culture, sectoral milieu, or even 'variety of capitalism'. Effective knowledge transfer involves consciousness of all these variables and capability to control them, in the knowledge, once again, that competitors may already be interested or active in adaptation activities. The political cycle is seldom able to accommodate long-term policy or culture change implied in policy learning of this kind. Rather, it is necessary to change the nature of the organization of knowledge transfer to one that is in constant interaction with its relevant environments. This reflexivity, monitoring and assessing of knowledge flows is precisely the model implemented in exemplary regional innovation systems (OECD, 2004a).

- The third element contributing to asymmetric knowledge relates to the scope and scale couplet. That is, in the same way that no national economy is self-sufficient in all the assets it requires to function effectively, *a fortiori* this is even less the case for regions. The key aim of regional innovation systems policy makers is to optimize on the knowledge asymmetries that privilege their regional economy and trade with firms, regions or countries privileged by other knowledge asymmetries. This involves both inter-industry and, importantly, intra-industry trade. The simple aim is a set of regional accounts that shows a surplus at the end of each trading year. 'Nicheing' in specialized 'regional knowledge domains' of this kind is inevitable.

However, it is also what, on the one hand, further undermines any crude notion of 'learning-by-cloning' while, on the other, undermining a perspective often promoted by national government policy makers to the effect that, for reasons of global competitiveness, knowledge assets should be concentrated in a few locations or a single region. This is the old 'economies of scale' perspective appearing in a different guise, whereas the 'economies of scope' perspective allows for variety, asymmetry and selection as a basis for innovation-based inter- and intra-industry trade. In an effective system, surpluses will arise from increasing returns to scope and eventually scale.

To conclude this section, a *regional knowledge capabilities* model of regional growth has been advanced (Figure 9.1) in which policy assists the evolution of 'constructed advantage' based on supporting privileged niches with specific asymmetric knowledge assets. It overcomes the weaknesses inherent in a possibly myopic 'learning economy' approach constrained by the existence of knowledge transfer asymmetries of the kind discussed. The elements not discussed in detail in the preceding paragraphs involve 'regional knowledge domains' of the kinds that arise with regional clustering of expertise in a sector. 'Increasing returns' of the kind discussed by Krugman (1995) mean specialist knowledge accumulates incrementally to give a cluster something approaching a 'spatial monopoly' in that sub-field

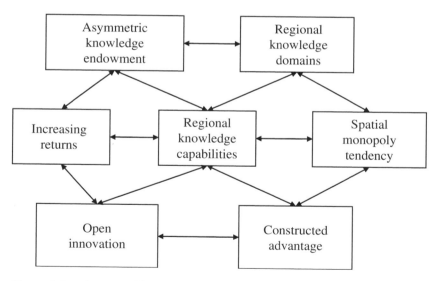

Figure 9.1   A regional knowledge capabilities model of 'Globalization 2' economic geography

of knowledge – hence 'asymmetric knowledge' of the regional kind. Such conditions are constructed in competitive places with further governance, talent and quality of life assets and inputs (Foray and Freeman, 1993). Regions with these advantages synchronized will be likely to support regional innovation systems (ERIS or IRIS).

6. CONCLUSIONS

This chapter has performed three main tasks: the first was to examine some problems associated with a broad 'learning' perspective, whether regarding learning in organizations, such as business firms, or even more complex and uncertain contexts such as regions. While the aspiration normatively to urge a learning predisposition upon agents in such complex organizations as regions seems hard to critique, nevertheless on closer inspection the focus is so blurred, the means so attenuated and the organizational meta-morphosis so daunting that the injunctions end up being meaningless. We noted how Hansen's (2002) investigation of learning missions in corporations showed how they floundered in the face of organizational inertia that simply resulted in excessive information demands of lower-order functionaries and further capture of whatever usable knowledge emerged from the process by top management for their own, possibly nefarious, motives. There is nothing intrinsically democratic about urging organizations to develop new 'learning' propensities absent organizational reform. This applies *a fortiori* to regions.

The second task attempted was to juxtapose the inherent weaknesses of the 'learning economy' perspective against a widely adopted approach proven, possibly surprisingly, to have stimulated enthusiasm and debate in both research and policy arenas. This is the broad 'innovation systems' perspective on the links between innovation and economic development. Operating at the regional scale, this proves to have major theoretical relevance both to understanding the detailed workings of the contemporary knowledge economy and to the construction of an overarching theory of contemporary economic growth. Important to this are ideas of 'open innovation' and 'regional knowledge capabilities'. We can understand much of the economic geography of contemporary economic development in 'Globalization 2' processes. Here, multinationals depend increasingly on *research* in their quest for global competitiveness. This happens by means of the conceptual and real interactions between 'open innovation systems' and the aforementioned *regional knowledge capabilities*.

Finally, a conceptual model was presented to show that regional innovation systems are an outcome of and a way of dealing with the problem of 'asymmetric knowledge' that is so fatal to a 'learning economy' perspective. Risk, time and scope were shown to be the proximate constraints on 'institutional borrowing' or 'learning by cloning'. Regional innovation systems perspectives recognize the need to manage risk by enhancing core regional capabilities. This entails setting up systems for constant monitoring and assessment of processes and policies of consequence to regional innovation. These seek to build 'constructed advantage' based on economies of scope that have a chance to generate a 'synergetic surplus' regarding knowledge, wealth and welfare of regional communities. This was shown to be intellectually and ethically superior to a viewpoint that scale impacts are the only abstraction worthy of study and a critique of multinationals, states and globalization the only practical way forward (MacKinnon et al., 2002). The latter approach is as weak analytically as it is in any prescriptive policy intent.

ACKNOWLEDGEMENTS

I express gratitude to Frans Boekema and Roel Rutten for stimulating me to articulate some problems I had found with the 'learning' approach, which nevertheless deserved credit for adding variety for a while to the 'new regionalism' gene pool. I also wish to thank the participants in the Lund University economic geography seminar in November 2004, where I first presented this critique of learning regions. Interjections from Bjørn Asheim, Ola Jonsson and Meric Gertler, in particular, made me think again, but I hope correctly. Finally, two policy bodies, VINNOVA (the Swedish Innovation Systems Agency), particularly Marit Werner and Lennart Stenberg, and the UK government's Department of Trade and Industry (Peter Bunn) are thanked for stimulating my thinking about the role of research in Europe's future economy.

NOTES

1. Thus, while leading agro-food clusters like Saskatoon in Canada have few DBFs, mainly large corporate R&D and Canadian national laboratories, a specialist knowledge centre such as The Netherlands' University of Wageningen has at least ten agro-food spinouts on its 'Food Valley' science park, along with numerous network linkages with both large and small Dutch and international agro-food firms through its Centre for Biosystems Genomics, a network of four universities, two research institutes and 15 firms in agro-food biotechnology.
2. As noted, on knowledge network capabilities, the early work of Penrose (1959) has given rise to the economics sub-field of studying 'dynamic capabilities' of firms to understand regional and other growth processes (Teece and Pisano, 1996).

3. This is a widely accepted norm in most locations testified to in research by Powell et al. (2002), among many others. It is because of the venture capitalist's need for a 'hands-on' relationship with its investment, possibly 'at the drop of a hat'. The greater the distance away from the investment, the greater the uncertainty about management control. As a case in point, Kleiner Perkins Caufield, Byers, the leading US venture capitalist, has 80 per cent of its so-called 'keiretsu' investments in biotechnology and ICT, within an hour's drive of its Sand Hills Road headquarters in Palo Alto (Cooke, 2001). The 'one-hour rule' was reasserted in all innocence by Oxford Technology venture capitalist, Matthew Frohn, in a BioLink project seminar held in Cardiff, 5 July 2004, eliciting consternation from assembled bioincubator managers and development agency personnel. The reasons given were precisely similar to those elicited by the American academics Powell et al. (2002).
4. In those days the leading DBFs were all associated with leading scientists. Alongside UCSF's Boyer with Genentech were Walter Gilbert of Harvard with Biogen, Ivor Royston of UCSD with Hybritech, Mark Ptashne of Harvard with Genetics Institute, and William Rutter of UCSF with Chiron. In the 1980s Nobel Laureate David Baltimore (MIT) founded SyStemix, Malcolm Gefter of MIT founded ImmuLogic, and Jonas Salk, Salk Institute San Diego, founded Immune Response (see Prevezer, 1998).
5. See http://www.eu.pg.com/news/2002/europeanresearch2002.html.
6. US National Science Foundation data show the share of US industrial R&D conducted by firms employing 25 000 and over declined from 71 per cent in 1981 to 36 per cent in 2000. Correspondingly, it rose for firms employing fewer than 1000 from 4 per cent to 22 per cent. Within the latter group it rose 120 per cent for firms employing fewer than 25 persons (1997–99). OECD (2004b) has the share of R&D spending in foreign affiliates rising from 22 per cent to 78 per cent in Hungary, reaching 75 per cent in Ireland and in Sweden and the UK rising to 40 per cent from an average of 25 per cent (1995–2001). In Japan it rose slightly, from 1 per cent to 4 per cent and in the USA 13 per cent to 17 per cent. This suggests that a 'research industry' is reconcentrating towards established and new 'knowledge economies'. Unfortunately, data on Brazil, India and China are not provided other than the observation that 'US [R&D] investments alone in China grew from $7 million to $500 million 1994–2000 ('Highlights', p. 11, OECD, 2004b).

REFERENCES

Akerlof, G. (1970), 'The market for "lemons": qualitative uncertainty and the market mechanism', *Quarterly Journal of Economics*, **84**, 488–500.
Amin, A. and Cohendet, P. (2003), *Architectures of Knowledge*, Oxford: Oxford University Press.
Argyris, C. (1962), *Interpersonal Competence & Organisational Effectiveness*, Homewood, IL: Dorsey.
Argyris, C. and Schon, D. (1978), *Organizational Learning*, Reading, MA: Addison-Wesley.
Arrow, K. (1962), 'The economic implications of learning-by-doing', *Review of Economic Studies*, **29**, 155–73.
Audretsch, D. and Dohse, D. (2004), 'The impact of location on firm growth', CEPR Discussion Paper no. 4332. London, Centre for Economic Policy Research. (http://www.cepr.org/pubs/dps/DP4332.asp)
Audretsch, D. and Feldman, M. (1996), 'Knowledge spillovers and the geography of innovation and production', *American Economic Review*, **86**, 630–40.
Bathelt, H. (2003), 'Growth regimes in spatial perspective 1: innovation, institutions and social systems', *Progress in Human Geography*, **27**, 789–804.

Brenner, N. (2001), 'The limits to scale? Methodological reflections on scalar struc-
turation', *Progress in Human Geography*, **25**, 591–614.
Breschi, S. and Lissoni, F. (2001), 'Knowledge spillovers and local innovation
systems: a critical survey', *Industrial & Corporate Change*, **10**, 975–1005.
Bunnell, T. and Coe, N. (2001), 'Spaces and scales of innovation', *Progress in
Human Geography*, **25**, 569–89.
Caniëls, M. and Romijn, H. (2005), 'What drives innovativeness in industrial clus-
ters? Transcending the debate', *Cambridge Journal of Economics*, **29**, 497–515.
Carlsson, B. (forthcoming), 'Innovation systems: a survey of the literature from a
Schumpeterian perspective', in H. Hanusch and A. Pyka (eds), *Elgar Companion
to Neo-Schumpeterian Economics*, Cheltenham, UK and Northampton, MA,
USA: Edward Elgar.
Chesbrough, H. (2003), *Open Innovation*, Boston, MA: Harvard Business School
Books.
Cooke, P. (1992), 'Regional innovation systems: competitive regulation in the new
Europe', *Geoforum*, **23**, 365–82.
Cooke, P. (2001), 'Regional innovation systems, clusters and the knowledge
economy', *Industrial & Corporate Change*, **10**, 945–74.
Cooke, P. (2002), *Knowledge Economies*, London: Routledge.
Cooke, P. (2003), 'The evolution of biotechnology in three continents:
Schumpeterian or Penrosian?', *European Planning Studies*, **11**, 789–804.
Cooke, P. (2004a), 'Biosciences and the rise of regional science policy', *Science and
Public Policy*, **31**, 185–97.
Cooke, P. (2004b), 'Globalisation of biosciences: knowledge capabilities and eco-
nomic geography', presented to the Centennial Conference of The American
Association of Geographers, Philadelphia, 16 March.
Cooke, P. (2004c), 'The substitution of in-house bioscience R&D by knowledge
value chain capabilities in a non-Schumpeterian sector: a Penrosian perspective',
presented at the 7th Uddevalla Symposium on 'Regions in Competition &
Cooperation', Östfold University College, Fredrikstad, Norway, 17–19 June.
Cooke, P. (2005), 'Rational drug design, the knowledge value chain and biosciences
megacentres', *Cambridge Journal of Economics*, **29**, 325–42.
Cooke, P., Heidenreich, M. and Braczyk, H. (eds) (2004), *Regional Innovation
Systems*, London: Routledge.
Cortright, J. and Mayer, H. (2002), *Signs of Life: the Growth of Biotechnology
Centres in the US*, Washington, DC: The Brookings Institution.
Dirckinck-Holmfeld, L. (2002), 'Problem oriented project pedagogy', in
L. Dirckinck-Holmfeld and B. Fibiger (eds), *Learning in Virtual Environments*,
Frederiksberg: Samfundslitteratur, pp. 56–70.
Etzkowitz, H. and Leydesdorff, L. (eds) (1997), *Universities and the Global
Knowledge Economy*, London: Pinter.
Foray, D. and Freeman, C. (1993), *Technology and the Wealth of Nations: The
Dynamics of Constructed Advantage*, London: Pinter.
Gibbons, J. (2000), 'The role of Stanford University: a Dean's reflection', in C. Lee,
W. Miller, M. Hancock and H. Rowen (eds), *The Silicon Valley Edge*, Stanford,
CA: Stanford University Press, pp. 200–217.
Gibbons, M., Limoges, C., Nowotny, H., Schwartzman, S., Scott, P. and Trow, M.
(1994), *The New Production of Knowledge*, London: Sage.
Haas, J. (1992), 'Introduction: epistemic communities and international policy
coordination', *International Organisation*, **46**, 1–37.

Hansen, M. (2002), 'Knowledge networks: explaining effective knowledge sharing in multi-unit companies', *Organisation Sciences*, **13**, 232–48.
Hirschman, A. (1958), *The Strategy of Economic Development*, New Haven, CT: Yale University Press.
Jaffe, A., Trajtenberg, M. and Henderson, R. (1993), 'Geographic localisation of knowledge spillovers as evidenced by patent citations', *Quarterly Journal of Economics*, **108**, 577–98.
Krugman, P. (1995), *Development, Geography & Economic Theory*, Cambridge, MA: MIT Press.
Latour, B. (1998), 'From the world of science to the world of research', *Science*, **280**, 208–9.
Levinthal, D. and March, J. (1993), 'The myopia of learning', *Strategic Management Journal*, **14**, 95–112.
Lorenzen, M. and Maskell, P. (2004), 'The cluster as a nexus of knowledge creation', in P. Cooke and A. Piccaluga (eds), *Regional Economies as Knowledge Laboratories*, Cheltenham, UK and Northampton, MA, USA: Edward Elgar, pp. 77–92.
Lundvall, B.-Å. (1994), 'The global unemployment problem and national systems of innovation', in D. O'Doherty (ed.), *Globalisation, Networking and Small Firm Innovation*, London: Graham & Trotman, pp. 35–48.
MacKinnon, D., Cumbers, A. and Chapman, K. (2002), 'Learning, innovation & regional development: a critical appraisal of recent debates', *Progress in Human Geography*, **26**, 293–311.
Malmberg, A. and Maskell, P. (2002), 'The elusive concept of localisation economies: towards a knowledge-based theory of spatial clustering', *Environment & Planning A*, **34**, 429–49.
March, J. (1991), 'Exploration and exploitation in organisational learning', *Organisation Sciences*, **2**, 71–87.
March, J. Sproull, L. and Tamuz, M. (1991), 'Learning from samples of one or fewer', *Organisation Science*, **2**, 1–13.
Myrdal, G. (1957), *Economic Theory & Underdeveloped Regions*, London: Duckworth.
Nowotny, H., Scott, P. and Gibbons, M. (2001), *Re-Thinking Science*, Cambridge: Polity.
OECD (1996), *The Knowledge-Based Economy*, Paris: OECD.
OECD (2004a), *Global Knowledge Flows & Economic Development*, Paris: OECD.
OECD (2004b), *Science, Technology & Industry Outlook*, Paris: OECD.
Oughton, C., Landabaso, M. and Morgan, K. (2002), 'The regional innovation paradox: innovation policy and industrial policy', *Journal of Technology Transfer*, **27**, 97–110.
Owen-Smith, J. and Powell, W. (2004), 'Knowledge networks as channels and conduits: the effects spillovers in the Boston biotechnology community', *Organization Science*, **15**, 5–21.
Penrose, E. (1959/1995), *The Theory of the Growth of the Firm*, Oxford: Oxford University Press.
Powell, W., Koput, K., Bowie, J. and Smith-Doerr, L. (2002), 'The spatial clustering of science and capital: accounting for biotech firm–venture capital relationships', *Regional Studies*, **36**, 291–305.
Prevezer, M. (1998), 'Clustering in biotechnology in the USA', in P. Swann, M. Prevezer and D. Stout (eds), *The Dynamics of Industrial Clustering*, Oxford: Oxford University Press, pp. 124–93.

Putnam, R. (1999), *Bowling Alone*, New York: Simon & Schuster.

Quéré, M. (2003), 'Knowledge dynamics: biotechnology's incursion into the pharmaceutical industry', *Industry & Innovation,* **19**, 255–73.

Rosenthal, S. and Strange, W. (2003), 'Geography, industrial organisation, and agglomeration', *The Review of Economics & Statistics*, **85**, 377–93.

Smith, K. (2001), 'What is the "knowledge economy"? Knowledge-intensive industries and distributed knowledge bases', Oslo, STEP Group.

Tavoletti, E. (2004), 'Higher education and high intellectual unemployment: does education matter? An interpretation and some critical perspectives', in P. Cooke and A. Piccaluga (eds), *Regional Economies as Knowledge Laboratories*, Cheltenham, UK and Northampton, MA, USA: Edward Elgar, pp. 20–37.

Teece, D. and Pisano, G. (1996), 'The dynamic capabilities of firms: an introduction', *Industrial & Corporate Change*, **3**, 537–56.

Valentin, F. and Lund-Jensen, R. (2003), 'Science-driven discontinuities and the organisation of distributed innovations: the case of biotechnology in food processing technologies', paper to DRUID Summer Conference 'Creating, Sharing & Transferring Knowledge', Copenhagen, 12–14 June.

Winter, S. (1984), 'Schumpeterian competition in alternative technological regimes', *Journal of Economic Behaviour and Organisation*, **5**, 287–320.

Wittgenstein, L. (1958), *Philosophical Investigations*, London: Macmillan.

Zeller, C. (2002), 'Regional and North Atlantic knowledge production in the pharmaceutical industry', in V. Lo and E. Schamp (eds), *Knowledge – the Spatial Dimension*, Münster: Lit-Verlag, pp. 131–66.

10. Localized learning and social capital

Mark Lorenzen

1. INTRODUCTION

This chapter discusses the importance of *social capital* (e.g. Bourdieu, 1986; Coleman, 1988; Burt, 1992; Putnam, 1993; Fukuyama, 1995; Woolcock, 1998; Baron et al., 2001; Lin, 2001; Lin et al., 2001; Field, 2003) for *localized learning* (i.e. processes of technological and institutional development taking place within confined regional spaces, such as clusters, as described by, for example, Malmberg and Maskell, 1999, Lorenzen, 2001 and Maskell, 2001).

Increasingly, scholars argue that persistent economic development differences among regions may be understood by focusing on social capital. In a resource-based view of regional economic development (see e.g. Foss, 1996; Maskell et al., 1998; Lorenzen, 2002), unique resource endowments of regions cause persistent differences in company performances, exports and economic growth. Obviously, regions' different locations, natural resource endowments, access to public or private venture capital, public educational programmes or knowledge transfers from universities often hugely influence their growth potential. However, taking all these resources into account is not sufficient to explain, for example, the persistent growth differences between Italian regions or Indian states, the emergence of successful clusters in hitherto predominantly rural areas around the world, or the success of some regions in restructuring their old industrial areas under the same conditions where others fail miserably.[1] Hence, some scholars argue that social capital is the 'residue' that may explain these regional performance differences, after we have taken other resource endowments into account.[2] In particular, social capital may facilitate *learning* at the regional level, thereby leading to product innovations and over-average export potential of local firms (Maskell et al., 1998; Lorenzen, 2002). In the following, I shall investigate and further develop this thesis.

With the rise of the knowledge economy (OECD, 1996; Lundvall and Maskell, 2000), traditional economic efficiencies of *production* (revolving around cost-cutting and stability) are giving way to efficiencies of *learning*.

This means a shift in economic organization. The abundance of flexible and temporary market-based forms (i.e. shifting interfirm relations and projects) is growing relative to integrated and stable forms (i.e. large firms and long-term networks). The chapter argues that the knowledge economy renders social capital increasingly valuable, because it organizes markets, serving as a social framework allowing business firms to connect and reconnect flexibly and to learn in both breadth and depth.

The chapter does not attempt to treat all aspects of the increasingly popular – and blurry – notion of social capital. Rather, providing a concise working definition of social capital, the chapter analyses why it is important for learning, regional competitiveness and economic development, why it has a regional dimension and how it is created. The chapter is structured as follows. Section 2 provides a workable definition of social capital. With other scholars, I suggest that a range of regional social phenomena arising from cooperative and reciprocal behaviour, such as altruism, trust, participation and inclusion, is preconditioned by the existence of *social relations* among agents (firms and persons), based on particular *social institutions* (shared conventions and codebooks). The chapter defines a dense amalgamation of different types of social relations and conventions cum codebooks as 'social capital'. Hence, contrary to some other scholars, I view trust and other benevolent social phenomena as outcomes of social capital, not parts of it. Furthermore, I emphasize the collective, non-proprietary dimension of social capital (as opposed to scholars who focus on single agents' or clubs' appropriation of the benefits of their social relations). I also emphasize the diversity, openness and social change that social capital allows for (contrary to scholars who view social capital as a stable phenomenon serving mainly to preserve established social traditions).

Section 3 takes as a starting point that competitiveness in the knowledge economy hinges on *technological learning*. It proceeds to analyse the impact of social capital on such learning. I argue that social capital facilitates interactive learning among business firms, because it lowers their incentive-related as well as cognitive *coordination costs*. Social capital is arguably an economically efficient framework for technological learning, because it offers a particularly diverse and flexible combination of knowledge resources.

Section 4 is devoted to a discussion of why stocks of social capital are often formed at the regional (rather than national or international) level. I point out that it is at the regional level that we find the densest configurations of weak and strong, *as well as* business-related and civic social relations – in other words, a regional *matrix* of different types of social relations, offering a wide and flexible framework for social interaction and learning processes. Hence *institutional learning*, bringing about (and adapting) social conventions and codebooks to further broaden the matrix of relations, is a predominantly regional phenomenon.

While a regional setting is necessary for social capital formation, it is clearly not sufficient. Some regions build large stocks of social capital and consequently experience growth in the knowledge economy, while others lag behind. Section 5 offers a discussion of why particular regions become richer in social capital than others. The section distinguishes between organic processes of social capital *accumulation* and policy processes of targeted *investments* in social capital.

The chapter is rounded off by a conclusion and brief investigation of how our discussion of social capital has added to a conceptualization of learning regions.

2.   A DEFINITION OF SOCIAL CAPITAL

Social Capital Defined

In recent literature, social capital has been assumed to mean many different things. A certain amount of terminological soup persists (for a discussion, see Woolcock, 1998). For example, altruism, trust, participation in different social activities (e.g. voluntary social work, leisure, or education), social inclusion and low crime levels have all been dubbed 'social capital'. Even if most of these social traits are obviously benevolent and important for economic development – and some of them are relatively easy to measure empirically – they seem to be chosen rather arbitrarily. Whether and how they are connected remains unclear.

For my purpose, I shall view trust and other benevolent social phenomena as *outcomes* of social capital, not parts of it, and revert to the relatively narrow definition of social capital employed by, for example, Coleman (1988, 1990) and Woolcock (1998). Social capital consists of 'Social relations among agents, resting on social institutions that allow for cooperation and communication.'[3] By 'social relations', I mean connections among two or more agents – in both business life and the civic sphere – that *affect behaviour*. Relations affecting behaviour need not be reciprocal (i.e. they may affect different agents in different ways. One agent may be forced to act due to the power distribution in a relation, while another agent may be inspired, but not forced, to act because of the information he receives through a relation). Nor do relations need to be direct (intransitive) to be effective. Especially in the civic sphere, indirect relations – relations mediated through third parties (e.g. friends of friends) – may be extremely influential due to the information they carry. I shall discuss the nature of social relations in more detail in Sections 3 and 4.

By 'agents', I mean persons (individuals), but these often represent the organizations (firms) in which they are employed. Hence social capital often benefits firms, and the effects on firms are the focus of discussion.

Social relations need not be particularly socially beneficial. As will become evident in the discussion in Section 5, some types of social relations may lead to collusion and economic stagnation. It is only in combination with particular social institutions that social relations become 'capital'. By 'social institutions', I refer to collective traits such as law, social conventions, languages, codes, or points of reference that through regulation, normative or cognitive alignment infuse social relations with cooperation and communication. Even if difficult to measure empirically (Abramovitz, 1986; Borgatti et al., 1998; Rotberg, 2001), such social relations with cooperation and communication arguably lead to the social traits mentioned above, such as trust, participation, low crime and so on.

Social Capital is Non-proprietary

Some scholars, keen on a methodological, individualist stance, view social capital as something that can be appropriated by single persons (Burt, 1992; Glaeser, 2001) or single firms (Gulati, 1999; Lin, 2001). While it is true that single persons or organizations may benefit from investing in their relations to others (just as they may benefit from investing in other types of capital, such as their employees' skills), focusing only on single agents' investments in social relations misses a key dimension of social capital.[4] Social capital is a powerful concept because it *supplements* methodological, individualist approaches to economic coordination, such as transaction-cost economics (Williamson, 1985, 2000). Pointing towards social capital as an institution, a *collective, non-proprietary asset* of a community of economic agents, helps to explain why individual rational agents make quite *different* choices in different regional settings and, consequently, how economic organization may differ between regions – an explanatory feat that, for example, transaction-cost economics is not able to pull off on its own.[5] This means that the social capital approach, by conceptualizing social capital as an asset with emergent properties, offers a powerful explanation of economic development differences. Exactly because social capital is collective and formed within communities through processes of interaction and institutional learning (see Section 4), it is a unique collective asset that is technically impossible to trade or imitate. Such collective assets are those that, if valuable, may form the basis for sustained competitive advantage for a community or region.

In the following, I shall discuss in more detail what is meant by social relations, social institutions, cooperation and communication, as well as formation of social capital. I begin by outlining why social capital is economically valuable.

3. THE VALUE OF SOCIAL CAPITAL

It is argued to the point of exhaustion by scholars and policy makers that we are entering the knowledge economy (e.g. OECD, 1996; Lundvall and Maskell, 2000) – an era in which competitiveness of firms, nations and regions is not only based on their efficiencies of producing cheaply and just in time, but also on continuous, flexible and cheap creation of knowledge, fostering product and process innovation (what we could call *technological learning*). Large-scale manufacturing is being automated and/or outsourced from former industrial regions to peripheral regions with low factor costs. Small-scale manufacturing becomes innovation-based and new consumer and supplier industries, revolving around product variety and economies of speed, spring up.

In this era, increasing globalization of demand and production, paired with a range of changes in facilitating technologies and international institutions, bring about a host of changes in the organization of economic activity – particularly in the OECD countries, where firms and industries need to change in order to cope with new forms of competition. As competitiveness hinges on efficiencies of learning more than efficiencies of production, firms implement new production methods, use different divisions of labour, changing their boundaries accordingly, depending on other types of institutions in order to coordinate their economic activities. It is in this setting that we can best understand the value of social capital. Below, I shall outline how particular social relations and social institutions, in turn, are valuable in the knowledge economy.

The Value of Social Relations

In economics, the innovation literature is replete with accounts of the interactive nature of technological learning. Eighteen years ago, von Hippel (1988) illustrated how firms use customers and suppliers when innovating. Since then, a whole literature has emerged, treating user–producer innovation, interactive learning, inter-organizational innovation and so on (for overviews and discussions, see e.g. Lundvall, 1992; Dyer and Singh, 1998; Ingram, 2002). The core argument is, of course, that collaborations – *relations* – among firms are drivers of technological learning. Firms may receive not only incentives for innovating along the vertical dimension of value chains, i.e. from customers and suppliers, but also valuable information feeding into the innovation process. Furthermore, firms may collaborate horizontally in alliances with other firms to innovate. The innovation literature points towards labour flows among firms as important sources of knowledge transfer.

Because many world markets are fluctuating and customer demands are increasingly ambiguous (or demanding in terms of customization), what is needed is not just stable, incremental learning or exploitation, but both exploitation and exploration (March, 1991). Such flexible learning makes it necessary for firms to connect to a range of diverse knowledge resources and constantly shift collaborations in order to learn in both breadth and depth (Lorenzen and Maskell, 2004). Consequently, we see how the nature of business relations shifts in an increasing number of industries. Whereas earlier efficiencies of production were often accomplished through integration or long-term networks, such as stable value chains or horizontal alliances, the efficiencies of learning in the knowledge economy render increasing economic value to a range of different flexible and temporary relations among firms – from the quintessential flexible specialization described by Piore and Sabel (1984) to project networks or temporary horizontal alliances (see e.g. Hobday 1998; Ekstedt et al., 1999; Grabher, 2002; Maskell and Lorenzen, 2004). For example, integrated pharmaceutical firms have given way to flexible outsourcing arrangements among specialized biotech firms; drug developers and drug producers and integrated Hollywood studios have been replaced by complex project networks of small-scale film-and-media production companies.

Whereas business relations among firms are particularly central to innovation in low-tech industries, studies of innovation systems (some of which are represented in other chapters of this book) point to the importance of a range of other relations. For example, relations among firms and universities and other public and semi-public knowledge centres may be important channels of information and knowledge. Particularly for firms in medium or high-tech industries, university training and research is a core input to learning.[6] A range of studies also addresses the learning effects of personal relations among managers and employees from different firms. Their collegial exchange of gossip and advice (often based on their belonging to the same professions, clubs or associations) may constitute an informal trade of information (von Hippel, 1987), or facilitate mutual monitoring among firms at the same stage in the value chain (Maskell and Lorenzen, 2004). Finally, sociological literature (e.g. Granovetter, 1973) notes that personal networks of families and friends may connect a social entity (such as a firm) with the outside world through socialization,

Table 10.1   Social relations and technological learning effects

Social relation	Learning effect
Value chains (vertical)	In-depth user–producer learning
Alliances (horizontal)	Knowledge built jointly
Flexible specialization	In-breadth learning
Interfirm project networks	Experimentation and customization
Industry–schools /universities relations	Research and education
Professions, clubs, associations	Informal know-how, trade, socialization, gossip
Families, friendships	Advice, passing on of information

exchanges of job-related and technical advice and gossip, therefore having important learning effects.

Table 10.1 summarizes these different social relations and their value for technological learning.

The Value of Social Institutions

Relations among business firms only lead to technological learning if information is exchanged openly and is well understood. However, specialized firms are typically different in terms of interests and goals, cultures, organizational designs and technologies. Differences between specialized firms make their trade valuable. They provide a potential for mutual learning. But these differences also raise huge potential *coordination* problems. There are two basic types of such problems (Lorenzen and Foss, 2003). First, differences in firms' goals and interests may cause *cooperation* problems. Rather than exchanging information openly, firms may lie and cheat, hence sacrificing technological learning for other, more short-sighted, goals. Second, even if firms are honest and seek to exchange information, differences in technologies, organizational designs, cultures or expectations may cause *communication* problems. Precisely when it is most valuable – i.e. under market uncertainty when demand and technological changes makes it necessary for firms to specialize, outsource and learn from each other – coordination is potentially most difficult. In order to overcome these obstacles to learning, firms rely on a range of *coordination mechanisms* of incentive alignment to solve cooperation problems and cognitive alignment to facilitate communication.

However, traditional coordination mechanisms, such as long-term contracts (Holmström and Milgrom, 1994; Hart, 1995; Williamson, 1985, 2000) or stable, partner-specific or dyadic trust (Lorenzen, 2002), which have proved efficient in a *production* logic because they lower costs and provide security and communication along value chains, are not particularly efficient in a *learning* logic, because they are designed to govern long-term relationships, rather than the more flexible and temporary relations needed in the knowledge economy. If firms rely on contracts, while at the same time needing to connect to a range of diverse knowledge resources to learn flexibly, they may be faced with huge dynamic transaction costs of constantly designing new contracts for shifting partners (Langlois and Robertson, 1995).

Hence, with the rise of the knowledge economy, other types of coordination mechanisms are valuable. What is needed for propagating technological learning are mechanisms that, rather that governing closed partnerships and stable networks (clubs), instead organize the market (Maskell and Lorenzen, 2004) and solve cooperation and communication problems for a large number of business firms that can flexibly connect and reconnect. In other words, whereas business firms may solve bilaterally many of their potential coordination problems in their long-term relations, their temporary and flexible relations are dependent on a social environment – *social institutions* (North and Thomas, 1973).[7]

There is a range of social (collective) institutions that may serve to lower cooperation problems through aligning incentives, from the regulative to the normative (Scott, 1995). National or international background law (such as trade legislation or patent law) is designed to regulate incentives in business relations, but such laws are too generic and have too high monitoring and sanctioning costs to stand alone in order to coordinate flexible and development-oriented relations. This is why, in many contexts, informal social contracts in the guise of social conventions (Granovetter, 1982; Taylor, 1982; Elster, 1989) serve to further coordinate social interaction, including business transactions, through social monitoring, gossip and reputation effects.[8] Such normative social institutions have demonstrated that they can efficiently allow for flexible business relations in different contexts (Macaulay, 1963; Lorenzen and Foss, 2003).

There is also a range of cognitive (Scott, 2002) social institutions that may lower coordination problems related to communication. In order to understand and learn from each other, business firms have to rely on some shared social codebooks that allow them to code and interpret information in the same way. Such social codebooks consist of shared languages (Lorenzen, 1998; Cowan et al., 2000; Lissoni, 2001) and common points of reference or focal points (Schelling, 1960) in the guise of shared experiences or myths. Social codebooks not only serve to increase firms' abilities to share information, but may also align their expectations about each other. One outcome of such cognitive coordination is social trust, where a whole collective group of agents takes mutual cooperation for granted, even if they have no direct experience with each other (Lorenzen, 2002, Lorenzen and Foss, 2003). Social trust is brought about in a cognitive process of automatically ascribing trust to a particular category of agents on the basis of their social characteristics, for example, employment, training, religion, or simply membership in the same social class or group (Fukuyama, 1995).[9]

As can be seen, social institutions (such as social conventions and social codebooks) are more conducive to learning than dyadic coordination mechanisms (such as contracts and partner-specific trust), simply because they allow for more – and more flexible – relations. But some social institutions may also be more conducive to learning than others. In fact, *cognitive* social institutions are likely to be better suited for learning than normative institutions: when firms align expectations and understand each other well, but are not necessarily constrained by narrow schemes for correct behaviour that social norms would impose on them, they are open to experiment freely with each other, in an intricate web of information-intensive and flexible relations. For example, social trust based on shared myths or expectations is collective and inclusive to a whole group of people and hence more efficient for flexible relations than dyadic trust (which would lock agents into long-lasting relations). Social trust is also more efficient for learning than tightly knit social norms, which would limit the types of relations and actions firms could undertake with each other.

4. THE REGIONAL DIMENSION OF SOCIAL CAPITAL

We have now established that social capital consists of social relations in combination with the social institutions that facilitate them. I have also made the point that flexible relations and cognitive social institutions are particularly valuable as social capital. Why, then, is social capital a regional phenomenon? In order to answer that question, let us further explore the nature of social relations and institutions.

The Regional Dimension of Social Relations

A key reason that social capital is often regional is that many social relations and, in particular, *combinations of different types of social relations*, are place-bound, because they are interdependent. For my purposes, I discuss two dimensions – and hence four main types – of social relations.

The first dimension of social relations (see Table 10.2) is their *realm*: the business realm versus the civic realm.[10] As *business relations* are the

Table 10.2   Types of social relations

Realm		
Nature	Business relations	Civic relations
Tightly coupled	Networks: Value chains Alliances	Strong ties: Families, friendships Clubs Universities and schools
Loosely coupled	Temporary organizations: Flexible specialization Projects	Weak ties: Families and friends of friends Professions Associations

relations in which technological learning and trade take place, they are also the type of relations that ultimately produce the most easily recognizable economic results. However, a much more abundant type of relations is, of course, relations that are established for many other reasons than profit making: *civic relations* among people in everyday life, knit through kinship; during school days (or reunions); through leisure and culture activities; in sports or in volunteer work and so on.

The second dimension in Table 10.2 is constituted by the *nature* of social relations: tightly coupled versus loosely coupled. *Tightly coupled* (Weick, 1979) relations bond agents together in relatively homogeneous social groups (Putnam, 2000). Tightly coupled relations are direct (with no intermediaries), encompassing frequent interactions among the agents involved, interdependent (participants are likely to influence each other when they act) and often firmly coordinated through regulation. In the business realm, this applies to long-term networks such as stable value chains and strategic alliances and in the civic realm to strong ties (Granovetter, 1973): families, long-term friendships and long-standing participation in schools/university programmes and some types of club memberships, where people meet frequently and interact directly.

Loosely coupled (Weick, 1979) relations are fluctuating (on–off) or short-lasting, with relatively little – or only temporary – interdependence. They typically bridge different social groups that are strongly coupled, internally (Putnam, 2000). In the business realm, an example of loosely coupled relations is temporary market organizations: business relations that are established quickly and are not meant to last, as when a furniture maker buys a shipment of standard components or an advertising agency uses a freelance photographer. Loosely coupled civic relations are weak ties: personal relations that are transitive – i.e. mediated through third parties, such as when people have common acquaintances (friends of friends) or because they share membership in an association based on professions or hobbies. Giving rise to casual, short-lasting and flexible interactions, weak ties are able to span the borders between the stable and closed relations constituted by strong ties, enriching agents with in-breadth information through gossip and opinions – and occasional favours – that strong ties do not provide them with (Granovetter, 1973).

Not all four types of social relations are equally sensitive to geographical distance, but they are all more abundant locally because those that are less dependent on proximity spring from those that are more so. Consequently, we see the densest configurations of *all* these types of relations within relatively small geographic areas. Let me explain this in more detail.

At the heart of the argument is the fact that tightly coupled civic relations – strong ties – are often extremely sensitive to distance. This is because they may be formally constrained to the geographical catchment area of a club; they may radiate from a particular place (such as a school, university, or other organization that encourages people to meet and talk); or may depend on place-specific physical artefacts or facilities (a golf course, a lake or a plaza). As they are not business relations and have no corporate sponsors sinking planned investments in maintaining them, strong ties hinge on frequent face-to-face meetings among people in the civic sphere. Such meetings are very sensitive to distance costs (Granovetter, 1982; Becattini, 1990; Brusco, 1992; Lorenzen, 1998) – to the point where Sweeney (1991) refers to the 'half-hour transport time contact potential'.

This distance sensitivity of tightly coupled civic relations (strong ties) rubs off on loosely coupled civic relations (weak ties). The scope of this type of relations is often claimed to be global. Weak ties among immigrants (such as the notorious personal relations among Chinese) are often able to span national borders. Members of some clubs will also gladly travel the world to participate in their events. Think of the global span and travel activities of Star Trekkies and golf fanatics, or the online communities of users of some exclusive software programs. But weak ties spring from strong ties. With more friends, there are also more friends' friends: friendly or family bonds as well as tightly knit networks of university alumni or club members recommend people to each other, thus adding 'halos' of weak ties to the strong ties. This means that strong ties' sensitivity to geographical distance can be traced in the patterns of weak ties: even if *single* weak ties have the potential to span distance, *patterns* of them have a regional dimension. It should of course also be noted that, with time, weak ties may also develop into strong ties. This interdependence of civic relations adds to their regionalization.

The fact that civic relations are more abundant regionally has a notable effect on business relations. First, let us consider loosely coupled such relations – temporary organizations. This type of relations is extremely dependent on speed. The furniture maker in the example above is likely to use a local supplier in order to minimize delivery time, just as the advertising firm is likely to choose a local freelancer, because it is easier and quicker. This need for speed when setting up temporary organization often brings firms to draw on civic relations – strong or weak ties – in order to identify and contact new suppliers and other partners. Because civic relations are local, temporary business organizations often become local, too.

Second, the distance sensitivity of civic relations rubs off on tightly coupled business relations – networks. This type of social relation is not sensitive to distance *per se* (Maskell and Lorenzen, 2004). Due to the direct and easily recognizable economic benefit of business relations, firms may sink asset-specific investments (Williamson, 1985) into them and thus be willing to pay transport costs and communication costs (which are diminishing anyway, due to new technologies), along with costs of travel and personnel exchanges associated with maintaining them (Gertler, 1995; Andersen, 1999). The types of business relations that firms are bound to be most willing to invest in and pay distance costs for are tightly coupled business relationships, such as strategic partnerships or long-term supplier relations. For example, General Motors thinks little of paying for airfare to maintain relations with Daewoo in Korea. Italian and German suppliers of machine tools constantly travel the world to service their customers. The fact is that, after being established, tightly coupled business relations may (seemingly paradoxically) demand relative rare face-to-face meetings between agents and, if the relation is tightly enough coupled, communication technology may substitute for much face-to-face contact. But nevertheless, many business networks are still regionalized. Some business collaborations may be facilitated by universities or public agencies that operate with geographically defined catchment areas. But more notably, such business relations also often spring from civic – and hence regional – relations among managers. This means that a great deal of them continue to be local, even with increasing global opportunities for trade and outsourcing. Adding to the regionalization of business networks is the fact that they sometimes spring from regionally abundant, loosely coupled business relations that develop into long-term value chains or alliances.

Table 10.3 sums up how, due to the interdependencies described above, different social relations are regionalized. Consider a matrix with a dense configuration of tightly coupled as well as loosely coupled, business-related and civic relations. Such a matrix of relations has, *ceteris paribus*, the strongest possible learning effects, as it holds a wide variety of opportunities for forming new types of flexible business relations with learning effects

Table 10.3   Regionalization of social relations

Realm		
Nature	Business relations	Civic relations
Tightly coupled	Networks: Not sensitive to distance – but more abundant in regions because they **spring from civic relations and temporary organizations**	Strong ties: **Highly sensitive to distance** because they depend on face-to-face contact
Loosely coupled	Temporary organizations: **Highly sensitive to distance** because they depend on speed	Weak ties: Not sensitive to distance – but more abundant in regions because they **spring from strong ties**

in breadth and in depth. Because many business relations depend on civic relations and many weak ties depend on strong ties, the distance sensitivity of civic relations and strong ties rubs off on business relations and weak ties, and they often also take on a distinct regional dimension. Hence a matrix of all four types of social relations is inevitably regional, a 'regional matrix of social relations'. Simply speaking, it is only in regions that we find, within the same group of firms and people, interconnected relations pertaining to money, work, sport and to a thousand other issues – some relations tight and long-lasting, others inspiring and loose.

The Regional Dimension of Institutions

A further reason that social capital is often confined to regions is that social institutions are also often regional. Quite simply, most regulatory institutions such as laws and rules have a defined catchment area – that of regional or city governments or of universities, clubs, etc. For example, contract law, police codes and membership rules apply to countries, counties and buildings, respectively. Cognitive institutions may also be place-bound, because they refer to local artefacts (e.g. buildings or sights). Without noticing it, we tend to behave in particular ways when we dine in the club or walk the plaza. But a more profound reason that social institutions are regional is that they not only serve to facilitate social relations; they are also *created* in social relations. Just as matrices of social relations facilitate technological learning, they also facilitate *institutional* learning. The results of such processes, in which groups of agents have interacted repeatedly, are normative and cognitive institutions. Social norms and codebooks have arisen as a result of regional problems, been tried out on regional problems and adapted over time to facilitate regional coordination (Lorenzen and Foss, 2003). Even if Silicon Valley is very different from a North Italian textile district in terms of market context, both regions take advantage of coordination among local firms made possible by an intricate local system of regulative, normative and cognitive institutions that has evolved over decades. Thus institutional learning processes create communities and, because learning is most efficient in matrices of social relations that are densest within regions, communities become regional. For example, Elster (1989) analyses how conventions arise and function in nation states and regional communities and – even if Holzner's (1972) original notion of communities coordinated by shared cognitive institutions – *epistemic* communities – was placeless and Haas (1989) analyses such communities (in the guise of business professionals) in a global context – there is ample evidence that many cognitive institutions and epistemic communities revolved around them are regional (Pyke et al., 1992; Braczyk et al., 1998; Lazaric and Lorenz, 1998; Keeble and Wilkinson, 2000; Lorenzen and Foss, 2003).

Because many social institutions are learned in social relations, they evolve regionally. But they also only *function* regionally, by virtue of regional social relations. For example, social conventions and reputation effects are only efficient if there are ample weak ties to spread around gossip and sufficient strong ties to facilitate social sanctions towards community members who breach social conventions. In a regional setting, there is not only a high number of both weak and strong ties, but also a finite number of agents, meaning better possibilities for identifying malefactors (Casson, 1997) and sanctioning them (Taylor, 1982). Whether a region's industry is low-tech and decentralized as in traditional industrial districts, or revolves around dominant firms or a university environment as in Cambridge, industry agents know each other and know *of* each other in the local industrial 'village'.

Hence we find particularly rich varieties of both social relations and institutions only in regions. It is true that most countries show an abundance of both business and civic interaction among people at the national level. It is also true that globalization has brought about new types of business-oriented as well as civic global communities. However, no such global, or even national, community can match a region's dense matrix of subcontracting, strategic alliances, informal know-how exchanges, plus interactions in employers' associations and in labour unions, in football clubs, at golf courses, or in the local pub or in the street – underpinned by unique local dialects and proverbs, local myths and local gossip and reputation effects. The potential regional wealth of such social capital and, hence, the regional scope for learning is unique.

5.   THE DYNAMICS OF SOCIAL CAPITAL

While the greatest scope for social capital and learning is regional, firms in
some regions have a modest learning rate and fall behind in the knowledge
economy. Clearly, while a regional setting is *necessary* for social capital
formation, it is not *sufficient*. In the following, I shall discuss why not all
regions are equally rich in social capital.

Some Regions Lack Social Capital

One reason for a region being relatively poor in social capital may be
poverty of social relations. For example, in the business realm, if dominant
('flagship') firms set up and coordinate supplier networks from the top
down, relations may be few and all tightly coupled. Many scale-intensive
industries, like shipbuilding, have thus been characterized by non-
reciprocal business relations and 'star'-type value chains (all directed at one
customer). But such patterns also seem to arise in a range of newer and
more knowledge-intensive industries that become coordinated by system
houses or a few dominant distributors. In all these cases, the potential for
interactive learning and experimentation across value chains is limited.
Another reason for a lack of relations or a dominance of tightly coupled
relations may simply be that an economic downturn has eradicated many
business relations, as in the case of shipbuilding in many OECD countries.
A lack of (venture) capital may also serve to hold down the number of business relations – clearly, in many cases social capital needs to be funded by
financial capital (Lorenzen, 2001). In the civic realm, relations may be fewer
and mostly benefiting a limited number of privileged insiders if closed,
exclusive clubs dominate leisure and society life. Extreme examples are how
the church and very closed and exclusive guilds have restricted and regi-
mented social as well as economic activities in some societies. The result of
such a dominance of a few tightly coupled social relations is collusion and
little and slow learning (technological as well as institutional), serving to
reproduce yesterday's technologies and old-fashioned traditions (Putnam,
2000; Florida, 2002).[11]

A region may also be rich in social relations, but poor in institutions.
Some regions experience institutional learning through social relations, but
rather than leading to socially beneficial institutions that promote openness
and dynamism, hence facilitating further institutional learning in a cumulative causation (and, of course, also facilitating technological learning),
institutional learning processes in these regions have amounted to misunderstandings and failed experiments with openness and collaboration. In
game-theoretic terminology, we could say that such a type of region where

institutions both impede collaboration and social learning has reached a low institutional equilibrium compared to equilibrium with socially beneficial and self-reinforcing social institutions (Lorenzen, 2002).[12] In the case of a low institutional equilibrium, conventions and expectations *prevent* cooperation and communication rather than facilitate it. Consequently, social relations are replete with distrust (which is different from and more costly than a lack of trust) and misunderstandings (which are more costly than a lack of communication). The dominance of the mafia and the general suspicion, hate and economic and institutional sclerosis this has brought about in some South Italian regions is a case in point (Putnam, 1993).

How can we explain, then, that some regions do manage to build social capital? When is a positive causation between social relations and institutional learning set in motion? Let us look into the processes in which social capital comes about. I shall distinguish between organic processes of social capital *accumulation* and strategic (or, at least, politically influenced) processes of social capital *investments*.

Accumulation of Social Capital

As social capital is a complex collective system of social relations and institutions, it is basically created in organic, non-planned, collective processes. Some scholars (e.g. Kristensen, 1992; Putnam, 1993) suggest that social capital accumulation is a process that may well take many decades and be deeply rooted in earlier institutions in the regional institutional sediment, which may well be one hundred years old. While it is likely that institutions have a history and often build on or draw analogies from each other (Lorenzen and Foss, 2003), it may be too conservative to suggest that accumulation of social capital takes decades or centuries: new industrial spaces (Scott, 1998), from high-tech Silicon Valleys to North European low-tech clusters, are examples of regions that accumulated developed and accumulated social capital much faster.

While social capital accumulation may thus happen in course of a decade or two, it may take external shocks (such as market developments or technological shifts) to set the process in motion. Experimenting with setting up both business and civic relations where few abounded earlier, and learning new institutions and practices, can be set off by a strong market pull or push (Lorenzen, 1998; OECD, 2001; Lorenzen and Foss, 2003). Hence (even this is likely to be of little comfort to policy makers) *chance* is bound to play an important role for social capital accumulation in many regions. But *key agents* may also spur the accumulation process. One example is the 'grand old men', fast-acting entrepreneurs whose firms create a regional

demand for sub-suppliers and spin off new firms by employing and training the people who later embark on own ventures. Another example is
visionary entrepreneurs, who through large, symbolic ventures (such as big
malls, museums, hotels, or the like), inspire others to conduct their own,
independent, economic experiments. Through such early events, whether
they be induced by chance or created by key regional agents, an initial stock
of social capital can breed more social capital: it stimulates technological
learning and economic success, which may build confidence in the very
strategies of interacting, openness and learning, inspiring new local agents
to build social relations and interact.

Investments in Social Capital

While social capital is built through organic, bottom–up accumulation,
public authorities and policy making may also play a vital role in setting
this process in motion. It is a misconception to define the civic as 'the non-
public' and to view social relations with public participation as a less
important constituent of social capital. It is equally wrong that private
agents always benefit social capital accumulation more than public agents.
In fact, public policy making is often important for social capital creation
because in some cases it takes deliberate investments – which may only be
undertaken or at least coordinated by public agents – to create social relations or set off institutional learning. Let us look at these types of investments in turn.

First, if social relations are few and reciprocity is modest (relations are
predominantly tightly coupled, serve dominant agents' interests, and information and goods do not flow freely but rather along directions set by dominant agents), public action may be necessary to 'loosen' social relations. If
public policy makers design rules for tenders in subcontracting, offer public
tenders, or offer incentives for outsider entrepreneurs to build new business
relations among themselves in order to challenge dominant firms and possibly short-circuit their relations, relations *within* the region can be de-
monopolized. The public may also play an important role in boosting civic
relations related to leisure, culture and various unions and associations.

There is also an important role for the public to play in regions with very
few relations to the *outside* world. While regions are typically open systems
(Braczyk et al., 1998) in terms of flows of goods and fiscal capital, it is still
an open question as to how open they are (or should be) in terms of social
capital flows. Some regions have built social relations among a limited
group of agents with local origins and formed social institutions in
predominantly closed local learning and investment processes, forming
social capital bases that typically support traditional industries. For such

regions that experience social as well as economic stability and maintain an acceptable rate of technological learning (expressed in exports) within traditional industries, the role of the public may well be to ensure stability and preserve the regional way of life. This type of social capital, along with the policy challenge that comes with it, is characteristic of many traditional industrial districts, e.g. in North Italy. However, other regions demonstrate quite another logic. The high social capital stocks of Silicon Valley, Cambridge and several Canadian regions demonstrate that a region may have a surprising capacity for successfully integrating a high number of immigrants into a regional system of social relations and institutional learning. Hence the role of policy makers who want to invest in and protect stocks of social capital is not to close a region to outside influences, competences and people, but rather to invite and propagate them, without undermining social stability and institutional learning, destabilizing social relations and dismantling social institutions.

Second, apart from addressing the social relations issue, a further role for policy making is to facilitate institutional *unlearning*. This is necessary if industrial history has resulted in a low institutional equilibrium of conventions of non-cooperation, as described above. In a game-theoretic perspective, a low institutional equilibrium can be viewed as one of two possible outcomes of a reciprocal (or tit-for-tat) game (Axelrod, 1984). If an agent cheats and everybody else reciprocates by cheating, the game ends in a low equilibrium. But if just one agent puts himself at risk and cooperates, other agents reciprocate by cooperating, thus pushing the equilibrium 'upwards'. In a region low on social capital, such *a first cooperative move* would, ideally, trigger an institutional learning process that will eventually redesign social conventions into cooperation (ultimately facilitating further institutional learning and social capital accumulation). The public can be the first agent that dares to cooperate, in order to set off a cumulative process of institutional learning.[13] Public–private partnerships are one way for policy makers to set off a new regional 'game' by playing 'Collaborate' first.

A relatively simple type of public investment in regional social capital is a large-scale construction project, as it may serve to create both an initial stock of social relations that spur further tie-building, plus act as artefact and symbol, creating a cognitive point of reference or even a myth that lays the foundation for later institution-building (OECD, 2001). The bridge built across the Swedish/Danish Øresund region, the Bluewater shopping centre built as a part of the regeneration of Kent Thames-side, or the museum and other cultural tourist attractions built in Bilbao are examples of attempts to invest in regional social capital, among other things. It is noteworthy, however, that not just any large-scale, prestige project will serve as a social capital investment. Many such large-scale projects incur few firms, spin-offs or social relations, as well as limited legitimacy, common interest or institution-building. Hence they are likely to remain short-term investments in personal prestige and political careers rather than long-term investments in social capital.

The Role of the Nation State

A basic role of the nation state has always been to form a foundation for the development of social capital at all national geographical levels. As mentioned, financial capital sometimes spurs social capital. National industry funds are often needed to support the formation of new business relations through start-ups. It also takes a nation to fight poverty. Belief in government has been and still is a crucial foundation on which social conventions of cooperation may rest (Lundvall and Maskell, 2000; Maskell, 2001). This role of the state is not at all trivial, which huge persisting national differences in social capital stocks demonstrate.[14]

But there may be a further role for the state related to the formation of social capital: to boost regional policy-making processes, inspiring and forcing regions with a low stock of social capital to invest in it. Even if cumulative causation among social capital, economic growth and public investments (meaning that even a modest initial investment in social capital may hugely influence a region's later economic performance) should make it very attractive for regional policy makers to invest in social capital, there are often barriers to such investments. Regional policy makers are often too locked in to particular policies (for instance, avoiding public–private partnerships) or lacking strategic thinking, involvement or legitimacy to invest in social capital, efficiently. Put simply, there may be a need for institutional unlearning at the regional *policy* level.

Global economic or political shocks can sometimes be conducive to setting off a regional policy process of investing in social capital (OECD, 2001). However, there is also great scope for national policy making here. For example, the Danish national planning law has for 50 years demanded that all Danish regions (counties) present plans for economic and social development. The latter years' increased planning pull has forced these regions to identify their key economic strengths and weaknesses and present coherent strategies for tackling them through economic, spatial and social policies. The pending regional reform (where municipalities are merged and regions are changed) is bound to spur this regional planning and investment process further. Moreover, regions compete for national funds for selected technology areas by setting up regional consortia. This has forced regional agents, private as well as public, to collaborate and form new types of social relations. Similar competitions among German *länder* (e.g. for biotech funds) have brought about new regional collaborations and institutions (OECD, 2001).

6. CONCLUSION

This chapter has contributed to our understanding of learning regions by looking at why society's most basic social infrastructure for learning – social capital – is a regional phenomenon. The chapter has argued that in the knowledge economy social capital 'finances' knowledge and skill assets. The chapter has uncovered how social capital – defined as a matrix of four types of social relations, along with institutions facilitating cooperation and communication – is a necessary precondition for localized learning. The chapter further suggested that social capital is a predominantly regional phenomenon, because it is either weak or strong at regional level; and civic and professional relations come together to facilitate institutional learning processes. Only with a certain stock of social capital, allowing for cooperation and communication, may a region be able to 'socially finance' technological learning. Social capital therefore has the potential for turning a region into a learning region.

Even if formation of social capital is a bottom–up process of building social relations and institutional learning, it plays an important role in public policy – through finance, public investments, public–private partnerships and symbolic and regulative efforts – at regional as well as national levels. There seems to be a division of labour of social capital policies. Whereas regional policy makers may need to invest in social capital formation through public projects, formation of public–private partnerships, influencing the nature of local relations and opening the region to external influences, national policy makers may provide background law and finance opportunities while provoking or otherwise moving regional policy makers to engage in social capital investments.

Research into learning regions has so far – quite naturally – drawn on diverse research fields such as education and learning studies (e.g. Rees et al., 1997; OECD, 2001), economic geography (e.g. Romer, 1986; Krugman, 1991; Fujuta et al., 1999); and regional studies (e.g. Brazyck et al., 1998; Cooke and Piccaluga, 2005). The literature on learning and education only focuses on select parts of learning regions, those connected to education, leaving out an analysis of business firms. Paradoxically, economic geography also has a tendency to ignore business firms, but for quite other reasons. Coming from a mainstream economic research tradition, economic-geography scholars often treat innovation and knowledge spillovers as phenomena that can be studied independently from the firms and other agents who bring them about. Furthermore, even if regional studies is now booming with studies of (and arguments about) knowledge-creating business firms and organizations (such as universities), many such studies often pay little more than lip service to the social embeddedness of business relations in civic society.

Digging into the problem of social capital clearly supplements these three research streams. Hence the social capital angle is an important constituent of an emerging theory of learning regions, as scrutinizing social capital's constituents – social relations and social institutions – reveals why so many learning processes are inherently regional. Furthermore, it uncovers the processes that are at the base of technological and institutional learning, facilitating a policy discussion that is so far relatively rare within the discourse on learning regions – or, for that matter, economic geography and regional studies.

NOTES

1. In development theory, scholars increasingly look for involvement, social ties and so on, as explanations for economic development differences, rather than trade regimes or government programmes (Hirschman, 1986; Miller, 1997). Another case in point is the rise of the Scandinavian welfare societies from being a part of the underdeveloped periphery of Europe to a GDP per capita that is among the highest in the world, while other European countries with a much stronger resource endowment lagged behind (Lundvall and Maskell, 2000).
2. Hall and Jones (1999) refer to 'social infrastructures' and Abramovitz (1986) uses the expression 'social capability'. In economics, social or institutional 'residue' is not a new idea (see e.g. Perroux, 1988).
3. This formulation is mine. Coleman (1988), for example, does not use the term 'institutions', as it is used here and in Woolcock (1998); the somewhat catchy phrase 'networks and norms' is used to denote what I refer to as 'relations and institutions'. In the following sections, it will become clear why I choose to use this terminology. It should be noted that defining social capital as social relations and institutions is at odds with Bourdieu's definition. In Bourdieu (1986), he views social capital as *resources that result from* social relations, not the social relations themselves.
4. This mode of analysing social capital is akin to the way *human* capital has been analysed by, for example, Becker (1964).
5. Williamson (1996) tends to explain social phenomena, such as collaboration and trust, as an outcome only of single rational choices of agents, not influenced by social institutions.
6. For a discussion of when such public knowledge centres are important, see Cooke's chapter in this book (Chapter 9).
7. While referring to social institutions as an 'environment', North and Thomas (1973) refer to partner-specific institutions such as contracts or dyadic trust as an 'arrangement'.
8. Elster (1989) uses the notion 'norms' instead of 'conventions'.
9. Hence I view social trust as an *outcome* of social capital (social ties and institutions), not a part of it, as many other authors would have it.
10. I juxtapose 'civic' with 'business'.
11. Whereas Putnam (2000) refers to the dominance of tightly coupled relations as 'negative' social capital, I simply call it a *lack* of social capital.

12. Of course, 'equilibrium' is meant as a metaphor for a particular type of development path. No social system – and least of all a region – can be said to be at rest.
13. Of course, this strategy hinges on other regional agents to play as Axelrod (1984) predicts: reciprocally.
14. Putnam's (1993) explanatory model can be criticized for its lack of state agency (Tarrow, 1996; Rothstein and Stolle, 2003).

REFERENCES

Abramovitz, M. (1986), 'Catching up, forging ahead and falling behind', *Journal of Economic History*, **46**, 385–406.
Andersen, P.H. (1999), 'Organizing international technological collaboration in subcontractor relationships: an investigation of the knowledge-stickiness problem', *Research Policy*, **28** (6), 625–42.
Axelrod, R. (1984), *The Evolution of Cooperation*, Princeton, NJ: Princeton University Press.
Baron, S. et al. (eds) (2001), *Social Capital: Critical Perspectives*, Oxford: Oxford University Press.
Beccatini, G. (1990), 'The Marshallian industrial district as a socio-economic notion', in F. Pyke, G. Beccatini and W. Sengenberger (eds), *Industrial Districts and Inter-firm Co-operation in Italy*, Geneva: International Institute for Labour Studies, pp. 37–51.
Becker, G.S. (1964), *Human Capital*, New York: Columbia University Press.
Borgatti, S.P. et al. (1998), 'Network measures of social capital', *Connections*, **21** (2), 1–36.
Bourdieu, P. (1986), 'The forms of capital', in J.G. Richardson (ed.), *Handbook of Theory and Research for the Sociology of Education*, New York: Greenwood Press.
Braczyk, H. et al. (eds) (1998), *Regional Innovation Systems: The Role of Governance in a Globalized World*, London: UCL Press.
Brusco, S. (1992), 'Small firms and the provision of real services', in F. Pyke and W. Sengenberger (eds), *Industrial Districts and Local Economic Regeneration*, Geneva: ILO, pp. 177–96.
Burt, R.S. (1992), *Structural Holes*, Cambridge: Cambridge University Press.
Casson, M. (1997), *Information and Organization*, Oxford: Clarendon Press.
Coleman, J.S. (1988), 'Social capital in the creation of human capital', *American Journal of Sociology*, **94** (supplement), S95–S120.
Coleman, J.S. (1990), *Foundations of Social Theory*, Cambridge, MA: Harvard University Press.
Cooke, P. and Piccaluga, A. (eds) (2005), *Regional Economies as Knowledge Laboratories*, Cheltenham, UK and Northampton, MA, USA: Edward Elgar Publishing.
Cowan, R. et al. (2000), 'The explicit economics of knowledge codification and tacitness', *Industrial and Corporate Change*, **9** (2), 211–53.
Dyer, J. and Singh, H. (1998), 'The relational view: cooperative strategy and sources of interorganizational competitive advantage', *Academy of Management Review* **23** (4), 660–79.
Ekstedt, E. et al. (1999), *Neo-industrial Organizing: Renewal by Action and Knowledge Formation in a Project-intensive Economy*, London: Routledge.

Elster, J. (1989), *The Cement of Society: A Study of Social Order*, Cambridge: Cambridge University Press.

Field, J. (2003), *Social Capital*, London: Routledge.

Florida, R. (2002), *The Rise of the Creative Class: And How it is Transforming Work, Leisure, Community and Everyday Life*, New York: Basic Books.

Foss, N.J. (1996), 'Higher-order industrial capabilities and competitive advantage', *Industry and Innovation (Journal of Industry Studies)*, **3** (1), 1–20.

Fujita, M. et al. (1999), *The Spatial Economy*, Cambridge, MA: MIT Press.

Fukuyama, F. (1995), *Trust: The Social Virtues and the Creation of Prosperity*, New York: Free Press.

Gertler, M. (1995), 'Being there', *Economic Geography*, **71** (1), 1–26.

Glaeser, E.L. (2001), 'The formation of social capital', *Isuma*, **2** (1), 34–40.

Grabher, G. (2002) 'Cool projects, boring institutions', *Regional Studies*, **36** (3), 205–14.

Granovetter, M. (1973), 'The strength of weak ties', *American Journal of Sociology*, **78** (6), 1360–80.

Granovetter, M. (1982), 'The strength of weak ties: a network theory revisited', in P.V. Marsden and N. Lin (eds), *Social Structure and Network Analysis*, Beverly Hills, CA: Sage, pp. 105–30.

Gulati, R (1999), 'Network location and learning: the influence of network resources and firm capabilities on alliance formation', *Strategic Management Journal*, **20** (5), 397–42.

Hall, R.E. and Jones, C.I. (1999), 'Why do some countries produce so much more output per worker than others?', *Quarterly Journal of Economics*, **114** (1), 83–116.

Hart, O. (1995), *Firms, Contracts and Financial Structure*, Oxford: Oxford University Press.

Haas, P.M. (1989), 'Do regimes matter? Epistemic communities and Mediterranean pollution control', *International Organisation*, **43**, 377–403.

Hirschman, A. (1986), *Getting Ahead Collectively*, New York: Pergamon Press.

Hobday, M. (1998), 'Product-complexity, innovation and industrial organisation', *Research Policy*, **26**, 689–710.

Holmström, B. and Milgrom, P. (1994), 'The firm as an incentive system', *American Economic Review*, **84** (4), 972–91.

Holzner, B. (1972), *Reality Construction in Society*, Cambridge, MA: Schenkma.

Ingram, P. (2002), 'Interorganizational learning', in J.A.C. Baum (ed.), *The Blackwell Companion to Organizations*, Oxford: Blackwell Business, pp. 642–63.

Keeble, D. and Wilkinson, F. (eds) (2000), *High-technology Clusters, Networking and Collective Learning in Europe*, Aldershot: Ashgate.

Kristensen, P.H. (1992), 'Industrial districts in West Jutland, Denmark', in F. Pyke and W. Sengenberger (eds), *Industrial Districts and Local Economic Regeneration*, Geneva: ILO, pp. 122–75.

Krugman, P. (1991), 'Increasing returns and economic geography', *Journal of Political Economy*, **99** (3), 483–99.

Langlois, R.N. and Robertson, P.L. (1995), *Firms, Markets and Economic Change: A Dynamic Theory of Business Institutions*, London: Routledge.

Lazaric, N. and Lorenz, E. (eds) (1998), *Trust and Economic Learning*, Cheltenham, UK and Northampton, MA, USA: Edward Elgar.

Lin, N. (2001), *Social Capital: A Theory of Social Structure and Action*, Cambridge, MA: Cambridge University Press.

Lin, N. et al. (eds) (2001), *Social Capital: Theory and Research*, New York: Aldine.
Lissoni, F. (2001), 'Knowledge codification and the geography of innovation: the case of Brescia mechanical cluster', *Research Policy*, **30** (9), 1479–500.
Lorenzen, M. (ed.) (1998), *Specialization and Localized Learning: Six Studies on the European Furniture Industry*, Copenhagen: CBS Press.
Lorenzen, M. (2001), 'Localized learning and policy: academic advice on enhancing regional competitiveness through learning', *European Planning Studies*, **9**, 163–85.
Lorenzen, M. (2002), 'Ties, trust and trade elements of a theory of coordination in industrial clusters, *International Studies of Management and Organization*, **31** (4), 14–34.
Lorenzen, M. and Foss, N.J. (2003), 'Cognitive coordination, institutions and clusters: an exploratory discussion', in T. Brenner and D. Fornahl (eds), *The Influence of co Operations, Networks and Innovations on Regional Innovation Systems*, Cheltenham, UK and Northampton, MA, USA: Edward Elgar, pp. 148–71.
Lorenzen, M. and Maskell, P. (2004), 'The cluster as a nexus of knowledge creation', in P. Cooke and A. Piccaluga (eds), *Regional Economies as Knowledge Laboratories*, Cheltenham, UK and Northampton, MA, USA: Edward Elgar, pp. 77–92.
Lundvall, B.-Å. (ed.) (1992), *National Systems of Innovation: Towards a Theory of Innovations and Interactive learning*, London: Pinter.
Lundvall, B.-Å. and Maskell, P. (2000), 'Nation states and economic development: from national systems of production to national systems of knowledge creation and learning', in G.L. Clark et al. (eds), *The Oxford Handbook of Economic Geography*, Oxford: Oxford University Press, pp. 353–72.
Macaulay, S. (1963), 'Non-contractual relations in business: a preliminary study', *American Sociological Review*, **28**, 55–67.
Malmberg, A. and Maskell, P. (1999), 'Localised learning and industrial competitiveness', *Cambridge Journal of Economics*, **23**, 167–86.
March, J.G. (1991), 'Exploration and exploitation in organizational learning', *Organization Science*, **2**, 71–87.
Maskell, P. (2000), 'Social capital and competitiveness', in S. Baron et al. (eds.), *Social Capital: Critical Perspectives*, Oxford: Oxford University Press, pp. 111–23.
Maskell, P. (2001), 'Towards a knowledge-based theory of the geographical cluster', *Industrial and Corporate Change*, **10** (4), 919–41.
Maskell, P. et al. (eds) (1998), *Competitiveness, Localised Learning and Regional Development: Specialisation and Prosperity in Small Open Economies*, London: Routledge.
Maskell, P. and Lorenzen, M. (2004), 'The cluster as market organization', *Urban Studies*, **41** (5/6), 991–1009.
Miller, D. (1997) *Capitalism: An Ethnographic Approach*, Oxford: Berg.
North, D.C. and Thomas, R.P. (1973), *The Rise of the Western World: A New Economic History*, Cambridge: Cambridge University Press.
OECD (1996), *The Knowledge Economy*, Paris: OECD.
OECD (2001), *Cities and Regions in the New Learning Economy*, Paris: OECD.
Perroux, F. (1988), 'The pole of development's new place in a general theory of economic activity', in B. Higgins and D.J. Savoie (eds), *Regional Economic Development: Essays in Honor of Francois Perroux*, Boston, MA: Allen and Unwin, pp. 48–76.
Piore, M.J. and Sabel, C.F. (1984), *The Second Industrial Divide: Possibilities for Prosperity*, New York: Basic Books.

Putnam, R.D. (1993), *Making Democracy Work: Civic Traditions in Modern Italy*, Princeton, NJ: Princeton University Press.

Putnam, R.D. (2000), *Bowling Alone: The Collapse and Revival of American Community*, New York: Simon & Schuster.

Pyke, F. et al. (eds) (1992), *Industrial Districts and Inter-firm Co-operation in Italy*, Geneva: ILO.

Rees, G. et al. (1997), 'History, place and the learning society: towards a sociology of lifetime learning', *Journal of Education Policy*, **12** (6), 485–97.

Romer, P. (1986), 'Increasing return and long run growth', *Journal of Political Economy*, **94**, 1002–37.

Rotberg, R.I. (ed.) (2001), *Patterns of Social Capital: Stability and Change in Historical Perspective*, Cambridge, MA: Cambridge University Press.

Rothstein, B. and Stolle, D. (2003), 'Social capital, impartiality and the welfare state: an institutional approach', in M. Hooghe and D. Stolle (eds), *Generating Social Capital: The Role of Voluntary Associations, Institutions and Government Policy*, New York: Palgrave Macmillan, pp. 191–210.

Schelling, T. (1960), *The Strategy of Conflict*, Cambridge, MA: Harvard University Press.

Scott, A.J. (1998), *New Industrial Spaces*, London: Pion.

Scott, W.R. (1995), *Institutions & Organizations*, London: Sage.

Scott, W.R. (2002), *Institutions and Organizations*, Thousand Oaks, CA: Sage.

Sweeney, G.P. (1991), 'Technical culture and the local dimension of entrepreneurial vitality', *Entrepreneurship & Regional Development*, **3**, 363–78.

Tarrow, S. (1996), 'Making social science work across space and time', *American Political Science Review*, **90**, 389–97.

Taylor, M. (1982), *Community, Anarchy and Liberty*, Cambridge: Cambridge University Press.

von Hippel, E. (1987), 'Cooperation between rivals: Informal know-how trading', *Research Policy*, **16**, 291–302.

von Hippel, E. (1988), *The Sources of Innovation*, Oxford: Oxford University Press.

Weick, K.E. (1979), *The Social Psychology of Organizing*, Reading, MA: Addison-Wesley.

Williamson, O.E. (1985), *The Economic Institutions of Capitalism*, New York: The Free Press.

Williamson, O.E. (1996), *The Mechanisms of Governance*, Oxford: Oxford University Press.

Williamson, O.E. (2000), 'The new institutional economics: taking stock, looking ahead', *Journal of Economic Literature*, **38**, 595–613.

Woolcock, M. (1998), 'Social capital and economic development: towards a theoretical synthesis and policy framework', *Theory and Society*, **27** (2), 151–208.

11. Learning about innovation in Europe's regional policy

Nicola Bellini and Mikel Landabaso[1]

INTRODUCTION

In the good old times, scholars and practitioners arguing in favour of a regional dimension of innovation policies wanted to be the avant garde of new, forward-looking thinking in contrast to the old-fashioned conventional wisdom, according to which 'grand' industrial policy inherently required the full strength of the nation state or – for some – the new European 'super state'. The former looked for answers from a new territorial and systemic perspective, paying particular attention to small and medium-sized enterprises (SMEs) and endogenous capacities rather than searching for exogenous help by, for example, luring inward investment, typically branch factories of multinational companies, through fiscal incentives. At the same time, the emphasis on innovation implied a departure from traditional regional policies, focused on the transfer of resources from 'rich' to 'poor' areas and on providing basic infrastructures to disadvantaged regions in the name of cohesion objectives.

Nowadays the need for regional innovation policy looks more commonplace, although policy makers and academics alike are still looking for the appropriate policy responses. Following the Lisbon agenda, there has been a general trend towards policy experimentation at regional level in the field of the economic exploitation of 'knowledge' and technological innovation as a means of promoting economic development.[2] Regional policy makers are trying to develop new innovation policies that focus much more on the provision of collective business and technology services to groups of firms in a way that can affect their innovative behaviour, rather than direct grants to individual firms through horizontal, automatic and traditional programmes of state aid. Furthermore, in most of these programmes, innovation is broadly defined, including finance, training, marketing, knowledge management, design, re-engineering, consulting, intellectual property rights, etc., rather than narrowly focusing on purely (pre-competitive) research and technology.

Moreover, providing the necessary linkages between the individual firm and a responsive knowledge base and facilitating the diffusion and absorption of knowledge figure prominently among these policies. The latter is especially relevant when referring to traditional sectors (e.g. textiles, wood, leather, agri-food, ceramics, metalworking, shoemaking etc.) and SMEs. Because of the critical relevance of geographical proximity in the transmission of tacit knowledge, traditional sectors and smaller firms are comparatively more dependent on the regional environment to innovate than other more technologically advanced sectors. On the contrary, for other more technologically advanced companies and sectors, codified knowledge and linkages to international research and technological development and innovation (R&TDI) networks of excellence is vital to keeping apace of the technology race.

This chapter outlines the contents and challenges of the learning processes that have been occurring in Europe's regional policy. The second section discusses the emerging conceptual framework for regional innovation policies in Europe, which are based on an 'innovation system' approach, significantly different from the US cluster approach *à la* Porter, mainly because of the different role attributed to public policies. The third section discusses new policy developments, inspired by the regional innovation systems and 'learning region' literature that have occurred since the mid-1990s. In the fourth section we show how these developments are leading to a serious reappraisal of the approach, policy delivery mechanisms and priorities of EU regional innovation policies. In the fifth section we discuss the implications in terms of policy and polity. Lastly, we suggest some challenges for research.

BEYOND THE CLUSTER APPROACH: INNOVATION SYSTEMS AS THE EMERGING POLICY CONCEPT

An established tenet of economic thinking is the vision of innovation as a multi-faceted behaviour, which is not limited to the development or adoption of new technologies. As a consequence, a new imperative has emerged that points to the need for innovation policy that is both sector and locality specific, at least in terms of delivery mechanisms. In this respect, regional innovation systems (and 'learning region') approaches are a significant evolution compared to the clusters approach, especially in its US variation, because they focus on a wider set of interrelationships among innovation actors (Cooke, 1998; Boekema et al., 2000). They do not concentrate solely on firms and factor conditions, paying particular attention to the way in which universities, educational and R&D institutions, technology centres, the public sector at different administrative levels and firms and SMEs in particular, interact with each other in a sort of 'interdependent economic ecology', and how they can jointly contribute, through networking, to foster regional competitiveness. In fact, it is more appropriate to talk about localized public–private networks that may have a sectoral, technological or thematic nature in Europe rather than of clusters in a strict sense.

These localized knowledge networks share a number of characteristics such as collective learning, 'co-opetition', embeddedness in a social/institutional infrastructure that fosters cooperation, trust and reciprocity, collective external economies etc. They are of course very diverse in nature, not least because radically different governance systems coexist in the present EU. Nevertheless, one may be talking about centres of expertise in Finland, competence centres in Sweden and Austria, clusters in the UK, networks of competence in Germany or regional technological networks in Spain, among others, but they all share key characteristics, objectives and challenges. They all attempt to promote development through innovation, and place emphasis on cooperation and networking and on increasing the interactive learning capacity of SMEs. They all try to reach critical masses and are confronted with the opportunities and threats of global markets. They all emphasize the need for better knowledge management in firms and improved knowledge-related business services.

Moreover, they also explicitly consider a larger role for the public sector than in the standard cluster approach (as pioneered by Michael Porter and practised in the USA). This approach has never seemed to have been at ease with the role to be assigned to the public sector, even if most of those that contracted out 'cluster' strategies were regional and national governments looking for policy advice about their own public policies. Policy recommendations stemming from this traditional cluster approach boil down mostly (with the important exception of the promotion of business cooperation) to standard regional policy tools, such as providing incentives for long-term investments, provision of (physical) infrastructures, and improving the business climate (taxes in particular). Indeed, we often hear, not without a smile, from the same American consultants that have been contracted by the public sector to develop publicly backed cluster strategies that clusters are 'spontaneous' in nature.

In Europe, on the contrary, there is an explicit recognition of the public sector role in the development or setting up of a cluster, sometimes going as far as to refer to it as 'indispensable' (EU Commission, 2001: 6) in some cases. In this sense the establishment of a network structure that makes possible the existence of a new cluster or the strengthening of an existing one, which may contribute to jobs and economic development in a region, is assimilated to the provision of a collective good. It is assumed that, since cluster generation does not have an immediate benefit for enterprises, they tend to under- (or not) invest in it, in particular in less favoured regions. In the early stages, it is thought that the necessary coordination and network structures must be sponsored by a third party representing the collective public interest and further maintained by a 'neutral' partner that can ensure a continuous flow of information and communication, achieve a balance of interests and conflict settlement among participants, create mutual trust between network partners, prepare decision making and build on and strengthen common interest.[3] Of course, this does not mean that clusters and regional innovation systems that can be generated by policy. They are too complex a construction to be designed by the enlightened hand of a policy maker. Yet policy cannot be hands-off, because it is likely to heavily determine the outcomes, both in the early phases (as we just said) and later on, by providing, especially through support services (Bellini, 2002), greater 'intelligence' of technological and market developments and new relations.

NEW POLICY DEVELOPMENTS

New policy developments in Europe, inspired by the regional innovation systems and 'learning region' literature, have taken place since the mid-1990s in an attempt to translate theory into practice and provide regional planners with a methodological tool to promote their regional economies through innovation. The Regional Innovation Strategies (RIS) pilot actions and the Regional Information Society Initiatives (RISI), started by the EU Commission and currently being developed in nearly 100 regions in Europe,[4] testify to this. Both sets of pilot actions follow the same methodological principles. RIS and RISI have been defined as 'social engineering' actions at the regional level whose main aim is to stimulate and manage cooperative links among firms and between firms and the regional R&TDI actors, which may contribute to their competitive position through innovation, notably by facilitating access to 'knowledge' sources and partners. In this sense, RIS/RISI social engineering means creating the right environmental conditions, institutional in particular, for increasing the innovative capacity of the regional economy (Landabaso et al., 2000).[5] They have also been termed a 'participative learning-for-policy approach', permitting policy decisions on an alignment of views of a broad group of stakeholders (Gavigan et al., 1999: 81). At the same time, with special reference to RITTS (Regional Innovation and Technology Transfer Strategies), it has been pointed out that these programmes do contribute to better structural innovation policies, but 'showed the difficulties in achieving success in regions where some form of successful innovation system was not already in place' (Charles and Benneworth, 2004, p. 1).

More recently, in January 2001, the European Commission offered each of the nearly 160 regions in the European Union of 15 the opportunity to develop a regional programme of innovative actions for a two-year period with grant of up to €3 million, at 50 per cent of total eligible costs.[6] This operation by the European Regional Development Fund has a total budget of €400 million for the period 2001–6 and is explicitly intended to help the less favoured regions to devise regional policies that effectively respond to fears that regional disparities could grow in the context of the knowledge-based economy (e.g. R&D capacity, 'digital divide', etc.) and more intangible competitive factors such as regional innovation capacity.

This is why the European Commission encouraged regions to test new, more indirect, policy approaches based on the creation of innovative environments related to non-cost-related competitive factors (e.g. innovation and entrepreneurship, quality, design, shortened product life cycles, speedier market response, new management techniques, enhanced business networking, etc.) and strengthened regional public–private partnerships for policy planning and implementation. Each proposal should contain a strategy for defining innovative actions agreed between the different regional actors. This strategy should provide the framework for the implementation of individual projects, the transfer of results to mainstream programmes financed by the European Regional Development Fund in the regions concerned and the exchange of experience between regions. The strategy may be based on one of the three strategic themes proposed by the Commission, or on a combination of these themes, in order to meet the specific needs of each region as fully as possible.

Out of the 107 responses by regional governments received by the European Commission in its first call for proposals ending May 2001, 73 applicants put forward proposals for regional programmes of innovative actions fully (20) or partly (53) based on the regional economies and on knowledge and technological innovation strands for a total amount of just over €200 million. Eighty-two regions focused fully (28) or partly (54) on the information society strand and only 43 dealt fully (3) or partly (40) with the regional identity and sustainable development topic.

Out of these 73, innovation-related, proposals, one in five applicants (16 in total), mainly from less favoured regions (defined as those with an average income per capita below 75 per cent of the EU average) submitted pilot actions under their regional programmes related to cluster-building and business network creation. It is important to note that out of the 60-odd proposals not putting forward cluster-type actions, most include some sort of networking. However, rather than emphasizing business cooperation, they try to promote the connection of SMEs to the regional knowledge base and/or facilitate the flow of knowledge from their R&TDI regional infrastructure to their local firms by better adapting supply to the regional demand for innovation. That is, they also focus to a large extent on linkages within the regional innovation systems but without concentrating on business networking/clustering as a specific field of action.

In all 16 cases the regional government was planning to fund the launching stage of the cluster-type initiatives by recruiting companies, acting as a 'facilitator' or 'broker', and providing the necessary institutional framework, which may involve an awareness campaign, the identification of relevant companies, common interests/needs (including database creation and printed/electronic communication tools) and tentative areas of joint action in the innovation field, the provision of a secretariat and technical assistance from external experts, good-practice identification abroad, etc. In practice, this involves funding consultant days, studies, workshops, technical assistance, communication tools, renting of premises and eventually providing the necessary electronic infrastructure in the case of IT-based business networks, among others.

Moreover, many regional governments see the cluster-type measures not as ends in themselves but as a means for identifying pilot projects in the innovation field that can be further financially supported by their existing regional development schemes, a way of aggregating (SMEs') innovation demand and as a source of information for the design of better adapted regional policy measures in the field. In all cases, special emphasis is laid on the planning and implementation of these actions in close partnership with the private sector, with public participation ranging from start-up or seed financing and 'first impulse' action to more hands-on involvement in the running of networks through direct participation in the cluster-type actions secretariat.

Finally, some of these actions are broader in scope than others, ranging from business-run business cooperations (e.g. based on the supply chain) to more open cluster-type actions involving other regional partners, such as universities, technology centres, development agencies, etc. as direct partners in the network (e.g. learning networks).

Three broad categories of publicly promoted cluster proposals have emerged. The first one includes most of the less favoured (Objective 1) regions that put forward a cluster-type action, from the so-called cohesion countries: Italy (Campania and Calabria), Spain (Aragón and Cantabria), Greece (Thessaly and Central Macedonia) and Portugal (Centro), and also including the North of Sweden (Mellesta Norreland). This category focuses on more traditional business networks and sectoral platforms that collectively design innovation action plans. Their business cooperation initiatives range from logistics, administrative management and joint marketing to advanced activities such as technology watch, technology acquisition, research, design, etc.

They also integrate the 'softer', more institutional aspects related to 'trust building' and sharing of strategic information through informal open meetings such as business forums, arenas, platforms and the like, with a built-in component of regional lobbying for more appropriate innovation-related public support. Moreover, some of them are seen as a means of raising, making explicit and aggregating innovation demand by SMEs in particular, in order to maximize the response by the existing regional R&TDI supply and infrastructure. Some of them also try to facilitate the participation of regional firms in international networks accessing state-of-the-art technological developments and best-practice examples.

Many are intended as a tool for overcoming the small (economic) size of regions and the absence of large firms that could help to structure a business network in the region around the partial subcontracting of the value chain.

The second category focuses on promoting information and communication technologies (ICTs) in SMEs, as a new tool for facilitating business networking, including the creation of virtual companies, joint software solutions, the promotion of business-to-business (B2B) Internet marketplaces, increased transparency of the availability of business services in the region through electronic one-stop shops, shared branch portals, data exchange and process integration among companies, among others. This category of cluster-type proposals is put forward by relatively more advanced regions that are willing to integrate information society tools in their regional productive fabrics. This is the case of Niederösterreich in Austria, South Tyrol (province of Bolzano) in Italy, Brandenburg in Germany, Etela-Suomi in Finland, and the South East and Eastern UK. It is interesting to note that within this category several of the proposals, notably the British proposals and South Tyrol, have as an explicit cohesion objective to link advanced and less favoured areas within the same region through ICT solutions that would make R&TDI resources existing in the advanced areas accessible to less favoured ones, including the creation of virtual networks and the replicability of good-practice cases.

Finally, a third cluster category, closer to the more traditional cluster model in a strict sense, could be identified, related to supply chain integration, in the automobile sector in particular, in the regions of Västsverige in Sweden, in one of the projects of Cantabria in Spain, in one of the projects in Central Macedonia in Greece and also in the case of Aragón in Spain.

STILL TIME FOR REGIONAL INNOVATION POLICIES?

In recent times advocates of regional innovation policies have been on the defensive. In Europe, the debate around the Sapir report (Sapir et al., 2004) has voiced doubts from a macroeconomic perspective, which are by no means limited to academic circles. The Sapir report (even in the absence of any analysis or reference to one single regional programme in the whole report!) has quite skilfully challenged not only the ability of regional policies to realize convergence objectives, but even their contribution to the growth of the targeted regions, as suggested by the comparison between Ireland and the Mezzogiorno. As is well known, Sapir and his colleagues have proposed that slimmed-down convergence policies should focus on countries rather than on regions, therefore de-legitimizing the 'standard approach' that has characterized European policies so far, while concentrating EU resources on standard R&D and other 'internal policies', in the absence once again of any serious analysis of the community value-added and economic impact these policies have actually had.

At approximately the same time, the British government's paper on *A Modern Regional Policy for the United Kingdom* (HM Treasury, Department of Trade and Industry, Office of the Deputy Prime Minister, 2003), contrary to the voiced opinion of several UK regions, reached similar conclusions. The paper emphasizes the 'inflexible' and centralized nature of EU regional policy[7] and advocates a new framework:

> Where Member States have the institutional structures and financial strength to develop and pursue their own modern regional policies, they should be enabled to do so. EU policies must support and encourage this, whilst assisting Member States [that] have not yet reached this position to do so, with the goal that these Member States would ultimately no longer need such support. (p. 26)

On the one hand, the attack on regional innovation policies involves different (but powerful and converging) critical arguments. First, regional innovation policies appear to be often too narrow in scope and too small in terms of resources to tackle the macro-dimensions of innovation in highly industrialized Europe (see MacKinnon et al., 2002). The supposed 'imperatives' of concentrating investment on R&D excellence, developing '*Grand Projets*' and scaling up resources to pursue major technological advances imply a greater role of national governments (under European 'soft' coordination, such as the so-called 'open method of coordination' established in the Lisbon Council[8]) and seem to relegate regional innovation policies to marginal tasks. Is 'grand' innovation policy out of reach for regional governments whose resources are below the minimum scale required? It must be emphasized that this criticism conceals at least one serious misunderstanding, namely that regional is not parochial but territorial in nature.

Second, some regional innovation policies appear to be too ambitious and too uncertain in their results. The objective of 're-creating Silicon Valley', which has been so influential in shaping the regional priorities in the past, now only belongs to the fantasy world of regional policy makers. Wide evidence now supports sound scepticism about the ability to originate high-tech clusters by decree. Similarly, policies have suffered from the 'best-practice' syndrome and have been subject to rapidly changing policy fashion: yesterday it was technology parks, today clusters, tomorrow . . . Sometimes too little thinking is devoted to careful adaptation of 'good practices' to each region's particular situation. Undoubtedly policies often would need objectives that are more realistic and more precisely defined.

Third, regional innovation policies appear too difficult to manage, in relation to planning as well as in policy delivery, both requiring strong public–private partnership and inter-institutional cooperation, vertically through the 'subsidiarity chain' as well as horizontally across ministries or regional departments. They are subject to many constraints, both in terms of legal powers of the regional governments and in terms of financial resources available to them. Regional policies imply complex governance systems, relying too much on the subsidiary role of private actors and too dependent on the smooth working of intergovernmental relations, both upwards (national governments, European Union) and downwards (municipalities and provincial governments). Furthermore, regional policies on the European scale involve too many actors with substantial quality variations in their ability to manage programmes and design policies. This problem is of course dramatized by the enlargement of the Union with new countries and many new regions, where a bottom–up strategic-planning method, rather than top–down dirigisme, is a radically new approach.

On the other hand, the 'missed convergence' argument could be easily dismissed. As emphasized by the *Third Cohesion Report* (EU Commission, 2004) growth and cohesion are mutually supportive: 'the concept of cohesion that has applied at the European level has not been a passive one that redistributes income, but a dynamic policy that seeks to create resources by targeting the factors of economic competitiveness and employment, especially where unused potential is high' (p. xxv). In this sense, for example, it is worth noting that 29 of the 33 regions in the so-called cohesion countries (Portugal, Greece, Spain and Ireland), including the three poorest member states, had growth rates above the community average between 1995 and 2001, with 19 regions growing over 50 per cent of this rate. It is also interesting to mention that, for example, in Objective 2 regions alone, the last generation of structural funds programmes (1994–99) contributed to the creation of some 500 000 new jobs (EU Commission, 2004: 151). The linkage between competitiveness and regional action is backed by factual evidence and is being challenged more on ideological grounds than in purely economic terms. Structural Funds have been revolutionary in transforming the economies and societies of countries such as Portugal, Greece or Spain in a historically unprecedented way within a short period of barely 15 years, as any economist familiar with these countries and their regions would easily acknowledge.

There is no inconsistency between the 'Lisbon objectives' and regional policies. In all regions innovation is critically important as part of the regional response to challenges posed by globalization and the so-called new economy. The fact is that there is no 'one-size-fits-all' regional innovation policy adapted to all sorts of regional environments. Regional characteristics linked to, among others, sector, firm size and 'isolation' do matter when addressing the need to formulate appropriate regional innovation policies (see Asheim and Isaksen, 2003).

In less advanced regions and in those regions that are undergoing industrial decline, regional innovation policies cannot be just about preconditions and implications. They deal directly with the issue of the relationship between innovation (and technological R&D) and economic development. It is interesting to note that innovation statistics based on R&D expenditures or personnel tend to underestimate innovation capacities in small firms in less favoured regions, not least because much of the innovation they actually produce has no connection with recorded R&D activities, since most statistical surveys do not consider firms under ten employees. For example, Martinez (2004) argues that, contrary to official statistics that show 20 per cent of the Murcia region's SMEs as innovative, in-depth research provides evidence that nearly 60 per cent of firms can be considered as innovative within the standard definition.

Does evidence then support the claim of these regions for basing their development on innovation? Is the further geographical concentration of R&D activities an inescapable rule of European development? The above-mentioned case of Murcia shows that it is misleading to interpret the distribution of R&D activities in the same way as distribution of innovation capacities. As a consequence, in policy terms, it would be wrong to infer from the concentration of R&D activities that such concentration must be maintained and even strengthened, so that a diffusion of innovation activities could be even detrimental to the overall innovative performance of the EU. After all, one key raw material of the knowledge economy, i.e. brain-power, is geographically evenly distributed across the territory. On the contrary, excessive geographic concentration of innovative activities could lead to under-utilization of the actual potential in Europe's regions.

Of course, no one could deny the existence of a high degree of geographical concentration of European R&D capacities and of very significant regional gaps, also within countries. However, innovation potential is more widely diffused and signs of innovative vitality increasingly come from the periphery of Europe. 'Vitality indicators', such as the level of participation in the Fifth Framework Programmes or the number of science parks do not coincide with the core–periphery relationship that is standard in the geography of innovation. The emergence of peripheral cores, which often specialize in specific 'niche' areas and can perform significant leaps forward, suggests that the knowledge factory is and can be more spatially dispersed, in particular within regions that are well connected physically and virtually to international R&D and technology excellence networks. The concept of marginality itself, which used to condemn certain regions to the periphery of development, must be revised.

Important opportunities for catching up (and in relatively short periods of time!) seem to be linked to the new geography of innovation. Well-targeted investments in public research and innovation promotion policies can tap the stock of qualified human capital, including entrepreneurs and scientists, which may be less mobile than standard economics would suggest. Other key factors for the knowledge-based economy are mobile and can be attracted to peripheral areas when infrastructures are available that guarantee quick communications, high-speed physical transportation and global cultural connections.

Within certain limits, the physical marginality of regions may be attractive when it supplies 'talent' with a greater quality of life than the one offered by overcrowded, congested and polluted metropolitan areas. Nature, health and education facilities, security, local culture, as well as leisure facilities, are vital in attracting knowledge workers (Florida, 2000), also considering that freedom of location increases thanks to ICTs (see Talvitie, 2003). Physical marginality itself (like in the extreme case of 'insularity') may push regions to invest heavily in ICT and to exploit the lesser relevance of distance in some ICT businesses.

Regional policies emerge therefore (surprisingly?) as one of those necessary actions to be undertaken 'to prevent Lisbon from becoming a synonym for missed objectives and failed promises' (Kok Report, p. 10). But to do so, it is necessary to learn from the lessons (positive and negative) of the past and to draw the correct conclusions both from factual evidence and from recent debates. In our view, the key conceptual (and political) issue is the need to radically reappraise the relationship between a situation characterized by enduring, but also evolving, disparities and the objective of cohesion. Rather than betting on the acceleration of growth by the core regions (and implicitly suggesting that resources devoted to other regions are ballast to Lisbon policies), it is necessary to find and activate the under-utilized growth potentials that are spread in the old and new peripheries of the Union. A defensive regional policy focuses on disparities as problems; an offensive regional policy looks for opportunities behind disparities, i.e. for underutilized resources. The former is a problem-centred approach, the latter an opportunity-centred one.

Such a radical change of approach has of course radical implications. First and foremost, a new policy menu is required. The availability of basic infrastructures must be complemented by the new competitiveness factors that suit the rules of the games of contemporary knowledge-based economies. The proposed new regulation of the European Regional Development Fund[9] clearly spells out a new policy priority, which is consistent with the objective of 'regional competitiveness and employment': 'innovation and the knowledge economy, by supporting the design and implementation of regional innovation strategies conducive to efficient regional innovation systems'.[10] Eventually the strategy of European regional policies reconnects with the outcomes of both research and policy practices during the last decade.

A POLITY FOR THE NEW POLICIES

The literature has already emphasized the new role of governments and has found unconventional labels for it (facilitator, broker, catalyst etc.). Undoubtedly, regional innovation policies escape the *étatiste* frame of mind and require a polity where 'intelligent government' is combined with good governance. The establishment, selection and retention of relationships with other actors within policy networks[11] constitute the essence of this kind of policy making. In fact, policy networks:

- reduce the governments' overload in both decision making and implementation;
- make available additional and/or scarce resources (financial, political, human, relational);
- make it possible to deal with policy making in uncertain scenarios.[12]

However, at the regional level, the learning process has not gone so far as to consolidate all the implications of this new approach. Building institutional and administrative capacity in tune with these new tasks is clearly an unaccomplished objective. For example, the intricacies of intergovernmental negotiations are too often labelled as inefficiencies. The standard culture of hierarchical policy making has problems in dealing with the need to accept not only a division of labour between institutions, but also some kind of competition and redundancy in order to guarantee a sufficient level of diversity to meet the challenges of rapidly changing scenarios.

Governments slowly learn the difficult art (and science) of managing complex policy networks, where they must gain the trust and respect of the two other sides of the 'triple helix' and where persuasion, partnership and consensus prime over 'dirigisme'. Difficulty derives from several factors, including the problems arising from the weakened legitimacy of public actors in a substantially neo-liberal political culture. This may be dangerous not so much because of the nostalgia for the strong technocratic state according to the Colbertian myth, but because it leads to an underestimation of the specificity and uniqueness of the resources that public actors can put into play. It neglects the important role public policy and institutions can play in economic outcomes, in particular where 'knowledge', as a public good, is concerned.

Another reason for complexity is that governance must be managed both at the social and at the cognitive level. In other words, exercises in 'institutional architecture' (e.g. the design of the 'ideal' regional development agency) are not sufficient and often secondary. In the imperfect world of governance, what counts is rather the ability to structure informal networks, to regulate the dynamics of openness of local systems, to activate (and de-activate) actors according to their potential positive (or negative) contribution to an innovative (and not necessarily agreed) project, to shape shared visions and manage expectations, often through lengthy exercises of interaction among key regional players through strategic planning and foresight.

Both in the USA and in Europe, the planning *process* itself, over and above projects or programmes, has increasingly gained the attention of economic development planners as a means of developing and strengthening clusters and public–private networks. This has to do with the new role the public sector is seen to be playing most effectively in economic development: an animator/facilitator of the strategic planning process, i.e. to co-create the framework conditions and the impulse for new economic activity, in partnership with the private sector as an equal but different partner. A continuous and dynamic, bottom–up and demand-led, broad-based and inclusive planning process offers an opportunity, by itself, to promote regional cooperation among key public and private actors.

In fact, strategic planning, developed as an iterative process built on a set of interactions among regional actors, allows each of them to progressively adapt its behaviour (agenda, objectives and actions) to the others voluntarily, thus maximizing synergies and avoiding duplications in the absence of a top–down *dirigisme* by a central planning authority. This can be achieved mainly through consensus and open discussion induced by the process of elaboration of a shared vision for the region (strategic objectives) and the design of the means to achieve them (action plan). This shared vision can progressively become the common reference by which the economic development relevance of each actor's agenda can be assessed. Moreover, through 'enlightened self-interest', becoming an active partner and aligning one's agenda with the shared one could have direct economic benefits in the form of public incentives and enhanced business opportunities, through new 'clustering' of business activities, for example.

Second, the planning process, including the implementation of a revolving action plan, offers a unique opportunity to build and strengthen links among key regional actors, which could develop into cooperation networks that, in turn, are vital to the strength and continuous revitalization of the regional economy through innovation. 'Social capital' is therefore, at the same time, a condition and an objective of effective policy making.

Initially, social capital was present mostly in political and social science literature. Subsequently, it was incorporated into economic writing as so-called intangibles became considered crucial factors for economic development.[13] This led some authors (Cooke, 2002) to state that social capital is a key missing ingredient of economic development that can be built up through efforts of policy makers. Hence social capital is considered an asset, just as other traditional forms of capital. It is attained through the processes of interaction and learning that take place in society. However, unlike other commodities, it cannot be traded or exchanged (Maskell, 2000). In the precise context of clusters, for example, it has been argued (Arzeni and Ionescu, forthcoming) that firms benefit from many elements associated with social capital, such as lower transaction costs, lower information costs and better coordination, leading to the 'know-who' that allows you to build the 'know-how' (Rosenfeld, forthcoming). Thus trust, collaboration and social–civic exchange associated with shared interests linked to social capital formation are central to cluster development, where innovation is based on collaboration, proximity and networks and spurs emulation, positive role models and personal contacts through a process of mutual learning.

Evidence from research and pilot-policy actions, such as RIS (Regional Innovation Strategies), suggests public policy can contribute to social capital building. One of the (possibly unexpected) conclusions of the evaluation of these projects was that their 'policy dimension' contributed significantly to promoting public and private partnerships and business networks, as well as to improving the institutional capacity of regional administrations in charge of innovation (Socintec, 2005). Building social capital is possible not only through inclusive procedures for regional innovation planning, but also through a wide variety of efforts to implement subsidiarity in all phases of policy making, particularly through the intensive use of working groups to identify R&D development needs, capacities and priorities, regional technology foresight exercises and the promotion of diffused and participative evaluation culture to ensure long-term commitment and shared visions.

The necessary reappraisal concerns not only the general approach to policy making, but also the contents of the innovation policy toolbox. Indeed, the intensive exchange of good practices for the last two decades has consolidated a standard toolbox that is shared by most regions in Europe. It includes traditional subsidies, public procurement and more 'fashionable' items such as business support services, human capital formation and technology transfer and the promotion of industry–university linkages.

The toolbox of regional innovation policy, however, is complemented by new sets of instruments that respond to apparently different policy objectives. We would like to call the reader's attention briefly to one of these new items that is, in many respects, one of the latest acquisitions of regional policy learning in Europe: *image* – or, more precisely – an attractive regional image with a distinct international profile.

Image is often associated with some inward investment promotion and with an (often superficial and incorrect) transfer of marketing and communication techniques to economic development. Our view is different. Image is both a result of real achievements of a region and a tool to improve its potential.

A global regional image has become critically important for innovation in the so-called new geography of talent. Recent empirical research in the USA and Canada has shown that the most innovative regions are those based on the '3 Ts': technology, talent and tolerance (Florida, 2002). They are capable of attracting talent or a so-called 'creative class' that is driven by the existence of a high quality of living, including cultural and sport amenities, as well as a well-developed research infrastructure, higher education establishments, technology centres and various open and tolerant societies.

As marketing research teaches us, image is a crucial factor in shaping expectations and filtering the perceptions of quality with regard to intangible goods. The same applies to territories. An attractive regional image, including an attractive regional identity and the values and attitudes that make up an open and tolerant 'mosaic' society, pays in the global economy, especially when it 'sells' both quality of life and the societal commitment to development and innovation ('the Guggenheim effect'). It is as important to attract inward investors as it is to attract students (i.e. the potential talents of the future) to the local university.

Building the image of a region is a complex process, not just the result of a contract with an advertising agency. It is a way of setting common targets and making them explicit to the local community as well as to the outside world. This may be risky: unrealistic images, when serious efforts are not in place to close the gap with reality, are bound to be disconfirmed, so that the reliability of the region as an innovation place is destroyed.

Image building and communicating is also a collective exercise that shows the level of awareness of a region about its own assets and its competitive position. The opposite gap may occur. Because of cognitive and political lock-ins, policy makers may be unwilling or unable to recognize innovative trends in the economy and society. Innovative potentials may be there, but locals and non-locals are both warned that policy makers are 'blind' and will not support innovation with the necessary consistency and commitment.

SOME CHALLENGES FOR RESEARCH

In conclusion, we would also like to stress some possible implications for research.

The first one regards the need for taking fully into account the complexity of regional innovation policies. In our opinion, a fundamental issue is the full recognition of knowledge spillovers to explain cumulative processes of (spatially bounded) economic growth. Given that inter-regional knowledge spillovers are considered to arise when actors involved in the innovation process, such as universities, the business sector and the government sector, form close links leading to fertilizations and feedback relations (Greunz, 2003), knowledge spillovers are generated and further developed within efficient regional innovation systems that facilitate 'links' and 'cross-fertilization' among the key innovation players, not least by connecting SMEs to a responsive R&TDI knowledge base. Thus public–private cooperation, business networks, university–enterprise connections and clusters can be of utmost importance in generating these spillovers and therefore in increasing the knowledge generation, diffusion and absorption capacities in a region. From a policy perspective, it also means that action-oriented, open, consensus-based and participatory strategic planning processes led by regional authorities, with a sufficient degree of autonomy/power and acting within a 'development coalition' (Asheim, 2001), can become key ingredients of the process of generating knowledge spillovers.

Policy, politics and polity matter (see Meyer-Stamer, 2004). But in what way? Both theory and empirical research provide only sketchy insights into how the interactions between knowledge spillover generation, regional governance and social capital operate. Why not try to integrate further the organizational, institutional, cultural and political aspects associated with this process into our economic theories about regional development?

A number of crucial dimensions of policy making would also be better understood, with obvious policy-learning benefits. Good examples are provided by two issues mentioned in this chapter. In the case of social capital, broadly understood as a 'local' capacity to form and nourish appropriate networks and interactions among regional stakeholders, we deal with a concept that has been discussed extensively in the literature, but requires operationalization. This means that we need to learn how to measure social capital in a way that allows comparison of different endowments of social capital in different regions and to monitor its evolution over time. These data could also help us to understand how policies can affect social capital in a region. In the case of the regional image, again, we need to understand better the social dynamics of image building and the role of the perceived attractiveness in shaping the region's opportunities to innovate.

A second implication concerns the need for better understanding, both in theory and in modelling, of the role of discontinuities in development. So far research (and especially economic research, both mainstream and evolutionary) has proved able to identify routines and regularities, which are of course fundamental in analytical terms. From the policy perspective, however, what triggers new cycles of development is the ability of regions to break path-dependency and reinvent their industrial vocations in a distinctive and unique way, *not* their compliance with general trajectories. In a sense, this also goes to the essence of the concept of 'learning region', allowing it to overcome the risk of being turned into a commonsensical catchword. This policy concept is really useful only to the extent that it describes (and prescribes) policies and processes that allow the unlocking of regional economies from negative path-dependencies.

A third and last implication concerns the relationship between academic work and regional practice. It may be worth reflecting more on the reasons for the exceptional success of Michael Porter's 'diamond' model. Its limitations (the partial explanations provided by its variables, the increasing relevance of factors such as globalization and digitalization, the underestimation of politics etc.) are known and, as a consequence, the model 'has generally proven to be more helpful in understanding clustering than in actually formulating policy' (Rosenfeld, forthcoming). Nevertheless, the 'diamond' has the advantage of being easily translated into a stand-ardized methodology, which has been widely used by local officials as well as by economic consultants internationally. It is interesting to note that many regional and national governments in Europe have turned their attention to this 'diamond' when looking for a way forward to promote their industrial/regional competitiveness, rather than drawing on the wealth of knowledge from the European regional schools of thought.

In Europe, there is an important and enduring divide between academic thinkers and regional planners. This has meant that many good economic theories and findings are of a diagnostic nature rather than clearly identifiable policy recommendations and tools amenable to testing and evaluation of results. Moreover, in the absence of the necessary feedback from practical policy experimentation to further policy theory reflection, much of the regional economic literature has tended to describe existing regional success stories, in an attempt to sketch a universal explanatory model, rather than helping planners to improve their policy making step by step in a realistic, effective and pragmatic way.

NOTES

1. The responsibility for the accuracy of the analysis and for the judgements expressed lies with the authors alone; this document does not constitute policy positions of the EU Commission.
2. Old industrial regions (Objective 2 regions in EU jargon), for example, have spent on average over 15 per cent of their total structural fund financial envelope during the period 2000–2006 in measures related to the knowledge-based economy, with some countries, like Spain, reaching nearly 33 per cent (EU Commission, 2004).
3. In this sense a recent empirical study (EU Commission, Agiplan, 1999, p. 93) concludes that 'in all the technology networks examined [in seven regional automobile clusters], initial expenses for setting up and running the network were covered by public funds, as enterprises showed little interest in investing in uncertain long-term projects'. Moreover, in another recent analysis of 55 business knowledge networks on an empirical base chosen from six European countries and Canada, it was found that 'in all, 90% of networks receive grants; and of this 90%, 45% receive grants from regional government or the State, one-third from local governments and one-third from other public organisations (chambers of commerce in particular) and 40% from EU programmes' (EU Commission, Lengrand and Chatrie, 1999: 20). In other words, public actors are 'almost always involved as content providers, partners or financiers'. Many of these networks have been launched at the initiative of public policies for economic development. Finally, a recent study by McKinsey & Co. (2001) on existing high-tech clusters success stories around the world, which is intended to inspire similar initiatives in Italy, identifies four key 'propulsive' or 'success' factors in cluster building: involvement of innovative companies, presence of 'talent', participation of venture capitalists, and availability of public funds, stating that 'the role of government and state institutions has been determinant in the initial phases of the (cluster building) process . . .'.
4. Most of the strategies, action plans, projects and evaluation studies resulting from these pilot actions can be found at http://www.innovating-regions.org for RIS and http://www.ispo.cec.be/risi, http://www.erisa.be for RISI.
5. For a practical guide for planners on the steps to follow, see EU Commission (1999).
6. Communication from the Commission: 'The regions in the new economy: guidelines for innovative actions under the European Regional Development Fund in 2000–2006', Brussels 31.01.2001 COM (2001) 60 final.
7. In effect, the paper disregards the fact that UK regions themselves are among the most vigorous defenders of EU regional policy and rather critical of the lack of 'subsidiarity' and sometimes of the lesser cost-effectiveness of its own national–regional policies, as publicly manifested in the III Cohesion Forum in Brussels in May 2004. See Frenz et al. (2003): 'when public support is split into national support measures and regional

support measures . . . it turns out that regional policy and European regional policy measures are highly significant while national policy measures are insignificant' (p. 36).

8. This is being challenged by the conclusions of the recently published 'Kok report' ('The Challenge: The Lisbon strategy for growth and employment', Report from the High Level Group chaired by Wim Kok, November 2004 http://europa.eu.int/comm/lisbon_strategy/pdf/2004-1866-EN-complet.pdf).

9. Proposal for a Regulation of the European Parliament and of the Council on the European regional development Fund, presented by the Commission. Brussels 14.7.2004 COM(2004) 495 final.

10. Art. 5 of the proposed regulation articulates this priority as follows: 'a) enhancing regional R&TD and innovation capacities directly linked to regional economic development objectives by supporting industry- or technology-specific competence centres, by promoting technology transfer, and by developing technology forecasting and international benchmarking of policies to promote innovation, and by supporting inter-firm collaboration and joint R&TD and innovation policies; b) stimulating innovation in SMEs by promoting university–enterprise cooperation networks, by supporting business networks and clusters of SMEs and by facilitating SMEs' access to advanced business support services, by supporting the integration of cleaner and innovative technologies in SMEs; c) promoting entrepreneurship by facilitating the economic exploitation of new ideas, and by fostering the creation of new firms by universities and existing firms; d) creating new financial instruments and incubation facilities conducive to the creation or expansion of knowledge-intensive firms.'

11. We define policy networks as '(more or less) stable patterns of social relations between interdependent actors, which take shape around policy problems and/or policy programmes' (Kickert et al., 1997, p. 6).

12. Uncertainty implies that policies may be unable to implement known techniques to reach agreed goals. Therefore, policy making needs to manage policy experimentation or even more complex 'social learning' processes, depending on the degree of consensus reached on the goals (see Christensen, 1999).

13. See, e.g., the July 2003 'Ostuni Declaration' on social capital signed by a dozen European academics. Download from: http://www.ebms.it/SS2003_speakers_present.asp.

REFERENCES

Arzeni, S. and Ionescu, D. (forthcoming), 'Social capital and clusters of enterprises: some essential questions', in A. Romano and M. Landabaso (eds), *Social Capital, Innovation and Regional Development.*

Asheim, B. and Isaksen, A. (2003), 'SMEs, innovation and regions: conceptual background', in B. Asheim et al. (eds), *Regional Innovation Policy for Small–Medium Enterprises*, Cheltenham, UK and Northampton, MA, USA: Edward Elgar, pp. 21–48.

Asheim, B.T. (2001), 'Learning regions as development coalitions: partnership as governance in European workfare states?', *Concepts and Transformation. International Journal of Action Research and Organizational Renewal*, **6** (1), 73–101.

Bellini, N. (2002), *Business Support Services. Marketing and the Practice of Regional Innovation Policy*, Cork: Oak Tree Press.

Boekema, F., Morgan, K., Bakkers, S. and Rutten, R. (eds) (2000), *Knowledge, Innovation and Economic Growth. The Theory and Practice of Learning Regions*, Cheltenham, UK and Northampton, MA, USA: Edward Elgar.

Charles, D. and Benneworth, P. (2004), 'From regional innovation strategies to the multi-level governance of science, technology and innovation', paper prepared for International Conference on Regionalization of Innovation Policy – Options & Experiences, Berlin, June.

Christensen, K. (1999), *Cities and Complexity. Making Intergovernmental Decisions*, Thousand Oaks, CA: Sage.

Cooke, P. (1998), 'Introduction. Origins of the concept', in H.-J. Braczyk et al. (eds), *Regional Innovation Systems*, London: UCL Press, pp. 2–27.

Cooke, P. (2002), *Knowledge Economies*, London: Routledge.

EU Commission (1999), *A Guide to Regional Innovation Actions*, mimeo.

EU Commission (2001), *Methodology for Regional and Transnational Technology Clusters: Learning with European Best Practices*, Brussels, March.

EU Commission (2004), *A New Partnership for Cohesion: Convergence, Competitiveness, Cooperation. Third Report on Economic and Social Cohesion*, Luxembourg.

EU Commission, Agiplan (1999), 'Cluster building and networking: analysis of transnational technology networking between existing clusters of SMEs and one or more technology poles', Final report by Agiplan for the European Commission – Directorate General Enterprise, Mulheim an der Ruhr, December (download: http://forum.europa.eu.int/irc/sme/euroinformation/info/data/sme/en/library/studies.html).

EU Commission, Lengrand L. and Chatrie, I. (1999), 'Business networks and the knowledge driven economy: an empirical study carried out in Europe and Canada', commissioned by the Enterprise Directorate-General, November (download: http://forum.europa.eu.int/irc/sme/euroinformation/info/data/sme/en/library/studies.html).

Florida, R. (2000), 'Competing in the age of talent: environment, amenities and the new economy', January (download: http://www.heinz.cmu.edu/~florida/talent.pdf).

Florida, R. (2002), *The Rise of the Creative Class*, New York: Basic Books.

Frenz, M., Michie, J. and Oughton, C. (2003), 'Regional dimensions of innovation: results from the third community innovation survey', paper presented at the UK Regional Innovation Network Conference, Belfast, June.

Gavigan, J., Ottitsch, M. and Mahroum, S. (1999), *Knowledge and Learning. Towards a Learning Europe*, European Commission – Joint Research Centre, Seville.

Greunz, L. (2003), *Knowledge Spillovers, Innovation and Catching Up of Regions*, doctoral thesis, ULB, Faculté des Sciences Sociales, Politiques et Economiques – Section des Sciences Economiques.

HM Treasury, Department of Trade and Industry, Office of the Deputy Prime Minister (2003), *A Modern Regional Policy for the United Kingdom*, March (www.dti.gov.uk/europe/consultation.pdf).

Kickert, W., Klijn, E.-H. and Koppenjan, J. (eds) (1997), *Managing Complex Networks. Strategies for the Public Sector*, London: Sage.

Landabaso, M. (2001), 'Reflections on U.S. economic development policies: meeting the new economy challenge', paper presented at the conference 'Learning from Comparing U.S. and European Experiences in Innovation and Competence Building', Lisbon, June (download: http://in3.dem.ist.utl.pt/inov2001/files/m_landabaso.pdf).

Landabaso, A. (2004), 'Invertir en investigación y desarrollo en la UE', paper presented at Santander at the Conference 'El futuro de la financiación comunitaria', November.

Landabaso, M., Oughton, C. and Morgan, K. (2000), 'Learning regions in Europe: theory, policy and practice through the RIS experience', in D. Gibson et al. (eds), *Systems and Policies for the Globalized Learning Economy*, Westport, CT: Quorum Books, pp. 79–110.

MacKinnon, D., Cumbers, A. and Chapman, K. (2002), 'Learning, innovation and regional development: a critical appraisal of recent debates', *Progress in Human Geography*, **26** (3), 293–311.

Martinez, R. (2004), Presentation at the III National Meeting of Spanish regions undertaking Regional Programmes of Innovative Actions in Badajoz, November.

Maskell, P. (2000), 'Social capital, innovation and competitiveness', in S. Baron, J. Field and T. Schuller (eds), *Social Capital, Critical Perspectives*, Oxford: Oxford University Press, pp. 111–23.

McKinsey & Company Italy (2001), 'I Cluster hi-tech e le aziende innovative'.

Meyer-Stamer, J. (2004), 'The theory and practice of policy, polity and politics around local economic development', in N. Bellini et al. (eds), *The Theory and Practice of Local Development*, Florence, pp. 135–54.

Rosenfeld, S. (1995), 'Industrial-strength strategies: regional business clusters and public policy', Washington, DC: The Aspen Institute, Rural Economic Policy Program.

Rosenfeld, S. (forthcoming), 'The social imperatives of clusters', in M. Landabaso et al. (eds), *Social Capital, Innovation and Regional Development*.

Sapir, A. et al. (2004), *An Agenda for a Growing Europe – The Sapir Report*, Oxford: Oxford University Press.

Socintec (2005), *Ex-post Evaluation of the RIS, RTTs and RISI ERDF Innovative Actions for the Period 1994–99*, Brussels, January.

Talvitie, J. (2003), 'The impact of mobile communication on land use planning' (download: http://www.fig.net/pub/fig_2003/TS_10/TS10_4_Talvitie.pdf).

12. The learning region: a constructive critique

Robert Hassink

1. INTRODUCTION

In the framework of the contemporary transformation from an industrial to a knowledge-based economy, the learning economy (Lundvall, 1996), learning regions and also learning cities have been propagated as future concepts for successful economic development in many countries of Europe (Morgan, 1997; Hassink, 2001; van Geenhuizen, 1999; Butzin, 2000; Scheff, 1999; Boekema et al., 2000; OECD, 2001; Landabaso et al., 2001; Fürst, 2001; MacKinnon et al., 2002; Kunzmann and Tata, 2003). The capacity of both individuals and organizations to engage successfully in learning processes is regarded as a crucial component of economic performance in the knowledge-based economy. Therefore, 'identifying and strengthening the factors that can support . . . economic learning have become critical goals for policymakers and academic researchers alike' (Benner, 2003: 1809). Oinas and Virkkala (1997) and Lagendijk (1997) even speak about the 1990s as being the era of the learning economy and the learning region, and Malmberg (1997: 576) refers to the 'learning turn' in economic geography. The debate about learning regions has not been confined to an academic and abstract one. Recently, both semi-academic empirical work on the learning region by the OECD (2001) and numerous policy initiatives launched under the label of learning regions (Lagendijk and Cornford, 2000) provide us with a considerable amount of empirical information on the learning region phenomenon. The OECD (2001) published a study called *Cities and Regions in the New Learning Economy*, which can be considered as the first in-depth empirical study on the concept of learning regions. With the help of an interesting mix of a quantitative correlation analysis and a qualitative analysis on the basis of case studies, several conceptual relationships of the learning region are investigated. Other recent empirical studies on the learning region include work on the central part of the Ruhr Area in Germany by Pommeranz (2000), on the Graz Region in Austria by Scheff (1999) and on Silicon Valley by Benner

(2003). Moreover, the learning region concept has arrived in one form or another on the desks of regional policy makers in Europe for quite some time now. At the national level, Germany's federal government, for instance, recently launched a programme called 'Learning Region', which is partly funded by the European Social Fund. Furthermore, partly based on the learning region concept, the EU has started a new generation of regional policies (Landabaso et al., 2001), which aim to improve the institutional capacity for innovation of less favoured regions, which, in turn, should lead to higher absorption capacity for innovation funds from the EU and national governments. It is therefore a positive sign that, since its launch a little less than ten years ago, the learning region has been much debated by academics and applied to regional innovation policies.

However, despite this positive sign, there have been critical voices as well (Lorentzen, 2005). Hudson (1999) asks what is new about the concept. Malmberg (1997: 576) observes another significant shortcoming: 'The questions in urgent need of an answer may thus be phrased: what are the precise characteristics of "learning regions"?' According to Cooke (2005), learning regions waxed and waned quickly because the concept is unreflective and leads to the absorption of old information. In a similar critical, but slightly more constructive, vein, this chapter will show that four weaknesses prevent the learning region from becoming a fully fledged theoretical concept in regional studies; that is, its fuzziness, its normative character, its strong overlapping with other similar concepts and its squeezed position between national innovation systems and global production networks. Before the main weaknesses are discussed in Section 3, there is a literature review on what has recently been written on the two main angles from which one can see this phenomenon: that is, regional learning and the learning region; this is presented in Section 2. Since I am convinced that, despite its weaknesses, the learning region concept is for several reasons a concept with great prospects, I will give my alternative view on how it should develop in the final section, Section 4, of this chapter.

2. REGIONAL LEARNING AND THE LEARNING REGION

Reading the rapidly expanding amount of literature on the learning region, two angles can be distinguished from which this concept has been launched. First, some authors have written about the relationship between entrepreneurial learning, innovation and spatial proximity at the micro-level (theoretical, actor-related perspective) (Section 2.1). Second, most authors have launched the concept as a theory-led regional development concept from an action-related perspective at the meso-level (Section 2.2).[1] This distinction bears resemblance to a distinction Boekema et al. (2000) made in a book on the theory and practice of learning regions, where they distinguish between regional learning (all cooperation between actors in a region through which they learn) and the learning region (institutional networks that develop and implement a regional innovation strategy).

2.1 Regional Learning

From a theoretical, actor-related perspective, the discussion about learning regions focuses on the relationship between entrepreneurial learning, innovation, institutional context and spatial proximity (Hausmann, 1996; Oinas and Virkkala, 1997; Boekema et al., 2000; Schamp and Lo, 2003). For their competitiveness firms depend on innovation processes. In order to come to such innovation processes, firms have to exchange information and reproduce this information into knowledge; in other words they have to learn. Innovation processes of firms can hence be regarded as learning processes of the firm's employees. These actors permanently collect information and compress it into innovations. The information and knowledge that is needed for innovations can be collected both inside and outside the firm. Due to increasing, cut-throat competition and shorter product life cycles, firms, particularly small and medium-sized enterprises (SMEs), are increasingly dependent on information and knowledge sources that are only available outside the firm. Firm innovation processes therefore increasingly take place in interaction with other organizations, be it with other business partners, such as customers, suppliers or competitors, or with public research establishments, higher education institutes, technology transfer agencies and regional development agencies. Innovation processes seldom take place now in isolation.

Innovations can thus be understood as manifest results of cumulative learning processes of firms (Hausmann, 1996: 82). This kind of learning is not the mere intra-firm learning by doing or learning by using, but much more learning by interacting, which is goal-oriented instead of just profit-oriented and which involves communicative and synergetic cooperation between at least two actors, who develop or affect innovation processes of companies (ibid.: 100). The synergy achieved through learning by interacting, which is so important for innovations, cannot be bought, but can only be achieved by personal commitment. The use of information, which is necessary for these learning processes, is dependent on existing human knowledge. Learning therefore is an evolutionary and context-dependent process. The spatial environment provides different institutional contexts for interactive learning. These contexts differ not only nationally, but also regionally and locally. Firms are therefore embedded in different institutional contexts for interactive learning.

The larger the proximity between at least two actors, the higher the probability that they will interact in a certain time period and that learning by interacting will take place (Hausmann, 1996; Oinas and Virkkala, 1997). Proximity particularly eases the formation of rules, norms and routines. Although spatial proximity might stimulate communicative interaction between actors, it is not a sufficient condition. In order to achieve this interaction, social proximity (equal or similar characteristics such as age, vocation, language and equal or similar views on values and norms) and organizational proximity (concerning structure, intrafirm and interfirm network structures) are necessary factors as well. The naive learning by 'being there' is fundamentally questioned: neither personal presence on the spot nor spillovers are sufficient factors to explain innovation-relevant communicative interaction between actors (Hausmann, 1996: 120). Proximity does not have to be a fixed conditioning factor; it can also be created by actors themselves. In addition to the static relational proximity (language, religion), there is dynamic relational proximity (for example, trust), which first has to be created by actors (Hausmann, 1996).

The knowledge form determines to what extent proximity is necessary for learning by interacting. Innovation-relevant information is typically not a publicly available, codified good, but private tacit knowledge: those parts of personal knowledge as well as personal skills that cannot be communicated in an impersonal way (Hausmann, 1996). Only through personal, communicative interaction between actors are there opportunities to exchange, understand and to apply this kind of information. This strongly selective transferability might be the deeper explanation for why learning by interacting is such an important form of learning for company innovation processes. In order to communicate tacit and, to a lesser extent, codified knowledge, 'code keys' are needed, which are only understandable if (social) coherence and proximity are available. According to Breschi and Malerba (1997: 136, 137): 'the more knowledge is . . . tacit, complex and part of a larger system, the more relevant are informal means of knowledge transmission, like "face-to-face" talks, personal teaching and training, mobility of personnel, and even acquisition of entire groups of people . . . Such means of knowledge transmission are extremely sensible to the distance among agents.' Although the simple dichotomy – i.e. tacit knowledge being only available at the local level and codified knowledge being globally available – might have been attractive, a whole series of empirical publications have dismissed it recently (Amin and Cohendet, 2003; Lo, 2003; Schamp and Lo, 2003; Gertler, 2003). In particular, the studies on the transnational community between Silicon Valley in the USA and Hsinchu

Science Park in Taiwan have shown that tacit knowledge might be built up in one region, but that it is transferable over large distances due to international migration (Saxenian and Hsu, 2001). Codified knowledge, on the other hand, is only accessible to people who know the codes.

Thus the conditions of learning by interacting between actors are institutional contexts, proximity and knowledge creation and transfer. From this perspective, regional learning can be considered as learning by interacting between actors who are linked to their locations or embedded in their regions: elsewhere, learning by interacting in its present form would not have been possible (Oinas and Virkkala, 1997: 270). Collective learning processes and a collective tacit knowledge are linked to the location because of the coinciding of social, cultural and spatial proximity (Keeble et al., 1999; Maskell and Malmberg, 1999; Cooke and Morgan, 1998). This collective, tacit knowledge in regions bears strong similarities to the concept of untraded interdependencies (Storper, 1997) and social capital (Field, 2003; OECD, 2001). They affect both individual and organizational learning (OECD, 2001). Low stocks of them can impede learning; high stocks, on the other hand, can lead to path dependency and lock-ins (Hassink and Shin, 2005; Grabher, 1993; OECD, 2001). Therefore, one can rightly ask to what extent regional learning processes distinguish themselves from path-dependent structurally weak regions, such as old industrial areas, which suffer from collective, tacit knowledge, untraded interdependencies or social capital. It is at this point that learning regions might come in (Schamp, 2000; OECD, 2001; Boschma and Lambooy, 1999), to which we turn now.

2.2 The Learning Region

Apart from authors who have explicitly used the term learning region in the context of the relationship between entrepreneurial learning, innovation and spatial proximity, most have launched the learning region as a new theory-led regional development concept that aims to achieve and/or support collective learning processes (Morgan, 1997; Fürst, 2001; Butzin, 2000; OECD, 2001).

In many countries a general shift of innovation and labour market policies can be observed from the national to regional levels of decision making, partly supported by supranational organizations such as the EU and the World Bank (OECD, 2001). The regional level is more and more seen as the level that offers the greatest prospect for devising governance structures to foster learning in the knowledge-based economy (Cooke and Morgan, 1998; Lorenzen, 2001; Boekema et al., 2000).

According to the OECD (2001: 23, 24), the learning region 'constitutes a *model* towards which actual regions need to progress in order to respond most effectively to the challenges posed by the ongoing transition to a "learning economy"'. It is 'characterised by regional institutions, which facilitate individual and organisational learning through the co-ordination of flexible networks of economic and political agents' (ibid.: 24). Regional policies are crucial for stimulating individual and organizational learning, because policy makers can address path dependency that goes beyond the interest of single agencies and firms (OECD, 2001). Both changing the industrial structure and institutional unlearning are issues that can fruitfully be addressed by regional policy makers. As the learning region is a model, it is not possible to identify examples of actually existing learning regions (ibid.). There are various trajectories towards the goal of becoming a learning region. Affecting social capital in regions is an important element of the learning region strategy.

In my view, a learning region can be defined as a regional innovation strategy in which a broad set of innovation-related regional actors (politicians, policy makers, chambers of commerce, trade unions, higher education institutes, public research establishments and companies) are strongly, but flexibly, connected with each other, and who stick to a certain set of 'policy principles' (OECD, 2001). The following 'policy principles', which are general in scope, leaving regional policy makers to adapt them to specific contexts and demand for innovation policies in the various regions, are a crucial part of a learning region strategy (OECD, 2001; Fürst, 2001):

- carefully coordinating supply of and demand for skilled individuals;
- developing a framework for improving organizational learning, which is not only focused on high-tech sectors, but on all sectors that have the potential to develop high levels of innovative capacity;
- carefully identifying resources in the region that could impede economic development (lock-ins);
- positively responding to changes from outside, particularly where this involves unlearning;
- developing mechanisms for coordinating both across departmental and governance (regional, national, supranational) responsibilities;
- developing strategies to foster appropriate forms of social capital and tacit knowledge that are favourable to learning and innovation;
- continuously evaluating relationships between participation in individual learning, innovation and labour market changes;
- developing an educational and research infrastructure for a knowledge society;
- encouraging openness to impulses from outside;
- fostering redundancy and variety;
- ensuring the participation of large groups of society in devising and implementing strategies.

Morgan (1997) calls learning regions the new generation of regional policy,
which, compared with traditional regional policy, focuses on 'infostructure'
instead of infrastructure, on opening minds instead of opening roads and
branch plants, and which devises policies with SMEs instead of just policies for SMEs. Other characteristics of this concept are the bottom–up
concept, transparent, face-to-face relations, integrated solving of problems
(crossing of policy fields) and permanent organizational learning with feedback effects. This network is open to learning, both intraregionally and
interregionally (Wink, 2003), and willing to unlearn. These characteristics
of a learning region, however, only describe the method of working and the
attitude of regional economic policy makers. The concrete contents of the
innovation policy need to vary according to the economic profile and
demand in individual regions (Tödtling and Trippl, 2005).

For the innovation policy of a learning region it is not enough to supply
technological knowledge (Butzin, 2000). Support is certainly also needed
to enhance the capacity of SMEs to accept, absorb and adapt this knowledge in a useful way. The SMEs' learning of how to become ready and able
to innovate – in other words the innovation competence of SMEs –
becomes the decisive determinant of regional development. In addition,
Butzin (2000) and Bellini (2000) stress the need for qualification measures
for regional actors. These measures should not focus on traditional, concrete expert knowledge, but on the readiness and ability to learn and to
'network', which should, in turn, lead to a consistency between regional
governments as participants in learning regions' interactions and regional
governments as learning organizations (Bellini, 2000: 111).

Since its launch some ten years ago, the learning region concept has been
arriving in one form or another – i.e. in an extremely wide variety of forms –
on the desks of regional policy makers in Europe for quite some time. A
short Internet and press survey carried out by Lagendijk and Cornford
(2000) in August 1998 revealed that nine regions labelled themselves as
learning regions. This number has dramatically increased since then. In May
2004, an Internet survey by the author of this chapter revealed a total of
5000 hits on 'learning region' in the World Wide Web and no less than 11 000
for the German equivalent 'lernende Region'. The Dutch and French equivalents ('lerende regio' and 'région apprenante') had only 218 and 185 hits,
respectively. The popularity of the German term can be explained through
the federal programme called Lernende Region, which is partly funded by
the European Social Fund (www.lernende-regionen.info), which supports
72 learning regions in Germany. A strong appeal to regional policy makers
has been that, with the help of the term 'learning region', they could
broaden out narrow technology policies to areas of business development,
labour market policies, skill improvement and particularly lifelong learning

(Lagendijk and Cornford, 2000: 216). Furthermore, partly based on the learning region concept, the EU has started a new generation of regional policies (Landabaso et al., 2001), which aim at improving the institutional capacity for innovation of less favoured regions, which, in turn, should lead to higher absorption capacity for innovation funds from the EU and national governments. EU strategic programmes, such as Regional Innovation and Technology Transfer Strategies and Infrastructures (RITTS), Regional Technology Plans (RTP) and Regional Innovation Strategy (RIS) aim at both intraregional and interregional learning. They support regions in Europe (re)organizing their innovation strategy in order to meet the demands of firms more than they did before. At the regional level, these programmes are bottom–up (demand-driven, dialogue with SMEs), regional (built on a consensus at regional level), strategic (plan-based on socio-economic objectives), integrated (both public and private sectors are involved) and international (international cooperation).

Although regional learning is clearly part of the learning turn in economic geography, it is confusing to speak about learning regions. Regional learning has clear similarities with concepts such as collective learning and 'untraded' interdependencies, and is only described by a few as a learning region. The learning region is therefore nothing more and nothing less than a regional innovation strategy.

3.   A CRITICAL STANCE ON THE LEARNING REGION

Following critical voices on the learning region by Hudson (1999) and Cooke (2005), I will show in the following that four weaknesses prevent the learning region from becoming a fully fledged theoretical concept in regional studies; that is, its fuzziness (3.1), its normative character (3.2), its strong overlapping with other similar concepts (3.3) and its squeezed position between national innovation systems and global production networks (3.4).

3.1   The Learning Region: A Fuzzy Concept

A fuzzy concept is a concept that 'posits an entity, phenomenon or process which possesses two or more alternative meanings and thus cannot be reliably identified or applied by different readers or scholars' (Markusen, 2003: 702). A fuzzy concept is typically characterised by both lacking conceptual clarity, rigour in the presentation of evidence and clear methodology and difficulties to operationalise the concept. Markusen (2003) observes a clear increase in fuzzy concepts in regional studies during the 1990s, an observation that has provoked reactions by Hudson (2003) and Peck (2003). In a similar vein, De La Mothe and Paquet (1998) talk about a balkanization of regional development concepts, which are difficult to distinguish from each other; as definitions are vague, scholars contradict themselves and empirical evidence is scarce or collected in an anecdotal way. Moreover, related to the fuzziness of concepts, there are concerns that research in economic geography is lacking policy relevance (Martin, 2001; Markusen, 2003). According to Markusen (2003: 705) 'under-researched fuzzy concepts are more tolerable the less we expect them to guide action'.

Is the learning region concept one of the fuzzy concepts Markusen (2003) talks about? In many ways the answer is yes. It is characterized both by lacking conceptual clarity, rigour in the presentation of evidence and clear methodology, and by difficulties of operationalization (Doloreux and Parto, 2004 observe exactly the same problems concerning regional innovation systems). The definitions of learning regions are still quite vague and diverse, since concrete examples can seldom be shown and since policy makers, who have been eager to use the concept as a label for their development plans, have made no efforts to define what they mean by learning regions. The concept seems to travel easily from academic circles to policy makers and back, without profound thoughts about its meaning (Hassink and Lagendijk, 2001). Small wonder, therefore, that Martin (2001: 198) considers learning regions, together with institutional thickness and untraded interdependencies, as fuzzy concepts. He calls these concepts 'vague and impressionistic neologisms'. In an edited book on learning regions, Boekema et al. (2000: 12) make this situation even worse when they want 'to avoid an unproductive discussion on what is or is not a "learning region"' and when they launch the learning region as a paradigm that does not need to be defined.

3.2   The Learning Region: A Normative Concept

Concepts differ in the extent to which they are normative in character, such as the learning region, or based on real situations in regions (industrial districts) (Hassink and Lagendijk, 2001). The learning region (and, according to Doloreux and Parto, 2004, also the regional innovation systems concept) is also in many ways a normative concept. As shown in Section 2.2, it is regarded as a model and it sticks to certain 'policy principles'. In contrast to other concepts with an analytical base, such as industrial districts, it clearly has a normative outlook. There is much written about *what* the ideal learning region is, but little is understood about *how* we get there. As long as we do not know enough about the learning processes that lead to a learning region strategy, we cannot speak about a learning region yet.

3.3 The Learning Region: An Overlapping Concept

As the learning region can be considered as an eclectic concept (Fürst, 2001), it strongly overlaps with several existing theory-led development models and policy-oriented, innovation stimulation concepts (for interesting overviews see Moulaert and Sekia, 2003; MacKinnon et al., 2002; Bathelt, 2005). Learning regions belong to a family of theory-led development models that emerged as reaction to the limited use of grand theories as an argumentative basis for regional innovation strategies. Other members of this family of so-called territorial innovation models (Moulaert and Sekia, 2003) are industrial districts (Pyke and Sengenberger, 1992), innovative milieux (Camagni, 1991; Crevoisier, 2004), regional innovation systems (Cooke et al., 2004; De La Mothe and Paquet, 1998) and clusters (Porter, 2000). They are situated somewhere in between the extremes of abstract theories and regional policy strategies. Based on experiences in growth regions such as Silicon Valley, Baden-Württemberg and the Third Italy, they consider the innovativeness of individual companies or industries as a factor insufficient to explain regional economic inequalities. In order to explain regional economic inequalities, it is not so important *what* is produced in a region (the production structure), but *how* and under which conditions. Some authors see learning regions as successors of these somewhat older, theory-led development models. According to Asheim (1996), for instance, learning regions are the successors of 'traditional' industrial districts. Butzin (2000) and Fürst (2001), on the other hand, see close links between the learning region and the innovative milieu concept.

Of all the above-mentioned models, it is particularly the regional innovation systems approach that most strongly overlaps with the learning region concept. The regional innovation system concept originates from discussions about national innovation systems (Edquist, 1997). Cooke et al. (1998: 1581) define regional innovation systems as systems 'in which firms and other organisations [such as research institutes, universities, innovation support agencies, chambers of commerce, banks, government departments] are systematically engaged in interactive learning through an institutional milieu characterised by embeddedness'. The aim of regional innovation systems, similar to that of learning regions, is to integrate traditional, context-linked, regional knowledge and codified, globally available knowledge in order to stimulate regional, endogenous potentials. Since the learning region and regional innovation concepts are very similar, it is not easy to distinguish them; Moulaert and Sekia (2003), for instance, consider them as one model in their family of so-called territorial innovation models. Only a few people have tried to distinguish the concepts from each other and what these few have written on the issue is contradictory. Fürst (2001: 72) even claims that it is for marketing reasons that Cooke and Morgan have given different labels to concepts that are more or less the same. Cooke et al. (1997) see regional innovation systems as learning regions with an added financial capacity. In a similar line, Cooke and Morgan (1998: 71) consider regional innovation systems as more advanced than learning regions, including the full range of innovation actors and tutoring functions. In contrast, Asheim (2001) sees learning regions as a broader concept than regional innovation systems. In other words, there is no consensus yet on what distinguishes the concepts from each other.

In my view, there are three main differences between the concepts. First, compared with the learning region, the regional innovation system concept is more operational in character. Although partly based on empirical insights (Morgan, 1997, in Wales, Great Britain; Butzin, 2000, in the Ruhr Area, Germany, and Asheim, 2001, in Jæren, Norway), the learning region concept is a conceptual model (Keeble et al., 1999: 321), whereas the regional innovation system concept has been far more empirically described and tested (Cooke et al., 2004; De La Mothe and Paquet, 1998). Second, the regional innovation system concept is a slightly broader concept than the learning region (Morgan, 1997). It contains more regional actors who have an impact on innovation, such as firms, than does the learning region, which focuses more on innovation support policies and agencies. Third, there might be a difference related to the focus on 'innovation' of regional innovation systems and 'learning' of the learning region concept. Compared with regional innovation systems, learning regions are more involved in learning from institutional errors made in the past and, by doing that, in avoiding path-dependent development (OECD, 2001). The latter point is illustrated by the research question Gertler and Wolfe (2004: 93) put in their study on a regional innovation system in Ontario, Canada: 'how reflexive is the [regional innovation] system as a whole in terms of monitoring its successes or failures and adopting the features associated with learning regions elsewhere?' Learning regions, therefore, seem to be reflective and monitoring or 'virtuous' (OECD, 2001: 11) regional innovation systems.

3.4   The Learning Region: Squeezed Between National Innovation Systems and Global Production Networks

Speaking about learning regions, one should not forget the role of nations and industries. In order to stay competitive, companies in regions must integrate locally specific competence with codified, generally available knowledge. In other words, they must link their own innovation systems with national innovation systems and international knowledge flows. According to Gertler (1996), the increasing impact of national regulatory and innovation systems on the behaviour and strategy of individual firms narrows the leeway for regional innovation policy. Furthermore, depending on national political–administrative systems, the leeway for developing learning regions strategies differs considerably. A learning region strategy, therefore, will not be successful if it ignores the impact of national and even international innovation systems on interfirm cooperation and innovative behaviour.

Moreover, the learning region concept does not pay much attention to industry differences and the position of firms in global production networks. By stressing the supply architecture for learning and innovation, it tends to neglect the fact that 'different kinds of products will "demand" different kinds of innovation systems' (Storper, 1997: 107, 108). Firms in different industries need different partners for technological learning (chemical industry – public research establishments; building industry – customers) at different distances (Thierstein, 1996). Regional learning processes, therefore, vary to a large extent, depending on the industry and the position of firms in global production networks. Most regional policy makers, however, have little knowledge about the global production networks in which regional firms are embedded (Herrigel, 2004). Since the economic well-being of firms is increasingly affected by their position in global production networks, policy makers have more and more difficulties updating the company and industry knowledge that is necessary for a tailored regional innovation policy. Regional learning is therefore less and less confined to the local (Bathelt et al., 2004), whereas learning region strategies mainly focus on supporting intraregional learning processes.

4.   BRIDGING THE GAP BETWEEN REGIONAL LEARNING AND THE LEARNING REGION: TOWARDS LEARNING CLUSTERS

As has been shown in this chapter, a large group of scholars in economic geography, regional economics and spatial planning have recently been widely published on learning from two perspectives. First, there are discussions going on about the relationship between entrepreneurial learning, innovation and spatial proximity (regional learning). According to that perspective, learning regions can be considered as areas in which inter-organizational learning by regionally embedded actors takes place. They could not achieve the same learning at another location in the way they achieve it now. Second, the learning region has been presented as a new theory-led policy concept for regional economic development. This concept is supposed to provide local and regional policy makers and economic development agencies with a framework for alternative strategies to link companies to their locations and to combat increasing unemployment.

This chapter has also shown that the learning region concept suffers from four main weaknesses: its fuzziness, its normative character, its strong overlapping with other similar concepts and its squeezed position between national innovation systems and global production networks. Despite these weaknesses, the learning region is highly relevant for two main reasons.

First, the concept has strengthened the relationship between economic geography, policy recommendations and consultancy. Learning regions and regional innovation systems can be seen as an 'intellectual basis for the development of particular forms of sub-national intervention' (OECD, 2001: 25). Therefore geographers and planners dealing with the learning region seem to belong to the 'significant numbers of economic geographers [who] have been working on policy-relevant topics and problems, including . . . local industrial clusters, local high-technology milieus' (Martin, 2001: 193). This clearly can be judged positively, seen against the background of the observed decrease in public policy relevance of geography research, in general (Martin, 2001). Arguably, no concept in economic geography, so far, has travelled as frequently between academic research and practical policy practice. Too strong involvement of academics in policy making in their home region even entails some danger of losing objectivity in their academic work (see Lovering, 1999 and Markusen, 2003 for a critical stand on this issue). Since the 'regional development industry has a seemingly inexhaustible thirst for concepts, notions, theories and models' (Lagendijk and Cornford, 2000: 209), the problem is not so much the lack of policy relevance, but far more the lack of theoretical and conceptual clarity and rigour (Butzin, 2000).

Second, the learning region concept could serve to solve the question of what distinguishes 'good' from 'bad' industrial agglomerations. Traditional theoretical concepts, as well as recent studies on regional networking and collective learning in Europe, not only focus too much on success regions, they also lack the equipment to distinguish 'good' industrial agglomerations, such as the Third Italy and Silicon Valley, from 'bad' ones, such as the Ruhr Area and Route 128 near Boston (Hassink and Shin, 2005; Grabher, 1993; Shapira and Fuchs, 2005). The limited learning ability of regional actors could be the explanatory factor of why coordination of inter-actor activities in some regions turns from a strength to a weakness (path dependence) (Lagendijk, 1997: 21; OECD, 2001; Fürst, 2001). Maskell and Malmberg (1999) distinguish 'good' from 'bad' agglomerations by pointing at their ability to 'unlearn', which involves the removal of formerly significant institutions that now act as obstacles to further development. There appears a great variation in the ability of regions to 'unlearn', 'which makes it possible in some regions but not in others to inaugurate new institutions and simultaneously dissolve ones' (ibid.: 179). The learning region is the first concept that gives policy clues on how to avoid path dependency (see the OECD principle in Section 2.2).

Due to the increasing gap between regional learning and the learning region and the above-described weaknesses, however, I have difficulties in using the term learning region. There are seldom regions that are characterized by only one dominant industry and a strong regional government (Bathelt and Depner, 2003). In reality, we find different clusters within one region, with differing learning processes, different global production networks and different national administrative systems and therefore a different leeway for learning region strategies. In order to develop a learning region strategy, we first need to understand the different learning processes that take place in the different clusters we find in regions.

Therefore a related, but slightly different, concept is proposed, namely that of the learning cluster (Hassink, 2005; see also Steiner and Hartmann, 1998). In my opinion, the learning cluster concept is able to bridge the gap between regional learning, which increasingly crosses the borders of regions and nations due to the globalization of production networks, and the learning region strategy, which focuses on the regional SMEs active in a variety of clusters with different characteristics.

On the basis of theoretical thoughts on geographic clustering by Porter (2000) and Enright (2003), a rapidly increasing number of policy initiatives to support clustering of industries has emerged in many countries of the world (see for instance Porter, 2000; Steiner, 1998). A cluster is a geographically proximate group of interconnected companies and associated institutions in a particular field, linked by commonalities and complementarities (Porter, 2000: 254). Cluster policy initiatives seem to be relevant to support and shape new forms of industrial organizations. Production clusters, therefore, like learning regions, seem to be an empirical and theoretical basis for newly oriented regional innovation policies. According to Lagendijk and Cornford (2000: 217), policy actors applying the cluster concept are more concerned about defining the concept than their counterparts are about using the learning region concept. The latter seems to be much more an undefined term in the regional development industry.

Nevertheless, Martin and Sunley (2003) are rightly very critical about the ambiguities and identification problems surrounding the cluster concept. In fact, clusters also bear many characteristics of a fuzzy concept. However, it is conceptually much further developed than the learning region concept. Enright (2003), for example, developed useful typologies of clusters according to their dimensions, such as the geographic scope, breadth, depth, geographical span of sales, the strength of competitive position, the innovative capacity, the ownership structure and, equally important, the stage of development. The last point refers to a life cycle of clusters, going from embryonic to emerging to mature and declining stages (see also Gilsing and Hospers, 2000). Related to this typology of the stages of development, clusters also vary in terms of their level of activity and self-realization (from working clusters to 'wishful thinking' clusters) (Enright, 2003). Finally, cluster initiatives differ in the type of government intervention, from non-existent to catalytic (bringing interest parties together without much support and direction), to supportive (catalytic plus cluster-specific investments in infrastructure, education and training), to directive (supportive plus more directive targeted programmes), to interventionist (government making the major decisions about the evolution of the cluster rather than the private actors) (Enright, 2003). A potential danger of regional cluster policy is that, by supporting specialization, negative lock-ins might emerge that hinder timely adaptation to changing external circumstances. Compared with the learning region concept, therefore, clusters are conceptually more developed and are put more in an evolutionary perspective, but lack ideas on how to react to changing circumstances and decline.

What then are the differences between a regional cluster strategy and a learning cluster strategy? In other words, what can the learning region add to the cluster concept? Although the danger of declining clusters is recognized in the cluster literature, the concept lacks strategies on how to prevent the emergence of negative lock-ins and path dependency in clusters. The learning cluster strategy, in contrast, does pay attention to these dangers, as it applies to the lock-in, avoiding principles of a learning region strategy. The main actors in such a learning strategy share a reflective attitude. The supporting institutions of such a learning strategy follow their companies along the lines of the global production network. By adopting learning cluster strategies, most of the learning region's weaknesses discussed in this chapter can be alleviated, without losing its main strengths – that is, its relevance for regional innovation policy makers and its institutional capabilities to avoid the emergence of negative lock-ins. There are therefore clear complementarities between the learning region and the cluster concept that need to be further developed and tested in the future with the help of the newly created learning cluster concept.

ACKNOWLEDGEMENT

Parts of this chapter were presented at the Regionalisation of Innovation Policy – Options and Experiences conference, 4 and 5 June 2004, Berlin. During that conference I learned a lot from criticism by Philip Cooke, David

Charles and Franz Tödtling on the learning region concept. I also benefited from comments made by Martina Hülz. The usual disclaimers apply, however, and responsibility for the chapter's content rests solely with me.

NOTE

1. One could add a third, theoretical–structural perspective, which considers the learning region as spatial outcome of grand societal changes at the macro-level. This perspective has been launched by Florida (1995), who broadly defines learning regions as the outcome of the shift from mass production capitalism to global, knowledge-intensive capitalism. However, these ideas have not been taken up by others to a large extent (one exception is Crevoisier, 1999).

REFERENCES

Amin, A. and Cohendet, P. (2003), 'Geographies of knowledge formation in firms', paper presented at the DRUID Summer Conference on Creating, Sharing and Transferring Knowledge, Copenhagen, 12–14 June.

Asheim, B.T. (1996), 'Industrial districts as "learning regions": a condition for prosperity', *European Planning Studies*, **4**, 379–400.

Asheim, B.T. (2001), 'Learning regions as development coalitions: partnership as governance in European workfare states?', *Concepts and Transformation*, **6**, 73–101.

Bathelt, H. (2005), 'Geographies of production: growth regimes in spatial perspective (II) – knowledge creation and growth in clusters', *Progress in Human Geography*, **29**, 204–16.

Bathelt, H. and Depner, H. (2003), 'Innovation, Institution und Region: zur Diskussion über nationale und regionale Innovationssysteme', *Erdkunde*, **57**, 126–43.

Bathelt, H., Malmberg, A. and Maskell, P. (2004), 'Clusters and knowledge: local buzz, global pipelines and the process of knowledge creation', *Progress in Human Geography*, **28**, 31–56.

Bellini, N. (2000), 'Planning the learning region: an Italian approach', in F. Boekema, K. Morgan, S. Bakkers and R. Rutten (eds), *Knowledge, Innovation and Economic Growth: The Theory and Practice of Learning Regions*, Cheltenham, UK and Northampton, MA, USA: Edward Elgar, pp. 95–114.

Benner, C. (2003), 'Learning communities in a learning region: the soft infrastructure of cross-firm learning networks in Silicon Valley', *Environment and Planning A*, **35**, 1809–30.

Boekema, F., Morgan, K., Bakkers, S. and Rutten, R. (2000), 'Introduction to learning regions: a new issue for analysis', in F. Boekema, K. Morgan, S. Bakkers and R. Rutten (eds), *Knowledge, Innovation and Economic Growth: The Theory and Practice of Learning Regions*, Cheltenham, UK and Northampton, MA, USA: Edward Elgar, pp. 3–16.

Boschma, R. and Lambooy, J. (1999), 'The prospects of an adjustment policy based on collective learning in old industrial regions', *GeoJournal*, **49**, 391–9.

Breschi, S. and Malerba, F. (1997), 'Sectoral innovation systems: technological regimes, Schumpeterian dynamics, and spatial boundaries', in C. Edquist (ed.), *Systems of Innovation: Technologies, Institutions and Organizations*, London and Washington: Pinter, pp. 130–56.

Butzin, B. (2000), 'Netzwerke, kreative Milieus und lernende Region: Perspektiven für die regionale Entwicklungsplanung', *Zeitschrift für Wirtschaftsgeographie*, **44**, 149–66.

Camagni, R. (1991), *Innovation networks. Spatial perspectives*, London: Belhaven.

Cooke, P. (2005), 'Learning regions: a critique', paper presented at the 4th European Meeting on Applied Evolutionary Economics, Utrecht, 19–21 May.

Cooke, P., Gomez Uranga, M. and Etxebarria, G. (1997), 'Regional innovation systems: institutional and organisational dimensions', *Research Policy*, **26**, 475–91.

Cooke, P., Heidenreich, M. and Braczyk, H.-J. (eds) (2004), *Regional Innovation Systems: The Role of Governance in a Globalized World*, London: Routledge.

Cooke, P. and Morgan, K. (1998), *The Associational Economy: Firms, Regions, and Innovation*, Oxford: Oxford University Press.

Cooke, P., Uranga, M.G. and Etxebarria, G. (1998), 'Regional systems of innovation: an evolutionary perspective', *Environment and Planning A*, **30**, 1563–84.

Crevoisier, O. (1999), 'Two ways to look at learning regions in the context of globalization: the homogenizing and particularizing approaches', *GeoJournal*, **49**, 353–61.

Crevoisier, O. (2004), 'The innovative milieus approach: toward a territorialized understanding of the economy?', *Economic Geography*, **80**, 367–80.

De La Mothe, J. and Paquet, G. (eds) (1998), *Local and Regional Systems of Innovation*, Boston, MA, Dordrecht and London: Kluwer Academic Publishers.

Doloreux, D. and Parto, S. (2004), 'Regional innovation systems: a critical review', paper presented at the XL Conference of the French-speaking Regional Science Association, 1–3 September, Bruselas.

Edquist, C. (1997), 'Systems of innovation approaches – their emergence and characteristics', in C. Edquist (ed.), *Systems of Innovation: Technologies, Institutions and Organizations*, London and Washington: Pinter, pp. 1–35.

Enright, M. (2003), 'Regional clusters: what we know and what we should know', in J. Bröcker, D. Dohse and R. Soltwedel (eds), *Innovation Clusters and Interregional Competition*, Berlin: Springer, pp. 99–129.

Field, J. (2003), *Social Capital*, London: Routledge.

Florida, R. (1995), 'Toward the learning region', *Futures*, **27**, 527–36.

Fürst, D. (2001), 'Die "learning region" – Strategisches Konzept oder Artefakt?', in H.-F. Eckey, D. Hecht, M. Junkernheinrich, H. Karl, N. Werbeck and R. Wink (eds), *Ordnungspolitik als konstruktive Antwort auf wirtschaftspolitische Herausforderungen*, Stuttgart: Lucius & Lucius, pp. 71–89.

Geenhuizen, M. van (1999), 'De lerende regio: hype of nieuw perspectief?', *Geografie*, **8**, December, 12–16.

Gertler, M.S. (1996), 'Barriers to technology transfer: culture and the limits to regional systems of innovation', paper presented at the EU-RESTPOR Conference 'Global Comparison of Regional RTD and Innovation Strategies for Development and Cohesion', 19–21 September, Brussels.

Gertler, M.S. (2003), 'Tacit knowledge and the economic geography of context, or the undefinable tacitness of being (there)', *Journal of Economic Geography*, **3**, 75–99.

Gertler, M.S. and Wolfe, D.A. (2004), 'Ontario's regional innovation system: the evolution of knowledge-based assets', in P. Cooke, M. Heidenreich and H.-J. Braczyk (eds), *Regional Innovation Systems: The Role of Governances in a Globalized World*, London and New York: Routledge, pp. 91–124.

Gilsing, V. and Hospers, G.-J. (2000), 'De levensloop van clusters', *Economische Statistische Berichten*, **85**, D12–D14.

Grabher, G. (1993), 'The weakness of strong ties: the lock-in of regional development in the Ruhr area', in G. Grabher (ed.), *The Embedded Firm; on the Socioeconomics of Industrial Networks*, London and New York: Routledge, pp. 255–77.

Hassink, R. (2001), 'The learning region: a fuzzy concept or a sound theoretical basis for modern regional innovation policies?', *Zeitschrift für Wirtschaftsgeographie*, **45**, 219–30.

Hassink, R. and Lagendijk, A. (2001), 'The dilemmas of interregional institutional learning', *Environment and Planning C: Government and Policy*, **19** (1), 65–84.

Hassink, R. (2005), 'How to unlock regional economies from path dependency? From learning region to learning cluster', *European Planning Studies*, **13**, 521–35.

Hassink, R. and Shin, D.-H. (2005), 'Guest editorial: the restructuring of old industrial areas in Europe and Asia', *Environment and Planning A*, **37**, 571–80.

Hausmann, U. (1996), *Innovationsprozesse von produktionsorientierten Dienstleistungsunternehmen und ihr räumlich-sozialer Kontext*. Dissertation No. 1750, Universität St Gallen, Bamberg.

Herrigel, G. (2004), *Space and Governance in New Old Economy Manufacturing Industries*, Bonn: Department of Geography, University of Bonn, SECONS Discussion Forum No. 7.

Hudson, R. (1999), 'The learning economy, the learning firm and the learning region: a sympathetic critique of the limits to learning', *European Urban and Regional Studies*, **6**, 59–72.

Hudson, R. (2003), 'Fuzzy concepts and sloppy thinking: reflections on recent developments in critical regional studies', *Regional Studies*, **37**, 741–6.

Keeble, D., Lawson, C., Moore, B. and Wilkinson, F. (1999), 'Collective learning processes, networking and "institutional thickness" in the Cambridge region', *Regional Studies*, **33**, 319–32.

Kunzmann, K.R. and Tata, L. (2003), 'Learning city initiatives: a review', University of Dortmund: Department of Spatial Planning in Europe (unpublished manuscript).

Lagendijk, A. (1997), *From New Industrial Spaces to Regional Innovation Systems and beyond. How and from whom should industrial geography learn?* Newcastle upon Tyne: CURDS, EUNIT Discussion Paper No. 10.

Lagendijk, A. and Cornford, J. (2000), 'Regional institutions and knowledge – tracking new forms of regional development policy', *Geoforum*, **31**, 209–18.

Landabaso, M., Oughton, C. and Morgan, K. (2001), 'Innovation networks and regional policy in Europe', in K. Koschatzky, M. Kulicke and A. Zenker (eds), *Innovation Networks: Concepts and Challenges in the European Perspective*, Heidelberg and New York: Physica Verlag, pp. 243–73.

Lo, V. (2003), 'Local codes and global networks: knowledge access as a location factor in the financial industry', in V. Lo and E.W. Schamp (eds), *Knowledge, Learning, and Regional Development*, Münster: LIT Verlag, pp. 61–81.

Lorenzen, M. (2001), 'Localized learning and policy: academic advice on enhancing regional competitiveness through learning', *European Planning Studies*, **9**, 163–85.

Lorentzen, A. (2005), 'The spatial dimensions of knowledge sourcing', paper presented at the Conference on Regional Growth Agendas, Regional Studies Association, Aalborg, 28–31 May.

Lovering, J. (1999), 'Theory led by policy? The inadequacies of the "new regionalism" (illustrated from the case of Wales)', *International Journal of Urban and Regional Research*, **23**, 379–95.

Lundvall, B.-Å. (1996), *The Social Dimension of the Learning Economy*, Aalborg: DRUID Working Paper No. 96-1.

MacKinnon, D., Cumbers, A. and Chapman, K. (2002), 'Learning, innovation and regional development: a critical appraisal of recent debates', *Progress in Human Geography*, **26**, 293–311.

Malmberg, A. (1997), 'Industrial geography: location and learning', *Progress in Human Geography*, **21**, 573–82.

Markusen, A. (2003), 'Fuzzy concepts, scanty evidence, policy distance: the case for rigour and policy relevance in critical regional studies', *Regional Studies*, **37**, 701–17.

Martin, R. (2001), 'Geography and public policy: the case of the missing agenda', *Progress in Human Geography*, **25** (2), 189–210.

Martin, R. and Sunley, P. (2003), 'Deconstructing clusters: chaotic concept or policy panacea?' *Journal of Economic Geography*, **3**, 5–36.

Maskell, P. and Malmberg, A. (1999), 'Localised learning and industrial competitiveness, *Cambridge Journal of Economics*, **23**, 167–85.

Morgan, K. (1997), 'The learning region: institutions, innovation and regional renewal', *Regional Studies*, **31**, 491–503.

Moulaert, F. and Sekia, F. (2003), 'Territorial innovation models: a critical survey', *Regional Studies*, **37**, 289–302.

Nooteboom, B. (2004), 'Innovation, learning and cluster dynamics', Tilburg University CentER Discussion Papers No. 2005-44.

OECD (2001), *Cities and Regions in the New Learning Economy*, Paris: OECD.

Oinas, P. and Virkkala, S. (1997), 'Learning, competitiveness and development: reflections on the contemporary discourse on "Learning Regions"', In H. Eskelinen (ed.), *Regional Specialisation and Local Environment: Learning and Competitiveness*, Stockholm: NordREFO, pp. 263–77.

Peck, J. (2003), 'Fuzzy old world: a response to Markusen', *Regional Studies*, **37**, 729–40.

Pommeranz, J.O. (2000), 'Lernende Region Ruhrgebiet – eine regionalpolitische Leitperspektive für das 21. Jahrhundert', *Zeitschrift für Wirtschaftsgeographie*, **44**, 183–200.

Porter, M.E. (2000), 'Locations, clusters and company strategy', in G.L. Clark, M. Feldman and M. Gertler (eds), *The Oxford Handbook of Economic Geography*, Oxford: Oxford University Press, pp. 253–74.

Pyke, F. and Sengenberger, W. (eds) (1992), *Industrial Districts and Local Economic Regeneration*, Geneva: International Institute for Labour Studies (ILO).

Saxenian, A. and Hsu, J.-Y. (2001), 'The Silicon Valley–Hsinchu connection: technical communities and industrial upgrading', *Industrial and Corporate Change*, **10**, 893–920.

Schamp, E.W. (2000), *Vernetzte Produktion: Industriegeographie aus institutioneller Perspektive*, Darmstad: Wissenschaftliche Buchgesellschaft.

Schamp, E.W. and Lo, V. (2003), 'Knowledge, learning, and regional development: an introduction', in V. Lo and E.W. Schamp (eds), *Knowledge, Learning, and Regional Development*, Münster: LIT Verlag, pp. 1–12.

Scheff, J. (1999), *Lernende Regionen: regionale Netzwerke als Antwort auf globale Herausforderungen*, Wien: Linde Verlag.

Shapira, P. and Fuchs, G. (eds) (2005), *Rethinking Regional Innovation and Change: Path Dependency or Regional Breakthrough*, New York: Springer.

Steiner, M. (ed.) (1998), *Clusters and Regional Specialisation: On Geography, Technology, and Networks*, London: Pion.

Steiner, M. and Hartmann, C. (1998), 'Learning with clusters: a case study from Upper Styria', in M. Steiner (ed.), *Clusters and Regional Specialisation*, London: Pion, pp. 211–25.

Storper, M. (1997), *The Regional World: Territorial Development in a Global Economy*, New York and London: Guilford.

Thierstein, A. (1996), 'Auf der Suche nach der regionalen Wettbewerbsfähigkeit – Schlüsselfaktoren und Einflußmöglichkeiten', *Raumforschung und Raumordnung*, **54**, 193–202.

Tödtling, F. and Trippl, M. (2005), 'One size fits all? Towards a differentiated regional innovation policy', *Research Policy*, **34**, 1203–19.

Wink, R. (2003), 'Transregionales Lernen – Leerformel oder regionalpolitische Zukunftsstrategie', *Gesellschaft für Regionalforschung, Seminarbericht*, **46**, 1–17.

PART III

Future

13. A future for the learning region

Roel Rutten and Frans Boekema

After discussing the foundations and the state of the art, it is time to turn to the future. So, what is the learning region? Now that the multitude of concepts identified in Chapter 6 has been methodically scrutinized in the previous chapters, how should the learning region be defined? Looking for consensus among the authors in the previous chapters could yield important clues in this respect. The most important one seems to be their concern with relations between actors. Oerlemans et al., Lorenzen and Hassink are most emphatic about this. Oerlemans et al. specifically argue in favour of considering both the structural and relational dimensions of innovation networks, as the learning part of innovation networks is found in their relational dimension. Lorenzen argues that, contrary to the assumption made in mainstream economics, innovation and knowledge spillovers cannot be studied independently from the agents that bring them about. Hassink, finally, argues in favour of learning clusters as alternatives for learning regions, his point being that clusters have an unambiguous unit of analysis, that of agents and their relations. This emphasis on relations is in line with what, for example, Morgan argued in the foundations part of this volume (Part I), that a region must be understood as a nexus of processes. So the important clues that can now be identified are the focuses on agents and on processes. This, in turn, corresponds to the conceptual model of Figure 6.1, where 'regional learning' was chosen as the dependent variable of the learning region. Every theory explains something; that is, it has a dependent variable. The learning region, we argue, explains the process of regional learning.

EMBEDDEDNESS: THE RELATIONAL PERSPECTIVE

In the literature on which the learning region builds, learning is inseparably linked to knowledge creation. On this issue, the consensus among the above authors is that the learning region subscribes to the resource-based perspective. In this perspective, knowledge is a key strategic resource for companies trying to achieve innovations and competitive advantage (see Maskell et al., 1998 and Lundvall, 1994, in Morgan, 1997). The resource-based perspective owes to Schumpeter the position that innovation is the outcome of a process of making combinations of means of production. In the knowledge-based economy, means of production, above all, pertain to knowledge (Schumpeter, 1943 and Rutten, 2003). In the knowledge-based perspective, 'learning' and 'the process of knowledge creation' are synonymous (Rutten, 2003). In fact, the literature on knowledge creation and learning offers a considerable choice in definitions for this phenomenon; but, essentially, all of them arrive at the same conclusion. In the words of Morgan (1997: 480), knowledge creation or learning refers to interactive processes that depend on the ability of agents to combine and recombine different pieces of knowledge into something new. It is this process that the learning region seeks to explain by making (the process of) regional learning its dependent variable.

To say that regional learning is the dependent variable of the learning region does not contradict our earlier claim that the two should be analytically separated (see Boekema et al., 2000: 246). On the contrary. What has changed, and, it is hoped, matured, is our conceptualization of the learning region. In our earlier work (Boekema et al., 2000) we proposed that the learning region be seen as a metaphor, a position criticized by Hassink (2001) as being unhelpful in providing conceptual clarity about the learning region. At the time, our position was that, conceptually, the learning region was immature to such an extent that to propose it as anything other than a metaphor would be ill conceived. However, given the current state of the art of the learning region, as laid down in this volume, we can comfortably agree with Hassink. We now propose the learning region as the theory that explains regional learning; that is, the process of knowledge creation between actors within a region while accounting for the characteristics of that region, its actors and the relations between them. In other words, the theory explains learning in regions, but the focus is on learning. Put differently, the level of analysis is regional learning, that is, the process of knowledge creation between regional actors. However, these actors are part of (i.e. embedded in) a wider regional context of actors and relations and they are affected by the characteristics of 'their' region. Therefore, in order to properly analyse the process of regional learning, we propose that the learning region should adopt an embeddedness perspective. The concept of embeddedness, as introduced into the socio-economic literature by Granovetter posits that

> Actors do not behave or decide as atoms outside a social context, nor do they adhere slavishly to scripts written for them by the particular intersection of

sociocultural categories they happen to occupy. Their attempts at purposive action are instead embedded in concrete, ongoing systems of social relations. (Granovetter, 1992: 32)

The embeddedness perspective thus looks at actors (or agents), the relations between them and their embeddedness in a social context. Applied to the learning region, this means that the focus is on regional actors and the learning processes that go on between them. Furthermore, it means that the embeddedness of these actors in their social context must be considered. According to Granovetter, embeddedness has both a structural and a relational dimension. 'Embeddedness refers to the fact that economic action and outcomes, like all social action and outcomes, are affected by actors' dyadic (pairwise) relations [relational embeddedness] and by the structure of overall network of relations [structural embeddedness]' (Granovetter, 1992: 33). Relational embeddedness affects the outcomes of (social and) economic action through the history of a particular relation. 'In ongoing relations, human beings do not start fresh each day, but carry the baggage of previous interactions into each new one' (ibid.: 34). Structural embeddedness, according to Granovetter, is more subtle. Narrowed down to its essence, structural embeddedness suggests that it is good to have friends who themselves have many friends. This creates high-density networks, the cohesiveness of which permits a quick and better dissemination of information and the generation of 'normative, symbolic, and cultural structures that affect our behavior' (ibid.: 35). The strength of Granovetter's argument is his keen understanding that (economic) actors cannot be understood without accounting for the network of social relations in which they are embedded. This puts him at odds with mainstream economics, which still subscribes to the idea that isolated market transactions are all that concern human agents (see Rutten, 2004). The weakness of Granovetter's argument is its leaning towards a network-biased view (see Oerlemans et al., Chapter 8 in this volume), although Granovetter (1985 and 1992), as well as others working in the embeddedness tradition (e.g. Uzzi, 1997 and Grabher, 1993), are aware of the potential perverse effects of embeddedness.

Another weakness of Granovetter's argument is his focus on dyadic relations. Social linkages other than dyadic relations, too, affect the behaviour of actors and, therefore, the outcome of economic action. Examples in this regard are social institutions, culture and affiliation to (social) groups. Although Granovetter (1985) warned against an over-socialized explanation of human behaviour on the basis of these very social linkages, to ignore them, arguably, would be a mistake. As long as Granovetter's main argument is observed – that actors are neither atoms outside a social

context, nor do they slavishly follow scripts – extending the embeddedness argument to include social linkages other than dyads does not seem to
be problematic. This is important, as it allows the continuation of a conceptual position where the level of analysis is the interactions of actors (in
our case, regional learning), while still accounting for (social) institutions,
cultures and other characteristics of their environment (in our case, the
characteristics of the region) when explaining actor behaviour. Therefore,
we propose that, in addition to structural embeddedness and relational
embeddedness, a third kind of embeddedness should be admitted: social
embeddedness. Social embeddedness accounts for actors' embeddedness in
a social context; that is, it accounts for the fact that actors' actions are
affected by the social context of which they are a part.

   When making a case for social embeddedness, we can borrow from Emile
Durkheim, one of sociology's founding fathers, who, like Granovetter,
appreciated the connection between association and obligation (Stedman
Jones, 2001: 186). Arguably, as a sociologist, Durkheim's interest for society
as a whole exceeds the scope of this volume. On the other hand, one of the
key messages of this volume is that learning is an inherently social process
and, in the first instance, that networks are networks of people. From this
perspective, a detour through sociology may be exotic, but not to the point
where it becomes irresponsible. In fact, sociology may deepen our understanding of the learning region, as economic explanations of it have thus
far dominated in the literature.

A CONCEPTUALIZATION OF EMBEDDEDNESS

For Durkheim, society is associative and relational. It consists of relations
that bind people. Durkheim, thus, has a thoroughly relational view of
reality. Relations slacken through distance and intensify through contact,
something that Durkheim refers to as social density. More contact
and more exchanges between members of a society increases the social
density of that society; that is, it makes the relations in and the coherence
of a society stronger (Stedman Jones, 2001: 93–4). Social density is thus
not unlike Granovetter's understanding of weak and strong ties. More
important in Durkheim's argument than density is the concept of social
solidarity. For Durkheim, to understand society in terms of relations is
solidarity, because solidarity expresses relations. Solidarity may follow
from mutually dependent relations that people in a society share. It also
follows from the collectively shared conventions and beliefs that
connect people within a society (Stedman Jones, 2001: 90). Moreover, the
collective conventions and beliefs also reflect the morality of a society.

This morality allows individuals in society to prosper (ibid.: 184). Or, in Durkheim's words:

> It is impossible for men to . . . be in regular contact with one another without their acquiring some feeling for the group . . . , without their becoming attached to it . . . And this attachment to something that transcends the individual . . . is the very well-spring of moral activity. (Durkheim, 1893/1997: xliii)

Although admitting to a relational perspective, Durkheim is not naive, as shown by his awareness that 'A life lived in common is attractive, yet at the same time it exerts coercion' (ibid.). This is Durkheim's way of reconciling solidarity with the autonomy of the individual or, in Granovetter's terms, to acknowledge that the individual does not slavishly follow scripts.

Durkheim distinguishes two forms of solidarity, mechanical solidarity and organic solidarity. Mechanical solidarity follows from similarity, that is, from the fact that individuals are part of the same group or society and therefore share relations, conventions and beliefs. Organic solidarity, on the other hand, is a function of the division of labour in society. The division of labour results in reciprocal relations and mutual dependence between members of a society (or group). Moreover, solidarity is also a moral phenomenon. It is what ought to follow from similarity and from the division of labour; it is what ought to happen in social relations. That is not necessarily the same as what is actually happening in social relations. In fact, Durkheim ascribed many of the social problems of the French Republic after 1871[1] to a lack of solidarity. Thus, for Durkheim, similarity and the division of labour in society do not automatically lead to solidarity as 'individuals do not fit automatically and unreflectively into structures' (Stedman Jones, 2001: 13). In other words, although Durkheim leaves us in no doubt that his concept of solidarity is collective in nature, it is by no means incompatible with agency, that is, the autonomous decision making of agents (actors) in a society. However, if present in a society, solidarity is beneficial for both the society and for the members of that society.[2]

Essentially, mechanical solidarity signals that the individual is part of a larger whole, a collective, be it a group or society. Being part of a collective means that people share characteristics, beliefs, conventions, etc. with other people in that particular collective; that is, to some extent, people within collectives are similar. Hence Durkheim's definition of mechanical solidarity as solidarity by similarity (Durkheim, 1893/1997). What this means is that, to use a contemporary concept, the social institutions[3] of a group (or society as a whole), that is, its norms, values, conventions etc., influence (but do not dictate) how individual members of that group (or society) behave. Or, as Durkheim put it:

> we all know that a social cohesion exists whose cause can be traced to a certain conformity of each individual . . . [All] members of the group are not only individually attracted to one another because they resemble one another, but they are also linked to what is the condition for the existence of this collective type, that is, to the society that they form by coming together. . . . Conversely, society insists upon its citizens displaying . . . basic resemblance because it is a condition for its own cohesion. (Durkheim, 1893/1997: 60–61)

Mechanical solidarity, thus, is a straightforward form of solidarity. Being part of a group is not without consequences for the behaviour of group members. For Durkheim, mechanical solidarity was a characteristic of primitive rather than of modern societies. Nevertheless, this form of solidarity does shed light on a basic mechanism that links association to obligation and, therefore, it should not be ignored. The second form of solidarity, organic solidarity, was, for Durkheim, a more complex but also a more profound form of solidarity.

As argued, organic solidarity follows from the division of labour in society. 'Clearly, interrelation and interdependence, through differentiated work relations, are essential for Durkheim; this is why the division of labour contributes to interdependence' (Stedman Jones, 2001: 97). As such, the division of labour is a necessary but not sufficient condition for organic solidarity to develop. For Durkheim, solidarity is a profoundly moral phenomenon. This can be explained by looking at his concept of the *conscience collective*, which is a key element in Durkheim's thinking. At face value, the *conscience collective* is just that. However, far from being a collectivist, Durkheim acknowledges that there are several *consciences collectives*, 'since we are members of several groups' (Durkheim, 1893/1997: 67n.). The *conscience collective*, thus, is an attribute of social relations and it 'demonstrates a form of moral relatedness which is distinct from self-interest'. Put differently, the *conscience collective* reflects the collective moral interest of a group of people (or of society as a whole). It also helps the group perceive and understand reality and, therefore, it is central to collective thinking (Stedman Jones, 2001: 98). In order to stress once more the importance in Durkheim's thinking of morality with regard to interdependence, solidarity and the *conscience collective*, we offer the following quote:

> [We] may state generally that the characteristic of moral rules is that they enunciate the basic conditions of social solidarity. Law and morality represent the totality of bonds that bind us to one another and to society, which shape the mass of individuals into a cohesive aggregate. We may say that what is moral is

everything that is a source of solidarity, everything that forces man to take account of other people, to regulate his action by something other than the promptings of his own egoism, and the more numerous and strong these ties are, the more solid is the morality. (Durkheim, 1893/1997: 331)

Organic solidarity thus requires not only that people develop interdependent and reciprocal relations, but also that they are aware of their interdependence and that, accordingly, they develop rules or codes of conduct (in Durkheim's words, morality) to guide their relations.

> For organic solidarity to exist it is not enough for there to be a system of organs necessary to one another that feel their solidarity in a general way. The manner in which they meet . . . must be predetermined. Otherwise, a fresh struggle would be required each time in order to bring them into a state of equilibrium with one another. (Ibid.: 301)

So, for Durkheim, morality, *conscience collective*, and interdependence are closely related. The stronger morality and *conscience collective* are present in interdependent relations, the better these relations function; that is, the higher their yields for both individuals and the group as a whole. What this means is that the Durkheimian argument goes a step further than the Granovetterian argument, without becoming over-socialized. Granovetter developed his embeddedness argument as a response to the transaction-cost discourse. Transaction-cost theory considers isolated transactions only. In response, Granovetter argued that the actors who engage in those transactions do not do so in a social vacuum but in a system of ongoing social relations (see Granovetter, 1985 and Rutten, 2004). What Durkheim shows is that this 'system of ongoing social relations' is a reality of its own for the actors within it; that is, they are part of a group, and groups have distinct characteristics that reflect on their members. It is a part of social reality that must not be ignored in the study of social relations. What Granovetter has in common with the transaction-cost theory is his focus on dyadic relations. Although he is aware of the wider social context of individual actors, his level of analysis is still the individual or individuals, and their dyadic relations and networks. The Durkheimian argument emphasizes that there is another level of analysis that must be accounted for when explaining the behaviour of individual actors, that of the group (or society as a whole). If anything, Durkheim's account of social solidarity demonstrates that groups matter. Looking at both dyadic relations and at groups effectively makes the explanation of the behaviour of individual actors a multi-level exercise. As Durkheim's own arguments show, this is not the same as resorting to an over-socialized explanation of human behaviour.

Durkheim signals a difference between mechanical and organic solidarity that is crucial in this respect. Whereas in the case of mechanical solidarity the *conscience collective* follows from uniformity and resemblance between group members, in the case of organic solidarity, differentiation between individuals (which is the result of the division of labour) leaves far more space for the individual conscience. As Durkheim put it:

> Whereas [mechanical] solidarity implies that individuals resemble one another, [organic solidarity] assumes that they are different from one another. The former type is only possible in so far as the individual personality is absorbed into the collective personality; the latter is only possible if each one of us has a sphere of action that is peculiarly our own. . . . The more extensive this free area is, the stronger the cohesion that arises from this solidarity. Indeed, on the one hand each of us depends more intimately upon society the more labour is divided up, and on the other, the activity of each one of us is correspondingly more specialised, the more personal it is. (Durkheim, 1893/1997: 85)

Durkheim then goes on to make an analogy with 'higher animals', i.e., biology, to support his argument:

> In fact each organ has its own special characteristics and autonomy, yet the greater the unity of the organism, the more marked the individualisation of the parts. Using this analogy, we propose to call 'organic' the solidarity that is due to the division of labour. (Ibid.)

In sum, the sociologist Durkheim has a pronounced relational view of society and in this view the behaviour of individuals cannot be understood but in terms of their connectedness to (or, embeddedness in) a social context, that is, the groups or the society that individuals are part of. This social context provides norms, rules, conventions, etc. (i.e. morality for Durkheim) that not only affect how individuals behave in social relations but also how they see the world around them. Although Durkheim stresses the collective, he does not ignore individuality. On the contrary, his is a balanced view of the collective and the individual where the individual sees his own interest through the lens of the collective, or social context, of which he is a part. The denser a person's relations with his social context, the more this person becomes aware of his being a part of a larger whole and, consequently, the more likely it is for this person to account for the rules, norms, conventions, etc. of his social context in his behaviour. In this case, social relations are characterized by a high level of solidarity. The fact that Durkheim recognized that society, in fact, suffered from a lack of solidarity means that he understood that the free will of individuals may lead them to choose not to let the rules, norms, conventions, etc. of their social context affect their behaviour.

Although nearly a century separates the works of Durkheim and Granovetter, the similarities between them are evident. It is difficult not to see Durkheim's 'solidarity' and Granovetter's 'embeddedness' as near equivalents. The differences between them, however, are also evident. Consider, for example, the following:

> [The] economic action of individuals as well as larger economic patterns . . . are very importantly affected by networks of social relationships. I think that for the economic action of individuals the embeddedness of individuals in networks of social relationships is in most contexts extremely important, and you rarely see this taken into account in economic arguments. (Granovetter, 1990: 100)

It looks similar. Durkheim and Granovetter have both identified the same mechanism, i.e., the relation between association and obligation. But there is a difference. As argued above, the difference is in the level of analysis. In the above quote, Granovetter does not, as Durkheim does, talk about social context. Instead, he talks about networks. For him, social relations are networks of individuals. What Durkheim says is that, if they are sufficiently dense, these networks of individuals become a social reality of their own. They become groups with a unique *conscience collective* that gives rise to a unique solidarity. To use Granovetter's words, individuals are not only embedded in ongoing systems of social relations – i.e. social networks – they are also embedded in groups, in a social context. To understand and explain the behaviour of individuals, therefore, is to understand how their social context affects their behaviour. Hence the addition of a third form of embeddedness, social embeddedness, to supplement the two forms already identified by Granovetter, i.e. relational embeddedness and structural embeddedness. Together, these three forms of embeddedness are a more complete conceptualization of the layers of social relations in which individuals are embedded.

- The first form of embeddedness, or layer of social relations, is Granovetter's relational embeddedness. It focuses on dyadic relations between actors and acknowledges that these relations often have a past and a future and that, therefore, considerations other than rent seeking play a role in economic exchange relations.
- The second form of embeddedness is structural embeddedness, which, in Granovetter's words, accounts for the fact that it helps to have friends who have friends. This form of embeddedness is about the position of actors in networks and about their access to resources, such as knowledge, and about the characteristics of these network relations, such as trust (see Uzzi, 1997 and Rutten, 2004).

- The final form of embeddedness is the one borrowed from Durkheim, social embeddedness. This form of embeddedness acknowledges that networks of social relations have a social reality of their own, characterized by interdependence and a unique set of norms, rules and conventions. By virtue of their being part of these social realities, actors see the world through a certain lens and this, arguably, affects their behaviour.

IMPLICATIONS FOR THE LEARNING REGION

If we argue that the learning region follows a relational perspective, it means that it must account for the above three forms of embeddedness in the explanation of regional learning. Looking at the variables as identified in Figure 6.1, it means that it must be clear on which level(s) each particular variable exercises its effect on the process of regional learning. This process takes place between individual actors, but these actors, of course, are embedded in webs of relations with other (regional) actors. That makes the relational perspective an embeddedness perspective. Conceptually, the challenge is to identify where in the layers of social context the different variables from Figure 6.1 should fit in.

Spatial Proximity

In so far as spatial proximity acts as a mechanism to facilitate the transfer of tacit knowledge, it is a characteristic of relations and, therefore, works on the level of relational embeddedness. In this perspective, spatial proximity is equivalent to the geography of knowledge. This means that the more tacit the knowledge, the more helpful spatial proximity is in transferring this knowledge from one person to another.[4] Notwithstanding the fact that other forms of proximity (such as cognitive proximity) may moderate the effect of spatial proximity in regional learning, spatial proximity as the geography of knowledge works at the lowest, most direct level of embeddedness, relational embeddedness. Additionally, spatial proximity may be seen as agglomeration advantages. Actors enjoy agglomeration advantages (or suffer from disadvantages) when they are linked to other regional actors and when these linkages yield benefits (or, in the case of disadvantages, frustrate them) without there necessarily being an exchange relation between these actors – for example, in the case of having access to a diverse regional knowledge pool. This form of spatial proximity typically works through linkages and, therefore, is an example of structural embeddedness.

Regional Interfirm Networks

From a purely organizational perspective, networks are a means of coordinating the allocation of resources and the creation of knowledge (embodied in products and services), as are markets and hierarchies. The organizational characteristics of these networks (e.g. formal or informal control and communication) are in large part responsible for the ability of networks to create knowledge, that is, to learn. This aspect of networks is structural embeddedness, as it has to do with the number and types of linkages between actors. Additionally, networks have a social side as, in varying degrees, they become social realities of their own and develop their unique set of norms, rules and conventions. This side of networks, arguably, is at the level of social embeddedness.

Regional Institutional Set-up

From the discussion of this variable in Chapter 6, it is clear that it must be understood as a regional innovation system or, narrower yet, as a regional knowledge infrastructure. Cooke also referred to it as a regional innovation system (in Chapter 9 in this volume). Seen simply in terms of 'what is there' with regard to knowledge centres, intermediary organizations, etc. and their connections to the regional business community, this variable is at the level of structural embeddedness. After all, it says something about the number and intensity of linkages among regional actors.

Social Capital

As Lorenzen (Chapter 10 in this volume) demonstrated, social capital is a multi-faceted concept. One way to look at it is in terms of regional institutional capacity and regionally embedded conventions, as in Figure 6.1. In this way, social capital is seen as a regional phenomenon (see Lorenzen, Chapter 10 in this volume) and pertains to regional norms, rules and conventions., etc. Regional social capital thus should be seen as an example of social embeddedness. Actors benefit from it (or are hampered by it) because they are linked to other actors in a particular region and because each particular region, in varying degrees, has developed its own way of doing things. However, social capital is also found on a lower level of abstraction, in concrete person-to-person relations. Since these relations tend to have a past and a future, people will invest in them (see Granovetter, 1985, 1992). Therefore, social capital is also a characteristic of relations and, hence, it can be studied on the level of relational embeddedness. Although networks, too, can become social realities of their own and thus develop their unique norms, rules and conventions, this should be seen as social embeddedness rather than structural embeddedness. Keeping in mind what we have said with regard to regional interfirm networks, structural embeddedness pertains to the number and density of relations; it does not say anything about their nature.

Regional Innovation Policy

Embeddedness is about relations. Regional policy, however, is not a relational variable; that is, it does not say anything about relations. The link between regional innovation policy, on the one hand, and relations between regional actors, on the other hand, is as follows. First, dense regional relations may make the formulation and implementation of regional innovation policy easier – but only if these regional relations are productive, not destructive. Second, regional innovation policy may further and strengthen linkages between actors, as has been the objective of many regional innovation strategies (see Bellini and Landabaso, Chapter 11, this volume). So, from a relational perspective, having a good regional policy is one thing; developing and implementing that policy is another matter. Since the latter is where relations are relevant, this is the learning region's focus with respect to regional innovation policy.

The result of the above discussion is summarized in Table 13.1. Regional innovation policy is not mentioned in this table since it is not a relational variable. Nor is it necessary to mention many relation variables identified in the previous chapters. The purpose of this table is to highlight the

Table 13.1   Relational perspective: levels of embeddedness

Relational embeddedness	Structural embeddedness	Social embeddedness
Spatial proximity (geography of knowledge)	Spatial proximity (agglomeration advantages)	
	Regional innovation networks (structural characteristics)	Regional innovation networks (social characteristics)
	Regional institutional set-up (knowledge infrastructure, regional innovation system)	
Social capital (norms, rules, conventions in a relationship)		Social capital (regionally embedded conventions, regional institutional capacity)

different layers of social context (embeddedness). With Granovetter, we argue that those layers are rarely accounted for in economic analysis; the field of regional economics is no exception. Following the above reasoning, researchers can list their variables under any one of the three forms of embeddedness, or decide that they are not relational variables. It is the logic that matters, and our logic says that the learning region is the theory that explains the process of regional learning from a relational perspective. That is, it sees learning as a process that takes place in actor-to-actor relations, or dyads. In order to explain how and why learning happens (or does not happen) in these dyads, it is essential that the three forms of embeddedness are taken into account. It is through the relations that these forms of embeddedness represent how a diverse set of phenomenon, such as innovative milieu, innovation systems and innovation policy, affect the process of regional learning.

THE LEARNING REGION, A PLACE IN THE LITERATURE

The relational perspective that we have proposed for the learning region does not automatically follow from the discussions in the state-of-the-art chapters in this volume. Instead, it is a choice that should answer the criticism that the learning region does not offer something new to the literature on learning, innovation and regions. By adopting a relational perspective, the learning region distinguishes itself from other theories in this literature on a conceptual level. The authors in Part II talked about many different theories, for example, innovative milieux, industrial districts, regional innovation systems and new industrial spaces. All of these theories, including what has been written about the learning region so far, address essentially the same phenomenon, which leads one to wonder what distinguishes one theory from another (e.g. Hassink, Chapter 12 in this volume). What the above theories have in common is that they take as their levels of analysis the region or regional networks. The strengths and weaknesses of these theories have been discussed elsewhere in this volume. A main weakness, though, that these theories share is that they do not specifically address the process of regional learning. Instead, their main focus, for example, is to explain the functioning of regional innovation systems or the coming about of an industrial district. Although the relevance of this is beyond doubt, it is somewhat puzzling that the regional innovation literature, thus far, has paid little attention to the actual process of learning. It is this gap that the learning region in our conceptualization seeks to fill. In our view, the process of regional learning is the starting point: how do regional actors create knowledge and how is this process affected by the layers of social context in which they are embedded? This means that the learning region can still study regional milieux or regional innovation systems, but that it does so from the perspective of the above questions – e.g. how do regional innovation systems affect the process of regional learning? (see also Rutten et al., 2003).

If the learning region would like an opportunity to stand out from the crowd, the relational perspective seems promising. At the very least, it is an approach that thus far has not been tried in the study of regions and innovation. Moreover, the sociological element that a relational perspective brings into the discussion may be a welcome addition to economic analysis, where real actors and their real relations sometimes seem to disappear behind such aggregates as a region's share of patents and the growth in R&D expenditure. Such studies seem to forget that it is the complex learning processes behind these aggregates that produces innovations.

This leaves two important issues to be discussed. First, the place of non-relational variables and, second, the role of non-regional or extra-regional relations. The non-relational variables, such as regional innovation policy, may affect regional learning in an indirect way. As argued above, it is not so much having a regional innovation policy that matters but developing and implementing one, as this requires interaction between regional actors and, therefore, is subject to the three forms of embeddedness. Moreover, the aim of regional innovation policy may be to further regional networking and hence interactions between regional actors. In other words, the way to deal with non-relational variables in a relational perspective is to propose and study causal mechanisms that link them to interactions between regional actors and, thus, to the three forms of embeddedness.

In the above we have discussed regional networks as if there were no non-regional or extra-regional networks that link regional actors to the global economy. Of course, such networks are vital. The most successful regions today are often highly connected to actors in a variety of locations elsewhere on the planet. How then to account for these linkages in the learning region? The answer is twofold, partially conceptual and partially practical. Conceptually, the learning region has as its focus regional learning between regional actors. The idea behind this is to explain why some regions fare better in the global economy than others. If the region matters, differences in regional learning should explain difference in regional performance, at least partially. Nevertheless – and this is the practical part of the answer – regional learning may include actors from outside the region. In the case of the development of new technologies and products, it often does. What is important, though, from the perspective of the learning region, is that the process of learning (i.e. the knowledge creation) takes place in the region.

The non-regional actors should be involved in learning with regional actors and they should benefit from it. A regional company that learns with global counterparts, but that is otherwise isolated from other actors in its home region, will not contribute much to regional learning. If, on the other hand, this company is embedded in its home region, the regional benefits of learning with global counterparts may be substantial. Therefore, involvement of non-regional actors in regional learning generally is a good sign. Regions that succeed in involving non-regional actors in their process of regional learning are likely to perform better than regions that are more isolated from the knowledge, skills and ideas from elsewhere in the world.

THE LEARNING REGION, WHERE NEXT?

At this point, the relational perspective of the learning region is scarcely more than a novel idea that, we believe, has potential. However, much work needs to be done to capitalize on that potential. In this volume, we have proposed the learning region as a comprehensive approach to regional innovation; therefore, we must also propose a comprehensive research agenda. In order to elaborate the relational perspective of the learning region, research efforts must be initiated on three fronts: theoretical, methodological and empirical.

The theoretical challenge is to further insight in and understanding of the process of regional learning. In addition, much theoretical work needs to be done to relate the process of learning to the different forms of embeddedness, the layers of social context within which actors learn. A number of theoretical questions must be answered for this purpose.

- How do actors learn; how can the process of regional learning be explained; which characteristics make this process run smoothly? Beginning with Nonaka and Takeuchi (1995), an extensive body of literature on (inter- and intra-) organizational learning as a process of knowledge creation has been developed. The learning region can borrow from this literature as it, too, focuses on the process of learning; that is, it focuses on those interactions between actors where the exchange and creation of knowledge actually take place.
- How do the three forms of embeddedness affect the process of regional learning? When does embeddedness facilitate learning and when does it frustrate it? How important are the different layers of social context for actors? Does embeddedness function differently in different regions? Even though it has been more than two decades since Granovetter (1985) (re)introduced the concept of embeddedness into

the socio-economic literature, this phenomenon still remains under-developed and misunderstood. Much theoretical work needs to be done in order to properly distinguish between the different levels of analysis implied by the three forms of embeddedness. Causal mechanisms must be studied at the right level of analysis and careful attention must be paid to how effects on one level trickle down to the next level. Much of the literature in the field of regions and learning has focused on a single level of analysis, such as the systems of innovation literature and the industrial districts literature. Therefore, the levels of analyses provide a formidable theoretical challenge: to understand and explain how the layers of social context affect the process of regional learning.

With regard to research methodology, the question is, which methods are best suited to empirically study the learning region in order to test hypotheses? Ironically, the two most obvious methods, surveys and case studies, are equally unsuitable. Surveys have great difficulties in distinguishing between different levels of analysis; they usually focus on one. Moreover, by their nature, they are extremely poorly equipped to shed light on processes, i.e., the process of regional learning. Although surveys yield correlations between variables, they do not examine actual causal mechanisms. Finally, most surveys are snapshots; they are rarely longitudinal. Case studies can overcome most of these difficulties. They are perfectly suited to study processes, following them over time and accounting for different levels of analysis. But their weaknesses are obvious, too. The number of observations in a case study is limited, which compromises generalizability. Moreover, case study results bear the stamp of the particular context of the case, which further reduces their generalizability. The popularity of surveys among researchers is largely due to the fact that generalizing survey results presents far less of a challenge. The obvious solution to this dilemma presents a formidable problem in terms of resources. The solution is to conduct case surveys, which combine the strengths of both surveys and case studies and, in doing so, overcome their weaknesses. However, the costs of conducting case surveys may be prohibitive. If case surveys were the exception, the methodological challenge would then be to refine both the survey and the case study methods in order to overcome at least some of their weaknesses.

The empirical challenge is to study and compare regions (see Rutten and Boekema, 2005). A notable difficulty in this respect is the definition of a region. For practical reasons, administrative regions are usually the subject of studies, whereas economic regions would be more appropriate. But they are more difficult to identify. However, from a relational perspective, one should study actual regional learning between actual regional partners. By tracing the layers of social context of these partners, the relevant regional scale should then emerge. Put differently, the starting point for empirical study is not the region but the learning relations between regional actors. As we argued earlier, the learning region studies regional learning. The aim of empirical research in the learning region tradition should be to compare many examples of regional learning. These comparisons might provide an answer to the above theoretical questions.

In short, the research agenda of the learning region is necessarily an ambitious one. It is the only way to get beyond what we have now: a fragmented understanding of regions and learning. The collection of theories in this field fails to make a conceptual connection between such phenomena as learning in dyads, innovation systems, regional innovation policy and innovative milieux. We have argued that starting with real actors, their real relations and their embeddedness in layers of social context is the most comprehensive and, therefore, most effective way to understand and explain why some regions fare better than others in the global economy. Ultimately, this is not merely about building a beautiful theory. Instead, it is about making companies more competitive, regions more prosperous and thus about increasing the chances of the people in those regions of having better lives. We consider the intimate link between science and practice that the field of regions and learning enjoys to be a strength. When the social and economic sciences forget that they are studying real human beings, this seems to us a contradiction in terms.

NOTES

1. Its defeat in the Franco-German war of 1870 and the peace terms imposed on it in 1871 plunged France into a political and social crisis.
2. In one of his best-known works, Durkheim argued that suicides occur most frequently in societies where solidarity is low. In this particular work he also presented empirical data to support his case. (Durkheim, É. (1897), *La Suicide: Étude de sociologie*, Paris: Alcan.)
3. Social institutions may be defined as 'patterns of behaviours that are collectively shared (from routines to social conventions to ethical codes)' (Coriat and Dosi, 1998: 6). They are habitual patterns of behaviour that help regulate economic life, for example by reducing uncertainty about how others behave (Morgan, 1997: 493).
4. 'To the extent that product and process innovation is based upon new ideas and that the creation of ideas is a social process involving discussion, then geographical proximity is important in innovation' (Best, 1990: 235).

REFERENCES

Best, M. (1990), *The New Competition: Institutions of Industrial Restructuring*, Cambridge: Polity Press.

Boekema, F., Bakkers, S., Morgan, K. and Rutten, R. (eds) (2000), *Knowledge, Innovation and Economic Growth: The Theory and Practice of Learning Regions*, Cheltenham, UK and Northampton, MA, USA: Edward Elgar.

Coriat, B. and Dosi, G. (1998), 'The institutional embeddedness of economic change: an appraisal of the "evolutionary" and "regulationist" research programmes', in K. Nielsen and B. Johnson (eds), *Institutions and Economic Change: New Perspectives on Markets, Firms and Technology*, London: Routledge, pp. 3–31.

Durkheim, É. (1893/1997), *The Division of Labour in Society*, New York: The Free Press.

Grabher, G. (ed.) (1993), *The Embedded Firm: On the Socioeconomics of Industrial Networks*, London: Routledge.

Granovetter, M. (1985), 'Economic action and social structure: the problem of embeddedness', *American Journal of Sociology*, **91** (3), 481–510.

Granovetter, M. (1990), 'Mark Granovetter', in R. Swedberg, *Economics and Sociology: Redefining their Boundaries: Conversations with Economists and Sociologists*, Princeton, NJ: Princeton University Press, pp. 98–114.

Granovetter, M. (1992), 'Problems of explanation in economic sociology', in N. Nohria and R. Eccles (eds), *Networks and Organizations: Structure, Form, and Action*, Boston, MA: Harvard Business School Press, pp. 25–56.

Hassink, R. (2001), 'The learning region: a fuzzy concept or a sound theoretical basis for modern innovation policies?', *Zeitschrift für Wirtschaftsgeographie*, **45** (3/4), 219–30.

Maskell, P., Eskelinen, H., Hannibalsson, I., Malmberg, A. and Vatne, E. (1998), *Competitiveness, Localised Learning and Regional Development: Specialisation and Prosperity in Small Open Economies*, London: Routledge.

Morgan, K. (1997), 'The learning region: institutions, innovation and regional renewal', *Regional Studies*, **31** (5), 491–503.

Nonaka, I. and Takeuchi, H. (1995), *The Knowledge-creating Company: How Japanese Companies Create the Dynamics of Innovation*, Oxford: Oxford University Press.

Rutten, R. (2003), *Knowledge and Innovation in Regional Industry: An Entrepreneurial Coalition*, London: Routledge.

Rutten, R., Boekema, F. and Kuijpers, E. (eds) (2003), *Economic Geography of Higher Education: Knowledge Infrastructure and Learning Regions*, London: Routledge.

Rutten, R. (2004), 'Inter-firm knowledge creation: a re-appreciation of embeddedness from a relational perspective', *European Planning Studies*, **12** (5), 659–74.

Rutten, R. and Boekema, F. (eds) (2005), 'Innovation, policy and economic growth: theory and cases', *European Planning Studies*, Special issue **13** (8).

Schumpeter, J. (1943), *Capitalism, Socialism and Democracy*, London: Allen & Unwin.

Stedman Jones, S. (2001), *Durkheim Reconsidered*, Cambridge: Polity Press.

Uzzi, B. (1997), 'Social structure and competition in interfirm networks: the paradox of embeddedness', *Administrative Science Quarterly*, **42** (1), 35–67.

Index